# International Differences in the Business Practices and Productivity of Firms

**A National Bureau
of Economic Research
Conference Report**

# International Differences in the Business Practices and Productivity of Firms

Edited by **Richard B. Freeman and Kathryn L. Shaw**

**The University of Chicago Press**

Chicago and London

RICHARD B. FREEMAN is the Herbert Ascherman Professor of
Economics at Harvard University and program director of labor
studies at the National Bureau of Economic Research. KATHRYN L.
SHAW is the Ernest C. Arbuckle Professor of Economics at Stanford
University Graduate School of Business and a research associate of the
National Bureau of Economic Research.

The University of Chicago Press, Chicago 60637
The University of Chicago Press, Ltd., London
© 2009 by the National Bureau of Economic Research
All rights reserved. Published 2009
Printed in the United States of America

18  17  16  15  14  13  12  11  10  09    1  2  3  4  5
ISBN-13: 978-0-226-26194-2 (cloth)
ISBN-10: 0-226-26194-8 (cloth)


Library of Congress Cataloging-in-Publication Data

International differences in the business practices and productivity of
    firms / edited by Richard B. Freeman and Kathryn L. Shaw.
        p. cm. — (A National Bureau of Economic Research
    Conference Report)
      Includes bibliographical references and index.
      ISBN-13: 978-0-226-26194-2 (alk. paper)
      ISBN-10: 0-226-26194-8 (alk. paper)
      1. Industrial productivity. 2. Industrial management.
    3. International business enterprises. I. Freeman, Richard B.
    (Richard Barry), 1943– II. Shaw, Kathryn. III. Series: National
    Bureau of Economic Research conference report
      HD56.I543 2009
      338'.06—dc22

                                                              2008048152

**Relation of the Directors to the
Work and Publications of the
National Bureau of Economic Research**

1. The object of the NBER is to ascertain and present to the economics profession, and to the public more generally, important economic facts and their interpretation in a scientific manner without policy recommendations. The Board of Directors is charged with the responsibility of ensuring that the work of the NBER is carried on in strict conformity with this object.

2. The President shall establish an internal review process to ensure that book manuscripts proposed for publication DO NOT contain policy recommendations. This shall apply both to the proceedings of conferences and to manuscripts by a single author or by one or more co-authors but shall not apply to authors of comments at NBER conferences who are not NBER affiliates.

3. No book manuscript reporting research shall be published by the NBER until the President has sent to each member of the Board a notice that a manuscript is recommended for publication and that in the President's opinion it is suitable for publication in accordance with the above principles of the NBER. Such notification will include a table of contents and an abstract or summary of the manuscript's content, a list of contributors if applicable, and a response form for use by Directors who desire a copy of the manuscript for review. Each manuscript shall contain a summary drawing attention to the nature and treatment of the problem studied and the main conclusions reached.

4. No volume shall be published until forty-five days have elapsed from the above notification of intention to publish it. During this period a copy shall be sent to any Director requesting it, and if any Director objects to publication on the grounds that the manuscript contains policy recommendations, the objection will be presented to the author(s) or editor(s). In case of dispute, all members of the Board shall be notified, and the President shall appoint an ad hoc committee of the Board to decide the matter; thirty days additional shall be granted for this purpose.

5. The President shall present annually to the Board a report describing the internal manuscript review process, any objections made by Directors before publication or by anyone after publication, any disputes about such matters, and how they were handled.

6. Publications of the NBER issued for informational purposes concerning the work of the Bureau, or issued to inform the public of the activities at the Bureau, including but not limited to the NBER Digest and Reporter, shall be consistent with the object stated in paragraph 1. They shall contain a specific disclaimer noting that they have not passed through the review procedures required in this resolution. The Executive Committee of the Board is charged with the review of all such publications from time to time.

7. NBER working papers and manuscripts distributed on the Bureau's web site are not deemed to be publications for the purpose of this resolution, but they shall be consistent with the object stated in paragraph 1. Working papers shall contain a specific disclaimer noting that they have not passed through the review procedures required in this resolution. The NBER's web site shall contain a similar disclaimer. The President shall establish an internal review process to ensure that the working papers and the web site do not contain policy recommendations, and shall report annually to the Board on this process and any concerns raised in connection with it.

8. Unless otherwise determined by the Board or exempted by the terms of paragraphs 6 and 7, a copy of this resolution shall be printed in each NBER publication as described in paragraph 2 above.

# Contents

# Acknowledgments

This book is derived from the grant entitled "Understanding Productivity Differences Between the U.S. and Europe by Combining Cross Country Industry Analysis with In-Depth Field Studies of Firms," from the Sloan Foundation to the NBER. We deeply appreciate the enthusiasm and vision that Gail Pesyna and Ralph Gomery of the Sloan Foundation had in encouraging economists to go "inside firms" to study how management and workers actually behave. Their support and enthusiasm has helped catalyze a flourishing of the "pin factory" research approach embodied in the book, in which researchers seek company data to analyze behavior and performance.

We also thank the researchers and conference attendees for persisting through many conferences and many revisions in their work, and through the lengthy research process. The tasks of interviewing at work sites, finding data, and modeling outcomes are time consuming, but ultimately revealing and rewarding.

# Introduction

Richard B. Freeman and Kathryn L. Shaw

Management practices toward workers differ substantially across countries and among the firms and establishments within countries. Some firms use work teams and employee involvement committees, have extensive personnel policies, and compensate workers in part through group incentives that link pay to company or workplace performance. Others operate under traditional hierarchical arrangements and pay hourly wages independent of performance. Practices differ by country within the same multinational firm in part because countries have different labor laws and institutions. Practices differ in the same country because firms choose different personnel management strategies and because within the same firm, management and labor implement policies differently in different worksites.

Labor productivity also varies widely among countries and among firms and establishments within countries. Some productivity differences reflect the differing skill of workers and differences in the machines and technology with which they work. Productivity also differs because managerial practices and worker responses to practices differ, with consequences for how workers do their jobs. At the industry level, productivity growth often takes the form of the entry of firms or establishments that have better practices and the exit of firms whose labor practices and productivity are worse than average, though this market culling still leaves a large dispersion in both practices and productivity.

In the 1990s to 2000s, globalization and the extension of information technologies associated with the computer and Internet reshaped many mana-

Richard B. Freeman is the Herbert Ascherman Professor of Economics at Harvard University and program director of labor studies at the National Bureau of Economic Research. Kathryn L. Shaw is the Ernest C. Arbuckle Professor of Economics at Stanford University Graduate School of Business and a research associate of the National Bureau of Economic Research.

gerial practices. Operating in different countries, multinational firms have had to adjust business practices to different legal regimes. Domestic firms have also had to reexamine their managerial practices in light of what foreign competitors do. Equally important, the new information technologies associated with the computer and Internet changed best practice methods of organizing work, paying compensation, and operating a business. Teamwork and group problem-solving, group incentive pay, and extensive modes of selecting workers became more prevalent along with lean manufacturing, better quality control, and better scheduling methods. Productivity grew rapidly in sectors that use information technology, resolving the Solow paradox that one observed computers everywhere but in the productivity statistics. There is also some evidence, but more conjecture, that the reason it took a long time before computerization impacted productivity was that organizations had to change business practices to make best use of the new technologies, which is more difficult and time-consuming than putting computers at work stations.

Taking the shocks of globalization and information technology and national labor relations regulations as exogenous, this book examines four questions that lie at the heart of ongoing debate about how firms contribute to economic growth and the degree to which national customs or regulations impede or spur growth-augmenting improvements in productivity.

1. How great is the *cross-country* variation of labor practices and productivity across firms and within a given multinational operating in the same sector across countries?

2. Do *country-specific rules and regulations* significantly affect the adoption or success of innovative management practices and the rate of productivity advance?

3. What slows the spread of best practices across firms and thus maintains the wide variation in productivity found in many sectors and firms?

4. Do the new labor practices associated with technological and managerial innovations benefit the workers directly affected by the changes or are firms (and ultimately consumers) the sole beneficiaries of improved productivity?

Many researchers examine these types of questions by relating measures of economic outcomes using industry-level or macroeconomic data to cross-country variation in labor regulations, investments in computer technology or other capital, and investments in labor skills. We take a more microeconomics approach, analyzing what goes on inside firms engaged in similar lines of business or sectors across countries when they face similar exogenous changes in technology or market conditions. Our primary focus is on establishments within multinational firms, because this controls for firm-based differences in technology or corporate strategy. But we also examine practices and productivity in sectors where many of the firms are domestic.

The first part of the book (chapters 1 through 3) report on studies of the practices and productivity across firms that operate in broadly similar markets and thus should face similar technological and market constraints and problems while operating in the United States and other advanced countries. The second part of the book (chapters 4 through 8) examines practices and productivity within multinational firms when they operate in different countries.

## Methods: Pin Factory or Insider Econometrics

All of the studies use a methodological approach that amalgamates econometric analysis of data on companies or sectors with the interviews and traditional business school or labor relations qualitative case studies. By combining the depth of knowledge about a particular firm or market from plant visits, interviews, and discussions with participants and statistical estimates of models of economic behavior from quantitative data, we hope to get closer to understanding business practices and their impact on productivity than we would get from either approach done separately. We call this combination of qualitative case studies and quantitative analysis *pin factory* or *insider econometrics.* The term pin factory comes from Adam Smith's famous example of the division of labor. The term insider econometrics refers to the use of information that is available only to persons with detailed knowledge of the firm or sector.

The first step in a pin factory/insider econometrics study calls for the researcher to interview managers, workers, and others at the relevant firm or firms to learn about the mode of production and the business practices and issues that face the firm. This gives the analyst a different perspective than he or she would have gotten from estimating production or cost functions or modeling firm behavior with little attention to actual processes or practices. It often leads the researchers to focus on different research questions or to choose a different research design than they envisaged before their pin factory visit. If, for example, the researcher learns that the big problem facing a firm is getting workers on one shift to work cooperatively with those on another shift, that could readily become the subject of study. Alternatively, if management reports that it changed compensation policies for some group of workers in a way that might readily provide the researcher with the pseudo-experimental variation from which to draw inferences about the impact of compensation on productivity, the researcher might concentrate on that issue (and so on).

The second step in a pin factory/insider econometrics study is to gather data from the firm or sector and to then test models or hypotheses of the factors that generate the behavior reflected in the data. In our volume, some of the insider econometrics data come from firm records (chapters 3, 5, 6, and 8); and some come from researcher-designed surveys of managers or workers (chapters 1, 2, 4, and 7). This step requires that top management open some of its books to the researcher and/or encourage lower level managers and workers to cooperate with the specially designed survey. The researcher usually agrees to some form of confidentiality regarding the use of data and identification of the firm in the study. In this volume, we do not provide the name of any of the firms that cooperated with our research team, but we are highly thankful to those firms. Without them we would have no study.

The third step in a pin factory/insider econometrics study is to formulate and estimate a model focused on key issues facing the firm/sector that illuminates their underlying cause or effect. This is standard econometric investigation, which has become increasingly sophisticated due to the availability of high-powered statistical programs and modes of data manipulation. What is nonstandard is the unique firm or establishment based data that reflects the information-gathering process in the firm and the issues facing it. Different researchers may use somewhat different techniques from the statistical tool-bag to analyze the data but the results rarely depend on the technique. It is the data itself—the variables measured and the quality of the measurements—that matters.

The principle scientific problem in our analyses (and in most others in economics and business) is that the data are generated by the decisions of management and workers rather than by a random assignment experiment designed to test, say, the impact of a particular work practice or new technology on the performance of the firm. We observe how an establishment fares with the business practices or technology that it chooses, not how it would have fared if it had chosen other practices. This does not rule out causal interpretations of observed patterns, but it makes them problematic.

In standard applied economics researchers usually conclude their work with their estimated model and interpretation of the estimated parameters. Ideally, they test for the robustness of results under different model specifications and consider alternative interpretations of the patterns in the data. Insider econometrics goes a step further by asking the informants in the firm/sector to assess the findings in light of the informants' knowledge. This step is critical because it provides nonstatistical independent verification or rejection of the story/conclusion of the analysis. When an informants' interpretation differs from that of the researcher, the researcher will try to close the gap by modifying the model or providing additional tests. But researchers need not take the views of the informants as gospel; sometimes the person closest to a phenomenon misses the critical factors that underlie it. By viewing the firm from outside and applying a broad economic perspective to issues, the economist may be closer to the truth than the informant. It is the tension between the qualitative and the quantitative that makes these types of studies challenging and stimulating.

There is one broad problem with the insider econometrics studies in this book and elsewhere that merits attention even in this brief introduction. This is the question of assessing how far, if at all, we can generalize results from a nonrepresentative sample of firms to the broader universe of firms. There is no gainsaying the nonrepresentative nature of virtually all case studies, whether they use econometric analysis or not. Some firms are open to having researchers study them. Others are not. Simply because one analyzes a nonrepresentative entity does not mean that the findings are limited to that entity. If the results of many studies from nonrepresentative samples with different sampling designs are similar, it seems reasonable to generalize beyond the particular companies or sectors covered. If the findings relate to basic economic behavior (for instance, buying less when prices or wages rise), it seems reasonable to generalize broadly just as psychologists generalize findings from experiments based on volunteers to all people. But when, as occurs between some chapters in this book, results differ across sectors or firms, we cannot make any broad generalization. Some results seem to reflect idiosyncratic differences among these units.

## Data Sets

Figure 1 provides a capsule summary of the data sets used in each chapter. The range of data sets is remarkable in its diversity. None of the studies uses "standard" statistical surveys as its main source of information. One chapter surveys 29,000 employees in a single multinational. Another asked management in 267 valve-making plants about the computer numerically controlled machines used in the business and about human resource practices associated with the technology. Another obtained data by interviewing managers in 732 manufacturing firms in four countries. Another chapter used internal firm data on inputs and outputs of hundreds of outlets of a fast food chain. Another obtained records on the hourly performance of individual workers from electricity generating firms, and so on.

Variety in the type of data studied is characteristic of pin factory/insider econometric analyses, in which the variables go far beyond those in the data sets that microeconomists investigate regularly (e.g., the Census of Population, labor force surveys, and surveys or censuses of business establishments), and diverge even more from the aggregate time series data that macroeconomists analyze. The diversity of data reflects the individuality of firms/sectors, each with its own history, management use of information technology for measuring performance, and firm or industry-specific practices and issues, and the microeconomic questions on which the researchers focused.

## Summary of Findings

Taken together, the studies in the book illuminate the four questions that motivated our research. Each study reports on the issues that it addresses,

**Table I.1    Data Sets and Major Findings of Studies in this volume**

| Chapter | Data sets used in chapter |
|---|---|
| *Studies Across Firms in Different Countries* | |
| 1. Work-Life Balance, Management Practices and Productivity (Bloom, Kretschmer, Van Reenen) | Own telephone survey of managers of 732 medium-sized manufacturing firms in the United States, France, Germany, and the United Kingdom; some are multinationals. |
| 2. International Differences in the Adoption and Impact of New Information Technologies and New HR Practices: The Valve-Making Industry in the United States and United Kingdom (Shaw, Bartel, Ichniowski, Correa) | Own survey of 267 valve-making plants in the United States and United Kingdom |
| 3. Personnel, Information Technology and the Productivity of Electricity Generation (Bushnell, Wolfram) | Company data on individual productivity of workers at five electricity generating facilities in the United States, with case material from the United Kingdom and Spain. |
| *Studies Within the Multinational* | |
| 4. Labor Practices, Compensation, and Establishment Performance in a Single Large Multinational (Blasi, Freeman, Kruse) | Own survey of 29,000 employees within a large manufacturing and service company with establishments in the United States and other countries. |
| 5. Within-firm Cross-country Labor Productivity Differences: A Case Study (Lafontaine, Sivadasan) | Company data on food outlets for 27 countries (including all of Europe) for 2002 and 2003. |
| 6. International Productivity Differences in a Pharmaceutical Firm (Eriksson, Westergaard-Nielson) | Company data on productivity of pharmaceutical plants in the United States and Europe within one company. |
| 7. Measuring the Productivity of Software Development in a Globally Distributed Company (Levenson) | Own survey of 200 developers as well as, site visits, and interviews, in four international locations. |
| 8. Comparing U.S. and European Operations of an Auto Parts Company (Helper and Kleiner) | Data on productivity of five auto parts production plants in the United States and the United Kingdom within one company. |

the particulars of the data analyzed, the methodology used, and the findings. Each also gives case study information about the firm or group of firms studied that will hopefully give the reader a memorable picture of the human resource issues and policies facing management in different settings and their link to productivity. Some of the studies explain the detailed technology in a given sector, such as how valve manufacturers use flexible manufacturing systems to coordinate computer numerically controlled machines to produce valves or how operators affect the efficiency of generation of electricity in utilities by turning on or off blowers to remove soot from machines. These studies use industry-specific measures, such as set-up time or the ratio of million British thermal units over mega watt hours of electricity produced, to measure productivity rather than generic value-added or sales per worker.

As an indication of what the reader will find in the chapters, we summarize next their main findings organized according to our four motivating questions.

*1. How great is the **cross-country** variation of labor practices and productivity across firms in the same sector or within a given multinational engaged in a similar business across countries?* As a broad generalization, the variation is great—certainly greater than most economists would expect on the basis of the standard theory of production that focuses on representative firms. Productivity differences across similar plants are substantial, due presumably to differences in management practices or the influences of historical (or possibly outdated) practices that persist over time. This appears to be true across firms in the same sector across countries, as in small auto parts production (Helper and Kleiner) and valve manufacturing (Bartel, Ichniowski, Shaw, and Correa); across firms in the same manufacturing industry (Bloom, Kretschmer, and Van Reenen); and across establishments in the same firm in manufacturing (Blasi, Freeman, and Kruse), and across countries in the same multinational retailer (Lafontaine and Sivadasan).

Even when multinational firms make similar products in similar plants across countries, differences in capital or in the quality of the managers produce different productivity outcomes in many situations. For instance, in auto parts U.S. plants have higher productivity compared to UK plants, which Helper and Kleiner attribute to differences in the quality of the plants' capital and the quality of the management. In electricity generation, Bushnell and Wolfram find considerable performance differences among workers in the same plants in the United States and report responses to incentive pay in the United Kingdom that seemingly diverge from that in the United States.

But not every study finds sizable variation in productivity. In some sectors multinationals operating with the same technology appear to compress productivity differences. Eriksson and Westergaard-Nielson report similar productivity in pharmaceutical establishments that produce the same products in the United States and Denmark. Human resource practices and labor market conditions differ between the United States and Danish plants, but management has found ways to work around these differences to keep operations in both countries near the productivity frontier. Similarly, Levenson finds that productivity does not vary substantially across different national sites of the same multinational software development firm. This firm maintains comparable productivity as it transfers some operations to international locations, some of which have lower labor costs than the United States. It incurs higher communications costs due to its setting up teams across countries but uses modern information and communication technology to maintain team effectiveness.

In sum, we find large variation among establishments across countries, which some multinationals seem to reduce or even virtually eliminate within their own business. The studies that examine data over time find trends toward improved productivity, be it through better information technologies, or capital, or improved labor practices.

2. *How much do* **country-specific rules and regulations** *affect the adoption or success of innovative management practices and/or productivity?* Analyses of why productivity differs among advanced countries that have access to similar technologies often stress the importance of national labor relations practices. In the 1980s, many American analysts and businesses looked longingly at Japan's job rotation and lifetime employment practices or at Germany's apprenticeship programs or the cooperative labor-management relations in the Nordic countries. In the 1990s to 2000, many analysts blamed the slower growth of productivity in advanced Europe than in the United States on Europe's greater reliance on labor regulations, collective bargaining, and institutions to determine labor market outcomes, compared to the United States's reliance on market-determination of outcomes.

Our analyses find that country-specific rules and regulations affect the personnel or human resource policies of firms but that these policies have relatively modest effects on productivity at the level of the firm or establishment. With respect to the impact of national policies on firm behavior, Bloom, Kretschmer, and Van Reenen find that while U.S. subsidiaries in Europe adopt the general management practices of their U.S. parent firm, they adopt the work-life balance practices in the country in which they operate. They offer work-life balance practices, such as part-time work, job-sharing, childcare, or work from home in EU countries but do so without reducing productivity. Looking within a single multinational Blasi, Freeman, and Kruse find large differences across countries in the work practices and attitudes of employees on such issues as their willingness to work hard for the company, willingness to monitor the behavior of their peers, and willingness to innovate on the job. But they also report that when the firm puts in comparable incentive practices in its establishments across countries that workers in different countries respond in qualitatively similar ways.

In pharmaceuticals the same multinational operates its U.S. plant non-union with a workforce that has considerable turnover while operating its Danish plant with a unionized workforce that has little turnover. Even with these differences, however, the plants have similar productivity levels and management has the same goal for managing labor: to increase its control and reduce worker (or team) empowerment. At the time of the Eriksson and Westergaard-Nielson case study, management had abolished work teams in the United States and was seeking to do so in Denmark. The differences in institutions seemingly affected the mode and speed by which management changed organizational practices more than the final outcomes. The chapters on valves (Shaw, Bartel, Ichniowski, and Correa) and on auto parts (Helper and Kleiner) also conclude that labor regulations had little impact on productivity. Blasi, Freeman, and Kruse report little relation between workers' attitudes and broad aggregate indices of country institutions. What matters in the multinational they study are labor policies and practices at the shop floor. Still, not every study found labor regulations to be largely irrelevant to productivity type outcomes. LaFontaine and Sividasan report that in the international retail food chain they studied how regulations covering hiring and firing costs across these countries affected outcomes. In countries with high firing and hiring costs, firms hired fewer workers, which raised labor productivity while lowering output by about 2 to 3 percent.

In sum, with one exception our studies find that the effects of labor market institutions on productivity are too small or unquantifiable to explain much of the difference in productivity in the data and accordingly attribute performance differences across plants to other factors. Managers and workers seem to find ways to minimize the potential adverse effects of regulatory or institutional constraints and thus achieve levels of productivity that are roughly independent of the labor codes.

*3. What slows the spread of best labor practices and prevents management from reducing the wide variation in productivity observed in many sectors and firms?* This is the most difficult of our four questions. The case investigations found that in some sectors managers were continually making changes in labor practices independent of the regulatory environment. They were either searching for best practice modes of operating or changing practices as economic conditions changed. In the valve industry, firms made huge progress between the 1980s and the 2000s in adopting new information technologies and human resource practices. These information technologies and the accompanying changes in the mode of work made these firms more productive. Still, there was considerable variation in productivity and in rates of adoption among firms and establishments. Even within the same firm some plants did not copy best practices even when it seemed fairly easy to do so. In electricity generating plants, management believed that individual operators could substantially affect plant efficiency and profits but it took the U.S. Environmental Protection Agency (EPA) regulations for them to produce the data that verified these claims (which limited the quantitative analysis in this chapter to the United States). Still, the firms did not use this data to target programs to improve the performance of individual operators and reduce the variance of performance across individuals. One firm developed an in-house computer program to guide operators that seemed to bring the less efficient up to speed, but others did not do this. The experience of the auto parts industry confirms the difficulty of transferring knowledge across plants.

In sum, in some sectors productivity varies widely among establishments in comparable production environments. Such factors as when the plant was built or the technologies in place or the idiosyncratic impact of having different managers or workers with different talents or objectives matters greatly in the speed with which best practices spread among plants in a given firm and across firms. In many cases, management does not analyze the outcomes from changes in practices nor have strong policies to bring laggard worksites or workers up to speed. Firms seem to leave rents on the table as long as they are not facing a financial crisis, either because they satisfice rather than maximize or because the transition costs of change are far greater than we would anticipate.

The absence in this volume of any study that uses random assignment experiments to study the introduction of practices or technology limits our ability to say more about what factors impede the spread of best practice techniques. We observe that learning is not sufficient to make firms or establishments identical, but we do not observe what these plants would have been like if they learned nothing at all from their counterpart. Absent experiments with randomly assigned practices, we can only conclude either that these establishments have not learned enough or that the low productivity workplaces had high unmeasured adoption costs. It is remarkable that U.S. states and the federal government often conduct random assignment experiments to determine what works or does not in welfare policies before changing those policies, while firms regularly alter labor practices that can affect bottom lines without any such evaluations.

*4. Do the new labor practices associated with technological and managerial innovations benefit the workers directly affected by the changes or are firms (and ultimately consumers) the sole beneficiaries of improved productivity?* Productivity change at a workplace can improve or harm the economic well-being of employees at that site. Technological change that raises demand for labor or skills should benefit workers while change that displaces labor or reduces or obsolesces skills is likely to harm some workers in the short or medium run, even though it should benefit workers as a whole in the long run. Changes in human resource practices that raise productivity can be beneficial or harmful to workers depending on how it affects their autonomy and working conditions.

The studies in this volume suggest that, with some exception, the technological and managerial changes in the period covered benefited workers as well as firms. Firms with good management practices in the Bloom, Kretschmer, and Van Reenan sample raised productivity more than others and were more likely to have work-life balance programs that benefit workers. By themselves, work-life balance programs had negligible effects on productivity, so it is their coincidence with better management that induces a positive association between those practices that benefit workers and productivity. In the multinational in the Blasi, Freeman, and Kruse study, workers paid by "shared capitalist" modes of compensation in the form of stock ownership or profit sharing or gain-sharing had better outcomes for workers than workers covered by standard modes of pay. The shared capitalist workers report greater work effort, employee cooperation, and willingness to act to reduce shirking by fellow employees, and lower the likelihood of leaving the firm—which should raise productivity and benefit the firm. But they also report better labor-management relationships, higher job satisfaction, greater loyalty and trust with the firm, and greater job security—all of which should benefit the workers.

In the valve industry, the adoption of new computer-based information technology increased the technical and problem-solving skill requirements of workers in the United States and United Kingdom (Bartel, Ichniowski, Shaw, and Correa). The use of teams, training programs, and bonus/incentive plans increased substantially along with the new technologies. Since employment in the valve industry fell, a full accounting of the impact of technology on the workforce in the sector requires some assessment of what happened to workers who might have had employment under the older technology, but at the least those employed seemed to have better jobs under the new technology. Still, on this point as on others, not all of the studies in the book found similar patterns. In the pharmaceutical firm examined by Eriksson and Westergaard-Neilson, management had eliminated teams in the U.S. establishment and was seeking greater managerial control over decisions in Denmark as well, which was probably not in the interest of workers.

## Conclusion

*International Differences in the Business Practices and Productivity of Firms* provides considerable insight and information into the way business practices vary across countries, firms, establishments, and among workers within establishments, but does not give definitive answers to the four questions around which our work focused. If there is a single conclusion to the volume, it is that there is a lot of heterogeneity or variation in practices and performance, and a lot of variation in the amount of variation among sectors that seems to require another level of analysis to explain. For the most part, our studies reject the simple story that differences in organizational practices and performance are largely caused by the legal restrictions. They illuminate the extent and nature of variation in practices and productivity but do not pin down the reasons for those differences nor offer ways to bring lower-productivity firms or worksites up to speed. We can imagine experiments that would identify barriers to the rapid spread of best practices and ways to reduce those barriers. In the not so distant future perhaps some firm(s) will take up the challenge of conducting such an experiment, not for the sake of academic research, important though that is, but to gain a competitive advantage in its business practices.

# I

## Cross-Firm Studies

# 1

# Work-Life Balance, Management Practices, and Productivity

Nick Bloom, Tobias Kretschmer, and John Van Reenen

## 1.1 Introduction

Does good management and higher productivity come at the expense of work-life balance (WLB), or is good work-life balance an important component of the management of successful firms? Some more pessimistic critics of globalization have argued that competition stimulates Anglo-Saxon management practices that may raise productivity but only at the expense of well-being at work. For example, Jacques Chirac, the French president, has stressed that:

> [Europe's] model is the social market economy, [the] alliance of liberty and solidarity, with the public authority safeguarding the public interest. [. . .] France will therefore never let Europe become a mere free-trade area. We want a political and social Europe rooted in solidarity.[1]

By contrast, a more optimistic view is often justified by citing the tangible and intangible business benefits of good WLB, sometimes espoused by the more optimistic Human Resource Management literature. For example, Tony Blair, the UK Prime minister, stated:

Nick Bloom is an assistant professor of economics at Stanford University and a faculty research fellow of the National Bureau of Economic Research. Tobias Kretschmer is a professor of management and director of the Institute for Communication Economics at the University of Munich. John Van Reenen is professor of Economics and director of the Centre for Economic Performance at the London School of Economics and a Faculty Research Fellow of the National Bureau of Economic Research.

Acknowledgments: We would like to thank the Anglo-German Foundation for their generous financial support.

1. Euractiv, "Blair, Chirac in drive to win citizens' support," October 27, 2005, (http://www.euractiv.com/Article?tcmuri=tcm:29-146484-16&type=News).

The UK has shown it is possible to have flexible labour markets combined with [. . .] family friendly policies to help work/life balance [. . .]. The result has been higher growth, higher employment and low unemployment.[2]

Given the slower productivity growth of Europe relative to the United States since the mid-1990s[3] this question features prominently in the implementation of "catching-up strategies." If productivity and WLB are in direct conflict, employees may be asked to make sacrifices of the quality of their work-life balance. On the other hand, if favorable work-life balance is not in the way of high productivity growth or is even productivity-enhancing, the European social model may have a brighter future.

Recent policy debates have focused on issues surrounding or directly addressing issues of WLB. For example, the European Working Time Directive has been under intense scrutiny recently, with several governments in Continental Europe challenging workers' right to opt-out of the maximum ceiling of forty-eight hours a week. At the same time, the European Services Directive (designed to liberalize the movement of service workers between countries) has been interpreted as intensifying foreign competition, which may exert a heavy toll on the work-life balance of workers.

On both sides of the argument, there seem to be underlying assumptions regarding the interaction between productivity and WLB. The question of WLB-enhancing practices, their implementation, and effectiveness has been taken up in the management literature, which generally finds that:

1. WLB measures have a positive effect on firm or workplace performance.[4]

2. WLB measures are more effective in situations demanding high employee flexibility and responsiveness.[5]

3. Firms with a more skilled workforce are more likely to implement WLB-enhancing practices.[6]

This leaves us with a dilemma: policymakers are concerned that firms are failing to introduce sufficient measures to ensure a sensible work-life balance for their employees because the costs of doing this are too high in competitive global markets. On the other hand, the academic literature

---

2. Toby Helm and David Rennie, "Blair attack on 'out-of-date' Chirac," *Daily Telegraph,* March 3, 2005, (http://www.telegraph.co.uk/news/main.jhtml?xml=/news/2005/03/25/weu25 .xml&sSheet=/news/2005/03/25/ixnewstop.html).

3. See, for example, O'Mahony and Van Ark (2003).

4. Delaney and Huselid (1996); Huselid, Jackson, and Schuler (1997); Konrad and Mangel (2000); Perry-Smith and Blum (2000); Guthrie (2001); Budd and Mumford (forthcoming); Gray (2002).

5. For example, in high-technology industries (Arthur 2003) or in highly differentiated firms (Lee and Miller 1999; Guthrie, Spell, and Nyamori 2002; Youndt et al. 1996).

6. Gray and Tudball (2003); Osterman (1995). The percentage of female employees has a weakly positive effect on the implementation of WLB practices—see Harel, Tzafrir, and Baruch (2003); Gray and Tudball (2003); Miliken, Martins, and Morgan (1998); Martins, Eddleston, and Veiga (2002); Perry-Smith and Blum (2000); Guthrie and Roth (1999).

seems to believe all firms should be adopting better WLB schemes given their apparently positive impact on firm performance, particularly in more competitive markets.

Our study sheds light on these contrasting views using a new large data set on over 700 firms in Europe and the United States that contains rich firm performance, management, and WLB variables. We are able to show that many of the prior results in the literature disappear when controls for management practice are included. We have already found in previous work (Bloom and Van Reenen 2007) that well managed firms tend to be more productive and more energy efficient; in this chapter we show that better managed firms also have better WLB practices. This can be seen in figure 1.1 where we simply plot our WLB outcome measure against an overall index of firm management quality (we explain the exact definitions in more detail following). Consequently, the association between firm productivity and WLB practices found elsewhere in the literature may simply be due to omitted variable bias—these regressions do not control for management quality. We show in this chapter that once we condition on management practices in the production function there is no independent role for WLB on productivity. Failure to control for the omitted variable of management leads to the spurious associations of better WLB with productivity.

The structure of the chapter is as follows: in section 1.2 we discuss our general models of management practices and firm performance. In section 1.3 we provide a detailed discussion of our data sets and the procedures

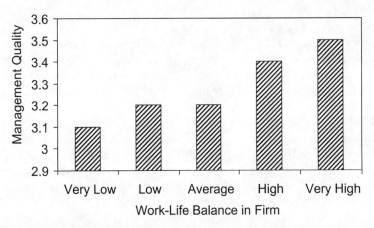

**Fig. 1.1    The correlation between work-life balance outcomes and managementpractices**

*Notes:* "Work-Life Balance in Firm" is the response to the question: *"Relative to other companies in your industry how much does your company emphasize work-life balance?"*, where scores are as follows: *"Much less"* (1); *"Slightly less"* (2); *"The same"* (3); *"Slightly more"* (4); and *"Much more"* (5). "Management quality" is the average score for the eighteen individual management practice questions with scores ranging from 1 (worst-practice) to 5 (best practice). Results from 530 firm observations.

used to collect this. In section 1.4 we discuss our results and in section 1.5 we provide some concluding comments. A detailed set of empirical appendices then follows.

## 1.2   Modeling Approach

Consider a simple approach of characterizing work-life balance, productivity, and management:

(1) $$w = f(X, M, D)$$

(2) $$y = g(X, M, D)$$

where w = Work-life Balance outcomes and y = (total factor) productivity outcomes. The variable $X$ is an index of "good" WLB practices (such as childcare flexibility and subsidies) and $M$ is an index of "good" management practices (such as better shop-floor operations or stronger incentives). We will model these as being composite measures of several underlying practices so $M = m(M_1, M_2, M_3, \ldots .)$ and $X = x(X_1, X_2, X_3, \ldots .)$. Finally, $D$ is other control variables such as firm size, firm age, industry effects and country dummies, and so forth.

We would expect that better management practices should be associated with improved productivity so $\partial y/\partial M \geq 0$ (see Bloom and Van Reenen [2007] for extensive evidence). We would also expect that better WLB practices should be associated with improved reported WLB outcomes so $\partial w/\partial X \geq 0$: this is the first thing that we examine empirically in the chapter.

What is much less clear are the cross partials in equations (1) and (2). Pessimists argue that improved WLB is costly in terms of productivity and will therefore be heavily resisted by employers, which is one reason for tough labor regulation.[7] In the context of equation (1) this implies $\partial y/\partial X \leq 0$. Similarly, pessimists argue that "Anglo-Saxon" management practices come at the expense of WLB so $\partial w/\partial M \leq 0$.

By contrast, optimists from some parts of the Human Resource Management field often argue for a win-win view that improving WLB practices will increase productivity as it improves employee well-being, leading to improved recruitment and retention (e.g., of women) and better morale and motivation. In this case, $\partial y/\partial X \geq 0$. They generally also argue that better management tends to be complementary with better WLB practices, and at a minimum, there is no obvious reason why they should be strong substitutes. Thus, $\partial w/\partial M \geq 0$.

These cross partials are with respect to endogenous variables chosen by firms, so it is not obvious how to interpret these relationships. Nevertheless,

---

7. Even if WLB practices improved productivity they may still be resisted by employers if the costs of implementing these policies were less than their productivity benefits.

the examination of the correlations with new data should be informative. More directly however, we also consider the more fundamental drivers of these practices. Consider a set of factors $Z( = Z_1, Z_2, Z_3, \ldots)$ that may exogenously affect the practices. We model management practices and WLB practices as functions of the exogenous variables as:

$$(3) \qquad\qquad X = h(Z, D) \text{ and } M = j(Z, D).$$

We are particularly interested in product market competition as one of the elements of $Z$. Under the pessimist view, tougher product competition caused by globalization, liberalization, and new technologies may increase productivity through improved management practices $\partial M/\partial Z \geq 0$, but this will be at the expense of worse WLB practices and outcomes (i.e., $\partial X/\partial Z \leq 0$). We examine these predictions directly in the empirical work. The optimists also view competition as a force promoting better management practices, but by contrast with the pessimists they argue that this should increase the use of good WLB practices. This is because, in their view, firms are making mistakes by not introducing better WLB practices and competition should make such profit-sacrificing strategies more costly.

To summarize, these two models yield a set of predictions laid out in table 1.1 that we subsequently test empirically. Of course, there can be "hybrid" positions between these positions. In short, we find that the evidence is inconsistent with the negative view: management practices are positively associated with WLB outcomes and there is no evidence that competition reduces WLB for workers. Nevertheless, the positive view does not receive unambiguous support: although better management and better WLB do sometimes go together, the positive correlation between WLB and productivity found elsewhere in the literature is not robust. Once we control for management we find no association of WLB with productivity. We find the evidence supports a hybrid view between the optimistic and pessimistic extremes.

### 1.3  Data

To investigate these issues we first have to construct robust measures of WLB, management practices, and competition. We discuss the collection of management and WLB data first (which was undertaken using a new firm survey tool) and then the collection of productivity and competition data (which was taken from more standard firm and industry data sources).

The data is detailed in table 1B.1 in Appendix B. Figures 1.2 and 1.3 plot some of the key cross-country averages. Looking at figure 1.2 there is a surprisingly large cross-country variation in hours worked, with French managers working about 68 percent of the annual hours worked by U.S. managers due to a combination of fewer hours per week, longer holidays, and more sick leave. United Kingdom and German managers work about

**Table 1.1**      **Empirical predictions of different models**

| | (1) | (2) | (3) | (4) | (5) | (6) |
|---|---|---|---|---|---|---|
| Symbol | $\dfrac{\partial w}{\partial X}$ | $\dfrac{\partial w}{\partial M}$ | $\dfrac{\partial y}{\partial X}$ | $\dfrac{\partial y}{\partial M}$ | $\dfrac{\partial X}{\partial Z}$ | $\dfrac{\partial M}{\partial Z}$ |
| Outcome | WLB outcomes | WLB outcomes | Productivity | Productivity | WLB practices | Management practices |
| Relationship | Derivative w.r.t. WLB practices | Derivative w.r.t. management practices | Derivative w.r.t. WLB practices | Derivative w.r.t. management practices | Derivative w.r.t. competition | Derivative w.r.t. competition |
| Pessimist | POSITIVE | NEGATIVE | NEGATIVE | POSITIVE | NEGATIVE | POSITIVE |
| Optimist | POSITIVE | POSITIVE | POSITIVE | POSITIVE | POSITIVE | POSITIVE |

*Note:* WLB = work-life balance; w.r.t. = with respect to.

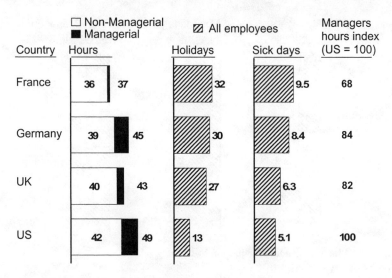

**Fig. 1.2    Managerial hours vary widely by country**

*Notes:* Country averages, per year except hours, which are per week. Average *managerial* hours. Assumes managers take "All employee" levels of holidays and sick leave, plus take ten days public holidays per year.

*Source:* Survey of 732 manufacturing firms.

82 percent and 84 percent of the U.S. managers' hours;[8] about equidistant between France and the United States.

In figure 1.3 we plot the share of women in the workforce at the managerial and nonmanagerial level. Looking first at *nonmanagerial* female involvement, we see this is higher in the United States, with around one third of nonmanagerial female workers in the United States, compared to about one quarter in Europe. While this difference is large, the gap at the *managerial* level is even greater. Only 12 percent of French managers are female compared to 31 percent in the United States. Hence, not only do U.S. firms have more female employees absolutely but they also appear to have relatively more female managers. Thus, at a first glance the French policy of regulating working hours does not seem to have been effective at ensuring female participation in the workforce, and particularly in the managerial workforce, which is often seen as an indirect indicator of work-life balance.

### 1.3.1    Scoring WLB and Management Practices

Measuring WLB and management practices requires codifying these concepts into something widely applicable across different firms. This is a hard

---

8. The surprisingly high hours are for German managers rather than workers—who work less than their UK counterparts.

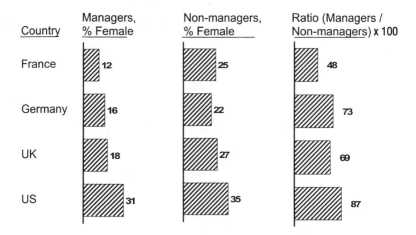

**Fig. 1.3    Manager gender distribution by country**
*Notes:* Country averages.
*Source:* Survey of 732 manufacturing firms.

task, as WLB and good management are tough to define. To do this we combined questions that have been used previously in the: (a) Workplace Employment Survey (WERS); (b) a management practice evaluation tool developed by a leading international management consultancy firm; and (c) the prior economics and management academic literature.

*Work-Life Balance*

In appendix A, table 1A.2, we detail the Human Resources Interview guide, which was used to collect a range of detailed WLB practices and characteristics from firms. We collected three types of key data:

- The first was the WLB perceptions data of individuals' on their own firms WLB versus other firms in the industry. This was used as our WLB *outcome* measure, defined as the response to the question: "Relative to other companies in your industry how much does your company emphasize work-life balance?", scored as: Much less (1); Slightly less (2); The same (3); Slightly more (4); Much more (5).
- The second was the WLB policies/practices data on key variables including childcare flexibility, home-working entitlements, part-time to full-time job flexibility, job-sharing schemes, and childcare subsidy schemes. This was used to construct our WLB *practice* measure defined as the average $z$ score[9] from the five questions: "If an employee needed to take

9. For comparability to the management $z$-score this WLB $z$-score (and the management $z$-score) were both renormalized to zero mean with standard deviation one. Hence, the coefficients on both the management and WLB practice $z$-scores in the tables of results both respond to one standard deviation change in both measures.

a day off at short notice due to childcare problems or their child was sick how do they generally do this?"; and the entitlements to "Working at home in normal working hours," "Switching from full-time to part-time work," "Job sharing schemes," and "Financial subsidy to help pay for childcare." These are all scored as yes/no.

* The third was workforce characteristic data on key variables including average employee age, hours, holidays, and proportion female, plus a full set of conditioning variables on skills (the proportion of college educated), training, and unionization. We used this data as a control for heterogeneity across firms.

*Management Practices*

In appendix A we detail the practices and the questions in the same order as they appeared in the survey, describe the scoring system, and provide three anonymous responses per question. These practices can be grouped into four areas: *operations* (3 practices), *monitoring* (5 practices), *targets* (5 practices), and *incentives* (5 practices). The *operations management* section focuses on the introduction of lean manufacturing techniques, the documentation of processes improvements, and the rationale behind introductions of improvements. The *monitoring* section focuses on the tracking of the performance of individuals, reviewing performance (e.g., through regular appraisals and job plans), and consequence management (e.g., making sure that plans are kept and appropriate sanctions and rewards are in place). The *targets* section examines the type of targets (whether goals are simply financial or operational or more holistic), the realism of the targets (stretching, unrealistic, or nonbinding), the transparency of targets (simple or complex), and the range and interconnection of targets (e.g., whether they are given consistently throughout the organization). Finally, *incentives* (or people management) include promotion criteria, pay and bonuses, and fixing or firing bad performers, where best practice is deemed to be an approach that gives strong rewards for those with both ability and effort. A subset of the practices has similarities with those used in studies on HRM practices, such as Ichniowski, Shaw, and Prenushi (1997), Black and Lynch (2001), and Bartel, Ichniowski, and Shaw (2004).

Since the scaling may vary across practices in the econometric estimation, we convert the scores (from the 1 to 5 scale) to $z$-scores by normalizing by practice to mean zero and standard deviation one. In our main econometric specifications, we take the unweighted average across all $z$-scores as our primary measure of overall managerial practice,[10] but we also experiment with other weightings schemes based on factor analytic approaches.

There is legitimate scope for disagreement over whether all of these mea-

---

10. This management $z$-score was then renormalized to zero mean and standard deviation one.

sures really constitute "good practice." Therefore, an important way to examine the external validity of the measures is to examine whether they are correlated with data on firm performance constructed from company accounts and the stock market.

### 1.3.2    Collecting Accurate Responses

With this evaluation tool we can, in principle, provide some quantification of firms' WLB and management practices. However, an important issue is the extent to which we can obtain unbiased responses to questions from firms. In particular, will respondents provide accurate responses? As is well known in the surveying literature (see, for example, Bertrand and Mullainathan [2001]), a respondent's answer to survey questions is typically biased by the scoring grid and anchored toward those answers that they expect the interviewer thinks is "correct." In addition, interviewers may themselves have preconceptions about the performance of the firms they are interviewing and bias their scores based on their *ex-ante* perceptions. More generally, a range of background characteristics, potentially correlated with good and bad managers, may generate some kinds of systematic bias in the survey data.

To try to address these issues we took a range of steps to obtain accurate data:

- First, the survey was conducted by telephone without telling the managers they were being scored.[11] This enabled scoring to be based on the interviewer's evaluation of the actual firm practices, rather than the firm's aspirations, the manager's perceptions, or the interviewer's impressions.[12] To run this blind scoring we used open questions (i.e., "Can you tell me how you promote your employees?"), rather than closed questions (i.e., "Do you promote your employees on tenure [yes/no]?"). These questions target actual practices and examples, with the discussion continuing until the interviewer could make an accurate assessment of the firm's typical practices. Typically, three to four questions were needed to score each practice.
- Second, the interviewers did not know anything about the firm's financial information or performance in advance of the interview. This was achieved by selecting medium-sized manufacturing firms and by providing only firm names and contact details to the interviewers (but no financial details). These smaller firms would typically not be known by

11. This survey tool has been passed by Stanford's Human Subjects Committee. The deception involved was deemed acceptable because it is: (a) *necessary* to get unbiased responses; (b) *minimized* to the management practice questions and is temporary (we send managers debriefing packs afterwards); and (c) *presents no risk* as the data is confidential.

12. If an interviewer could not score a question it was left blank, with the firm average taken over the remaining questions. The average number of unscored questions per firm was 1.3 percent, with no firm included in the sample if more than three questions were unscored.

name and are rarely reported in the business media. The interviewers were specially trained graduate students from top European and U.S. business schools, with a median age of twenty-eight and five years prior business experience in the manufacturing sector.[13] All interviews were conducted in the manager's native language.

- Third, each interviewer ran over fifty interviews on average, allowing us to remove interviewer fixed effects from all empirical specifications. This helped us to address concerns over inconsistent interpretation of categorical responses (see Manski 2004), standardizing the scoring system.

- Fourth, the survey instrument was targeted at plant managers, who are typically senior enough to have an overview of management practices but not so senior as to be detached from day-to-day operations of the enterprise.

- Fifth, a detailed set of information was also collected on the interview process itself (number and type of prior contacts before obtaining the interviews, duration, local time-of-day, date, and day-of-the week), on the manager (gender, seniority, nationality, company and job tenure, internal and external employment experience, and location), and on the interviewer (we can include individual interviewer fixed effects, time-of-day, and a subjective reliability score assigned by the interviewer). Some of these survey controls are significantly informative about the management score (see table 1B.2),[14] and when we use these as controls for interview noise in our econometric evaluations the coefficient on the management score typically increased (see Bloom and Van Reenen 2006).

### 1.3.3    Obtaining Interviews with Managers

The interview process took about fifty minutes on average, and was run from the London School of Economics. Overall, we obtained a high response rate of 54 percent, which was achieved through four steps.

- First, the interview was introduced as "a piece of work"[15] without discussion of the firm's financial position or its company accounts, making it relatively uncontroversial for managers to participate. Interviewers did not discuss financials in the interviews, both to maximize the par-

---

13. Thanks to the interview team of Johannes Banner, Michael Bevan, Mehdi Boussebaa, Dinesh Cheryan, Alberic de Solere, Manish Mahajan, Simone Martin, Himanshu Pande, Jayesh Patel, and Marcus Thielking.

14. In particular, we found the scores were significantly higher for senior managers when interviews were conducted later in the week and/or earlier in the day. That is to say, scores were highest, on average, for senior managers on a Friday morning and lowest for junior managers on a Monday afternoon. By including information on these characteristics in our analysis, we explicitly controlled for these types of interview bias.

15. Words like "survey" or "research" should be avoided as these are used by switchboards to block market research calls.

ticipation of firms and to ensure our interviewers were truly "blind" on the firm's financial position.

- Second, management questions were ordered to lead with the least controversial (shop-floor management) and finish with the most controversial (pay, promotions, and firings). The WLB questions were placed at the end of the interview to ensure the most candor in the response to this.
- Third, interviewers' performance was monitored, as was the proportion of interviews achieved, so they were persistent in chasing firms (the median number of contacts each interviewer had per interview was 6.4). The questions are also about practices within the firm that any plant manager can respond to, so there were potentially several managers per firm who could be contacted.[16]
- Fourth, written endorsement of the Bundesbank (in Germany) and the Treasury (in the United Kingdom), and a scheduled presentation to the Banque de France, helped demonstrate to managers this was an important exercise with official support.

### 1.3.4  Sampling Frame and Additional Data

Since our aim was to compare across countries we decided to focus on the manufacturing sector, where productivity is easier to measure than in the nonmanufacturing sector. We also focused on medium-sized firms, selecting a sample where employment ranged between fifty and 10,000 workers (with a median of 700). Very small firms have little publicly available data. Very large firms are likely to be more heterogeneous across plants, and it would be more difficult to get a picture of managerial performance in the firm as a whole from one or two plant interviews. We drew a sampling frame from each country to be representative of medium-sized manufacturing firms and then randomly chose the order of which firms to contact (see appendix B for details). We also excluded any clients of our partnering consultancy firm from our sampling frame.[17]

Comparing the responding firms with those in the sampling frame, we found no evidence that the responders were systematically different to the nonresponders on any of the performance measures. They were also statistically similar on all the other observables in our data set. The only exception was on size, where our firms were slightly larger than average than those in the sampling frame.

---

16. We found no significant correlation between the number, type, and time span of contacts before an interview is conducted and the management score. This suggests while different managers may respond differently to the interview proposition, this does not appear to be directly correlated with their responses or the average management practices of the firm.

17. This removed thirty-three firms out of our sampling frame of 1,353 firms.

### 1.3.5    Evaluating and Controlling for Potential Measurement Error

To quantify possible measurement error in the WLB and management practice scores obtained using our survey tool, we performed repeat interviews on management practice data on sixty-four firms—contacting different managers in the firm, typically at different plants, using different interviewers. To the extent that our measures are truly picking up general company-wide practices these two scores should be correlated, while if our measures are driven by noise these should be independent.

Figure 1.4 plots the average firm-level management scores from the first interview against the second interview, from which we can see that they are highly correlated (correlation 0.734 with $p$-value 0.000). Furthermore, there is no obvious (or statistically significant) relationship between the degree of measurement error and the absolute score. That is to say, high and low scores appear to be as well measured as average scores, and firms that have high (or low) scores on the first interview tend to have high (or low) scores on the second interview. Thus, firms that score below two or above four on the 1 to 5 scale of composite management scores appear to be genuinely badly or well managed rather than extreme draws of sampling measurement error.

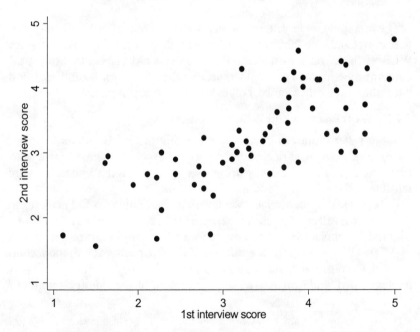

**Fig. 1.4    The management scoring appears reliable**

*Note:* Scores from sixty-four repeat interviews on the same firm with different managers and different interviewers.

### 1.3.6    Productivity and Competition Data

Quantitative information on firm sales, employment, capital, materials, and so forth came from the company accounts and proxy statements, and was used to calculate firm level productivity. The details are provided in appendix B. To measure competition we follow Nickell (1996) and Aghion et al. (2005) in using three broad measures. The first measure is the degree of import penetration in the country by three-digit industry measured as the share of total imports over domestic production. This is constructed for the period 1995 to 1999 to remove any potential contemporaneous feedback. The second is the country by three-digit industry Lerner index of competition, which is (1 − profits/sales), calculated as the average across the entire firm level database (excluding each firm itself).[18] Again, this is constructed for the period 1995 to 1999 to remove any potential contemporaneous feedback. The third measure of competition is the survey question on the number of competitors a firm faces (see appendix A, table 1A.2), valued zero for "no competitors," one for "less than 5 competitors," and two for "5 or more competitors".[19]

## 1.4    Results

The first thing we look at is whether our key measures of WLB outcomes were correlated with the practices that we might expect to improve employee WLB. If this did not turn out to be true, we would suspect that the WLB outcome measure was not really reflecting the actual events on the ground but rather some other unobservable firm-specific characteristic.

### 1.4.1    WLB Practices and WLB Outcomes

Table 1.2 examines this issue by regressing the WLB outcome indicator on a number of variables that we would expect to be associated with better work-life balance. Reassuringly we find that all the associations are sensible.

Column (1) simply correlates WLB with average hours worked per week in the firm across all employees. An extra ten hours a week worked is associated with a 0.4 points lower WLB score (about 12 percent lower than the mean of 3.21). This association is significant at the 5 percent level. In the second column we control for four country dummies, firm size, whether the firm is publicly listed, and firm age. With the exception of the country dummies[20]

---

18. Note that in constructing this we draw on firms in the population database, not just those in the survey.

19. This question has been used by inter alia Nickell (1996) and Stewart (1990).

20. The pattern of the country dummies suggests that conditional on other factors, Germans report the worst work-life balance and Americans report the best work-life balance. It is difficult to interpret these results, however, as the WLB question is relative to the industry

**Table 1.2**     **Work-life balance outcomes and WLB practices (dependent variable = WLB outcome score)**

| | (1) | (2) | (3) | (4) | (5) | (6) | (7) | (8) | (9) | (10) |
|---|---|---|---|---|---|---|---|---|---|---|
| Explanatory variable | Hours (all employees) | Hours (all employees) | Days holiday per year | WLB practices z-score | Working from home | Full-time/ part-time job | Job sharing | Childcare flexibility | Childcare subsidy | Share female managers |
| Explanatory coefficient | −0.038** | −0.037** | 0.026** | 0.230*** | 0.286** | 0.185* | 0.369** | 0.321** | 0.265** | 0.005** |
| | (0.012) | (0.012) | (0.007) | (0.041) | (0.098) | (0.094) | (0.151) | (0.094) | (0.106) | (0.002) |
| Controls | No | Yes | Yes | Yes | Yes | Yes | Yes | Yes | Yes | Yes |
| Firms | 525 | 525 | 523 | 477 | 489 | 489 | 484 | 513 | 486 | 521 |

*Notes:* In all columns, standard errors are in parentheses under coefficient estimates and allow for arbitrary heteroskedasticity. WLB outcome score is the response to the question: "Relative to other companies in your industry how much does your company emphasize work-life balance?", where scores are as follows: "Much less" (1); "Slightly less" (2); "The same" (3); "Slightly more" (4); and "Much more" (5). WLB practices z-score is the average z-score for the five practice "working from home allowed," "job switching allowed," "job sharing allowed," "childcare flexibility," and "childcare subsidy," normalized so this measure has a mean of 0 and standard deviation of 1. Controls include country dummies, log of employees, a dummy for public listing, and the ln(age) of the firm.

***Significant at the 1 percent level.

**Significant at the 5 percent level.

*Significant at the 10 percent level.

and firm size[21] all other variables are insignificant. The coefficient on managerial hours stays essentially the same.[22] Column (3) includes the number of days' holiday per year—more holidays are associated with a higher WLB score.

We next consider the composite WLB practices $z$-score (the average $z$-score across the five practices—working from home, job switching, job sharing, childcare flexibility, and childcare subsidy). When we include this WLB practice score in the regression in column (4), the variable is positive and highly significant. The next five columns show the correlation of WLB with each of the five practices individually.

Firms that are flexible and allow some working from home (column [5]), job switching (column [6]), and job sharing (column [7]) also have higher reported WLB outcomes. The next two columns show that firms who have more family-friendly policies with regard to allowing flexibility for employees to take time off for children[23] or offer childcare subsidies also score more highly on WLB. All of these correlations are significant and consistent with the notion that the WLB outcome measure reflects something real about the WLB policies in the firm.

The final column includes the proportion of female managers in the regression. Firms who have a greater proportion of female managers are also more likely to report a higher WLB outcome. This correlation is specifically related to the proportion of female managers, not females in the workplace as a whole. The share of females in nonmanagerial positions is not correlated with WLB. This suggests that the correlation does not simply arise from the fact that women are more or less attracted to different firms. More likely is some combination of: (a) in firms with more female managers there is greater decision-making support for improved WLB because the balance of power is more with women; and (b) female managers are attracted to firms with better WLB.

### 1.4.2   Work-life Balance and Management

Table 1.3 examines the correlation between WLB and our composite measure of good management described in the previous section. In previous

---

average so this implicitly removes the country effect if managers compare themselves to other firms in the same sector in the same country. The systematically lower score in Germany could reflect a "more negative" cultural bias in answering these questions.

21. Firm size is always strongly correlated with WLB, for example in column 2 of table 1.2 the coefficient (standard error) on log of employees is 0.104 (0.036), respectively.

22. If we split total hours into average hours worked by managers and average hours worked by nonmanagers both variables are negatively related to WLB at the 10 percent significance level or higher, suggesting WLB is related to the hours worked by both workers and managers.

23. Response to the question "If an employee needed to take a day off at short notice due to childcare problems or their child was sick how do they generally do this?", where this variable was ordered conceptually as: 1 = Not allowed; 2 = Allowed but unpaid; and 3 = Allowed and paid. Hence, we allocated the responses to the scores as follows: A score of 1 for "Not Allowed" or "Never been asked;" a score of 2 for "Take as leave without pay" or "Take time off but make it up later;" and a score of 3 for "Take as annual leave" or "Take as sick leave."

**Table 1.3    Work-life balance outcome scores, WLB practices, and management best practices (dependent variable = WLB outcome score)**

|  | (1) | (2) | (3) | (4) | (5) | (6) | (7) | (8) |
|---|---|---|---|---|---|---|---|---|
| Management practices z-score | 0.139*** | 0.106*** | 0.097** | 0.079* | | | | |
|  | (0.039) | (0.039) | (0.043) | (0.044) | | | | |
| WLB practices z-score | | 0.219*** | 0.206*** | 0.187*** | 0.196*** | 0.191*** | 0.191*** | 0.176*** |
|  | | (0.037) | (0.045) | (0.046) | (0.046) | (0.046) | (0.046) | (0.046) |
| Type of management |  |  |  |  |  |  |  |  |
| Operations | | | | | 0.023 | | | |
|  | | | | | (0.035) | | | |
| Monitoring | | | | | | 0.035 | | |
|  | | | | | | (0.037) | | |
| Targets | | | | | | | 0.042 | |
|  | | | | | | | (0.037) | |
| People | | | | | | | | 0.113** |
|  | | | | | | | | (0.045) |
| Standard controls | No | No | Yes | Yes | Yes | Yes | Yes | Yes |
| Full controls | No | No | No | Yes | Yes | Yes | Yes | Yes |
| Firms | 477 | 477 | 477 | 477 | 475 | 475 | 475 | 475 |

*Notes:* In all columns, standard errors are in parentheses under coefficient estimates and allow for arbitrary heteroskedasticity. WLB outcome score is the response to the question: "Relative to other companies in your industry how much does your company emphasize work-life balance?," where scores are as follows: "Much less" (1); "Slightly less" (2); "The same" (3); "Slightly more" (4); and "Much more" (5). Management practices z-score is the average z-score for the eighteen individual management practice scores, normalized so this measure has a mean of 0 and standard deviation of 1. WLB practices z-score is the average z-score for the five practice "working from home allowed," "full-time/part-time job switching allowed," "job sharing allowed," "childcare flexibility," and "childcare subsidy," normalized so this measure has a mean of 0 and standard deviation of 1. Standard Controls include country dummies, a dummy for public listing, the ln(age) of the firm plus the management measure noise controls. Full Controls includes controls for percentage employees with degrees, percentage of employees with MBAs, and a U.S. multinational and a non-U.S. multinational dummy.

***Significant at the 1 percent level.

**Significant at the 5 percent level.

*Significant at the 10 percent level.

work, we have found this a reliable metric of the overall degree of managerial quality in the firm and the management score is strongly correlated with superior firm performance. Is it the case that firms who adopt these better "Anglo-Saxon" management practices do so at the expense of employees' work-life balance?

In the first column of table 1.3, we regress our WLB outcome measure on the average management score and nothing else. There is a strong positive and significant correlation between the two variables. The second column then includes the composite score of the WLB practices. This is also positive and highly significant. The third column includes the "standard" vector of controls (firm size, firm age, country dummies, listing status, and controls for measurement error in the survey such as interviewer fixed effects). Both variables remain positive and significant. The fourth column includes skills and multinational status as additional controls. The skills measure—the proportion of workers with degrees—is significant at the 5 percent level. Hence, firms with higher skilled employees also tend to have better work-life balance practices. After including these additional controls, the management coefficient falls further and is now only significant at the 10 percent level. Hence, while WLB practices play a strong role in influencing the WLB outcomes, management practices per se play only a weak role in influencing these, after including a full set of control variables.

We then disaggregate our management measure into four components—operations, monitoring, targets, and people management (incentives). Interestingly, the WLB measure is correlated with each of these positively when entered individually into the regression (columns [5] through [8]), but only people management/incentives is significant at the 5 percent level. Thus, it appears that while WLB practices are linked with good management, this is much stronger for people management practices than other types of management practices.

### 1.4.3   Competition, Work-Life Balance, and Management

Having established the correlations of WLB with several factors, we now turn to the key hypotheses on competition and productivity. Our previous research found that tougher product market competition drives higher productivity[24] and at least part of this seems to work through improving management practices (Bloom and Van Reenen 2006). Nevertheless, does competition damage work-life balance?

Table 1.4 examines this question in detail. We measure competition by the degree of openness to trade (columns [1] and [2]), the degree of "excess profit" in the industry (columns [3] and [4]), or simply the number of competitors (columns [4] and [5]). In column (1) import competition is weakly

---

24. On the relationship between productivity and competition see also inter alia Nickell (1996) and Syverson (2004a, 2004b).

Table 1.4          Work-life balance outcomes and product market competition
(OLS estimation, dependent variable = WLB outcome score)

|  | (1) | (2) | (3) | (4) | (5) | (6) |
|---|---|---|---|---|---|---|
| Import penetration | 0.147* | 0.073 | | | | |
| (5-year lagged) | (0.079) | (0.145) | | | | |
| Lerner index of competition | | | 0.463 | 0.306 | | |
| (5-year lagged) | | | (0.858) | (1.118) | | |
| Number of competitors | | | | | 0.009 | −0.000 |
| | | | | | (0.081) | (0.084) |
| Firms | 492 | 492 | 486 | 486 | 524 | 530 |
| Country controls | Yes | Yes | Yes | Yes | Yes | Yes |
| Full controls | No | Yes | No | Yes | No | Yes |

*Notes:* Coefficients from OLS regressions with standard errors in parentheses (robust to arbitrary heteroskedasticity and clustered by country × industry pair); single cross-section. Country controls includes four country dummies. Full controls includes ln(firm size), ln(firm age), a dummy for being listed, the share of workforce with degrees, the share of workforce with MBAs, a dummy for being consolidated, and the survey noise controls. Import Penetration = ln(Import/Production) in every country industry pair. Average over 1995 to 1999 used. Lerner index of competition constructed, as in Aghion et al (2005), as the mean of (1 − profit/sales) in the entire database (excluding the firm itself) for every country industry pair. Number of competitors constructed from the response to the survey question on number of competitors, and is coded as 0 for "none" (1 percent of responses), 1 for "less than 5" (51 percent of responses), and 2 for "5 or more" (48 percent of responses). Columns (4) through (6) include the "noise controls" of column (2) in table 1A.2 (seventeen interviewer dummies, the seniority, gender, tenure, and number of countries worked in of the manager who responded, the day of the week the interview was conducted, the time of the day the interview was conducted, the duration of the interviews, and an indicator of the reliability of the information as coded by the interviewer).

***Significant at the 1 percent level.
**Significant at the 5 percent level.
*Significant at the 10 percent level.

and positively associated with better WLB, but this association disappears when we include the additional controls in column (2). A similar picture emerges in the other columns—competition is essentially uncorrelated with WLB outcomes. We conclude that although competition seems to improve management, it does *not* seem to reduce WLB.

We also estimated the relationship between competition and the WLB practices examined later in section 1.4.4—working from home flexibility, job switching flexibility, flexibility for childcare time off, and childcare subsidies—and found *no* significant relationships. We could not find any relationship between average hours worked per week or days holidays per year and competition. So we confirm the earlier conclusion that although competition seems to improve management, it does *not* seem to be associated with worse WLB outcomes or practices. While higher competition appears to increase management practices by removing the worst managed/least productive firms from the market it does not seem to affect WLB. This is presumably because—as we show in the next section—WLB practices and

Table 1.5          **Work-life balance practices are unrelated to productivity (All countries, OLS estimation, dependent variable = Ln (Sales$_{it}$))**

|  | (1) | (2) | (3) |
|---|---|---|---|
| WLB practices | 0.048** | 0.034 | −0.005 |
| z-score | (0.023) | (0.023) | (0.018) |
| Management z-score |  | 0.064*** | 0.038*** |
|  |  | (0.023) | (0.015) |
| Ln(Labor$_{it}$) | 0.983*** | 0.978*** | 0.500*** |
|  | (0.018) | (0.018) | (0.032) |
| Ln(Capital$_{it}$) |  |  | 0.122*** |
|  |  |  | (0.027) |
| Ln(Materials$_{it}$) |  |  | 0.370*** |
|  |  |  | (0.032) |
| Basic Controls | Yes | Yes | Yes |
| Full controls | No | No | Yes |
| Firms | 481 | 481 | 481 |

*Notes:* In all columns, standard errors are in parentheses under coefficient estimates and allow for arbitrary heteroskedasticity. Basic controls include country and industry dummies, log(firm age), public listing, and consolidated dummy. Full controls include industry dummies, log(firm age), public listing, percent of workforce with degrees, percent of employees with MBAs, U.S. multinational dummy and non-U.S. multinational dummy. Management practices z-score is the average z-score for the eighteen individual management practice scores, normalized so this measure has a mean of 0 and standard deviation of 1. WLB practices z-score is the average z-score for the five practice "working from home allowed," "full-time/part-time job switching allowed," "job sharing allowed," "childcare flexibility," and "childcare subsidy," normalized so this measure has a mean of 0 and standard deviation of 1.

*Source:* Bloom, Kretschmer, and Van Reenen (2008).

***Significant at the 1 percent level.
**Significant at the 5 percent level.
*Significant at the 10 percent level.

productivity are essentially unrelated, so that the selection effects of competition have no bearing on typical WLB practices.

### 1.4.4    Productivity, Work-Life Balance, and Management

Perhaps the most important issue is the association of WLB with productivity. We address this issue in table 1.5, which shows the results from simple production functions. We must always remember the caveat that these are associations and *we cannot infer causality.*[25] The dependent variable is the log of real sales and because we control for the factor inputs (labor, capital, and materials) the coefficient on WLB practices should be interpreted as the association with Total Factor (or revenue) Productivity (TFP). These variables are taken from company accounts as measured by the number of employees for labor, the net-tangible fixed assets for capital, and the reported materials

25. We are currently running field experiments in India to randomize improvement in management practices across firms to evaluate its causal impact on energy use.

costs. For labor we also control for the average hours worked in the firm. Of course one issue is the measurement error around these inputs that could lead to attenuation, which could potentially bias the results, particularly if this was correlated with the WLB measures (e.g., Siegel 1997).

Column (1) of table 1.5 reports the first specification that also includes country and industry dummies and basic controls (firm age, listing status, and a consolidation dummy). The association of WLB and productivity is positive and significant at the 5 percent level. This is the kind of regression highlighted in the Human Resource Management literature that is often used to justify policies to introduce better WLB practices.

Column (2) of table 1.5 simply conditions on our management $z$-score, which enters the production function with a positive and highly significant coefficient. The WLB practices variable, by contrast, falls in magnitude and is no longer significant at even the 10 percent level. When we condition on a wider set of controls in the next column (skills, multinational status, listing, and firm age), the management variable remains positive and significant (see Bloom and Van Reenen 2006) but the WLB practices variable is now negative, albeit completely insignificant.

Table 1.5 suggests that the significant association of WLB with productivity is spurious and arises because WLB is correlated with an important omitted variable—good management. Firms with better management practices will tend to have both higher productivity and better work-life balance. This gives rise (in column [1]) to the mistaken impression that better WLB causes higher productivity.

### 1.4.5   Multinationals, Work-Life Balance, and Management

Finally, in table 1.6 we examine some of the cross-country differences in WLB practices and management practices. The first column simply regresses the composite WLB practice measure on the country dummies (the United States is the omitted base). It is clear that the United States has less generous WLB practices than the European countries and France has more generous WLB practices than the United Kingdom or Germany. The second column includes dummy variables indicating whether for the European based firms they are a U.S. multinational or a non-U.S. multinational (European domestic firms are the omitted base).[26] The WLB does not seem worse in U.S. multinationals located overseas as indicated by the insignificant variable on the dummy than on the local domestic firms (and indeed the non-U.S. multinational dummy). This does not change when we condition on the more extended covariate set in column (3). Therefore, U.S. multinationals in Europe appear to adopt local work-life balance practices.

In contrast, columns (4) to (6) show that U.S. multinationals in Europe

26. Our U.S. firms are all publicly traded so we have no multinational subsidiaries in the U.S. Hence, these regressions compare between different types of European firms. Restricting the estimates to only European firms thus does not change the point estimates on the U.S. and non-U.S. multinationals.

Table 1.6    **Work-life balance and management practices in domestic and multinational firms (All countries, OLS estimation)**

| | Dependent variable = WLB practices z-score | | | Dependent variable = Management practices z-score | | |
|---|---|---|---|---|---|---|
| | (1) | (2) | (3) | (4) | (5) | (6) |
| Baseline is U.S. | | | | | | |
| Country is France | 1.066*** | 1.052*** | 1.284*** | −0.270*** | −0.302*** | −0.091 |
| | (0.0115) | (0.117) | (0.179) | (0.103) | (0.104) | (0.156) |
| Country is Germany | 0.306*** | 0.288*** | 0.368** | −0.093 | −.0142 | −0.067 |
| | (0.109) | (0.111) | (0.155) | (0.098) | (0.099) | (0.156) |
| Country is UK | 0.336*** | 0.320*** | 0.439*** | −0.359*** | −0.396*** | −0.290** |
| | (0.120) | (0.121) | (0.166) | (0.099) | (0.100) | (0.138) |
| U.S. Multinational in | | 0.229 | −0.059 | | 0.828*** | 0.679*** |
| (Europe) | | (0.255) | (0.215) | | (0.220) | (0.242) |
| Non-U.S. multi- | | 0.149 | 0.059 | | 0.077 | −0.223 |
| national (in Europe) | | (0.286) | (0.291) | | (0.251) | (0.316) |
| Basic controls | No | No | Yes | No | No | Yes |
| Firms | 492 | 492 | 492 | 732 | 732 | 732 |

*Notes:* In all columns, standard errors are in parentheses under coefficient estimates and allow for arbitrary heteroskedasticity. Basic controls include country and industry dummies, log(firm age), public listing, percent of workforce with degrees, and percent of employees with MBAs. Management practices z-score is the average z-score for the eighteen individual management practice scores, normalized so this measure has a mean of 0 and standard deviation of 1. WLB practices z-score is the average z-score for the five practice "working from home allowed," "full-time/part-time job switching allowed," "job sharing allowed," "childcare flexibility," and "childcare subsidy," normalized so this measure has a mean of 0 and standard deviation of 1.

***Significant at the 1 percent level.
**Significant at the 5 percent level.
*Significant at the 10 percent level.

bring over their better U.S. *management* practices. So in column (4) we see that on management practices the United Kingdom and France have significantly worse management practices than the United States and Germany. Including the multinational controls in column (5) we see when U.S. multinationals are located in Europe they appear to have significantly better management practices than equivalent non-U.S. multinationals and domestic firms (column [5]). In column (6), we see this result is robust to including additional covariates.

An interpretation of table 1.6 is that U.S. firms in general have better management practices but worse WLB policies. There are many complex reasons for these patterns. For example, although competition appears to be a reason for better U.S. management practices it cannot seem to explain its worse WLB outcomes as we showed that competition was unrelated to WLB in table 1.4. What is clear is that although U.S. firms appear to be able to transport their better management practices to Europe (column [6]), they do *not* transfer their worse WLB practices to Europe (column [3]). One rationale for this could be that European regulations require U.S. multinationals based in Europe to adopt these more worker-friendly practices. However, the work-life balance practices we measure—working from home, job-sharing, switching from full- to part-time, childcare flexibility, and childcare subsidies—are typically not directly regulated in Europe. Thus, our belief is that social norms explain much of this localization by U.S. multinationals, with this an area of ongoing research.

## 1.5    Conclusions

A debate is raging all over the developed world about quality of work issues. As unemployment has fallen in the United States and United Kingdom, attention has focused more on the quality rather than quantity of jobs. This has sharpened as women's participation has risen and issues of work-life balance and family-friendly policies have risen up the political agenda. This chapter has tried to shed some empirical light on these debates.

We characterized two opposing views of globalization, entitled the pessimistic and the optimistic view. The pessimists argue that "savage neo-liberalism" encapsulated by tougher product market competition, globalization, and "Anglo-Saxon" managerial policies are undesirable. Although these forces will raise productivity, they come at the expense of misery for workers in the form of poor work-life balance (long hours, job insecurity, and intense and unsatisfying work). The optimistic Human Resource Management literature argues that better work-life balance will, in fact, improve productivity (and even profitability) and employers are mistakenly failing to treat their workers as assets and implement better work-life balance policies.

We find evidence for a hybrid view between these two extremes. Using originally collected data, we show that we have a useful firm specific measure of WLB. The pessimists' argument that "Anglo-Saxon" management practices are negatively associated with worse WLB is rejected—there is a positive association as suggested by the optimists. Similarly, the pessimists' theory that competition is inevitably bad for workers' WLB is also rejected: there is no significantly negative relationship. Larger firms—which are typically more globalized—also have better WLB practices on average. However, the view that WLB will improve productivity is also rejected: there is no relationship between productivity and WLB once we control for good management. Neither is there support for the pessimists' prediction that WLB is negatively associated with productivity.

Finally, looking at U.S. multinationals based in Europe we find an intriguing result that these firms appear to bring over their superior U.S. management practices with them to Europe but then adopt more worker-friendly European work-life balance practices. Why U.S. firms internationalize their management practices but localize their work-life balance practices appears to be due to a combination of regulations and social norms, an area of ongoing research.

# Appendix A

## Management practice interview guide and example responses

Any score from 1 to 5 can be given, but the scoring guide and examples are only provided for scores of 1, 3, and 5. Multiple questions are used for each dimension to improve scoring accuracy.

(1) Modern manufacturing, introduction
  a) Can you describe the production process for me?
  b) What kinds of lean (modern) manufacturing processes have you introduced? Can you give me specific examples?
  c) How do you manage inventory levels? What is done to balance the line? What is the Takt time of your manufacturing processes?

| | Score 1 | Score 3 | Score 5 |
|---|---|---|---|
| Scoring grid: | Other than JIT delivery from suppliers few modern manufacturing techniques have been introduced, (or have been introduced in an ad-hoc manner). | Some aspects of modern manufacturing techniques have been introduced, through informal/isolated change programs. | All major aspects of modern manufacturing have been introduced (Just-in-time, autonomation, flexible manpower, support systems, attitudes, and behavior) in a formal way. |
| Examples: | A UK firm orders in bulk and stores the material on average six months before use. The business focuses on quality and not reduction of lead-time or costs. Absolutely no modern manufacturing techniques had been introduced. | A supplier to the army is undergoing a full lean transformation. For twenty years, the company was a specialty supplier to the army, but now they have had to identify other competencies forcing them to compete with lean manufacturers. They have begun adopting specific lean techniques and plan to use full lean by the end of next year. | A U.S. firm has formally introduced all major elements of modern production. It reconfigured the factory floor based on value stream mapping and 5-S principles, broke production into cells, eliminated stockrooms, implemented Kanban, and adopted Takt time analyses to organize workflow. |

(2) Modern manufacturing, rationale
  a) Can you take me through the rationale to introduce these processes?
  b) What factors led to the adoption of these lean (modern) management practices?

| | Score 1 | Score 3 | Score 5 |
|---|---|---|---|
| Scoring grid: | Modern manufacturing techniques were introduced because others were using them. | Modern manufacturing techniques were introduced to reduce costs. | Modern manufacturing techniques were introduced to enable us to meet our business objectives (including costs). |
| Examples: | A German firm introduced modern techniques because all its competitors were using these techniques. The business decision had been taken to imitate the competition. | A French firm introduced modern manufacturing methods primarily to reduce costs. | A U.S. firm implemented lean techniques because the chief operating officer (COO) had worked with them before and knew that they would enable the business to reduce costs, competing with cheaper imports through improved quality, flexible production, greater innovation, and just in time (JIT) delivery. |

(3) Process problem documentation
   a) How would you go about improving the manufacturing process itself?
   b) How do problems typically get exposed and fixed?
   c) Talk me through the process for a recent problem.
   d) Do the staff ever suggest process improvements?

| | Score 1 | Score 3 | Score 5 |
|---|---|---|---|
| Scoring grid: | No, process improvements are made when problems occur. | Improvements are made in one week workshops involving all staff, to improve performance in their area of the plant. | Exposing problems in a structured way is integral to individuals' responsibilities and resolution occurs as a part of normal business processes rather than by extraordinary effort/teams. |
| Examples: | A U.S. firm has no formal or informal mechanism in place for either process documentation or improvement. The manager admitted that production takes place in an environment where nothing has been done to encourage or support process innovation. | A U.S. firm takes suggestions via an anonymous box, they then review these each week in their section meeting and decide any that they would like to proceed with. | The employees of a German firm constantly analyze the production process as part of their normal duty. They film critical production steps to analyze areas more thoroughly. Every problem is registered in a special database that monitors critical processes and each issue must be reviewed and signed off by a manager. |

(4) Performance tracking
   a) Tell me how you track production performance.
   b) What kind of KPI's would you use for performance tracking? How frequently are these measured? Who gets to see this KPI data?
   c) If I were to walk through your factory could I tell how you were doing against your KPI's?

| | Score 1 | Score 3 | Score 5 |
|---|---|---|---|
| Scoring grid: | Measures tracked do not indicate directly if overall business objectives are being met. Tracking is an ad-hoc process (certain processes are not tracked at all). | Most key performance indicators are tracked formally. Tracking is overseen by senior management. | Performance is continuously tracked and communicated, both formally and informally, to all staff using a range of visual management tools. |
| Examples: | A manager of a U.S. firm tracks a range of measures when he does not think that output is sufficient. He last requested these reports about eight months ago and had them printed for a week until output increased again. | At a U.S. firm every product is bar-coded and performance indicators are tracked throughout the production process; however, this information is not communicated to workers. | A U.S. firm has screens in view of every line. These screens are used to display progress to daily target and other performance indicators. The manager meets with the shop floor every morning to discuss the day past and the one ahead and uses monthly company meetings to present a larger view of the goals to date and strategic direction of the business to employees. He even stamps napkins with key performance achievements to ensure everyone is aware of a target that has been hit. |

(*continued*)

**(5) Performance review**

a) How do you review your KPIs?
b) Tell me about a recent meeting.
c) Who is involved in these meetings? Who gets to see the results of this review?
d) What are the typical next steps after a meeting?

| | Score 1 | Score 3 | Score 5 |
|---|---|---|---|
| Scoring grid: | Performance is reviewed infrequently or in an unmeaningful way (e.g., only success or failure is noted). | Performance is reviewed periodically with successes and failures identified. Results are communicated to senior management. No clear follow-up plan is adopted. | Performance is continually reviewed, based on indicators tracked. All aspects are followed up ensure continuous improvement. Results are communicated to all staff. |
| Examples: | A manager of a U.S. firm relies heavily on his gut feel of the business. He will review costs when he thinks there is too much or too little in the stores. He admits he is busy so reviews are infrequent. He also mentioned staffs feel like he is going on a hunt to find a problem, so he has now made a point of highlighting anything good. | A UK firm uses daily production meetings to compare performance to plan. However, clear action plans are infrequently developed based on these production results. | A French firm tracks all performance numbers real time (amount, quality, etc.). These numbers are continuously matched to the plan on a shift-by-shift basis. Every employee can access these figures on workstations on the shop floor. If scheduled numbers are not met, action for improvement is taken immediately. |

**(6) Performance dialogue**

a) How are these meetings structured? Tell me about your most recent meeting.
b) During these meetings do you find that you generally have enough data?
c) How useful do you find problem-solving meetings?
d) What type of feedback occurs in these meetings?

| | Score 1 | Score 3 | Score 5 |
|---|---|---|---|
| Scoring grid: | The right data or information for a constructive discussion is often not present or conversations overly focus on data that is not meaningful. Clear agenda is not known and purpose is not stated explicitly. | Review conversations are held with the appropriate data and information present. Objectives of meetings are clear to all participating and a clear agenda is present. Conversations do not, as a matter of course, drive to the root causes of the problems. | Regular review/performance conversations focus on problem solving and addressing root causes. Purpose, agenda, and follow-up steps are clear to all. Meetings are an opportunity for constructive feedback and coaching. |
| Examples: | A U.S. firm does not conduct staff reviews. It was just "not the philosophy of the company" to do that. The company was very successful during the last decade and therefore did not feel the need to review their performance. | A UK firm focuses on key areas to discuss each week. This ensures they receive consistent management attention and everyone comes prepared. However, meetings are more of an opportunity for everyone to stay abreast of current issues rather than problem solve. | A German firm meets weekly to discuss performance with workers and management. Participants come from all departments (shop floor, sales, R&D, procurement, etc.) to discuss the previous week's performance and to identify areas to improve. They focus on the cause of problems and agree topics to be followed up the next week, allocating all tasks to individual participants. |

(7) Consequence management
  a) What happens if there is a part of the business (or a manager) who is not achieving agreed upon results? Can you give me a recent example?
  b) What kind of consequences would follow such an action?
  c) Are there any parts of the business (or managers) that seem to repeatedly fail to carry out agreed actions?

| | Score 1 | Score 3 | Score 5 |
|---|---|---|---|
| Scoring grid: | Failure to achieve agreed objectives does not carry any consequences. | Failure to achieve agreed results is tolerated for a period before action is taken. | A failure to achieve agreed targets drives retraining in identified areas of weakness or moving individuals to where their skills are appropriate. |
| Examples: | At a French firm no action is taken when objectives are not achieved. The president personally intervenes to warn employees but no stricter action is taken. Cutting payroll or making people redundant because of a lack of performance is very rarely done. | Management of a U.S. firm reviews performance quarterly. That is the earliest they can react to any underperformance. They increase pressure on the employees if targets are not met. | A German firm takes action as soon as a weakness is identified. They have even employed a psychologist to improve behavior within a difficult group. People receive ongoing training to improve performance. If this does not help they move them in other departments or even fire individuals if they repeatedly fail to meet agreed targets. |

(8) Target balance
  a) What types of targets are set for the company? What are the goals for your plant?
  b) Tell me about the financial and nonfinancial goals.
  c) What do CHQ (or their appropriate manager) emphasize to you?

| | Score 1 | Score 3 | Score 5 |
|---|---|---|---|
| Scoring grid: | Goals are exclusively financial or operational. | Goals include nonfinancial targets, which form part of the performance appraisal of top management only (they are not reinforced throughout the rest of organization). | Goals are a balance of financial and nonfinancial targets. Senior managers believe the nonfinancial targets are often more inspiring and challenging than financials alone. |
| Examples: | At a UK firm performance targets are exclusively operational. Specifically, volume is the only meaningful objective for managers, with no targeting of quality, flexibility, or waste. | For a French firm strategic goals are very important. They focus on market share and try to hold their position in technology leadership. However, workers on the shop floor are not aware of those targets. | A U.S. firm gives everyone a mix of operational and financial targets. They communicate financial targets to the shop floor in a way they found effective—for example, telling workers they pack boxes to pay the overheads until lunchtime and after lunch it is all profit for the business. If they are having a good day the boards immediately adjust and play the "profit jingle" to let the shop floor know that they are now working for profit. Everyone cheers when the jingle is played. |

*(continued)*

## (9) Target interconnection

a) What is the motivation behind your goals?
b) How are these goals cascaded down to the individual workers?
c) What are the goals of the top management team (do they even know what they are)?
d) How are your targets linked to company performance and their goals?

| | Score 1 | Score 3 | Score 5 |
|---|---|---|---|
| Scoring grid: | Goals are based purely on accounting figures (with no clear connection to shareholder value). | Corporate goals are based on shareholder value but are not clearly communicated down to individuals. | Corporate goals focus on shareholder value. They increase in specificity as they cascade through business units ultimately defining individual performance expectations. |
| Examples: | A family-owned firm in France is only concerned about the net income for the year. They try to maximize income every year without focusing on any long term consequences. | A U.S. firm bases its strategic corporate goals on enhancing shareholder value, but does not clearly communicate this to workers. Departments and individuals have little understanding of their connection to profitability or value with many areas labeled as "cost-centers" with an objective to cost-cut despite potentially disproportionately large negative impact on the other departments they serve. | For a U.S. firm, strategic planning begins with a bottom-up approach that is then compared with the top-down aims. Multifunctional teams meet every six months to track and plan deliverables for each area. This is then presented to the area head that then agrees or refines it and then communicates it down to his lowest level. Everyone has to know exactly how they contribute to the overall goals or else they will not understand how important the ten hours they spend at work every day is to the business. |

## (10) Target time horizon

a) What kind of time scale are you looking at with your targets?
b) Which goals receive the most emphasis?
c) How are long-term goals linked to short-term goals?
d) Could you meet all your short-run goals but miss your long-run goals?

| | Score 1 | Score 3 | Score 5 |
|---|---|---|---|
| Scoring grid: | Top management's main focus is on short term targets. | There are short- and long-term goals for all levels of the organization. As they are set independently, they are not necessarily linked to each other. | Long-term goals are translated into specific short-term targets so that short-term targets become a "staircase" to reach long-term goals. |
| Examples: | A UK firm has had several years of ongoing senior management changes—therefore senior managers are only focusing on how the company is doing this month versus the next, believing that long-term targets will take care of themselves. | A U.S. firm has both long- and short-term goals. The long-term goals are known by the senior managers and the short-term goals are the remit of the operational managers. Operations managers only occasionally see the longer-term goals so are often unsure how they link with the short-term goals. | A UK firm translates all their goals—even their five-year strategic goals—into short-term goals so they can track their performance to them. They believe that it is only when you make someone accountable for delivery within a sensible time frame that a long-term objective will be met. They think it is more interesting for employees to have a mix of immediate and longer-term goals. |

(11) Targets are stretching
a) How tough are your targets? Do you feel pushed by them?
b) On average, how often would you say that you meet your targets?
c) Are there any targets that are obviously too easy (will always be met) or too hard (will never be met)?
d) Do you feel that on targets that all groups receive the same degree of difficulty? Do some groups get easy targets?

| | Score 1 | Score 3 | Score 5 |
|---|---|---|---|
| Scoring grid: | Goals are either too easy or impossible to achieve; managers provide low estimates to ensure easy goals. | In most areas, top management pushes for aggressive goals based on solid economic rationale. There are a few "sacred cows" that are not held to the same rigorous standard. | Goals are genuinely demanding for all divisions. They are grounded in solid economic rationale. |
| Examples: | A French firm uses easy targets to improve staff morale and encourage people. They find it difficult to set harder goals because people just give up and managers refuse to work people harder. | A chemicals firm has two divisions, producing special chemicals for very different markets (military and civil). Easier levels of targets are requested from the founding and more prestigious military division. | A manager of a UK firm insisted that he has to set aggressive and demanding goals for everyone —even security. If they hit all their targets he worries he has not stretched them enough. Each KPI is linked to the overall business plan. |

(12) Performance clarity
a) What are your targets (i.e., do they know them exactly)? Tell me about them in full.
b) Does everyone know their targets? Does anyone complain that the targets are too complex?
c) How do people know about their own performance compared to other people's performance?

| | Score 1 | Score 3 | Score 5 |
|---|---|---|---|
| Scoring grid: | Performance measures are complex and not clearly understood. Individual performance is not made public. | Performance measures are well defined and communicated; performance is public in all levels but comparisons are discouraged. | Performance measures are well defined, strongly communicated, and reinforced at all reviews; performance and rankings are made public to induce competition. |
| Examples: | A German firm measures performance per employee based on differential weighting across twelve factors, each with its own measurement formulas (e.g., Individual versus average of the team, increase on prior performance, thresholds, etc.). Employees complain the formula is too complex to understand, and even the plant manager could not remember all the details. | A French firm does not encourage simple individual performance measures as unions pressure them to avoid this. However, charts display the actual overall production process against the plan for teams on regular basis. | At a U.S. firm, self-directed teams set and monitor their own goals. These goals and their subsequent outcomes are posted throughout the company, encouraging competition in both target setting and achievement. Individual members know where they are ranked, which is communicated personally to them biannually. Quarterly company meetings seek to review performance and align targets. |

(continued)

(13) Managing human capital

a) Do senior managers discuss attracting and developing talented people?
b) Do senior managers get any rewards for bringing in and keeping talented people in the company?
c) Can you tell me about the talented people you have developed within your team? Did you get any rewards for this?

| | Score 1 | Score 3 | Score 5 |
|---|---|---|---|
| Scoring grid: | Senior management do not communicate that attracting, retaining, and developing talent throughout the organization is a top priority. | Senior management believe and communicate that having top talent throughout the organization is a key way to win. | Senior managers are evaluated and held accountable on the strength of the talent pool they actively build. |
| Examples: | A U.S. firm does not actively train or develop its employees, and does not conduct performance appraisals or employee reviews. People are seen as a secondary input to the production. | A U.S. firm strives to attract and retain talent throughout the organization, but does not hold managers individually accountable for the talent pool they build. The company actively cross-trains employees for development and challenges them through exposure to a variety of technologies. | A UK firm benchmarks human resources practices at leading firms. A cross-functional HR excellence committee develops policies and strategies to achieve company goals. Bimonthly directors' meetings seek to identify training and development opportunities for talented performers. |

(14) Rewarding high-performance

a) How does you appraisal system work? Tell me about the most recent round.
b) How does the bonus system work?
c) Are there any nonfinancial rewards for top performers?
d) How does your reward system compare to your competitors?

| | Score 1 | Score 3 | Score 5 |
|---|---|---|---|
| Scoring grid: | People within our firm are rewarded equally irrespective of performance level. | Our company has an evaluation system for the awarding of performance-related rewards. | We strive to outperform the competitors by providing ambitious stretch targets with clear performance-related accountability and rewards. |
| Examples: | An East Germany firm pays its people equally and regardless of performance. The management said to us that "there are no incentives to perform well in our company." Even the management is paid an hourly wage, with no bonus pay. | A German firm has an awards system based on three components: the individual's performance, shift performance, and overall company performance. | A U.S. firm sets ambitious targets, rewarded through a combination of bonuses linked to performance, team lunches cooked by management, family picnics, movie passes, and dinner vouchers at nice local restaurants. They also motivate staff to try by giving awards for perfect attendance, best suggestion, etc. |

(15) Removing poor performers

a) If you had a worker who could not do his job what would you do? Could you give me a recent example?

b) How long would underperformance be tolerated?

c) Do you find any workers who lead a sort of charmed life? Do some individuals always just manage to avoid being fixed/fired?

| | Score 1 | Score 3 | Score 5 |
|---|---|---|---|
| Scoring grid: | Poor performers are rarely removed from their positions. | Suspected poor performers stay in a position for a few years before action is taken. | We move poor performers out of the company or to less critical roles as soon as a weakness is identified. |
| Examples: | A French firm had a supervisor who was regularly drinking alcohol at work but no action was taken to help him or move him. In fact, no employee had ever been laid off in the factory. According to the plant manager HR "kicked up a real fuss" whenever management wanted to get rid of employees, and told managers their job was production not personnel. | For a German firm it is very hard to remove poor performers. The management has to prove at least three times that an individual underperformed before they can take serious action. | At a U.S. firm, the manager fired four people during last couple of months due to underperformance. They continually investigate why and who are underperforming. |

(16) Promoting high performers

a) Can you rise up the company rapidly if you are really good? Are there any examples you can think of?

b) What about poor performers—do they get promoted more slowly? Are there any examples you can think of?

c) How would you identify and develop (i.e., train) your star performers?

d) If two people both joined the company five years ago and one was much better than the other would he/she be promoted faster?

| | Score 1 | Score 3 | Score 5 |
|---|---|---|---|
| Scoring grid: | People are promoted primarily upon the basis of tenure. | People are promoted upon the basis of performance. | We actively identify, develop, and promote our top performers. |
| Examples: | A UK firm promotes based on an individual's commitment to the company measured by experience. Hence, almost all employees move up the firm in lock step. Management was afraid to change this process because it would create bad feelings among the older employees who were resistant to change. | A U.S. firm has no formal training program. People learn on the job and are promoted based on their performance on the job. | At a UK firm each employee is given a red light (not performing), amber light (doing well and meeting targets), a green light (consistently meeting targets, very high performer), and a blue light (high performer capable of promotion of up to two levels). Each manager is assessed every quarter based on his succession plans and development plans for individuals. |

*(continued)*

(17) Attracting human capital
   a) What makes it distinctive to work at your company as opposed to your competitors?
   b) If you were trying to sell your firm to me how would you do this (get them to try to do this)?
   c) What don't people like about working in your firm?

| | Score 1 | Score 3 | Score 5 |
|---|---|---|---|
| Scoring grid: | Our competitors offer stronger reasons for talented people to join their companies. | Our value proposition to those joining our company is comparable to those offered by others in the sector. | We provide a unique value proposition to encourage talented people to join our company above our competitors. |
| Examples: | A manager of a firm in Germany could not give an example of a distinctive employee proposition and (when pushed) thinks the offer is worse than most of its competitors. He thought that people working at the firm "have drawn the short straw." | A U.S. firm seeks to create a value proposition comparable to its competitors and other local companies by offering competitive pay, a family atmosphere, and a positive presence in the community. | A German firm offers a unique value proposition through development and training programs, family culture in the company, and very flexible working hours. It also strives to reduce bureaucracy and seeks to push decision making down to the lowest levels possible to make workers feel empowered and valued. |

(18) Retaining human capital
   a) If you had a star performer who wanted to leave what would the company do?
   b) Could you give me an example of a star performer being persuaded to stay after wanting to leave?
   c) Could you give me an example of a star performer who left the company without anyone trying to keep them?

| | Score 1 | Score 3 | Score 5 |
|---|---|---|---|
| Scoring grid: | We do little to try and keep our top talent. | We usually work hard to keep our top talent. | We do whatever it takes to retain our top talent. |
| Examples: | A German firm lets people leave the company if they want. They do nothing to keep those people since they think that it would make no sense to try to keep them. Management does not think they can keep people if they want to work somewhere else. The company also will not start salary negotiations to retain top talent. | If management of a French firm feels that people want to leave the company, they talk to them about the reasons and what the company could change to keep them. This could be more responsibilities or a better outlook for the future. Managers are supposed to "take-the-pulse" of employees to check satisfaction levels. | A U.S. firm knows who its top performers are and if any of them signal an interest to leave it pulls in senior managers and even corporate HQ to talk to them and try and persuade them to stay. Occasionally they will increase salary rates if necessary and if they feel the individual is being underpaid relative to the market. Managers have a responsibility to try to keep all desirable staff. |

**Table 1A.1**         **Question level averages by country**

| Countries | Question number | Question type | Average value by country (United States = 100) | | | Regression coefficients |
|---|---|---|---|---|---|---|
| | | | (1) United Kingdom | (2) Germany | (3) France | (4) All |
| Modern manufacturing, introduction | 1 | Operations | 90.0 (3.50) | 86.4 (3.47) | 101.3 (3.63) | 0.017** (0.008) |
| Modern manufacturing, rationale | 2 | Operations | 92.9 (3.35) | 101.5 (3.32) | 101 (3.47) | 0.012 (0.009) |
| Process documentation | 3 | Operations | 89.0 (3.51) | 106.9 (3.49) | 99 (3.64) | 0.030*** (0.009) |
| Performance tracking | 4 | Monitoring | 98.3 (3.19) | 109.5 (3.17) | 111 (3.32) | 0.018** (0.009) |
| Performance review | 5 | Monitoring | 94.7 (2.99) | 110.2 (2.97) | 104 (3.10) | 0.016* (0.009) |
| Performance dialogue | 6 | Monitoring | 93.0 (3.19) | 103.3 (3.11) | 99 (3.27) | 0.019** (0.009) |
| Consequence management | 7 | Monitoring | 96.5 (3.02) | 108.7 (3.01) | 94 (3.13) | 0.019** (0.009) |
| Target breadth | 8 | Targets | 91.1 (3.53) | 93.3 (3.51) | 94 (3.66) | 0.027*** (0.009) |
| Target interconnection | 9 | Targets | 93.7 (3.56) | 97.3 (3.54) | 78 (3.68) | 0.023*** (0.009) |
| Target time horizon | 10 | Targets | 91.9 (3.69) | 98.6 (3.66) | 92 (3.83) | 0.021** (0.009) |
| Targets are stretching | 11 | Targets | 87.8 (3.34) | 104.9 (3.32) | 101 (3.45) | 0.015* (0.009) |
| Performance clarity and comparability | 12 | Monitoring | 93.7 (3.53) | 80.7 (3.49) | 83 (3.65) | 0.008 (0.009) |
| Managing human capital | 13 | Targets | 89.4 (3.94) | 99.0 (3.92) | 89 (4.08) | 0.023** (0.009) |
| Rewarding high performance | 14 | Incentives | 81.6 (3.42) | 85.2 (3.42) | 85 (3.55) | 0.022** (0.010) |
| Removing poor performers | 15 | Incentives | 89.4 (3.04) | 92.5 (3.02) | 83 (3.15) | 0.011 (0.009) |
| Promoting high performers | 16 | Incentives | 90.2 (2.86) | 104.9 (2.85) | 92 (2.97) | 0.017* (0.010) |
| Attracting human capital | 17 | Incentives | 90.4 (2.89) | 95.1 (2.88) | 85 (2.99) | 0.029*** (0.009) |
| Retaining human capital | 18 | Incentives | 93.6 (2.74) | 97.7 (2.73) | 97 (2.84) | 0.007 (0.009) |
| Unweighted average | | | 91.5 | 98.7 | 93.8 | 0.019 (0.009) |

*Notes:* In columns (1) to (3) standard deviation of each question's average response are reported below in brackets. Calculated from full sample of 732 firms. Management $z$-scores used in these calculations. In column (4) results from eighteen OLS estimations following exactly the same specification as column (1) in table 1.2 except estimated with each individual question $z$-score one-by-one rather than the average management $z$-score. So every cell in column (4) is from a different regression with 5,350 observations from 709 firms where: standard errors in parentheses allow for arbitrary heteroskedacity and correlation (clustered by firm), and regression includes "full controls" comprising of "firm" controls and "noise controls" as detailed in table 1.2.

***Significant at the 1 percent level.
**Significant at the 5 percent level.
*Significant at the 10 percent level.

**Table 1A.2**     **Human Resources interview guide (Run in parallel as the management survey but targeted at the HR department)**

| Workforce characteristics | |
| --- | --- |
| Data field | Breakdown |
| Total number of employees (cross check against accounts) | (All employees) |
| % with university degree | (All employees) |
| % with MBA | (All employees) |
| Average age of employees | (All employees) |
| % of employees | (Managerial/Nonmanagerial) |
| Average training days per year | (Managerial/Nonmanagerial) |
| Average hours worked per week (including overtime, excluding breaks) | (Managerial/Nonmanagerial) |
| Average holidays per year | (All employees) |
| Average days sick-leave | (All employees) |
| % part-time | (Managerial/Nonmanagerial) |
| % female | (Managerial/Nonmanagerial) |
| % employees abroad | (All employees) |
| % union membership | (All employees) |
| Are unions recognized for wages bargaining [yes / no] | (All employees) |

| Work-life balance outcome measure: | |
| --- | --- |
| Question | Response choice (all employees) |
| Relative to other companies in your industry how much does your company emphasize work-life balance? | [Much less / Slightly less / The same / Slightly more / Much more] |

| Work-life balance practices: | |
| --- | --- |
| Question | Response choice (managerial/nonmanagerial) |
| If an employee needed to take a day off at short notice due to childcare problems or their child was sick how do they generally do this? | [Not allowed / Never been asked / Take as leave without pay / Take time off but make it up later / Take as annual leave / Take as sick leave] |
| What entitlements are there to the following | Breakdown |
| Working at home in normal working hours? | (Managerial/Nonmanagerial) |
| Switching from full-time to part-time work? | (Managerial/Nonmanagerial) |
| Job sharing schemes? | (Managerial/Nonmanagerial) |
| Financial subsidy to help pay for childcare? | (Managerial/Nonmanagerial) |

| Organizational Characteristics | |
| --- | --- |
| Question | Response choice (all employees) |
| Who decides the pace of work? | [Exclusively workers / Mostly workers / Equally / Mostly managers / Exclusively managers] |
| Who decides how tasks should be allocated? | [Exclusively workers / Mostly workers / Equally / Mostly managers / Exclusively managers] |
| Do you use self-managing teams? | [V. heavily / Heavily / Moderately / Slightly / None] |

**Table 1A.2**          (continued)

| Market and firm questions: | Response choice |
| --- | --- |
| No. of competitors | [None / Less than 5 / 5 or more] |
| No. of hostile take-over bids in last three years | [None / One / More than one] |

| Interviewer's assessment of the scoring reliability |
| --- |

1 to 5 scoring system calibrated according to:
1 = Interviewee did not have enough expertise for interview to be valuable; I have significant doubts about most of the management dimensions probed.
3 = Interviewee had reasonable expertise; on some dimensions I am unsure of scoring.
5 = Interviewee had good expertise, I am confident that the score reflects management practices in this firm.

# Appendix B

## Data

Sampling Frame Construction

Our sampling frame was based on the Amadeus data set for Europe (United Kingdom, France, and Germany) and the Compustat data set for the United States. These all have information on company accounting data. We chose firms whose principal industry was in manufacturing and who employed (on average between 2000 and 2003) no less than fifty employees and no more than 10,000 employees. We also removed any clients of the consultancy firm we worked with from the sampling frame thirty-three out of 1,353 firms).

Our sampling frame is reasonably representative of medium-sized manufacturing firms. The European firms in Amadeus include both private and public firms whereas Compustat only includes publicly listed firms. There is no U.S. database with privately listed firms with information on sales, labor, and capital. Fortunately, there are a much larger proportion of firms listed on the stock exchange in the United States than in Europe so we were able to go substantially down the size distribution using Compustat. Nevertheless, the U.S. firms in our sample are slightly larger than those of the other countries, so we were always careful to control for size and public listing in the analyses. Furthermore, when estimating production functions we could allow all coefficients to be different on labor, capital, materials, and consolidation status by country.

Another concern is that we conditioned on firms where we have information on sales, employment, and capital. These items are not compulsory for firms below certain size thresholds so disclosure is voluntary to some extent for the smaller firms. Luckily, the firms in our sampling frame (over fifty workers) are past the threshold for voluntary disclosure (the only exception is for capital in Germany).

We achieved a response rate of 54 percent from the firms that we contacted: a very high success rate given the voluntary nature of participation. Respondents were not significantly more productive than nonresponders. French firms were slightly less likely to respond than firms in the other three countries and all respondents were significantly larger than nonrespondents. Apart from these two factors, respondents seemed randomly spread around our sampling frame.

Firm Level Data

Our firm accounting data on sales, employment, capital, profits, shareholder equity, long-term debt, market values (for quoted firms), and wages (where available) came from Amadeus (France, Germany, and the United Kingdom) and Compustat (United States). For other data fields we did the following.

*Materials.* In France and Germany these are line items in the accounts. In the United Kingdom these were constructed by deducting the total wage bill from the cost of goods sold. In the United States these were constructed following the method in Bresnahan, Brynjolfsson, and Hitt (2002). We start with costs of goods sold (COGS) less depreciation (DP) less labor costs (XLR). For firms who do not report labor expenses expenditures we use average wages and benefits at the four-digit industry level (Bartelsman, Becker, and Gray [2000] until 1996 and then Census Average Production Worker Annual Payroll by four-digit North American Industry Classification System [NAICS] code) and multiply this by the firm's reported employment level. This constructed measure is highly correlated at the industry level with materials. Obviously there may be problems with this measure of materials (and therefore value-added), which is why we check robustness to measures without materials.

Industry Level Data

This comes from the Organization for Economic Cooperation and Development (OECD) STAN database of industrial production. This is provided at the country International Standard Industrial Classification (ISIC) Rev. 3 level and is mapped into US Standard Industrial Classification (SIC) (1997) three (which is our common industry definition in all four countries).

**Table 1B.1       Descriptive statistics**

| | All | France | Germany | United Kingdom | United States |
|---|---|---|---|---|---|
| Number of firms | 732 | 135 | 156 | 151 | 290 |
| Work-life balance | 3.21 | 3.44 | 3.03 | 3.19 | 3.22 |
| Management (mean z score) | −0.001 | −0.084 | 0.032 | −0.150 | 0.097 |
| Employment (mean) | 1,984 | 1,213 | 1,816 | 1,735 | 2,569 |
| Labor share of output (%) | 26.4 | 23.5 | 28.2 | 27.2 | 28.0 |
| Tobin's Q | 1.71 | 1.16 | 1.86 | 2.01 | 0.88 |
| Nominal sales growth rate (%) | 6.0 | 5.4 | 3.8 | 6.8 | 7.2 |
| Age of firm (years) | 53.4 | 38.6 | 86.8 | 44.7 | 48.4 |
| Listed firm (%) | 57.2 | 16.1 | 41.0 | 28.5 | 100 |
| Multinational subsidiary (%) | 5.1 | 8.9 | 7.1 | 9.3 | 0 |
| Share workforce with degrees (%) | 21.2 | 15.5 | 14.3 | 14.0 | 31.0 |
| Share workforce with an MBA (%) | 1.36 | 0.23 | 0.09 | 1.28 | 2.73 |
| Sickness, days per year | 6.80 | 8.16 | 8.51 | 6.21 | 5.01 |
| Hours, hours per week | 40.7 | 35.6 | 38.6 | 40.8 | 44.1 |
| Holidays, days per year | 22.7 | 32.2 | 29.7 | 26.9 | 12.4 |
| Union density (%) | 19.9 | 9.7 | 41.4 | 25.3 | 9.4 |
| Number of competitors index, 1 = none, 2 = a few, 3 = many | 2.47 | 2.32 | 2.35 | 2.53 | 2.56 |
| Lerner index, excluding the firm itself | 0.055 | 0.040 | 0.071 | 0.040 | 0.060 |
| Trade openness (imports/output) | 0.31 | 0.33 | 0.32 | 0.42 | 0.24 |
| Childcare flexibility (see table 1A.2; 1 is none and 3 is maximum) | 2.82 | 2.75 | 2.85 | 2.82 | 2.85 |
| Working from home (% that allow this) | 31.6 | 23.4 | 31.7 | 44.1 | 30.1 |
| Switching from full-time to part-time (% that allow this) | 48.0 | 76.5 | 61.5 | 43.7 | 27.8 |
| Job-sharing (% that allow this) | 10.0 | 21.0 | 7.7 | 15.5 | 3.6 |
| Childcare subsidy (% that provide this) | 16.6 | 58.5 | 5.3 | 3.4 | 8.4 |

*Notes:* Data descriptive calculated on the full sample of 732 firms for which management information is available.

**Table 1B.2**      **Controls for measurement error**

| Explanatory variable | Definition | Mean | Coefficient (s.e.) | Coefficient (s.e.) |
|---|---|---|---|---|
| Male | Respondent is male | 0.982 | −0.277 (0.128) | −0.298 (0.127) |
| Seniority | The position of manager in the organization (1 to 5) | 3.08 | 0.074 (0.026) | 0.073 (0.026) |
| Tenure in this post | Years with current job title | 4.88 | −0.011 (0.007) | −0.009 (0.006) |
| Tenure in the company | Years with the company | 11.7 | 0.002 (0.004) | |
| Countries | Total number of countries worked in over last ten years | 1.19 | 0.085 (0.048) | 0.092 (0.043) |
| Organizations | Total number of organizations worked in over last ten years | 1.66 | −0.009 (0.032) | |
| Manager is foreign | Manager was born outside the country s/he works | 0.032 | −0.048 (0.142) | |
| Ever worked in United States | The manager has worked in the United States at some point | 0.425 | 0.103 (0.152) | |
| Location of manager | Manager based onsite (rather than in corporate HQ) | 0.778 | 0.011 (0.063) | |
| Tuesday | Day of the week that interview was conducted (Monday base) | 0.181 | 0.011 (0.062) | 0.016 (0.086) |
| Wednesday | Day of the week that interview was conducted (Monday base) | 0.280 | 0.017 (0.084) | 0.014 (0.080) |
| Thursday | Day of the week that interview was conducted (Monday base) | 0.195 | 0.183 (0.088) | 0.176 (0.088) |
| Friday | Day of the week that interview was conducted (Monday base) | 0.165 | 0.059 (0.090) | 0.054 (0.090) |
| Local time for manager | The time of the day (24 hour clock) interview conducted | 12.45 | −0.023 (0.010) | −0.022 (0.010) |
| Days from start of project | Count of days since start of the project | 39 | 0.001 (0.001) | |
| Duration of interview | The length of the interview with manager (in minutes) | 46.0 | 0.008 (0.003) | 0.007 (0.003) |
| Number of contacts | Number of telephone calls to arrange the interview | 5.73 | 0.007 (0.006) | |
| Reliability score | Interviewer's subjective ranking of interview reliability (1 to 5) | 4.15 | 0.326 (0.034) | 0.327 (0.033) |
| 17 Interviewers Dummies | | | $F_{(15,699)} = 3.05$ $p$-value $= 0.000$ | $F_{(15,699)} = 3.46$ $p$-value $= 0.000$ |

*Notes:* Dependent variable is Management $z$-score. Coefficients from ordinary least squares (OLS) regressions with standard errors (s.e.) in parentheses (robust to arbitrary heteroskedasticity); single cross section; 3 country dummies and 108 three-digit industry dummies included in the regression; 732 observations.

# References

Aghion, P., N. Bloom, R. Blundell, R. Griffith, and P. Howitt. 2005. Competition and innovation: An inverted U relationship. *Quarterly Journal of Economics* 120 (2): 701–28.

Arthur, M. 2003. Share price reactions to work-family initiatives: An institutional perspective. *Academy of Management Journal* 46 (4): 497–505.

Bartel, A., C. Ichniowski, and K. Shaw. 2004. Using "insider econometrics" to study productivity. *American Economic Review* 94 (2): 217–23.

Bartelsman, E., R. Becker, and W. Gray. 2000. The NBER manufacturing productivity database. *National Bureau of Economic Research.* Available at http://www.nber.org/nberces/nbprod96.htm.

Bertrand, M., and S. Mullainathan. 2001. Do people mean what they say? Implications for subjective survey data. *American Economic Review Papers and Proceedings* 91 (2): 67–72.

Black, S., and L. Lynch. 2001. How to compete: The impact of workplace practices and information technology on productivity. *Review of Economics and Statistics* 83 (3): 434–45.

Bloom, N., and J. Van Reenen. 2007. Measuring and explaining management practices across firms and countries. *Quarterly Journal of Economics* (November): 1351–1408.

Bloom, N., C. Genakos, R. Martin, and R. Sadun. 2008. Modern management: Good for the environment or just hot air? NBER Working Paper no. 14394. Cambridge, MA: National Bureau of Economic Research, October.

Bloom, N., T. Kretschmer, and J. Van Reenen. 2009. Determinants and consequences of family-friendly workplace practices—An International Study. LSE/Stanford mimeo.

Bresnahan, T., E. Brynjolfsson, and L. Hitt. 2002. Information technology, workplace organization, and the demand for skilled labor: Firm-level evidence. *Quarterly Journal of Economics* 117 (1): 339–76.

Budd, J., and K. Mumford. Forthcoming. Family-friendly work practices in Britain: Availability and effective coverage. *Human Resource Management.*

Delaney, J., and M. Huselid. 1996. The impact of human resource management practices on perceptions of organizational performance. *Academy of Management Journal* 39 (4): 949–69.

Gray, H. 2002. Family-friendly working: What a performance! An analysis of the relationship between the availability of family friendly policies and establishment performance. Centre for Economic Performance Discussion Paper no. 529.

Gray, M., and J. Tudball. 2003. Family-friendly work practices: Differences within and between workplaces. *Journal of Industrial Relations* 45 (3): 269–91.

Guthrie, J. 2001. High-involvement work practices, turnover, and productivity: Evidence from New Zealand. *Academy of Management Journal* 44 (1): 180–90.

Guthrie, J., and L. Roth. 1999. The state, courts and maternity policies in US organizations: Specifying institutional arrangements. *American Sociological Review* 64:41–63.

Guthrie, J., C. Spell, and R. Nyamori. 2002. Correlates and consequences of high involvement work practices: The role of competitive strategy. *International Journal of Human Resource Management* 13 (1): 183–97.

Harel, G., S. Tzafrir, and Y. Baruch. 2003. Achieving organizational effectiveness through promotion of women into managerial positions: HRM practice focus. *International Journal of Human Resource Management* 14 (2): 247–63.

Huselid, M., S. Jackson, and R. Schuler. 1997. Technical and strategic human resource management effectiveness as determinants of firm performance. *Academy of Management Journal* 40 (1): 171–88.

Ichniowski, C., K. Shaw, and G. Prenushi. 1997. The effects of human resource management practices on productivity: A study of steel finishing lines. *American Economic Review* 87 (3): 291–313.

Konrad, A., and R. Mangel. 2000. The impact of work-life programs on firm productivity. *Strategic Management Journal* 21 (12): 1225–37.

Lee, J., and D. Miller. 1999. People matter: Commitment to employees, strategy and performance in Korean firms. *Strategic Management Journal* 20 (6): 579–93.

Manski, C. 2004. Measuring expectations. *Econometrica* 72 (5): 1329–76.

Martins, L., K. Eddleston, and J. Veiga. 2002. Moderators of the relationship between work-family conflict and career satisfaction. *Academy of Management Journal* 45 (2): 399–409.

Miliken, F., L. Martins, and H. Morgan. 1998. Explaining organizational responsiveness to work-family issues: The role of human resource executives as issue interpreters. *Academy of Management Journal* 41 (5): 580–92.

Nickell, S. 1996. Competition and corporate performance. *Journal of Political Economy* 104 (4): 724–46.

O'Mahony, M., and B. van Ark, eds. 2003. *EU productivity and competitiveness: An industry perspective. Can Europe resume the catching-up process?* Luxembourg: Office for Official Publications of the European Communities.

Osterman, P. 1995. Work/family programs and the employment relationship. *Administrative Science Quarterly* 40 (4): 681–700.

Perry-Smith, J., and T. Blum. 2000. Work-family human resource bundles and perceived organizational performance. *Academy of Management Journal* 43 (6): 1107–17.

Pfeffer, J. 1983. *Competitive advantage through people.* Cambridge, MA: Harvard University Press.

Schuler, R., and I. MacMillan. 1984. Gaining competitive advantage through human resource practices. *Human Resource Management* 23 (3): 241–55.

Siegel, D. 1997. The impact of investments in computers on manufacturing productivity growth: A multiple-indicators, multiple causes approach. *The Review of Economics and Statistics* 79:68–78.

Stewart, M. 1990. Union wage differentials, product market influences and the division of rents. *Economic Journal* 100 (4): 1122–37.

Syverson, C. 2004a. Market structure and productivity: A concrete example. *Journal of Political Economy* 112 (6): 1181–1222.

Syverson, C. 2004b. Product substitutability and productivity dispersion. *Review of Economics and Statistics* 86 (2): 534–50.

Youndt, M., S. Snell, J. Dean, and D. Lepak. 1996. Human resource management, manufacturing strategy, and firm performance. *Academy of Management Journal* 39 (4): 836–66.

# 2

# International Differences in the Adoption and Impact of New Information Technologies and New HR Practices
## The Valve-Making Industry in the United States and United Kingdom

Ann Bartel, Casey Ichniowski, Kathryn L. Shaw, and
Ricardo Correa

## 2.1  Introduction

There is now a well-developed body of macroeconomic evidence that information technology (IT) investments are likely to have paid-off with higher levels of productivity growth in industries that invested more heavily in IT in recent years.[1] In our own work (Bartel, Ichniowski, and Shaw 2007), we have documented that plants that adopt new IT are in fact the same ones that increase the customization and reliability of their products and the speed and efficiency of their operations, thereby providing an explanation of what lies behind the macro-level trends. Other researchers have also reported micro-level evidence on the relationship between IT and productivity.[2] An important question is whether plants outside of the United States gain as much from IT as U.S. plants. This chapter contributes to that literature by providing comparative evidence on the adoption rates and impact of new

Ann Bartel is the A. Barton Hepburn Professor of Economics at Columbia University Graduate School of Business and a research associate of the National Bureau of Economic Research. Casey Ichniowski is the Carson Family Professor of Business Management at Columbia University Graduate School of Business and a research associate of the National Bureau of Economic Research. Kathryn L. Shaw is the Ernest C. Arbuckle Professor of Economics at Stanford University Graduate School of Business and a research associate of the National Bureau of Economic Research. Ricardo Correa is an Economist in the Division of International Finance at the Board of Governors of the Federal Reserve System.

We are grateful for the support of the Alfred P. Sloan Foundation, the Russell Sage Foundation, and the managers and employees of the firms we visited.

1. See Jorgenson, Ho, and Stiroh (2003) and Oliner and Sichel (2000).

2. See Bloom and Van Reenen (2007); Brynjolfsson and Hitt (2000); Athey and Stern (2002); Hubbard (2003); and McGuckin, Streitwieser, and Doms (1998).

information technologies (and related HR practices) in the valve industry in the United States and United Kingdom.[3]

The microeconomic evidence in this chapter is based on data obtained from plant visits and our own detailed survey of plants in the valve-making industry in the United States and United Kingdom. By using our own personally designed survey we are uniquely able to identify precise ways in which firms have both adopted and benefited from the investments in IT. Ours is the first study to have detailed microeconomic evidence linking IT, HR, productivity, and skill demand for plants in the same industry in two different countries. Our data enable us to address the following questions: Have valve-making plants in the United States and United Kingdom adopted new IT and new HR practices at the same rate? What has been the impact of new IT and new HR on productivity in the two countries? Has the adoption of new IT influenced skill demand and has this impact differed in the United States and United Kingdom?

Our main findings can be summarized as follows. The plants in the United Kingdom and United States are not identical in their characteristics: the UK plants are more unionized, smaller, and thus have fewer advanced machines, sell more to wholesalers, and less directly to a primary customer. However, in the five years that we follow these plants (1997 to 2002), they have moved in virtually identical directions, as is evident in the means of the variables and the regression results. We find the following results:

1. While U.S. valve-makers adopted computer numerically controlled (CNC) technology earlier than plants in the United Kingdom, by 2002, UK plants were just as likely to be using CNC technology as their U.S. counterparts. Over the last five years, in both countries there was pronounced growth in IT technology, new HR practices, and increased skill demand. There has also been nearly identical and substantial increases in the efficiency of production and the customization of the products.

2. The impact of CNC technology on the efficiency of production is virtually identical in the two countries; plants in both countries have experienced reductions in setup-times, runtimes, and inspection times as a result of the new information technologies.

3. As a result of the adoption of new IT-enhanced equipment, plants in both countries have shifted production to customized products.

4. In both countries, there is a positive correlation between the adoption of new IT and the adoption of new HR practices.

5. The adoption of new computer-based IT increases the technical and problem-solving skill requirements of workers in both countries and this effect is stronger in the United Kingdom.

---

3. See Bloom and Van Reenen (2007) for broader firm-level evidence on the impact and adoption of management practices in which they show differences between the United States and United Kingdom.

These findings lead us to conclude that even though the United Kingdom has a different history of labor market institutions, small valve-making firms are operating in much the same way in the United Kingdom as in the United States. This suggests that plants in both countries have been responsive to similar market pressures following a decline in the price of computerization.

The chapter is organized as follows. Section 2.2 describes the valve-making production process and the data that we collected in our survey of the industry. Section 2.3 compares the adoption rates of new IT and HR practices in the United States and United Kingdom and recent trends in the efficiency of production in the two countries. Sections 2.4 through 2.6 present econometric evidence on the relationship of new IT investments to process efficiency, product innovation, worker skills, and employment practices in the United States and United Kingdom. Section 2.7 concludes.

## 2.2   Survey Data on the Valve-Making Industry in the United States and United Kingdom

In this section, we provide background on the valve-making industry and describe the findings from plant visits that proved critical to the design of an accurate industry survey.[4]

### 2.2.1   The Production Process and Information Technologies in Valve Manufacturing

A valve is a metal device attached to pipes to regulate the flow of liquids or gases—such as the flow of natural gas in a heating system, or the control of liquids in a chemical factory. Valves can be a commodity product—as when they control the flow of air in standard air conditioners—or they can be a highly customized product—as when they are built to order for a new chemical plant or a submarine. The production process in valve making is a machining operation.[5] A simple valve is made by taking a steel block or pipe and completing several processes on one or more machines, such as: etching grooves at each end for screwing the valve to pipes; boring holes at different spots to attach control devices; and making and attaching various devices that control the flow.

### *IT and Capital Machinery*

Thirty years ago, the reshaping of the steel pipe or block would be done on a workbench by a highly skilled machinist using manual tools. Today, much of valve making is highly automated with new computer-based IT features

4. See Bartel, Ichniowski, and Shaw (2004) for a discussion of methods to use for assembling detailed organization-level data.
5. Other processes are welding and assembly of multiple machined parts and final packaging and shipping.

embedded directly in valve-making equipment. The central piece of equipment in the valve-making production process is a *computer numerically controlled (CNC) machine* that lines up the block on the pallet of the machine and automatically drills and chips in the proper places based on directions entered into the machine's operating software.[6] The CNC machines are now in widespread use in the industry, as will be shown in our data following.

As information processing technologies improve, greater computing power is embedded directly into newer CNC machines, computing power that can reduce setup-time substantially and, to a lesser extent, reduce runtime. Because the computing power is intangible (or embedded in the capital), only descriptive field research can reveal the source of the IT gains. Therefore, we offer numerous examples to explain the IT gains.

The key IT element of the CNC machine is in the CNC *controller,* or box that controls the machine. The controller tells the machine exactly what to do to make each particular valve—where to cut, how deep, the angle of the cut, the diameter, how many times to cut, how to move the steel to recut, and so forth. Improvements in software go hand-in-hand with setup-time reduction. More precisely, after 1998, CNC were equipped with fusion control that is much easier to program and much easier for operators to understand (more conversational) and this control technology became standard in 2003 for new vintage CNC machines.[7] While the computerization in the CNC label began when the CNC machines were introduced in the 1970s, at that time the CNC was controlled by computer tapes that were programmed off-line by computer programmers and fed to the machine for the operator to run. Today, the computers in the CNC machines are controlled and programmed by the operators, and are dramatically faster and cheaper.

The computerization of the CNC has also reduced the runtime of the machines when they are doing the cutting and drilling, though to a lesser extent than setup reduction (since runtime is ultimately limited by how fast you can cut steel). The cost reduction for controllers has enabled CNC to add axis capabilities: a five-axis CNC machine tool can drill holes into a valve at several different angles (or axes) while a three-axis CNC machine tool would require the valve to be manually repositioned within the machine tool for each new drill angle. Thus, computerization has directly enabled the machine to increase the number of axes on which it can operate, and this has directly reduced the runtime (and setup-time) and increased the flexibility of the machine. There have also been advances in the IT component of CNC controllers that allow the controller to use its computing resources more efficiently. An example is curve interpolation, which allows CNC machine

6. The CNC machines were predated by numerically controlled (NC) machines in which fixed computer programs for a given run, originally input on tape, controlled the action of machines during that run. Manual, NC, and CNC machines of different vintages all still exist in the industry, but sophisticated CNC are now dominant.

7. As stated by the chief operating officer of a plant that we visited.

tools to create smooth curves on a valve instead of having to approximate curves using a large number of linear cuts. This reduces the software program size, which decreases the amount of memory needed to perform a given task, thus lowering setup-time and runtime.

Overall, increases in computing power improved the capabilities of CNC machines considerably. Operators can now program a modern CNC machine more easily through much simpler software interfaces, and each machine can now perform a much wider variety of tasks on the block of steel. *Most important for our empirical work following, plant managers and engineers demonstrated how investing in technologically more capable CNC machines leads to a reduction in the number of CNC machines needed to produce a given product.* For example, in 1980 a typical product at one plant required seven machines; by 2002 that same product would be made on two more advanced CNC machines. The only way that the same product can be produced on fewer machines is if the quality of the CNC has improved through the purchase of new CNC machines that are IT intensive. Thus, when the number of CNC machines falls over time, CNC quality must be rising (according to our experts).

A second technology, *flexible manufacturing systems* (FMS), coordinates machining operations across different CNC machines. To implement FMS, a separate computer is installed and hooked up to the control boxes on the CNC machines so that the FMS system can control the coordination of the production tasks across different CNC machines. By coordinating across machines, it clearly reduces setup-time—setup instructions are given directly to the machines it is coordinating when the production of a valve requires multiple machines. The FMS also does a better job of optimizing which part of the valve should be produced on which CNC machine. In addition, FMS also reduces runtime. The FMS also typically monitors the machine tools themselves (that are in the CNC) using its centralized data. The coordination process reduces the number of tool changes that are required as it allocates jobs across CNC machines, and it reduces the cost of calibrating each cutting step, which increases cutting accuracy and speed and thus reduces runtime.[8]

Finally, plant tours and interviews identified new IT-based advances that have reduced the time it takes to inspect valves in the quality control process. Each dimension of a complicated valve often must be produced to an accuracy rate of 1/1000 of an inch, so inspection is a critical part of the production process. For many years, inspection was done with hand-measuring devices, which was very time-consuming. Over the last several years, *automated inspection* machines have been introduced that use a laser

---

8. Note also that plants that implement FMS are also likely to put higher quality control boxes on their CNC machines, which reduces setup-time and runtime and will show up in our regressions as a return to FMS.

probe technology, so that the operator touches each surface (interior, exterior, holes, etc.) of the valve with a probe that develops a three-dimensional picture and measures all dimensions and automatically compares measurements to the desired specifications.[9]

Another technology that is becoming more common in valve-making plants is *three-dimensional computer-aided design* (3D-CAD). This is a constantly advancing IT method for turning customers' valve specifications into a specific design, thereby reducing the time that elapses from order placement to design presentation to the customer.

Thus, during our site visits and interviews, managers routinely identified as important sources of improved operational efficiency one or more of the following three specific technologies: advances in the capabilities of the CNC machines themselves through the use of more advanced controllers; flexible manufacturing systems (FMS) that coordinate the operations of multiple machines; and new automated inspection equipment. All three technological advances are a direct result of improvements in microprocessor, storage, and software computer technologies.

*Production Efficiency Gains and Product Customization*

Many of those interviewed during our plant visits underscored two key operational imperatives for remaining competitive in this industry. First, production efficiency gains are important since many plants can make a wide variety of customer orders. In describing the computer-based technology previously, we have identified the three primary elements that cause production efficiencies by reducing production times in machining a valve: the *setuptime* of a machine, or the time it takes to program the machine so that it will perform the right combination of tasks to produce the specified valve; the *runtime* of the machine to complete the machining of each unit of valve; and the *inspection time* to verify the quality of the valve.[10] Second, managers also observed that their plants were increasingly relying on a strategy of customizing their production to meet customer needs. Production of commodity valves is increasingly moving abroad to low wage countries. Therefore, many U.S. valve makers are increasing the number of customized products they produce and are relying less on selling directly from their catalogs. Information technology advances play a critical role in the move to product customization. More sophisticated controllers will not only reduce the cost of customizing products, but technologies that reduce setup-times will also increase the speed and reduce the cost of making changeovers between product runs.

9. The most recent inspection technology, which became available in 2004, now enables the inspection to be done without any human contact; the inspection machine surrounds the valve and operates the probe to measure its features and check them against required specifications.

10. When reductions in these times are achieved with the same or fewer workers, productivity also rises.

The plant visits and interviews with experienced industry practitioners help identify concrete examples of new IT-based equipment, and identify what parts of the overall machining process these IT advances would impact. To examine the impacts of IT investments on performance more broadly throughout the entire industry, we developed a customized survey for valve plants. This survey measures process improvements in each of the three production stages, product improvements and increasing customization of valves, and investments in new IT-enhanced production machinery. The survey also asks for information on worker skills and human resource management (HRM) practices.

### 2.2.2    Survey of the Valve-Making Industry

*The Sample of Valve Industry Plants*

Using the insights from our field research, we designed, pretested, and conducted a customized industry survey in 2002.[11] To identify the population of U.S. valve-making plants for this survey, we collected contact information from Survey Sampling, Inc. for any plant in a valve-making industry class (Standard Industrial Classifications [SICs] 3491, 3492, 3494, and 3593) with more than twenty employees. Of a potential universe of 416 valve-making plants in the United States, 212 plants, or 51 percent, provided responses to the survey questions described in this section via telephone interviews.[12] In the United Kingdom, there was a potential universe of 120 valve-making plants, of which 46 percent responded, resulting in a sample of fifty-five plants. The respondents to the survey were the managers of the plants. Since valve-making plants are quite small (see table 2.1), plant managers are very likely to be familiar with all aspects of production. Empirical results in the study are based on the responses from the 212 valve-making plants in the United States and the fifty-five valve-making plants in the United Kingdom.[13]

*Production Efficiency Measures*

Efficiency gains in machining processes are *product-specific* measures. We asked each respondent to look up data for "the product you have produced

11. The Office for Survey Research at the Institute for Public Policy and Social Research at Michigan State University conducted the pretests and final surveys by telephone from July 31, 2002 through March 30, 2003. Interviews lasted an average of twenty minutes with an average of 7.6 phone contacts needed to complete the survey.

12. Of 762 plants that Survey Sampling Inc. lists in the four valve-making SIC classifications, 200 were determined to have no production and another seventy were no longer in business. Assuming a similar rate of survey ineligibility for other plant names that could not be contacted yields the number of 416 valve-making plants.

13. The respondents to the survey were the plant managers. Since valve-making plants are quite small (mean employment is seventy-four in the United Kingdom and ninety-six in the United States), plant managers are very likely to be familiar with all aspects of production.

**Table 2.1**　　　　　**Variable means**

| | United Kingdom | United States |
|---|---|---|
| No. of shop employees, 2002 | 74[a] | 96 |
| No. of shop employees, 1997 | 100 | 106 |
| No. of CNC operators, 2002 | 14 | 25 |
| No. of CNC operators, 1997 | 10 | 19 |
| No. of CNC machines | 10[a] | 15 |
| No. of conventional machines | 22 | 25 |
| Unionized establishment | 0.33[a] | 0.21 |
| Age of plant (years) | 42.69 | 34.27 |
| New CNC | 0.63[a] | 0.74 |
| New flexible manuf. system | 0.25[a] | 0.15 |
| New automated sensors | 0.18 | 0.14 |
| New 3-D CAD | 0.49[a] | 0.39 |
| Percent of products ordered from catalog (PCT CAT) | 46[a] | 61 |
| Percent catalog up | 16 | 13 |
| Percent catalog down | 27 | 24 |
| Educational requirements up since 1997 | 0.44[a] | 0.22 |
| Minimum education required for CNC operators (dummy response) | | |
| 　High School | 0.47[a] | 0.71 |
| 　Technical School | 0.07 | 0.04 |
| 　Apprenticeship | 0.09 | 0.05 |
| 　None | 0.32[a] | 0.09 |
| Training sources (dummy variable responses yes = 1) | | |
| 　Government-sponsored training | 0.35[a] | 0.24 |
| 　Vendor | 0.78 | 0.80 |
| 　Firm-basic | 0.18[a] | 0.33 |
| 　Firm-technical | 0.80 | 0.75 |
| 　Firm-local schools | 0.50 | 0.50 |
| Type of customer for key product (dummy variables) | | |
| 　Customer | 0.35[a] | 0.22 |
| 　Wholesaler | 0.04[a] | 0.18 |
| 　Distributor | 0.11[a] | 0.18 |
| 　Mixture | 0.50 | 0.42 |
| Percent of revenue | | |
| 　From primary customer | 27% | 26% |
| 　From top 4 customers | 47% | 48% |
| Competition | | |
| 　No. of competitors | 21 | 21 |
| 　No. of competitors-up | 0.22 | 0.33 |
| 　No. of competitors-down | 0.44[a] | 0.29 |

*Note:* The sample size for most variables is 212 for the United States and 55 for the United Kingdom.

[a]United Kingdom different from United States at 5 percent or higher.

the most over the last five years" for the following key indicators of production efficiency:

*Setup-Time:* About how much setup-time does (did) it take to produce one unit of this product today (and in 1997)?

*Runtime:* About how much runtime does (did) it take to produce one unit of this product today (and in 1997)?

*Inspection Time:* About how long does (did) it take to inspect one unit of this product today (and in 1997)?

### Product Customization Measures

Increases in customization imply changes in the number of products a plant makes, so these measures are *plant-specific* measures. To measure whether plants had increased customization of their products, the survey asks the following question.

*Percent Catalog:* In 2002 (1997), what percent of your customer orders are directly from your catalog with no design change?

Although the response rate for 1997 was only 33 percent for this question, virtually all the plants were able to answer a companion question that indicated whether the percent catalog increased, decreased, or stayed the same between 1997 and 2002.

### Information Technology Measures

To measure investments in new IT, the survey asks the following questions:[14]

*Number of Machines:* In order to produce one unit of this product today (and in 1997) how many machines do (did) you employ?

*New CNC Machines:* How many CNC machines does the plant have and how many are less than five years old (new cnc), five to ten years old, and more than ten years old?

*Flexible Manufacturing Systems (FMS):* Does the plant have FMS technology (where two or more machines are controlled by computers) and what was the year of adoption?

*Automatic Inspection Sensors (Auto Sensors):* Does the plant have automated inspection sensor equipment and what was the year of adoption?

*Three-Dimensional CAD software:* Does the plant use three-dimensional CAD software for designing new products and in what year was this software first used?

14. Due to limited responses to any questions about costs or prices in a survey pretest and to a need to limit the length of the survey, we did not ask questions about the costs of adopting the various production technologies.

The first IT question concerning number of machines is a *product-specific* question, and pertains to the plant's main valve product over the last five years. The other IT questions are *plant-specific* questions.

*Human Resource Management Practices*

To measure the use of various human resource management practices at the plant, the survey asks the following questions.

*Basic Training:* Does your plant provide formal training in basic reading and/or math skills and in what year was this introduced?

*Technical Training:* Does your plant provide formal training in technical skills and in what year was this introduced?

*Formal Meetings:* Do you have meetings with shop floor workers to discuss the shop's performance and in what year was this introduced?

*Teams:* Do you have problem-solving teams for shop floor workers and when was this introduced?

*Incentive Pay:* Do you have a formal incentive pay plan for your machine operators or do you give occasional special bonuses and when was this introduced?

*Skill Requirements*

To measure how the demand for various skills has changed over time, the survey asks whether a particular skill's importance increased between 1997 and 2002. Data on five types of skills were collected: math skills, computer skills, skills for programming machine operations, problem-solving skills, and engineering cutting tool knowledge.

### 2.3   Trends in IT Investments, Work Organization, and Productivity in the Valve-Making Industry

Before turning to the trends in the adoption of new technologies and work practices, we look first at the conditions in the plants in the United Kingdom versus the United States. Tables 2.1 and 2.2 show descriptive statistics and indicate when the mean (or median) values for the United Kingdom differ from those of the United States.

There are some significant differences between the plants in the two countries. In the United Kingdom, the plants are smaller, more likely to be unionized, and appear to have lower skill requirements. Their product mix is also different: the UK firms produce more for an intended final customer ("customer" = 1) and less for wholesalers and distributions. As a result, the UK firms had fewer of their products ordered from their catalog ("percent of products ordered from catalog")—46 percent versus 61 percent for the United Kingdom versus the United States. Yet despite these differences, the same trends apply: in both countries, there was an equal move toward

**Table 2.2    Changes in product—specific production efficiency measures, 1997–2002**

| Product-specific production efficiency measures | Medians | | | | Means | | | | Mean of log (2002 production time) minus log (1997 production time) | |
| --- | --- | --- | --- | --- | --- | --- | --- | --- | --- | --- |
| | United Kingdom | | United States | | United Kingdom | | United States | | United Kingdom | United States |
| | 1997[a] | 2002[a] | 1997[a] | 2002[a] | 1997[a] | 2002[a] | 1997[a] | 2002[a] | | |
| Setup-time | 3.00 | 2.00 | 3.00 | 1.50 | 6.07 | 4.46 | 11.03 | 6.04 | -0.52 | -0.68 |
| Runtime | 0.50 | 0.42 | 0.25 | 0.17 | 5.61 | 3.83 | 10.77 | 9.32 | -0.25 | -0.37 |
| Inspection time | 0.10 | 0.08 | 0.17 | 0.14 | 2.63 | 1.46 | 1.22 | 0.84 | -0.34 | -0.33 |

*Source:* Authors' survey of value manufacturing plants (see section 2.2).

[a]Production times are measured in hours and pertain to the typical time to setup, run, or inspect the product that the plant produced the most in the period 1997 to 2002. Setup-time is measured per batch while runtime and inspection time are per unit to adjust for differences in batch sizes across plants. The difference between median and mean production times is due to a very small number of observations with large production times.

greater product customization ("Percent catalog down") as described following. And both countries have key customers that dominate their sales: percent of revenue from one customer is 26 to 27 percent in both countries, and from the top four customers, it is 47 to 48 percent (where customers can be wholesalers or distributors).

### 2.3.1   The Adoption of Information Technologies

Figure 2.1 shows the adoption rates of the four types of IT-enabled equipment in valve-making plants in the United States and United Kingdom between 1980 and 2002. In the case of CNC machines, we see that in the United States the highest rates of adoption for the plant's first CNC machines occurred during the 1980s, but throughout the 1990s, plants invested heavily in new CNC machines—74 percent of plants purchased new CNC machines from 1997 to 2002 (see fig. 2.2). Plants in the United Kingdom adopted CNC machines somewhat later than U.S. plants; whereas in 1990, 66 percent of the U.S. plants had CNC machines, only 44 percent of the UK plants had this technology. The first half of the 1990s was a catch-up period for the UK plants, so that by 1995, 71 percent of the UK plants were using CNC machines, compared to 78 percent of their U.S. counterparts. And, like the U.S. plants, the UK plants invested heavily in new CNC machines from 1997 to 2002; 63 percent of UK plants purchased new CNC machines from 1997 to 2002 compared to 74 percent of the U.S. plants (see fig. 2.2). In both countries, investments in other new computer-based technologies—in automated

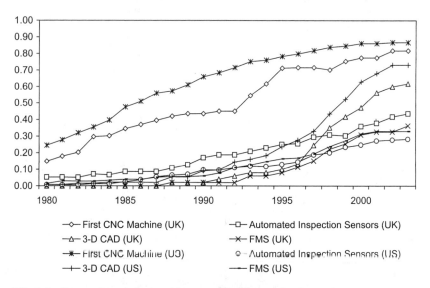

**Fig. 2.1   Proportion of plants with computer-aided production technologies (United Kingdom vs. United States)**

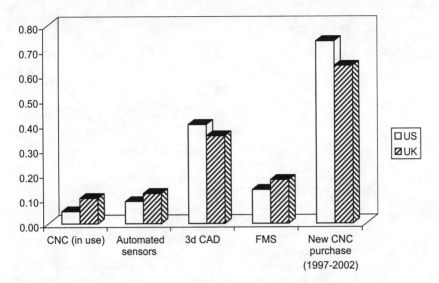

**Fig. 2.2    Fraction of observations adopting equipment between 1997 and 2002**

inspection sensors, flexible manufacturing systems, and 3D-CAD—show the largest growth after 1995. The adoption rates for the time period 1997 through 2002 (the years for which we measure production times) are shown in figure 2.2. In both countries, there was significant adoption of these new technologies during the 1997 to 2002 time period. There are two interesting differences in the current usage of these technologies. By 2002, UK plants were significantly more likely to have adopted automated inspection sensors than U.S. plants (44 percent compared to 28 percent) while U.S. plants were significantly more likely to have adopted 3D-CAD than UK plants (73 percent compared to 62 percent).

As discussed in section 2.2, bringing new more advanced CNC machines on-line results in a reduction of the number of CNC machines it takes to produce a given product. On average, in the U.S. it took 19 percent fewer machines to produce a given valve product in 2002 compared to 1997, while in the U.K. the number of machines needed to produce a given valve product fell by 24 percent between 1997 and 2002.

### 2.3.2    The Adoption of New HRM Practices

Figure 2.3 shows that the use of teams, training programs, and bonus/incentive pay plans all increased substantially in both countries since 1980 with the highest rates of adoption of these practices occurring after 1990. Figure 2.4 shows adoption rates for the 1997 to 2002 time period. Valve plants in both countries increasingly adopted new training programs and

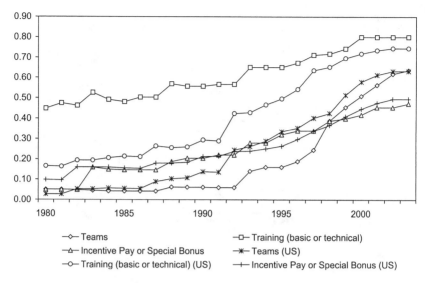

**Fig. 2.3   Proportion of plants with new HRM practices (United Kingdom vs. United States)**

more team-based methods of job design, and more meetings with operators. Direct incentive pay plans, excluding bonus payments, are less common than the other HRM practices.[15]

### 2.3.3   Trends in Measures of Production Efficiency

Table 2.2 shows that plants in both countries realized large declines in production times at each stage of production when making their most common product. Setup-time and runtime fell by a larger percentage in the United States than in the United Kingdom.

### 2.3.4   Summary

The patterns in figures 2.1 through 2.4 show that in both the United States and the United Kingdom the 1990s in the valve industry was a decade marked by rapid adoption of new machinery that incorporates many IT-based technological improvements and a growing reliance on new methods of work organization. While these trends demonstrate that production efficiency gains and product customization increases are happening at the same time

15. Interviews suggested that direct incentive pay is difficult to adopt in an industry that makes customized products. The increase in the use of incentive pay is smaller than the increase in other HRM practices in the valve industry. By 2002, incentive pay is used by 31 percent of plants and special bonuses by 36 percent of plants, so about 50 percent of plants have one or the other (see table 2.1), but interviews suggest that these incentives are a very small percent of total pay and are used rather erratically. As a result, we do not focus on the incentive pay plans in our HR analysis following.

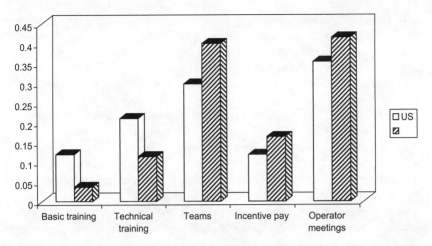

**Fig. 2.4    Fraction of observations adopting HRM practices between 1997 and 2002**

that the industry is investing in new IT-enhanced machinery and new HRM practices, the empirical work to follow examines whether the improvements in various aspects of machining times or increases in customization over this period are concentrated in those plants that have made investments in these new technologies and work practices.

## 2.4    The Impact of IT and HRM on Productivity at the Product Level

We estimate the following first difference productivity models in which time-based efficiency measures are expressed as a function of the adoption of new machining technologies and new HRM practices to see if production efficiency gains occur in those plants that adopt new technologies or work practices.

$$(1) \quad \Delta\ln(\text{ProductionTime}) = a + b_1\Delta(\text{NewTechnology})$$
$$+ b_2\Delta(\text{NewTechnology}) \cdot \text{UK}$$
$$+ b_3\Delta(\text{NewHRM}) + b_4\text{UK} + b_5\text{X} + e_1.$$

The dependent variable in (1) is the log change in Production Time between 1997 and 2002—where Production Time refers to setup-time, runtime, and inspection time *for a given product.* The vector $\Delta$(New Technology) measures the 1997 to 2002 adoption of new technologies expected to reduce these machining times—the adoption of higher-quality CNC machines (as measured by the change in the number of CNC machines needed to produce the plant's main product), FMS, and automated inspection sensors. The vector $\Delta$(NewHRM) measures the 1997 to 2002 adoption of new HRM practices, such as work teams and training programs, and X is a vector of controls including the age of the plant, union status, and plant size measured as number of workers to test whether the change in production efficiency is affected by these additional factors. To test for differences in the effects of new IT between the United States and United Kingdom, the vector Δ(NewTechnology) is interacted with a dummy for UK plants. The UK dummy is also entered separately in the regression.

The results in table 2.3 demonstrate that investments in new IT-machinery have improved production efficiency by reducing all components of production times. The results are remarkably straightforward and striking: the adoption of new CNC technologies reduces production times significantly. The variable "Increase CNC Quality" is defined as the reduction in the number of CNC machines used to produce the product (using the survey variable defined previously, "in order to produce one unit of this product today (and in 1997) how many machines do (did) you employ."[16] The adoption of higher-quality CNC machines reduces setup-time (column [1] and [2]) and runtime (columns [3] and [4]). Inspection time declines with the introduction of new automated inspection sensors (column [5]). The UK dummy, as well as the UK-interactions with CNC-quality and other technology variables (which are not shown in the table), are all insignificant.

The insignificance of the differences in the United Kingdom and United States could simply arise because of the small sample size of the UK data, which falls to thirty-nine plants in the regressions using production data. However, if the production regressions are run for just the UK sample, the results are the same as in the entire sample for the setup-time and runtime regressions. On just these observations, in the setup-time regression, the coefficient on "increase CNC Quality" is −.63 (t-statistic = −10.3), and in the runtime regression, the coefficient is −.35 (t-statistic = −1.60) for the median regressions. In contrast, while the dummy for the presence of automatic inspection sensors has a negative coefficient in the inspection time equation, the coefficient is not significantly different from zero for the UK sample.

### 2.4.1    The Impact of HRM Practices on Product-Level Efficiency Measures

According to the results in table 2.3, in both the United States and the United Kingdom, plants that introduce technical training programs also realize an additional reduction in setup and runtimes. While these efficiency regressions find no effects of teams, it is important to remember that we are modeling the efficiency gains over time for one specific product, not the overall efficiency of the plant. Teams may be less likely to have a direct effect on product efficiency as compared to overall plant efficiency.

---

16. Our measure of the increase in CNC quality (number of machines down) is significantly correlated with a dummy variable that indicates whether the plant bought a new CNC machine since 1997.

**Table 2.3    The effects of IT and HRM on production efficiency, 1997–2002[a]**

| Dependent variable | Percentage change in setup-time | | Percentage change in runtime | | Percentage change in inspection time |
|---|---|---|---|---|---|
| | (OLS) | (Median regression) | (OLS) | (Median regression) | (OLS) |
| UK dummy | 0.095 | −0.029 | 0.039 | 0.009 | 0.097 |
| | (0.155) | (0.113) | (0.161) | (0.094) | (0.191) |
| Log (change in "CNC quality")[b] | −0.651*** | −0.659*** | −0.406* | −0.404*** | −0.180 |
| | (0.249) | (0.099) | (0.153) | (0.078) | (0.178) |
| Adopted flexible manuf. system | −0.018 | −0.148 | −0.037 | −0.080 | 0.165 |
| | (0.177) | (0.113) | (0.206) | (0.092) | (0.205) |
| Adopted automated inspection sensors | −0.172 | −0.132 | 0.062 | 0.025 | −0.610** |
| | (0.208) | (0.136) | (0.214) | (0.111) | (0.332) |
| Adopted technical training | −0.387*** | −0.385*** | −0.391*** | −0.345*** | −0.191 |
| | (0.177) | (0.122) | (0.166) | (0.097) | (0.280) |
| Adopted teams | 0.204 | −0.014 | 0.050 | 0.058 | −0.243 |
| | (0.162) | (0.099) | (0.168) | (0.085) | (0.255) |
| Observations | 185 | 185 | 177 | 177 | 192 |
| $R^2$/Pseudo $R^2$ | 0.13 | 0.12 | 0.14 | 0.14 | 0.07 |

*Notes:* Huber-White robust standard errors in parentheses. Dependent variables: Product-specific production times.

OLS = ordinary least squares.

[a]All regressions include controls for age of plants (five age dummies), number of shop floor workers, a dummy for unionization, and two dummy variables indicating whether the number of competitors that produce a product that competes with the firm's main product went up or down.

[b]Log (change in "CNC quality") is measured by the percentage decrease in the number of CNC machines used to produce the plant's main product; or, log(# of CNCs used to produce the main product in 2002) − log(# of CNC's used to produce the main product in 1997). A decrease in the number of CNC machines used to produce a given product indicates an increase in the quality of the CNC machines being used. See section 2.4 of text for explanation.

***Significant at the 1 percent level.

**Significant at the 5 percent level.

*Significant at the 10 percent level.

## 2.5    The Impact of IT on Customization in the Valve-Making Industry

In addition to reducing production times, new IT is also valuable because it allows plants to design and make new valves that are more complex. These effects of new IT are not captured in any estimated reduction in the time it currently takes to produce the plant's single most common valve product. In this section, we analyze the effect of IT-enhanced equipment on increased product customization. The extent to which a plant customizes its products is measured in our survey with questions on the percent of the plant's output that is ordered directly from their catalog. Because many respondents did not report a 1997 value of this variable, we measure the changes in customization of production in a plant between 1997 and 2002 with the related survey question that asks whether the percent of output from the catalog increased, decreased or stayed the same over this period which was answered by nearly all respondents. The dummy variable for an increase in product customization (percent catalog down) equals one if the plant reports that the percentage of output ordered from their catalog fell between 1997 and 2002. Twenty-five percent of the U.S. plants and 27 percent of the UK plants reported that their percentage of output ordered from their catalog fell during this period.

The IT measures that are most likely to facilitate a move toward customization are 3D-CAD and new CNC machines. The former reduces the time it takes to translate a customer's specifications into an actual product design, thereby making it easier for the plant to produce products that are not in its catalog. Since new CNC machines reduce setup-time, this should also make it easier for the plant to accept orders for custom products. The results in table 2.4 show that in both countries the introduction of 3D-CAD and the purchase of a new CNC machine are both associated with an increase in product customization, as reflected in the decline in the percentage of orders directly from the plant's catalog. The results do not reveal any differences between the U.S. and UK firms in the effects of new CNC or 3D-CAD technology on customization. In particular, the UK dummy in line 1 of table 2.4 is always insignificantly different from zero, as are the UK-technology interaction terms (not shown in the table). An unexpected result in table 2.4 is the negative and significant coefficient on the introduction of flexible manufacturing systems, which would not be expected to have an effect on product customization.[17]

When we again look only at the UK subsample of fifty plants for the

---

17. In considering this result, it is worth noting that the results in table 2.3 concerning the adoption of FMS adoption on setup-time are insignificant. In contrast, all model specifications show setup-times declining after plants begin using higher-quality CNC machines. If FMS adoption does not reduce setup-times as new CNC machines do, then the theoretical reason to expect that FMS adoption would lead to an increase in customization is less clear. While this can explain why FMS would not have a positive and significant effect in table 2.4, it cannot explain why the coefficient is negative.

**Table 2.4    The effects of IT on change in product customization, 1997–2002[a]**

| Dependent variable | Percent catalog up[b] (1a) | Percent catalog down[b] (1b) | Percent catalog up[b] (2a) | Percent catalog down[b] (2b) | Percent catalog up[b] (3a) | Percent catalog down[b] (3b) | Percent catalog up[b] (4a) | Percent catalog down[b] (4b) |
|---|---|---|---|---|---|---|---|---|
| UK dummy | 0.427 (0.489) | 0.334 (0.404) | 0.414 (0.487) | 0.158 (0.402) | 0.372 (0.493) | 0.453 (0.412) | 0.525 (0.504) | 0.614 (0.433) |
| Bought new CNC machine | 0.558 (0.469) | 0.795** (0.409) | | | | | 0.617 (0.477) | 0.989*** (0.441) |
| Adopted 3D-CAD | | | −0.332 (0.435) | 0.660** (0.334) | | | −0.251 (0.442) | 0.738*** (0.353) |
| Adopted flexible manufacturing system | | | | | 0.046 (0.511) | −1.630*** (0.596) | 0.031 (0.525) | −1.610*** (0.598) |
| Adopted automated inspection sensors | | | | | | | −0.888 (0.720) | −0.525 (0.504) |
| Observations | 233 | | 233 | | 233 | | 233 | |
| Pseudo $R^2$ | 0.075 | | 0.077 | | 0.088 | | 0.119 | |

*Note:* Huber–White robust standard errors in parentheses.

[a]Each pair of columns reports estimated coefficients from one multinomial logit model. Regressions include interactions between the technology variables and the UK dummy, controls for age of plants (five age dummies), number of shop floor workers, and dummy for unionization.

[b]The dependent variable has three categories: the percent catalog down category includes plants that report that the percentage of customer orders that were valves in the product catalog with no modifications went down between 1997 and 2002; the *percent catalog up* category includes plants that report that this percentage went up between 1997 and 2002; and the (omitted) category includes plants that reported that this percentage was unchanged between 1997 and 2002. The percent catalog up (down) category identifies plants with decreases (increases) in customized production over this five-year period.

***Significant at the 1 percent level.

**Significant at the 5 percent level.

*Significant at the 10 percent level.

customization regressions, the basic results hold, but the impacts of new technology on customization are less significant. The coefficients on the technology variables are still negative but the t-statistics are insignificant.

### 2.6    The Impact of the Adoption of New HRM Practices and the Demand for Worker Skills

In this section, we examine whether the adoption of new IT is correlated with the adoption of new HRM practices, and whether IT raises the demand for skills. An increase in IT would increase the use of innovative HRM practices, such as team-production, if IT requires more problem solving by operators.[18] And as with any IT adoption, the demand for skills could rise or fall. The demand for skills could rise for either of two reasons. First, the use of more sophisticated machines could increase the level of skills required, as it increases the demand for computer skills or programming skills, and possibly problem-solving skills. Second, it could increase skill demand indirectly. On our plant visits, we heard that there are two types of operators—those who program and those who simply run machines but have less knowledge of the machining operations. If the new machines require fewer simple operators, overall skill demand will increase. On the other hand, we also heard stories of substitution effects—that computers on CNC machines now solve machining problems so well that the need for creative knowledge of tools and machining has decreased.

Regarding skill demand, in table 2.5 we present regressions in which the dependent variable equals one if the plant reported that a particular skill's importance increased between 1997 and 2002. We collected data on five types of skill increases: math skills, computer skills, skills for programming machine operations, problem-solving skills, and engineering knowledge.

In both the United States and the United Kingdom, there is a substantial increase in the demand for computer skills, programming skills, problem-solving skills, and engineering skills when the plant increases its IT use (columns [2] through [5]). That is, the purchase of a new CNC machine is correlated with the plant's response that they increased the demand for these skills. In the United Kingdom, increased IT adoption in CNC machines had an even greater effect on the increase in demand for computer skills and programming skills than in the United States (row 3, columns [2] and [3]). Moreover, on average, the UK plants did not increase their skill demand as much as the U.S. plants unless they increased their IT use: the UK dummy variables are negative for several skills.[19] Our finding that the introduction

18. Bresnahan, Brynjolfsson, and Hitt (2002); Autor, Levy, and Murnane (2003); Boning, Ichniowski, and Shaw (2007).
19. The same is true for cutting-tool knowledge—UK plants that did not adopt IT did not increase their demand for skills.

**Table 2.5**     **The effects of IT adoption on increased importance of different types of skills[a]**

| | Math (1a) | Computer (2) | Programming (3) | Problem-solving (4) | Engineering knowledge (5) |
|---|---|---|---|---|---|
| UK dummy | −0.022 | −0.432*** | −0.308** | 0.032 | −0.391*** |
| | (0.139) | (0.126) | (0.143) | (0.129) | (0.123) |
| Bought new CNC machine | 0.107 | 0.139** | 0.270*** | 0.144** | 0.195*** |
| | (0.084) | (0.082) | (0.086) | (0.083) | (0.081) |
| UK * New CNC | −0.0203 | 0.310*** | 0.331** | 0.057 | 0.216 |
| | (0.166) | (0.067) | (0.145) | (0.148) | (0.185) |
| Adopted 3D-CAD | −0.038 | 0.103 | 0.081 | −0.114 | −0.018 |
| | (0.069) | (0.064) | (0.071) | (0.096) | (0.070) |
| Adopted flexible manufacturing system | 0.236*** | 0.177 | −0.053 | 0.084 | 0.133 |
| | (0.075) | (0.070) | (0.090) | (0.075) | (0.089) |
| Adopted automated inspection sensors | 0.068 | −0.015 | −0.082 | −0.101 | 0.071 |
| | (0.100) | (0.095) | (0.104) | (0.097) | (0.100) |
| Pseudo-$R^2$ | 0.072 | 0.132 | 0.142 | 0.055 | 0.088 |
| Sample Size | 255 | 254 | 249 | 253 | 252 |
| Mean UK | 0.45 | 0.60 | 0.44 | 0.63 | 0.30 |
| Mean U.S. | 0.57 | 0.71 | 0.53 | 0.68 | 0.52 |

*Note:* Huber-White robust standard errors in parentheses. Dependent variable: Equals one if skill's importance increased between 1997 and 2002.

[a]Probit coefficients evaluated at the mean are shown. Regressions include controls for age of plants (five age dummies), number of shop floor workers, and dummy for unionization.

***Significant at the 1 percent level.

**Significant at the 5 percent level.

*Significant at the 10 percent level.

of IT increases the demand for certain types of worker skills provides an interesting counterpoint to Doms, Dunne, and Troske (1997). In their study, the cross-sectional correlation between worker skill (as measured by the nonproduction worker share and the average wage) and technology adoption disappeared in a longitudinal analysis.

These results show that the effect of new CNC technology on increased importance of certain skills is more pronounced in the United Kingdom than in the United States. Consistent with this pattern, when we restrict the analysis to the UK plants only, the CNC variable remains large and significant in the computer, programming, and engineering skill regressions.

Note that if we look back at our variable means in table 2.2, the United Kingdom started at lower educational demand levels than the United States—they had few educational requirements. However, 44 percent of the UK firms said they increased their educational requirements from 1997 to 2002, whereas in the United States only 22 percent of the firms increased their educational requirements. Virtually all U.S. firms required a high school degree or more but 32 percent of UK firms said they had no educational

Table 2.6           The effects of IT adoption on the adoption of new HRM practices, 1997–2002[a]

| Dependent variable | Teams (1) | Shopfloor meetings (2) | Technical training (3) |
|---|---|---|---|
| UK dummy | 0.151 | 0.125 | 0.013 |
| | (0.097) | (0.098) | (0.133) |
| Bought new CNC machine | 0.279*** | 0.191** | 0.212*** |
| | (0.081) | (0.105) | (0.091) |
| Adopted 3D-CAD | 0.068 | 0.076 | 0.236*** |
| | (0.083) | (0.084) | (0.098) |
| Adopted flexible manufacturing system | −0.005 | −0.029 | 0.161 |
| | (0.110) | (0.110) | (0.114) |
| Adopted automated inspection sensors | −0.070 | 0.110 | 0.375*** |
| | (0.121) | (0.105) | (0.149) |
| Observations | 173 | 119 | 128 |
| Log likelihood | −102.8 | −66.9 | −64.06 |
| Pseudo $R^2$ | 0.136 | 0.059 | 0.233 |
| Mean UK | 0.52 | 0.81 | 0.32 |
| Mean U.S. | 0.42 | 0.69 | 0.36 |

*Notes:* Huber-White robust standard errors in parentheses. Dependent variable: Equals one if plant adopted the HRM practice between 1997 and 2002.

[a]Probit coefficients evaluated at the mean are shown. Regressions include controls for age of plants (five age dummies), number of shop floor workers, and dummy for unionization

The samples for these probit models include those plants that did not have the given practices as of 1997, and the dependent variable equals one for those plants that adopt the given practice by 2002.

***Significant at the 1 percent level.

**Significant at the 5 percent level.

*Significant at the 10 percent level.

requirements. Looking at the training sources in table 2.2, virtually all firms offer technical training, and half of all firms send workers to local schools for updated training.

Turning to HRM practices, in the United States the purchase of new CNC machines with imbedded IT is correlated with new HR practices (table 2.6).[20] The sample size for the UK firms falls too much for us to check for significant differences between the countries.

In sum, we find that there is an increase in the demand for skills when there is an increase in information technologies, where the skill needs are for both increased computer skills and increased mechanical machining knowledge to complement them. This would be in keeping with the rising demand for skills in the U.S. economy: even within narrowly defined occupations, wage inequality has risen, and the demand for cognitive skills has risen.[21] Moreover, there is also an increase in the demand for innova-

20. Siegel, Waldman, and Youngdahl (1997) found a positive correlation between the adoption of advanced manufacturing technology and employee development and empowerment practices in a sample of Long Island, New York manufacturers.

21. Katz and Autor (1999); Autor, Levy, and Murnane (2003).

tive HRM practices—including training and teamwork—when there is an increase in computerization.[22]

## 2.7 Conclusion

We pose the following three questions. Is there international microeconomic evidence that information technologies have increased productivity at the firm level? If so, what is the mechanism for increased performance? And finally, has IT increased skill demand or the demand for more innovative human resource management practices, like training or teamwork?

We find that, despite differences in the current and historical patterns of institutions in the United Kingdom and United States, both countries exhibit comparable patterns of gains to IT at the plant level. Using very detailed data on the valve-making industry, we show that investments in IT that are embedded in the production process do yield increases in productivity. However, new IT investments also introduce a new strategic focus, moving to produce the products that are more customized, given the greater ease of designing and producing custom-designed products. Thus, the performance of the firm is enhanced due to both new strategies and higher levels of productivity. This is true for the United Kingdom as well as the United States, and our trends show that plants in both countries substantially increased their use of new IT-based technologies. Finally, those plants that purchase more IT-embedded capital also are more likely to increase their demand for skills.

## References

Athey, S., and S. Stern. 2002. The impact of information technology on emergency health care outcomes. *RAND Journal of Economics* 33 (3): 399–432.

Autor, D., F. Levy, and R. Murnane. 2003. The skill content of recent technological change: An empirical exploration. *Quarterly Journal of Economics* 118 (4): 1279–1333.

Bartel, A., C. Ichniowski, and K. Shaw. 2004. Using "Insider Econometrics" to Study Productivity. *American Economic Review* 94 (2): 217–22.

Bartel, A., C. Ichniowski, and K. Shaw. 2007. How does information technology affect productivity? Plant-level comparisons of product innovation, process improvement, and worker skills. *Quarterly Journal of Economics* 122 (4): 1721–58.

Bloom, N., and J. Van Reenen. 2007. Measuring and explaining management prac-

22. Interviews during plant visits indicated that the use of teamwork (and not IT investments themselves) made problem-solving skills more important. Consistent with this claim, an increase in the importance of problem-solving skills is correlated with the introduction of teams (correlation = 0.14, significant at 5 percent level), but teams were also fairly widespread prior to 1997 (35 percent had teams).

tices across firms and countries. *Quarterly Journal of Economics* 122 (4): 1351–1408.

Boning, B., C. Ichniowski, and K. Shaw. 2007. Opportunity counts: Teams and the effectiveness of production incentives. *Journal of Labor Economics* 25:613–50.

Bresnahan, T., E. Brynjolfsson, and L. Hitt. 2002. Information technology, work organization, and the demand for skill labor: Firm-level evidence. *Quarterly Journal of Economics* 14 (4): 23–48.

Brynjolfsson, E., and L. Hitt. 2000. Beyond computation: Information technology, organizational transformation and business performance. *Journal of Economic Perspectives* 14 (4): 23–48.

Doms, M., T. Dunne, and K. R. Troske. 1997. Workers, wages and technology. *Quarterly Journal of Economics* 112 (1): 253–90.

Hubbard, T. N. 2003. Information, decisions and productivity: On-board computers and capacity utilization in trucking. *American Economic Review* 93 (4): 1328–53.

Jorgenson, D. W., M. C. Ho, and K. Stiroh. 2003. Growth of U.S. industries and investments in information technology and higher education. Paper presented at NBER/CRIW Conference on Measurement of Capital in the New Economy. 26–27 April, Washington, D.C.

Katz, L. F., and D. H. Autor. 1999. Changes in the wage structure and earnings inequality. In *Handbook of labor economics,* vol. 3A, ed. O. Ashenfelter and D. Card, 1463–1555. Amsterdam: North-Holland.

McGuckin, R. H., M. L. Streitwieser, and M. Doms. 1998. The effect of technology use on productivity growth. *Economics of Innovation and New Technology* 7: 1–26.

Oliner, S. D., and D. E. Sichel. 2000. The resurgence of growth in the late 1990s: Is information technology the story? *Journal of Economic Perspectives* 14 (4): 3–22.

Siegel, D. S., D. A. Waldman, and W. E. Youngdahl. 1997. The adoption of advanced manufacturing technologies: Human resource management implications. *IEEE Transactions on Engineering Management* 44 (3): 288–98.

# The Guy at the Controls
# Labor Quality and Power Plant Efficiency

James B. Bushnell and Catherine Wolfram

## 3.1 Introduction

In this chapter, we explore the impact of labor policies on the operations of electric power plants. At first glance, it might seem that workers should have little scope to influence the performance of the electricity industry and that this should be particularly true of the generation sector, where costs are dominated by the capital required to build plants and the fuel required to operate them. Overall, labor costs constitute a small fraction of generation costs. Yet in extensive interviews with plant managers and utility executives in the United States and Europe, most expressed the belief that the individual skill and effort of key personnel could make a significant difference in the performance of generating plants.

We focus on the role of the plant operator, an individual whose decisions have direct impact on many facets of plant operation. We describe both anecdotal evidence drawn from our interviews and empirical analysis documenting that individual operators do influence the efficiency of plant operations. The existence and tolerance of such an "operator effect" might seem counterintuitive. The cost of fuel in power plant operations is orders of magnitude greater than the salary of any individual operator. The sav-

James B. Bushnell is director of research at the University of California Energy Institute, Berkeley California, and a faculty research fellow of the National Bureau of Economic Research. Catherine Wolfram is an associate professor of economics at the Haas School of Business, University of California, Berkeley, and a research associate of the National Bureau of Economic Research.

This research was generously supported by the Sloan Foundation-NBER International Productivity Project. We are grateful to Rob Letzler, Amol Phadke, and Jenny Shanefelter for excellent research assistance.

ings in fuel costs reaped by highly skilled operators far outweigh any pay premiums they earn.

Having documented the existence of an operator effect, we describe circumstances where companies have taken steps to foster the practices of efficient operators and discourage those of inefficient ones. Generally, however, these appear to be the exception more than the rule. Because labor makes up such a small fraction of industry costs, it is possible that managers have not made human resource polices a priority. Further, it seems likely that the history of regulation in the industry dampened the incentives for operational efficiencies both among managers and workers. This trend may begin to change with the adoption of various forms of regulatory restructuring throughout the industry.

This chapter is related to an emerging empirical literature that uses high frequency data to measure productivity differences across workers (see, e.g., Hamilton, Nickerson, and Owan 2003; Bandiera, Barankay, and Rasul 2005; and Mas and Moretti 2009). While the previous work has focused on measuring the impacts of the workers' environments on their productivity (e.g., teams, compensation scheme, and coworkers), we focus on the size of the differences in productivity across workers at the same firm. Worker heterogeneity is not ordinarily captured in descriptions of firm efficiency based on production functions, but may be an important component of technical efficiency differences across firms. We also place a straightforward economic value on the productivity differences across power plant operators, and show that it is quite large relative to the pay received by the workers.

We begin by giving a general description and historical overview of the electricity industry. We then describe the power production process and the key role of plant operators in that process. We present empirical evidence, drawn from shift and production data from several U.S. power plants, that operators can indeed have a nontrivial impact on plant efficiency. We then conclude with a discussion of labor policies in the industry and describe some isolated attempts to confront and take advantage of the differences in operator skill and effort levels.

The bulk of the information described in this chapter is derived from interviews with power plant efficiency experts and visits to power plants in the United States, United Kingdom, and Spain. Overall, we conducted site visits to five power plants: two gas plants in California, a large coal plant in Alabama, and two coal plants in central England. We also conducted interviews at the offices of three other firms involved in the management of power plants. Our empirical analysis is dependent upon observations of hourly plant productivity that are available only in the United States as a product of regulations under the U.S. Clean Air Act. Equivalent data for European power plants do not exist. These hourly performance data are matched to data on labor shifts acquired through plant visits at U.S. plants.

The management practices and trends described throughout the chapter are drawn from interviews with managers at all of the facilities visited.

## 3.2    The Electricity Industry

The electricity industry provides a foundation for much of the industrial and commercial activity in the developed world. In the United States, total sales in 2004 were nearly $300 billion per year, making electricity industry revenues comparable to those in the automotive, petroleum products, and telecommunications industries. Yet the industry has typically been viewed as a sleepy one, where innovation, quality improvement, and efficiency efforts have not yielded the rewards garnered in other industries.

Historically, the electricity industry was viewed as a natural monopoly. Typically, a single utility company generated, transmitted, and distributed all electricity in its service territory. In much of the world, the monopoly was a state-owned utility. Within the United States, private investor-owned companies supplied the majority of customers, although federally- and municipally-owned companies played an important minority role. These companies operated under multiple layers of local, state, and federal regulation.

A primary feature of regulation or government ownership was that revenues were based on costs rather than market factors. Under a typical rate-of-return regulatory structure, electric utilities would be responsible for making investments and operating power systems such that the demand of its franchise customers was met. In return, operating expenses would be recovered fully from rates, and capital expenditures would earn a guaranteed rate-of-return. Typically, only the most egregiously wasteful expenditures would be overturned by regulators. It has long been observed that this form of "cost-plus" pricing structure naturally weakens incentives for cutting costs and improving efficiency of operations.[1] The lack of direct competition also made the industry relatively amenable to unionization. The electricity industry has traditionally featured one of the highest union membership rates among U.S. industries. Although deregulation and restructuring has reduced that rate somewhat, as of 2001 the membership rate was around 30 percent, higher than telecommunications and trucking, and more than twice the level of the U.S. workforce overall.[2]

### 3.2.1    Industry Structure

The electricity industry is comprised of three main sectors: generation, transmission, and distribution. The generating sector encompasses the

---

1. Joskow (1997) gives a detailed overview of the history and performance of the industry in the United States, and of the forces pushing regulatory restructuring and reform.
2. See Niederjohn (2003).

power plants where electricity is produced from other energy sources. The transmission system transports the electricity over high-voltage lines from the power plants to local distribution areas. The distribution system includes the local system of lower voltage lines, substations, and transformers, which are used to deliver the electricity to end-use consumers. Administrative activities associated with billing retail customers are often included with distribution. Each sector is strongly differentiated from the others in operating characteristics. Transmission is capital intensive, with minimal labor and operating costs. While the natural monopoly arguments for distribution point to the large capital costs associated with replicating the distribution system, from an accounting perspective, most of the capital in the sector is extremely long-lived, so the main accounting costs are related to operating and maintaining the distribution system. In the United States in 2006, about 40 percent of the over 400,000 employees in the industry worked in distribution and, aside from approximately 25,000 in transmission, the remaining worked in generation.[3]

Within the generation sector, fuel accounts for the bulk of the expenses. For fossil-fired steam generation units, fuel accounted for about 75 percent of power plant operating costs in 2003 and still over half of the expenses when capital costs are included.[4] By contrast, labor expenses are less than 10 percent of total generation costs. Although power plants can be extremely large, complex, and expensive facilities, the fundamental process is the conversion of fuel (usually fossil fuel) into electricity. Since fuel is the dominant input into this production process, even small improvements in the efficiency at which fuel is converted into electricity (usually through an intermediate conversion into steam), can result in significant cost savings.

However, within the paradigm of cost-of-service regulation, efficiency of fuel conversion is usually taken to be an immutable, exogenous characteristic of operations rather than a parameter within management's control. In the United States, rates often contained *fuel adjustment clauses* that would allow for automatic adjustment to electricity rates based upon the costs of fuel consumed by the utility. Thus, fuel costs for many utilities were automatically passed on to customers. Although incentive mechanisms have been applied to certain activities, they have rarely extended to fuel consumption within the regulatory framework. One plant manager interviewed for this project indicated that, under regulation, management would not seriously consider an investment aimed solely at improving the efficiency of fuel conversion.

By contrast, environmental considerations can be powerful drivers of

3. This information is from the Bureau of Labor Statistics, "Employment, Hours, and Earnings from the Current Employment Statistics" survey. Information for the industry overall is based on NAICS code 2211, while the generation, transmission, and distribution sectors are five-digit subsets of this.
4. This figure is also taken from the Energy Information Administration's (EIA's) Electric Power Annual.

investment and operational decisions, both under regulation and competition. A common theme to our interviews was the high degree of focus on how plant operations could be modified to deal with emissions restrictions, or other environmental concerns such as water temperature. The design of the plant and the actions of individual operators can have impacts on these environmental factors. In many cases the goals of fuel-efficiency and emissions mitigation are in conflict with each other. For example, an oxygen-rich fuel mix can reduce NOx emissions, but also reduce fuel efficiency.

### 3.2.2  Regulatory Restructuring and Market Liberalization

Over the last two decades, governments in many countries have privatized and restructured their electricity industries. Restructured electricity markets now operate in much of Europe, North and South America, New Zealand, and Australia. These changes were primarily motivated by the perception that the previous regimes of either state ownership or cost-of-service regulation yielded inefficient operations and poor investment decisions. Restructuring of the electricity industry also reflected the natural progression of a deregulation movement that had already transformed infrastructure industries—including water, communications, and transportation—in many countries.

Within the United States, electricity restructuring has proceeded unevenly, driven by state-level initiatives. Restructuring has reached an advanced level in much of the Northeast, California, Illinois, and Texas. By contrast, the organizational and economic structure of the industry in most of the Northwest and Southeastern United States remains unchanged from the 1980s.

Restructuring is primarily aimed at the generation sector. Within restructured markets, wholesale electricity is sold at market-based, rather than cost-based, prices. Many power plants have been divested to nonutility owners, many of which have been unregulated affiliates of the former utility owners. During the period from 1998 through 2004, the industry has also experienced an enormous amount of investment in new generation facilities by nonutility operators.

There is some evidence that restructuring and liberalization, and the ensuing changes in the incentives of generation firms, has had an effect on efficiency in the industry. Bushnell and Wolfram (2005) find that fuel efficiency rates at divested U.S. power plants improved roughly 1 to 2 percent, relative to nondivested plants. Aggregate statistics suggest that employment in the U.S. electricity industry has declined substantially, from over 550,000 in 1990 to 400,000 in 2005. Figure 3.1 plots employment relative to 1990 both for the whole industry, and, beginning in 1997 when employment is broken out by five-digit NAICS code, distinguishing between the generating sector and the transmission and distribution sector of the industry. At least post-1997, the major cuts in the industry were driven by employment reductions at power plants. While these trends are suggestive of a regulatory

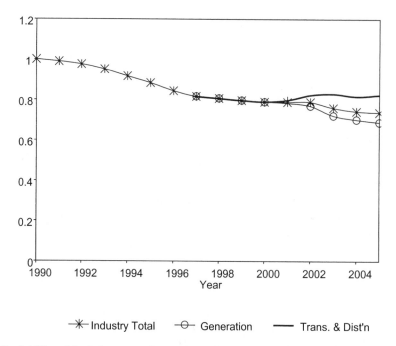

**Fig. 3.1 Electricity industry employment relative to 1990**
*Source:* Bureau of Labor Statistics, "Employment, Hours, and Earnings from the Current Employment Statistics" survey.

restructuring effect, there could have been other factors driving the reductions. The results in Fabrizio, Rose, and Wolfram (2007) suggest that restructuring was at least partially responsible for the decline, as they demonstrate that regulated power plants operating in states that passed restructuring legislation reduced the number of employees and the level of nonfuel operating expenses by more than both power plants in states that did not pass restructuring legislation and municipally-owned power plants. Similarly, Newbery and Politt (1997) attribute substantial efficiency improvements to liberalization in England and Wales.

The broad reach of economic regulation and government ownership has combined with the extremely localized character of electricity markets to yield an industry that has largely resisted the effects of globalization. Electricity can be transported across large regions, but this requires extensive and extremely expensive infrastructure. The international coordination of electricity network operations is still in its infancy and, with few exceptions, "national" grids remain, as their name implies, focused on transporting electricity within, rather than between, countries. For the most part, electricity producers have little to fear from international competition.

Liberalization has also opened the door to the acquisition by well-funded electricity firms of power plant facilities in other countries. The multinational electricity firm is therefore still a relatively new and evolving phenomenon. There is evidence that cross-national ownership is leading to some level of standardization in management practices. The Spanish firm we visited was developing several facilities in Mexico, and many English power plants are now owned by large French and German companies. However, the emerging trend of multinational ownership is offset somewhat by several factors. First, regulation still plays a far more prominent role in the electricity industry than most others, even in the markets that have been liberalized. The prominent role of regulators combines with a relatively strong position of labor unions to create an effective resistance to rapidly changing operational practices. Last, as we document, improved power plant efficiency appears to be a surprisingly low priority for newly liberalized power plant owners. Rather, the volatility of liberalized electricity markets appear to have placed more of a focus on trading operations and plant availability than on reducing the costs of these assets.

### 3.3   Plant Operators and Generator Efficiency

In this section, we will focus on the largest single cost in the electricity industry, the consumption of fuel in power plants. Despite the fact that billions of dollars are invested in the research, design, and construction of power plants, and the fact that labor is a relatively small component of power plant costs, there is a widespread belief in the industry that the *quality* of the workforce can have a nontrivial impact on performance. In particular, the decisions of one key employee, the plant operator, can affect the efficiency with which the plant converts fuel into electricity.

As described previously, power plant operations are fundamentally the process of converting potential energy in fuel into electrical energy. In general, this process can be further separated into the handling and processing of fuel, the combustion of the fuel, and the generation of electricity from either the exhaust heat or steam produced by the combustion. Depending upon the fuel type, technology, and location of the plant, the processing and monitoring of emissions and other waste products can be another significant component of plant operations. The complexity of these individual processes depends upon the specific technology of the plant. The materials handling and processing is very involved at coal facilities and relatively straightforward at natural gas plants. The combustion process can either entail burning the fuel in boilers to heat water into steam, which in turn rotates a turbine, or the direct use of hot exhaust from combustion to rotate a turbine. The former technology is often described as steam combustion and the latter a combustion turbine (CT).

While power plants employ teams of widely varying sizes and roles, all fossil fired conventional power plants staff a plant operator, whose responsibilities are central to the performance of the plant. The plant operator is primarily responsible for the monitoring and control of the combustion process.

At more complex plants, such as coal facilities, an operator controls several aspects of the process that can influence both fuel-efficiency and emissions. These include the rate at which coal mills feed pulverized fuel to burners, or even the number of mills and burners in operation. The operator controls the mix of oxygen in the combustion process, and through dampers the mix of air and fuel in the mills. Some boilers also allow for adjustment of the angle or tilt of the burners within the boiler chamber.

In all cases, these settings are automated to some degree, but the operator has the ability and responsibility to adjust or override automatic settings in the context of monitoring the operational status of the generation unit. The degree to which these decisions have been automated and optimized varies greatly across facilities. As we discuss at the end of the chapter, development of automated combustion optimization systems is an area of active commercial and research interest.

In many interviews plant managers and executives expressed a belief that individual operators can have a nontrivial impact on the combustion process. Each facility has idiosyncratic aspects that experienced and motivated operators learn to account for. The act of balancing all of these input parameters was described by one manager as "playing the piano," and one star operator was considered a virtuoso on the instrument.

Another important responsibility of plant operators that was often cited in interviews at coal plants is the operation of soot blowers within boilers. In the combustion process, pressurized water is run through pipes or tubes and heated by the boilers into steam. As a by-product of the combustion, various impurities and uncombusted material form into soot that settles onto the tubes. The soot forms an insulating layer on the tube that reduces the transfer of heat from the boiler to the water. To counteract this effect, boilers are equipped with soot blowers to jet steam at the tubes and knock off the soot.

While the operator needs to ensure that soot does not accumulate to a detrimental level on tubes, the manner in which the soot is removed can also impact boiler performance. Ideally, blowers would be operated in a sequence that is calibrated to current boiler operations. Alternatively, one unmotivated operator would "trigger all the blowers at once and go have a sandwich," as described in interviews. Triggering all the blowers can cause excess soot to circulate throughout the boiler and also reduce the efficiency of combustion.

Overall, most managers we spoke to believed that operators could have a nontrivial impact on the performance of plants. In the next section we present empirical evidence that this is in fact the case.

## 3.4   Measuring Efficiency Differences across Operators

In this section we develop an empirical model to test whether individual shifts or operators impacted the fuel efficiency of their power plants. This task is facilitated by the continuous emissions monitoring system (CEMS) data set collected by the U.S. Environmental Protection Agency (EPA). The CEMS program was developed to monitor power plant emissions systematically in order to implement environmental controls such as the cap-and-trade system for SOx. The CEMS data track many attributes of generation unit performance on an hourly basis, including the fuel burned and the power output of each facility. We can use these data to obtain an hourly measure of the fuel efficiency of each generation unit.[5] We combine the fuel efficiency data with shift information we obtained from several power companies.[6] Power plants typically comprise multiple boilers and turbines, and each boiler-turbine pair is usually referred to as a generating unit. Some multiunit plants are organized around a single control room, so that the same plant operator controls multiple units (up to seven in our data). By contrast, some plants, typically plants with larger units, have separate control rooms for each unit. To mask their identity, we will refer to the five entities from which we received shift schedule information as Plant A through Plant E, recognizing that in some cases, the operator controls less than the entire plant. The key characteristics of the plants are described in table 3.1. Although by no means a comprehensive sample of U.S. generation technology, they do represent some of the standard technologies in use in the United States today.

### 3.4.1   Empirical Strategy

To test for efficiency differences across operators, we estimate versions of the following equation:

$$(1) \quad \ln(HEAT\_RATE_{ijt}) = \alpha_i + \beta_1 \ln(OUTPUT_{ijt}) + \beta_2 \Delta \ln(OUTPUT_{ijt}) \\ + \beta_3 X_{ijt} + \kappa_j + \varepsilon_{ijt},$$

where $t$ indexes an hour, $i$ indexes the operator, and $j$ a generating unit. We estimate this equation for each plant for which we have shift-schedule information.

The dependent variable, $HEAT\_RATE_{ijt}$, is a generation unit's heat-rate,

---

5. We used a compilation of the CEMS data set obtained from Platts. The data are described in more detail in the appendix.
6. In all cases, the specific identity of the operators was masked in the data.

Table 3.1          Characteristics of units analyzed

|  | Plant A | Plant B | Plant C | Plant D | Plant E |
|---|---|---|---|---|---|
| Units under operator's control | 1 | 2 | 2 | 7 | 1 |
| Unit(s) characteristics |  |  |  |  |  |
| Size (MW) | 950 | 700 | 700 | 2,000 | 250 |
| Primary fuel | Coal | Gas | Gas | Gas and Oil | Gas |
| Year installed | 1975 | 1965 | 1965 | 1955–1970 | 1965 |
| Operating statistics |  |  |  |  |  |
| Average capacity factor (%) | 90 | 56 | 43 | 43 | 45 |
| Starts/year | 14 | 26 | 31 | 42 | 6 |
| Efficiency (MMBtu/MWh) |  |  |  |  |  |
| Average | 8.9 | 10.2 | 10.5 | 11.4 | 10.4 |
| Standard deviation | .5 | 1.0 | 3.7 | 3.8 | 1.3 |
| Positive output (MW) |  |  |  |  |  |
| Average | 826 | 181 | 144 | 184 | 92 |
| Standard deviation | 110 | 82 | 93 | 163 | 60 |
| Output$_t$/Output$_{t-1}$ |  |  |  |  |  |
| Average | 1.02 | 1.05 | 1.08 | 1.06 | 1.02 |
| Standard deviation | .85 | .78 | 1.00 | .73 | .27 |
| Combustion optimization In use? | No | In later periods | In-house version |  |  |
| Shift schedule information |  |  |  |  |  |
| Source | Operator logs | Bi-weekly schedule | Annual schedule |  |  |
| Period covered | 2003 | 2001–2003 | 2002–2003 |  |  |
| Shift length | 8 hour | 12 hour | 12 hour |  |  |
| Total operators | 12 individuals | 11 individuals | 4 teams |  |  |
| N | 7,578 | 33,490 | 18,003 | 28,790 | 15,339 |

*Note:* Unit size rounded to 50MW increments, and unit installation years rounded to half-decade.
$N$ = number of observations.

measured as the ratio of the heat content of the fuel input (in Btus) per units of electricity output (measured in kWh). It is inversely proportional to a unit's fuel efficiency and is the industry standard measure of fuel use. We obtained information on the hourly heat rates from the EPA's Continuous Emissions Monitoring System (CEMS) database. As part of the Sulfur Dioxide (SO2) Emissions Permit program, all electric power plants larger than 25 MWs were required to install pollution monitoring devices in their smokestacks. They transmit the data from the monitoring devices to the EPA on a quarterly basis, and the EPA posts it on their web site. For some types of units, the fuel input is calculated based on the carbon in the smokestack, while for others, it is measured directly.

The main variables of interest for this study are the $\alpha_i's$, the operator-specific effects. These capture the mean difference in heat rates across operators, controlling for the other variables in the regression. To code them, we needed information on exactly which person was in the control room during a particular hour. We obtained this kind of detailed shift information from three U.S. companies covering five fossil-fuel fired plants. Table 3.1 summarizes information on the five plants.

For Plant A, a large coal plant in the Southeast, company personnel transcribed entries from the operator logs for one unit at the plant for 2003. Though there are two approximately 1,000 MW units at the plant, each unit has its own control room and its own operator at any given hour. Operators are asked to sign into the log when they begin their shift, although for 33 percent of the hours (24 percent of the hours when the plant is producing power), the operator did not sign the log. We estimate a single operator effect for all hours when the operator information is missing. The plant operates on a three-shift schedule, with a morning shift (7:00AM to 3:00PM), afternoon shift (3:00PM to 11:00PM), and a night shift (11:00PM to 7:00AM). We have information on a total of twelve people, who logged anywhere from 120 to 780 hours over the course of the year. Operators who logged few hours did not necessarily have less industry experience since they could have been assigned mainly to the second "sister" unit at the plant.

For Plant B, a gas plant with two units in the West, company personnel sent us three years' worth of spreadsheets with the planned shift schedules. The plant operator controls both units at the same time, so we estimated versions of equation (1) including observations for each unit. We also include a unit fixed effect to capture mean efficiency differences across the two units. These will impact our operator effect estimates to the extent the allocation of output across units varies systematically by operator. There was a fair amount of operator turnover over the three years we analyze, as the time period followed the divestiture of the plant from a regulated utility to a nonregulated merchant firm. Some of the more senior employees at Plant B left to take jobs with the utility parent in part to maintain their favorable treatment in the company benefits programs. Also, for some shifts, two people were scheduled as the operator. We estimate a separate operator effect for each team, giving us sixteen total operator effects, though only twelve distinct individuals are represented in the data. Plant personnel work twelve-hour shifts, either from 7:00AM to 7:00PM or 7:00PM to 7:00AM. Plant B installed combustion optimization software in August 2002 at unit 3 and in August 2003 at unit 4.

Plants C, D, and E are all owned by the same firm (Firm X), but the information we have from this firm is the sparsest. Company personnel gave us two single page printouts with the schedules for their four different shifts over two years. The same shift schedules apply to the three Firm X plants that are located in the same state. This means that shift A is always working at the same time at all three plants, but the employees on shift A at Plant C are different from the employees on shift A at Plant D, and the composition of shift A at a particular plant no doubt varies over time. Unfortunately, we do not know anything about the turnover of the personnel working on the shift. Shifts are worked for twelve hours at a time, either from 7:00AM to 7:00PM or from 7:00PM to 7:00AM. The three plants are also quite different from one another. Plant C has two natural gas-fired units that were still in operation as of 2004, with a combined capacity of 760MW (five of the units at the plant were already retired). Plant D is a large plant with seven total natural gas- or oil-fired units ranging in size from 100 to 700 MWs, with the combined potential to generate over 2,000MW of total capacity. Some of the units are quite old and run infrequently. Plant E is a natural gas-fired unit with one unit still in operation.

For all units, we control for the unit output level ($\ln[OUTPUT]$), change in output over the previous hour ($\Delta \ln[OUTPUT]$) and the ambient temperature.[7] The output variables are taken from the EPA CEMS database. We obtained hourly temperature (dry bulb temperature measured in Fahrenheit) by picking the closest weather station from the National Oceanic and Atmospheric Administration (NOAA) surface weather database (available at http://www.ncdc.noaa.gov/servlets/ULCD). We also include dummy variables for the four hours directly after the unit is started and dummy variables for the type of shift (e.g., night shift versus day shift).

Equation (1) can be formalized as part of a production function if we assume that power production is Leontief in fuel and other inputs, suggesting that a plant cannot substitute labor or materials for fuel to produce electricity. Under this assumption, we can estimate equation (1) without including other factors. While there may be a limited extent to which hiring more employees and spending more on materials can help a plant use less fuel, we assume that the primary use of labor and materials in the production process is to keep the plant available. (See Fabrizio, Rose, and Wolfram [2007] for a further discussion of the Leontief assumption.)

One issue we confront in estimating equation (1) is the possibility that the choice of output level is correlated with the unit's efficiency. This would be the case if, for instance, the plant operator scaled back output when malfunctioning equipment reduced the unit's efficiency. This is equivalent to the endogeneity problem faced in estimating production functions (see, e.g., Griliches and Mairesse 1998; Olley and Pakes 1996; Levinsohn and Petrin 2003). To account for the possibility that both $\ln(OUTPUT)$ and $\Delta \ln(OUTPUT)$ are endogenous, we instrument for them using electricity demand within each plant's state ($\ln[STATE\ DEMAND]$ and $\Delta \ln[STATE$

---

7. Personnel at one of the plants we visited in the United Kingdom showed us calculations they do to benchmark the plant versus a target efficiency value, and the main adjustments they make are for unit load, starts, and ambient temperature.

*DEMAND*]). Since electricity is not storable, plants are dispatched to meet hourly demand. Depending on congestion on the transmission grid, a plant may serve anywhere from a very local geographic area to a multistate area. We take the state level as a reasonable representation of the average geographic area a plant could serve.

This selection problem is not unique to our context and has been discussed extensively in the production function literature. While many papers have estimated production or cost functions for electric generating plants, from the classic analyses in Nerlove (1963) and Christensen and Greene (1976) to very recent work such as Kleit and Terrell (2001) and Knittel (2002), electricity industry studies typically have not explicitly treated the selection problem.

While it might be interesting to examine whether there are differences in the extent to which individual operators adjust output in response to efficiency shocks, we leave that for future work. Based on our discussions with plant personnel, we perceive that individual operators have some (but by no means complete) discretion to respond to efficiency shocks. Some of the output adjustments are purely mechanical; for instance, when a malfunctioning pulverizer reduces the amount of fuel that can be fed into a plant boiler. Also, many decisions about output are made by personnel outside the plant, since deciding by exactly how much production should be scaled back when efficiency drops requires coordination across plants in the same geographic area.

### 3.4.2  Empirical Results

The $\alpha_i's$ from an instrumental variables estimation of equation (1) for Plant A are summarized in figure 3.2. The squares are at the mean effect for the operator and the vertical lines are drawn over the 95 percent confidence interval. Operator 27 collects all of the missing log entries. Four of the eleven operators (five including operator 27) had statistically significantly lower average heat rates than operator 4, the operator with the highest average heat rate. The estimates suggest that the best operator achieved an average heat rate that was more than 3 percent lower than the average heat rate achieved by the worst operator. To gain perspective on the magnitudes of the estimated effects, consider that if every operator were able to achieve the same average heat rate as the best operator, the unit would save approximately $3.5 million in fuel costs each year.[8] These savings are no doubt considerably larger than the annual payroll costs for operators.

The coefficient estimates on the control variables associated with the specification of equation (1) depicted in figure 3.2 are reported in column (1)

---

8. This calculation assumes the plant operates at a 90 percent capacity factor, with fuel costs of $25/MWh, and that the best operator worked for 10 percent of the time.

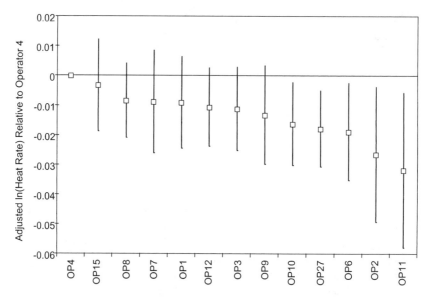

**Fig. 3.2 Relative heat rates by operator—Plant A**

*Note:* The squares are drawn at the estimated $\alpha_i$ from equation (1) for each operator, while the vertical lines are drawn over the 95 percent confidence interval. Low values of $\alpha_i$ indicate that an operator achieved a lower average heat rate; that is, was more efficient, relative to the least efficient operator (Operator 4).

of table 3.2. The second-to-last row in table 3.2 also reports the F-statistic on the joint test that all of the operator effects are zero.[9] For Plant A, the F-statistic is 2.23, suggesting that we can reject the hypothesis that all operators are the same at the 1 percent level.

Figure 3.3 summarizes the operator effects estimated for personnel at Plant B, and column (2) of table 3.2 reports the coefficient estimates and F-statistic for the specification used to generate the effects summarized in figure 3.3. As with Plant A, eight of the fifteen operators are significantly different from the worst operator and the F-statistics suggests that we can reject that all operators are the same at better than the .1 percent significance level. The operator effects may be more significant at Plant B than they were at Plant A because we have three times as long a time period for Plant B, so the estimates are tighter. The range of operator effects is smaller for Plant B than it is for Plant A, with the most efficient operator only 1.9 percent better than the least efficient operator. We spoke with engineers from both coal and gas plants who suggested that operator decisions are likely to have more impact on efficiency at coal plants.

9. The F-test for Plant A excludes operator 27, the operator effect used to collect all hours when the operator log was left blank.

**Table 3.2**          **Efficiency regressions**

|  | Plant A | Plant B | Plant C | Plant D | Plant E |
|---|---|---|---|---|---|
| ln(Output) | −0.040 | −0.119*** | −0.118*** | −0.191*** | −0.071*** |
|  | (0.040) | (0.002) | (0.003) | (0.003) | (0.003) |
| Δ ln(Output) | 0.084*** | 0.051*** | 0.039*** | 0.024*** | 0.022*** |
|  | (0.019) | (0.003) | (0.007) | (0.006) | (0.007) |
| $Start_{t-2}$ | −0.141 | 0.327*** | 0.278*** | 0.222*** | 0.261*** |
|  | (0.132) | (0.021) | (0.079) | (0.038) | (0.055) |
| $Start_{t-3}$ | −0.155** | 0.143*** | 0.096** | 0.077*** | 0.091*** |
|  | (0.074) | (0.013) | (0.043) | (0.015) | (0.024) |
| $Start_{t-4}$ | −0.061 | 0.060*** | 0.083* | 0.035*** | 0.045*** |
|  | (0.051) | (0.009) | (0.043) | (0.007) | (0.015) |
| Day shift | −0.008 | < 0.001 | −0.004*** | 0.002* | −0.001 |
|  | (0.006) | (0.001) | (0.001) | (0.001) | (0.001) |
| Evening shift | −0.001 |  |  |  |  |
|  | (0.007) |  |  |  |  |
| Temperature | 0.0005*** | 0.0003*** | 0.0005*** | 0.0003*** | 0.0007*** |
|  | (0.0002) | (0.00009) | (0.00006) | (0.00008) | (0.0001) |
| Number of distinct operators | 11 | 16 | 4 | 4 | 4 |
| F-statistic on operator effects |  |  |  |  |  |
| (p-value) | 2.23 | 3.90 | .39 | .11 | .42 |
|  | (.01) | (< .0001) | (.76) | (.95) | (.74) |
| N | 7,578 | 33,490 | 18,003 | 28,790 | 15,339 |

*Notes:* Dependent variable: ln(Efficiency). All specifications estimated using instrumental variables with ln(State Load) and Δ ln(State Load) used as instruments for ln(Output) and Δ ln(Output). Unit fixed effects are included where operators control multiunit plants and year-effects are included where data span multiple years. Standard errors (in parentheses) are robust to serial correlation within a day. N = number of observations.

***Significant at the 1 percent level.
**Significant at the 5 percent level.
*Significant at the 10 percent level.

Unlike for Plants A and B, the operator effects at Plants C, D, and E (recall that they are all owned by Firm X) were estimated to be small and statistically indistinguishable from zero. The largest difference between the best and worst shifts was .0020 (standard error [s.e.] .0019) at Plant C. This point estimate is an order of magnitude smaller than the similar measures at Plants A and B. Overall, the results suggest there are no discernible differences between the four shifts at any of Firm X's plants. It is instructive to consider why we might find differences across operators at Plants A and B, but not at Plants C, D, and E. For one, the shift information that we received from Firm X is much less precise than the information for Plants A or B, so the estimates could be biased to zero because of classical measurement error. For instance, since we only have information on four shifts, the operators were scheduled to work almost 2,200 hours per year. No doubt

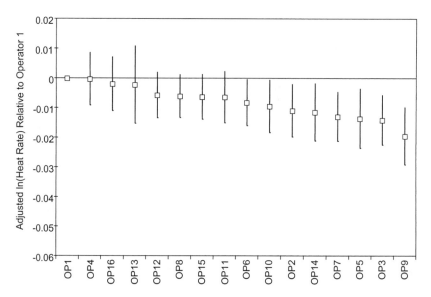

**Fig. 3.3 Relative heat rates by operator—Plant B**
*Note:* See figure 3.2.

operators, especially those with considerable seniority, are working much less than this per year, suggesting that each shift contains more than a single operator. Also, as we noted in comparing Plant A to Plant B, operators have less room to affect efficiency at gas plants. Finally, plant personnel at Plant C described an in-house computer program that they used to instruct operators about the optimal setting for plants, suggesting that operators at the Firm X plants are less likely to make different decisions about plant operations.

Note that there is reason to believe that all of the operators effects we measured are biased to zero. For one, we only have information on the operator and not the plant staff supporting him (all of the operators we have on record were male). It is possible that we could see larger differences if we could control for the supporting staff as well. Second, even for Plant A, where we have operator log information, there may be measurement error in our independent variable.

The coefficient estimates on the control variables summarized in table 3.2 are for the most part as expected. For all plants except Plant A, the coefficient on $\ln(OUTPUT)$ are negative and statistically significant, suggesting that plants are more fuel efficient at higher output levels. Also, as would be expected if operators are reducing output in response to negative efficiency shocks, instrumenting for $\ln(OUTPUT)$ causes the coefficient to fall toward zero. For example, an ordinary least squares (OLS) estimate of equation (1) using data on Plant B yields a coefficient on $\ln(OUTPUT)$ of −.121 (s.e. =

.002).[10] Similarly, the coefficient on $\Delta \ln(OUTPUT)$ is positive and statistically significant at all plants, suggesting that increases in output degrade efficiency and reductions improve efficiency.[11] Also, the F-statistics on the first stages are large, suggesting that our instruments work quite well.

The coefficient estimates on $TEMPERATURE$ are all positive and statistically significant, consistent with what engineers told us to expect. Only two of the five $DAYSHIFT$ variables are significantly different from zero, and one is positive and small and the other is negative and quite small (suggesting at most a .5 percent difference across shifts). Except at Plant A, the $START_{t-X}$ for $X \subset 2, 3, 4$ dummies are positive, suggesting that fuel efficiency is compromised after starts. There were only thirteen starts at Plant A, so these variables are imprecisely estimated. Also, since starts are associated with rapid changes in output, the heat rate variable can be very noisy.

## 3.5   Labor Policies and Operator Performance

We have described the critical role that plant operators play in the operation of power plants, and presented anecdotal and empirical evidence that operators can have a significant impact on the efficiency of plant operations. Given this evidence, two important questions arise. Why is such a variation in performance tolerated by firms, and what can firms do to take advantage of the skills and experience of the strong performers?

### 3.5.1   Human Resource Policies

Aggregate statistics and our interviews with power plant managers both suggest that labor policies in electricity generation have been undergoing a dramatic transformation over the last ten to twenty years. This transformation has coincided with the rise of nonutility power producers, the privatization of publicly-owned utilities outside of the United States, and the advent of regulatory restructuring. It is reasonable to conclude that the competitive pressures created by these developments provided the impetus for these changes. However, it is worth noting that these changes have not been limited to regions where power plants have been divested or deregulated. Also, many interviewees cited the adoption of automated monitoring technology beginning in the late 1980s as a factor in the declining employment rates.

In general, the historic labor picture at power plants was heavily unionized with inflexible work rules and promotion policies. There were several layers of

10. The significance of the operator effects are not sensitive to the estimates of $\ln(OUTPUT)$. In addition to the specifications we report, we also estimated other specifications that allowed $OUTPUT$ to take different nonlinear forms. The estimates of the F-statistics on the operator effects were qualitatively very similar; that is, they suggested that operators at Plants A and B differed from one another but those at Firm X's plants did not.

11. We also estimate specifications that allowed the effect of an output change to differ for positive and negative changes. Both effects were positive, suggesting that a reduction in output does lead to a lower heat rate (more efficient).

job categories and restrictions on utilizing employees in roles outside of their categories. Staffing levels were also, by today's standards, quite high. Promotion was largely based upon tenure at a plant or with the company. Certainly a minimum level of competence was required for promotion, particularly to the operator level. However, among those employees able to exceed a certain minimum threshold of performance, there was little effort to differentiate among the quality of employees when determining promotions.

Since the mid-1980s employment levels have steadily declined. Plant F, a coal plant in England visited for this project, is representative of this trend. There were 285 employees at the plant when we visited, down from a peak of over 700 before the plant was privatized in the early 1990s. This trend is shared among most liberalized electricity markets, but not restricted to those facing full competitive pressures. Plant G, a coal plant in Alabama also visited for this project, reported 320 employees in 2004, down from a peak of over 450 despite the fact that its regulatory status has remained unchanged. Among the positions eliminated was a full-time groundskeeper, cited to us as an example of previous excesses given the paucity of grass around the plant.

As mentioned previously, aggregate statistics suggest a pronounced reduction in power plant employment throughout the United States. These reductions are most pronounced in areas actively pursuing some form of deregulation (see Fabrizio, Rose, and Wolfram 2007). The largest reductions overall appear to be a plants divested from regulated utilities to nonutility operators (see Bushnell and Wolfram 2005).

The reduction in employment has coincided, at least in restructured states, with a declining influence of unions and increasingly flexible work rules. In two separate interviews, managers described how previously, a shift was staffed with a number of specialists, including mill workers, electricians, and boilermakers. Union work rules prohibited job sharing. In the late 1990s, management had been able to renegotiate union contracts, in some cases when the plants were divested to new owners, to allow workers to be classified generally as power plant operators. As a result, workers at the restructured plants we visited were valued for their broad skill sets, and staffing levels fell.

According to managers at some plants, wage levels have in many cases risen as the number of employees has been reduced and responsibilities expanded.[12] Promotion policies have also become less rigid. One operator at Plant F in England rose to his position in just over two years, much faster than would have been possible under the plant's previous tenure-based promotion scheme. The merchant owner of Plant B replaced a large fraction of the employees it inherited from the regulated utility when it purchased the plant, drawing its new employees largely from ex-Navy technicians and

---

12. Shanefelter (2006) uses Bureau of Labor Statistics (BLS) data to describe a picture consistent with these claims.

engineers. By contrast, Firm X, also a merchant company operating plants it had purchased from regulated utilities, has retained most of the employees at the plants it purchased.

Despite these broad trends that indicate increasing productivity at power plants in liberalized electricity markets, in most cases we found little focus on the quality of specific employees, beyond standard promotional policies. In particular, in most cases there were no specific initiatives designed to address the operator effects on fuel efficiency that have been described previously, despite a widespread consensus that such effects are meaningful. That said, there were some efforts at linking bonuses to corporate or plant performance, and one specific effort to link employee pay to the efficiency of the plant. We describe these programs in section 3.5.2.

### 3.5.2 Performance Pay

All plants we visited paid bonuses to their employees loosely based upon some measure of performance. In some cases, as with Plant G in Alabama, these bonuses were largely linked to corporate financial performance and therefore were more a version of "profit-sharing" than incentive pay. Bonuses at many plants also reflected conventional HR policies, such as a linkage to favorable performance reviews by supervisors, the completion of assigned tasks on time, and limited absenteeism. In several cases, such as Plant F, bonuses were linked to aggregate measures of plant's performance, such as the achievement of certain fuel efficiency and availability targets. For the most part, however, such bonuses did not attempt to distinguish between the performance of specific employees within a given plant.

One notable exception to these policies was a performance pay initiative attempted at Plant F in England in the mid-1990s. Plant F is a large coal-fired plant that had been built by the government-owned Central Electricity Generation Board (CEGB) and privatized in the early 1990s. The plant has since changed hands multiple times. Since before privatization, substantial efforts were made to monitor and document the plant's performance along a large number of efficiency measures. These efforts evolved into an automated system able to monitor, quantify, and report the "cost of [efficiency] losses" at the plant. The cost of losses calculation was highly sophisticated and attempted to control for all relevant exogenous impacts on plant operations, such as fuel quality, ambient temperature, and the output level of the plant. It generated detailed reports, breaking down efficiency losses to specific processes within the plant.[13] Initially (and currently) these data were aggregated into monthly performance reports and utilized by managers as a general tool for helping to focus efficiency efforts. These measures would be

13. The cost of losses report would decompose performance measures to report the losses due to several factors including turbine losses, boiler efficiency, fuel feed trains, and exhaust pressure.

reviewed at monthly meetings of all section heads, including representatives from operations, commercial performance, and maintenance.

In 1995, managers attempted to utilize the cost of losses system in a more direct fashion by linking it to performance bonuses for specific shifts. Recognizing the disparity in performance and losses between shifts, managers believed that the incentives provided by such a linkage would help to focus underperforming operators and shifts and help to improve their efficiency at least to levels attained by higher performing shifts. In doing so, managers implicitly expressed a belief that these performance disparities were largely effort-based, rather than a result of differences in the inherent acumen or talent of the operators. The pay differentials created by the bonuses were still quite modest, amounting to about 1 percent of annual pay.

Even with this modest incentive, however, managers did notice marked changes in performance between shifts. Unfortunately they were not the kinds of effects that they intended to induce. The incentive scheme was based upon the *relative* performance in the cost of losses of each shift. Operators quickly discovered that a degradation in the performance of *other* shifts could be as rewarding as an increase in their own efficiency. It appears that there are more and easier options for sabotaging other shifts than for improving own performance. Managers found that operators would sometimes avoid blowing soot throughout their shift, forcing excessive blowing upon the next shift, or triggering all the blowers simultaneously at the very end of their shift, leaving the next shift to deal with the resulting residue. In such an environment there was growing acrimony between shifts and operators. Eventually, managers at Plant F dropped the incentive scheme, and shifted toward a system of rewarding the pooled performance of all shifts. Although the direct influence of individual effort and performance on such pooled incentives is diluted, managers claimed that efficiency improved roughly half a percent under this new scheme.

### 3.5.3   Combustion Optimization Software

The experiment with performance pay at Plant F can be viewed as an attempt to elevate the efficiency of underperforming operators at least up to the level observed in the better operators by applying incentives intended to increase focus and effort. A more recent trend at power plants may also result in more balanced performance among operators by reducing the impact of their individual performance. This trend is the adoption of automated combustion optimization software and systems. In general, these systems use learning algorithms to attempt to customize operating protocols to the specific idiosyncrasies of a specific plant. The more ambitious of these systems take much of the influence over burner angles, fuel flow, oxygen content, and so forth out of the hands of the operator. In theory, such systems should reduce the disparities between operator performance. Indeed, the vendor of one such system, NeuCo, claims that its systems can help to "make the worst operator at least as good as the best." The adoption of these systems is still in its early stages, and we were not able to attain sufficient data to adequately evaluate such claims.

However, two factors that were raised during our interviews indicate that, at least in the near future, the impact of such systems on fuel efficiency may be small. First, these systems are being utilized primarily for the purpose of reducing emissions, rather than improving fuel efficiency. Second, in many cases operators have been hostile to yielding control over operations to these systems. In one plant we visited, an installed control system had been converted to an "advisory mode" that provided recommendations, but direct control was left to the human operator.

That said, managers at the Firm X plants firmly believed that the optimization systems they had installed would significantly reduce if not eliminate any operator effects. Our empirical analysis supports their view. By contrast, Plant B installed a NeuCo system in the middle of our sample period. The system had been installed to help the plant address NOx emissions, rather than fuel efficiency. When we included a dummy variable equal to one after the adoption of the optimization software, we did not detect a statistically significant impact on either the overall fuel efficiency of the units or on the relative operator effects at the plant, although we observed only nine operators who worked before and after the installation.

### 3.6    Conclusions

Labor policies in the electricity industry have been significantly impacted by its historical status as either a publicly owned or regulated utility business. At the same time, evaluating and improving labor practices may have been given low priority due to the fact that labor costs constitute a small portion of industry costs. We present evidence that, despite the fact that overall labor costs are small, the *quality* of certain workers can have a significant impact on the operations of power plants. Power plant operators, in particular, can influence the fuel-efficiency of the plants under their control in a myriad of individually small, but in aggregate consequential, ways. There is good reason to believe that this effect is more prominent in the more complex coal facilities than in gas-fired power plants.

In our examination of performance data from U.S. power plants we find that the individual operators could influence fuel efficiency by more than 3 percent. While this figure may sound modest, it translates into a difference worth millions of dollars in annual fuel costs at larger facilities. Despite what appears to be a widespread belief in an "operator effect" amongst plant managers, there have been relatively few attempts to address the impacts of these effects. We have documented one failed attempt at performance-based incentive pay, and described how the advent of automated combustion optimization systems may reduce or eliminate operator effects. Even the roll-out of such automated systems has been relatively slow, and more focused on environmental considerations than on efficiency concerns. It is worth noting that market incentives have only recently been introduced in the industry. The process of regulatory restructuring is less than a decade old in most of the world, and this is a relatively short time in a historically slow-moving industry. It remains to be seen whether firms facing more exposure to market incentives will prove to be more adept at taking advantage of operator effects, or whether such effects are an immutable characteristic of the power generation business.

More generally, our results provide a clean measure of the extent of worker heterogeneity within the same job description at a particular plant. It is possible that other industries would show less heterogeneity, perhaps because labor practices have received little attention in the electricity industry relative to other industries, where labor is a larger fraction of overall employment. It is also possible that the true heterogeneity across workers would be larger in other industries, and the fact that managers have clean measures of worker output in electricity helps keep it in check. For example, Mas and Moretti (2009) report a 21 percent difference between supermarket cashiers in the top and bottom deciles. At any rate, worker heterogeneity is not ordinarily captured in descriptions of firm efficiency based on production functions, but may be an important component of technical efficiency differences across firms.

# Data Appendix

Our primary data sources are BaseCase and PowerDat, two databases produced by Platts (see www.Platts.com). Platt's compiles data on power plant operations and characteristics from numerous public sources, performs limited data cleaning and data analysis, and creates cross references so that the data sets can be linked by numerous characteristics (e.g., power plant unit, state, grid control area, etc.). We relied on information from Platts for the following broad categories.

### Unit Operating Profile

BaseCase contains hourly power plant unit-level information derived from the Continuous Emissions Monitoring System (CEMS) database collected by the Environmental Protection Agency. The EPA assembles this detailed, high quality data to support various emissions trading programs. The CEMS data are collected for all fossil-fueled power plant units that operate more than a certain number of hours a year. The data set contains hourly reports on heat input, gross electricity output, and pollutant output.

We calculate the heat rate by dividing heat input (measured in mmBtus) by gross electricity output (measured in MWh). By construction of the heat rate variable, our sample is limited to hours in which the unit was producing positive gross electricity output.

**System-level Demand Characteristics**

Data on system level demand are taken from the PowerDat database, also compiled by Platts. These data report the monthly minimum, maximum, mean, and standard deviation of load by utility, as well as the average daily maximum over a month. Platts compiles this information from survey data collected by the EIA and reported in its form 714.

**Plant and Unit Characteristics**

Unit characteristics are taken from the "Base Generating Units" and "Estimated Fossil-Fired Operations" data sets within BaseCase.

We merged data from Platts to several additional sources.

**Shift Schedules**

We obtained shift schedules from three companies covering operations at five power plants. For Plant A, company personnel transcribed entries from the operator logs for one unit at the plant for 2003. Though there are two approximately 1,000 MW units at Plant A, each unit has its own control room and its own operator at any given hour. Plant operators are asked to sign into the log when they begin their shift. For Plant B, a gas plant with two units, company personnel sent us three years' worth of spreadsheets with the planned shift schedules. The plant operator controls both units at the same time. The information we have from Firm X is the sparsest. Company personnel gave us two single page printouts with the schedules for the four different shifts over two years. The same shift schedules apply to all three of Plant X's plants in the same Western state. This means that shift A is always working at the same time at all three plants, but the employees on shift A at plant 1 are different from the employees on shift A at plant 2, and the composition of shift A at a particular plant no doubt varies over time.

**Ambient Temperature-Hourly**

We obtained hourly temperature data by weather station from the Unedited Local Climatological Data Hourly Observations data set put out by the National Oceanographic and Atmospheric Administration. Further documentation is available at: http://www.ncdc.noaa.gov/oa/documentlibrary/ulcd/lcdudocumentation.txt.

We calculated the Euclidean distance between each weather station-power plant combination, using the latitude and longitude for each power plant and for each weather station. Then, for each month, we found the weather station closest to each power plant that had more than 300 valid temperature observations. For hours when the temperature was missing, we interpolated an average temperature from adjoining hours.

# References

Bandiera, O., I. Barankay, and I. Rasul. 2005. Social preferences and the response to incentives: Evidence from personnel data. *Quarterly Journal of Economics* 120 (3): 917–62.

Bushnell, J., and C. Wolfram. 2005. Ownership change, incentives and plant efficiency: The divestiture of U.S. electric generation plants. The Center for the Study of Energy Markets (CSEM) Working Paper WP-140. University of California Energy Institute, March. Available at www.ucei.org.

Christensen, L. R., and W. H. Greene. 1976. Economies of scale in U.S. electric power generation. *Journal of Political Economy* 84 (4): 655–76.

Fabrizio, K., N. Rose, and C. Wolfram. 2007. Do markets reduce costs? Assessing the impact of regulatory restructuring on U.S. electric generation efficiency. *American Economic Review* 97 (4): 1250–77.

Griliches, Z., and J. Mairesse. 1998. Production functions: The search for identification. In *Econometrics and economic theory in the 20th Century,* ed. Steiner Strom, 169–203. Cambridge: Cambridge University Press.

Hamilton, B. H., J. A. Nickerson, and H. Owan. 2003. Team incentives and worker heterogeneity: An empirical analysis of the impact of teams on productivity and participation. *Journal of Political Economy* 111 (3): 465–97.

Joskow, P. 1997. Restructuring, competition, and regulatory reform in the U.S. electricity sector. *Journal of Economic Perspectives* 11 (3): 119–38.

Kleit, A., and D. Terrell. 2001. Measuring potential efficiency gains from deregulation of electricity generation: A Bayesian approach. *The Review of Economics and Statistics* 83 (3): 523–30.

Knittel, C. R. 2002. Alternative regulatory methods and firm efficiency: Stochastic frontier evidence from the U.S. electricity industry. *The Review of Economics and Statistics* 84 (3): 530–40.

Levinsohn, J., and A. Petrin. 2003. Estimating production functions using inputs to control for unobservables. *Review of Economic Studies* 70 (2): 317–41.

Mas, A., and E. Moretti. 2009. Peers at work. *American Economic Review* 99 (1): 112–45.

Nerlove, M. 1963. Returns to scale in electricity supply. In *Measurement in economics,* ed. C. F. Christ, M. Friedman, L. A. Goodman, Z. Griliches, A. C. Harberger, N. Liviatan, J. Mincer, et al. Stanford, CA: Stanford University Press.

Newbery, D. M., and M. G. Pollitt. 1997. The restructuring and privatisation of the CEGB—Was it worth it? *The Journal of Industrial Economics* 45 (3): 269–303.

Niederjohn, M. S. 2003. Regulatory reform and labor outcomes in the U.S. electricity sector. *Monthly Labor Review* 126 (5): 10–19.

Olley, S., and A. Pakes. 1996. The dynamics of productivity in the telecommunications equipment industry. *Econometrica* 64 (6): 1263–97.

Shanefelter, J. 2006. Restructuring, ownership and efficiency: The case of labor in electricity generation. CSEM Working Paper WP-161, University of California Energy Institute, November. Available at www.ucei.org.

# II

## Within-Firm Studies

# 4

# Labor Practices and Outcomes across Countries
## Analysis of a Single Multinational Firm

Richard B. Freeman, Douglas Kruse, and Joseph Blasi

Consider a multinational firm producing similar goods and services in the same industry in many countries. How much do labor practices, employee attitudes, and worker behavior differ among the establishments of the firm across countries? Do workers in different countries respond similarly to policies? Are aggregate measures of labor practices across countries related to differences in worker behavior and outcomes, or do the specifics of the firm trump such measures of conditions?

This chapter examines these questions using data from a 2005 to 2006 web-based and paper survey of workers in a large multinational manufacturing firm in 272 establishments in nineteen countries. The firm convened employee meetings in each facility to induce employees to respond, which led to a sample of 29,353 respondents, with a response rate of greater than 60 percent.[1] This gives us one of the largest individual level data sets on labor practices, employee attitudes toward work, and self-reported workplace per-

Richard B. Freeman is the Herbert Ascherman Professor of Economics at Harvard University and program director of labor studies at the National Bureau of Economic Research. Douglas Kruse is a professor of Human Resource Management at Rutgers University and a research associate of the National Bureau of Economic Research. Joseph Blasi is a professor of Human Resource Management and Labor Studies and Employment Relations at Rutgers University and a research associate of the National Bureau of Economic Research.

1. The web surveys were submitted directly to our website and not to company administration. To protect the confidentiality of workers who filled out paper surveys, each worker placed his or her anonymous survey in a sealed envelope that went into a box controlled by a committee of three nonmanagement employees who were instructed to drive it to an express mail/shipping facility immediately. These protections of confidentiality set the stage for a high "comfort zone" for open responses to the questions. In addition, the surveys were translated into the language of each country so that it would be accessible to most of the workers filling out the surveys who were native speakers. The company's policy is to rely on local management teams and workers with very selective and infrequent use of expatriates. To the extent there are immigrants in the company's workforce, this will mute the estimates of country differences.

formance across countries in a single firm since Geert Hofstede's (1984, 1991) study of IBM based on surveys in 1968 and 1972.[2] Our study differs from Hofstede's classic work in three ways. Hofstede's surveys focused on European and Middle Eastern countries; our sample contains many observations from the United States and from countries in Latin America and Asia as well as from Europe. Hoftstede's 1968 study included many workers outside manufacturing and his 1972 sample excluded manufacturing; our data are for manufacturing. Finally, Hofstede looked at employee values and beliefs as they related to organizations and national culture or character, while our focus is on employment relations, the organization of work, and the economic behavior of workers in response to labor policies.

Our analysis shows:

1. Large cross-country differences in work practices, worker attitudes, and employee performance, evinced by significant country dummy variables for all variables.

2. Qualitatively similar responses of workers to work policies and practices across countries, as evinced in positive slope terms in regressions linking measures of worker performance to the quality of labor-management relations and the presence of a "high performance" work system, although with differing magnitudes.

3. A strong relation between reported employee performance and quality of labor-management relations at the level of establishments. This relation is similar among establishments outside the United States as among establishments within the United States.

4. Taking country as the unit of observation, countries where workers report better employee-management relations and compensation above market levels have better employee performance. In contrast, measures of worker performance are negatively or insignificantly correlated with country level indices of labor practices from the Economic Freedom of the World Index and the Global Competitiveness Index.

## 4.1   The Data and Research Strategy

Columns (1) and (2) of table 4.1 give the sample size and number of establishments by country in our survey. The source notes to the table show the specific questions on which we focus, and the way in which we coded them for analysis. Because the firm is headquartered in the United States and expanded from the United States to other countries, the United States has the largest number of establishments (73 percent of the total) and workers (72 percent of the total). The company began expanding internationally in the 1960s through acquisitions and accelerated its international presence

2. Hofstede collected about 60,000 employee surveys in each year for a total of 116,000 surveys.

**Table 4.1**    Country means of key variables and questions that define them

| | No. of employees | No. of facilities | Workplace policies | | | Own performance | | | | Coworker/facility performance | |
|---|---|---|---|---|---|---|---|---|---|---|---|
| | | | Grade on ee-mgt. relations 0–4 scale | High-perf. index 0–6 scale | Total comp relative to mkt 1–5 scale | Likely to stay 1–4 scale | Willing to work hard 1–5 scale | Willing to innovate 1–4 scale | Antishirking index 4–16 scale | Coworkers work hard 0–10 scale | Facility effectiveness 0–4 scale |
| Overall | 29,353 | 272 | 2.27 | 2.93 | 2.69 | 0.59 | 3.94 | 3.01 | 9.78 | 6.89 | 2.69 |
| Argentina | 28 | 1 | 2.96 | 3.33 | 2.50 | 3.46 | 4.27 | 3.39 | 12.13 | 8.00 | 3.16 |
| Australia | 103 | 2 | 1.72 | 2.83 | 2.46 | 2.96 | 3.44 | 2.94 | 9.75 | 6.07 | 2.31 |
| Brazil | 1,126 | 5 | 2.31 | 3.38 | 2.75 | 3.21 | 4.04 | 3.16 | 10.68 | 8.19 | 2.52 |
| Canada | 415 | 2 | 2.46 | 3.98 | 2.94 | 3.60 | 3.95 | 3.06 | 9.66 | 6.79 | 2.84 |
| China | 937 | 7 | 2.01 | 3.14 | 1.98 | 3.04 | 3.94 | 2.86 | 10.13 | 7.62 | 2.66 |
| Czech Republic | 87 | 1 | 2.55 | 3.69 | 2.61 | 3.47 | 3.88 | 3.12 | 11.16 | 7.18 | 2.75 |
| Finland | 101 | 1 | 2.28 | 2.45 | 2.58 | 2.63 | 3.28 | 2.76 | 9.16 | 7.08 | 2.57 |
| France | 215 | 5 | 2.08 | 3.32 | 2.55 | 3.52 | 3.33 | 2.66 | 9.60 | 5.80 | 2.63 |
| Germany | 479 | 14 | 2.46 | 3.19 | 2.75 | 3.60 | 3.69 | 3.35 | 11.15 | 7.04 | 2.53 |
| Italy | 808 | 3 | 1.79 | 2.35 | 2.43 | 3.50 | 4.14 | 2.94 | 10.45 | 7.20 | 2.79 |
| Korea | 445 | 3 | 2.08 | 2.92 | 2.38 | 3.43 | 3.88 | 2.60 | 9.18 | 7.55 | 2.60 |
| Mexico | 2,460 | 7 | 2.32 | 2.98 | 2.69 | 3.25 | 3.97 | 3.03 | 11.05 | 7.34 | 2.92 |
| Netherlands | 74 | 6 | 2.39 | 2.67 | 2.52 | 3.68 | 2.96 | 3.07 | 11.65 | 6.79 | 2.51 |
| South Africa | 49 | 1 | 2.70 | 2.83 | 2.59 | 3.65 | 4.43 | 3.33 | 10.47 | 7.50 | 3.09 |
| Sweden | 234 | 4 | 2.13 | 2.91 | 2.24 | 3.47 | 3.48 | 2.52 | 9.02 | 7.03 | 2.51 |
| Switzerland | 115 | 1 | 2.33 | 3.66 | 2.31 | 3.62 | 3.67 | 2.68 | 9.91 | 6.27 | 2.74 |
| Taiwan | 27 | 1 | 2.52 | 3.63 | 2.48 | 2.89 | 4.00 | 2.78 | 9.32 | 6.63 | 2.33 |
| United Kingdom | 415 | 9 | 2.08 | 3.41 | 2.66 | 3.33 | 3.78 | 3.35 | 10.10 | 6.85 | 2.56 |
| United States | 21,235 | 199 | 2.29 | 3.28 | 2.75 | 3.44 | 3.95 | 3.01 | 9.59 | 6.72 | 2.67 |
| F-stat. for differences | | | 18.20 | 29.49 | 38.39 | 30.86 | 25.24 | 24.13 | 32.63 | 49.56 | 24.06 |
| P-value for differences | | | 0.00 | 0.00 | 0.00 | 0.00 | 0.00 | 0.00 | 0.00 | 0.00 | 0.00 |

*Source:* Obtained from firm-based survey questions as given in the appendix.

*Note:* ee-mgt. = employee-management.

in the 1980s and 1990s. The large number of U.S. establishments allows us to estimate with some precision the level and interrelation of variables in the United States and use this as a base for seeing how institutional and economic environments outside the United States influence operations but limits comparisons of operations among other countries. It dictates the structure of ensuing analysis in which we take the U.S. mode of operating as an "original type" and treat the practices in other countries as "varieties" that depart from the original type in response to differing regulatory and economic environments. This mimics the way Wallace and Darwin examined how species developed from existing populations across geographic areas.[3]

The survey asked about employee opinions and attitudes on the organization of work, labor-management relations, supervision, employee involvement, and compensation systems; expected turnover, behavior toward coworkers, the effort of workers at their job, and the effort of fellow employees, plus a module of unique questions regarding worker perception and responses to seeing fellow workers shirk, their willingness to take innovative action at their workplace, and their views of how their facility performs. In addition, the survey contained measures of demographic and job characteristics. Most of the survey questions asked workers to rate how their establishment or they operate using a five-point Likert scale, with higher numbers reflecting more positive assessments, though some questions are dichotomous.[4]

We have structured our analysis around the distinction between policies/practices that in principle the firm's management controls, which we take as exogenous to workers, and outcome or behavioral variables that reflect worker decisions, which will in part respond to these policies/practices. One way to analyze a survey with many questions in particular domains is to focus on a subset of variables that reflect responses to specific questions. An alternative mode of analysis is to form indices of variables by compressing the data through factor analyses or through summated rating or other indices. In this chapter, we choose the former procedure in most cases, analyzing single variables as measures of practice or behavior. Where research has found that certain practices fit together in a group, such as in the form of "high performance workplaces," however, we analyze an index of several variables. To make sure that our results do not depend on the specific variables we chose or the indices that we form, we also estimated models with variables from all of the questions in the relevant modules and note the results.

3. Alfred Russel Wallace (July 1858).

4. In addition to the worker survey, we obtained administrative records from the firm on the economic performance of seventy-nine divisions, with each division containing facilities producing a similar product, or in some cases, geographic units that report performance to top management. Here we relied on data that the firm normally gathers from its facilities to assess their performance.

Our primary measures of management policies/practices are employee-management relations, the work practices that contribute to high performance work systems, and total compensation relative to the market. While employer-employee relations reflects the behavior of workers and management, management usually sets the tenor of the relationship, to which workers or unions respond, by choosing work practices or policies. Since research has found complementarities in the effects of these practices (Ichniowski, Shaw, and Prennushi 1997), we formed an index of high performance workplace based on six questions relating to worker reports on: employee involvement teams, training; information sharing; employee selection; profit or gain sharing; and job rotation, as described in the source to table 4.1. Finally, management decides on pay relative to the market. While in principle it cannot obtain workers below market rates, it can pay above market rates, either to reduce turnover or give workers an incentive to work harder (Akerlof 1982).

On the workers' side, we focus on four measures of individual behavior or potential behavior: whether workers are likely to look for a new job in the next six months, their willingness to work hard for the company, their willingness to innovate, and an index of the worker's willingness to intervene with a shirking coworker. We also analyze their view on how hard coworkers work, and of the overall effectiveness of their facility. The likelihood of leaving a workplace is a widely studied variable in analyses of job satisfaction. Our question on the workers' willingness to try to develop innovative products and services is designed to get at the more creative dimension of work, which has arguably become more important over time in most workplaces.

The measure of workers' willingness to intervene when they see fellow workers not working up to speed is the most innovative measure of this study. It is designed to cast light on modern team production and group incentive employment systems (Kruse, Blasi, and Park 2006) that must overcome free-riding and shirking to succeed. Since workers often have better information than management on what fellow workers are doing, worker responses to shirking are critical to the success or failure of these approaches to the organization of work. The antishirking measure comes from a question about the likelihood that a worker responds to seeing a fellow employee not working as hard or well as he or she should: talking directly to the employee, speaking to a supervisor or manager, talking about it in a work group or team, or doing nothing. By asking about responses in four ways, we obtained a more finely graded measure than if we had asked about any single response. Freeman, Kruse, and Blasi (2006) provide a detailed analysis of this variable for random samples of all U.S. workers in 2002 and 2006 based on the General Social Survey and for the aggregated sample of employees across fourteen companies in this data set. The key finding is that antishirking behavior is greater when workers are paid by group incentive systems and is correlated with how workers assess the effectiveness of their workplace and the effort of fellow workers. Building on these findings, we seek to determine whether there are any country differences in this behavior.

## 4.2   Empirical Strategy

We have undertaken a two-step analysis of our data. First, we seek to identify differences in employment practices, employee attitudes, and worker and establishment performance that we can attribute to operating in different countries. Without such differences, this study would come to a rapid conclusion. The statistical problem with identifying country effects in our data is that the survey has only a few establishments per country outside the United States (the largest number of establishments in a non-U.S. country is nine, while there is just one establishment in five countries). This makes it difficult to differentiate the effects of country institutions on outcomes from the effects of establishments per se. We address this problem by contrasting the variation in estimated country effects across all non-U.S. establishments with the variation in the same variables across U.S. states. Since firms in the United States operate under essentially the same legal regulations and institutions, variation among states/regions will be due to regional economic conditions or historic labor practices in geographically contiguous areas rather than to different national labor regulations. This variation is thus an indicator of differences independent of national institutions. Assuming an additive model in which regional factors are orthogonal to national institutions, and in which regional differences are comparable in countries, the variation in variables in our country analysis would equal regional differences as in the United States plus differences due to different national labor institutions. Accordingly, our research strategy is to estimate within-U.S. state/region; and then compare the variation in the U.S. regional effects with the variation in country effects. If country institutions matter, the variation across countries should exceed the variation in the same variable across U.S. states. Since regional effects are likely to be larger in the United States than in other countries, both because of the lack of national wage bargaining and geographic reach of the country, by subtracting the variation in variables in U.S. states from the variation in variables across countries to measure what we might call the "region adjusted" country variation, we potentially underestimate variation due to country effects.

We next want to see whether estimated country effects in worker outcomes are related to estimated country effects in labor practices and policies. The problem here is that the firm operates in only nineteen countries, and has only one establishment in five of them, which makes obtaining statistically trustworthy results difficult. We deal with this problem by contrasting all of the non-U.S.-based establishments with all of the U.S. establishments. In addition, we estimated the relation between country differences in labor outcomes and measures of country labor practices from the Fraser Institute's "indices of economic freedom" and the World Economic Forum's measures of competitiveness.

Second, we assess how management practices affect worker behavior by regressing four measures of worker behavior on the measures of company policy and practice. The problem in this analysis is that both the independent and dependent variables are self-reports from workers. It is possible that workers would report practices/policies based on their idiosyncratic position or views rather than on the overall situation at the workplace. For instance, worker A at establishment E might report that the establishment has good work practices and that they are willing to work hard while worker B at the same establishment might report that the establishment has bad work practices and that they are unwilling to work hard. This pattern would produce a strong relation between work practices and willingness to work hard at the individual level that would not generalize to the workplace. We deal with this problem by calculating and analyzing establishment averages, as well as the responses of individual workers. Averaging responses across establishments eliminates the danger that the happy (unhappy) worker reports only good (bad) things about the establishment even when other workers have different perceptions.

## 4.3   Cross-country Patterns

Columns (3) through (5) of table 4.1 report the average level of our three indicators of workplace policy: how the worker grades the firm on the quality of labor management relations; the index of high performance workplace policies; and a measure of whether the firm pays compensation above that in the local market.[5] The note to table 4.1 presents the exact questions used in each case. The means for the policy/practice measures show sizable country differences. For example, workers in the Czech Republic and Taiwan give higher ratings to the quality of labor-management relations than those in Italy or Australia (column [3]); workers in Canada report that their establishments have more policies associated with high performance workplaces than those in France (column [4]); workers in China report that their total compensation relative to the market is significantly lower than workers in the United States (column [5]), and so on. The F-statistics for differences in country means at the bottom of the table are sizable and highly significant.

Columns (6) through (9) of the table give the means for the four measures of the performance of individuals at their workplace: the likelihood that they will stay at the job; their willingness to work hard; their willingness to offer

---

5. These are self-reported measures and not objective measures of company practices; however, these perceptions may be the key to worker behavior because they reflect on important dimensions of the entire employment relationship.

innovative thoughts; and their willingness to take action against a shirking fellow employee. Again, the table note gives the specific questions used to define these outcome measures. These columns also show sizable differences in the country means and F-statistics that indicate that the differences are statistically significant.

Finally, columns (10) and (11) turn to how workers assess the activity of other employees and the effectiveness of their facility, based on the questions given in the table note.[6] We asked these questions to differentiate workers as observers of their workplace from their perceptions of their own behavior. To see if the reports on how other workers are doing differ from the self-reports, we correlated the two variables. The measure of perceptions of the willingness to work hard of coworkers is correlated at only .122 with the measures of the worker's own work effort, so the two measures are indeed reflecting different perceptions. The mean values for the worker assessment of the work effort of fellow employees and of the effectiveness of their facility show substantial country differences. Employees in Brazil are more likely to report that fellow workers work hard than employees in Australia. Employees in Argentina are more likely to report that their establishment operates effectively than employees in Taiwan, and so on. Because the characteristics of workers differ across establishments, however, it is possible that the differences among establishments by country in management policy/practice variables and worker behavior are due to differences in the characteristics of workers and jobs rather than to differences in institutions across the countries of concern to us. To see whether observable worker and job characteristics explain the country differences, we estimated the following equation:

$$(1) \qquad Y_{ijc} = a + bX_{ijc} + \mathbf{D}_c + u_{ic},$$

where $Y$ is a specified practice or outcome variable; $i$ refers to the worker; $j$ to the establishment employing the worker, $c$ to the country in which the establishment is located, and where $X_{ijc}$ are covariates for the individual, $\mathbf{D}_c$ is a vector of dummy variables for the country in which the establishment is located, and $u_{ic}$ is an error term. The coefficients on $\mathbf{D}_c$ capture the country effect relative to the deleted country, which is the United States. Because establishments are located in only a single country, the estimated country effects are averages of establishment effects for the establishments in the country. The survey gives us detailed information on employee characteristics such as age, gender, marital status, family size, number of children, education, ethnicity, and whether the employee has a disability or not. There is also detailed information on occupational and job characteristics

---

6. Division performance data supplied by the company is strongly correlated with these worker reports of facility effectiveness aggregated to the division level, indicating that these reports appear to measure an operational variable.

**Table 4.2**    **Statistical tests for country effects compared to regional effects in U.S. establishments**

| | F-stat for country diffs. (1) | F-stat for U.S. state diffs. (3) | Variance of dummy coefficients | | |
| --- | --- | --- | --- | --- | --- |
| | | | Countries (4) | U.S. states (5) | Ratio (4/5) (6) |
| Policies | | | | | |
| Grade on ee-mgt relations | 18.43 | 11.27 | 0.072 | 0.015 | 4.94 |
| High-perf. index | 26.85 | 10.13 | 0.168 | 0.026 | 6.48 |
| Total comp relative to mkt. | 20.27 | 10.78 | 0.053 | 0.014 | 3.78 |
| Own performance | | | | | |
| Likely to stay | 18.17 | 15.36 | 0.075 | 0.011 | 6.85 |
| Willing to work hard | 23.56 | 8.93 | 0.111 | 0.008 | 13.91 |
| Willing to innovate | 18.06 | 6.05 | 0.055 | 0.005 | 10.17 |
| Antishirking index | 12.50 | 10.34 | 0.687 | 0.081 | 8.51 |
| Coworker/facility performance | | | | | |
| Coworkers work hard | 18.47 | 6.22 | 0.292 | 0.041 | 7.04 |
| Facility effectiveness | 11.65 | 10.90 | 0.051 | 0.011 | 4.45 |
| All 79 outcomes | | | | | |
| Average F-statistic (37 outcomes) | 24.86 | 10.43 | 7.891 | 1.904 | 4.14 |
| Average Chi-sq. statistic (42 outcomes) | 259.65 | 160.34 | 0.078 | 0.013 | 5.84 |
| Percent of outcomes with higher statistics for country dummies (79 outcomes) | | 83% | | | 100% |
| No. of country/state dummies | 19 | 19 | 19 | 19 | |

*Notes:* ee-mgt. = employee-management. Based on regressions that control for job and demographic characteristics.

such as fixed pay, tenure, supervisory status, managerial level, and whether the employee is hourly or salaried or is engaged in administrative support, production, professional/technical, sales, or customer service work. We estimated two functional forms for equation (1): ordered probits when the outcomes have several values with a natural ordering (e.g., "not at all true, not very true, somewhat true, and very true"), and ordinary least squares (OLS) regressions with the dependent variables measured from 1 to 5, reflecting the five-point scales used in the survey. The statistical results were similar. Here we use the OLS regressions for ease in comparing F-statistics.

The first column in table 4.2 presents the F-statistics for the country dummies with the establishments from all countries in the data set. They are sizable and significant.[7] As noted, however, with the small number of establish-

7. In addition, we also estimated the ANOVA model for the thirteen countries for which we have more than a single establishment and obtained larger F-statistics. The F-statistics for the thirteen country sample are: 26.04, 38.00, 29.08, 20.42, 31.05, 24.30, 17.43, 26.08, and 14.30.

ments outside the United States, the differences could reflect differences in local management practices and employee behavior among establishments that are closer geographically within a country than those in a foreign country. To see whether the estimated country differences reflect more than the regional variation in practices/performance in a single country, we estimated the state/region effects in practices and outcomes in the United States. We formed nineteen state/regional dummy variables for the United States (thus mimicking the number of countries in our country data set) and estimated the contribution of these dummies to the variation in U.S. outcomes using the analysis of variance (ANOVA) model of equation (1). The computations show significant differences in the value of the variables among the U.S. regions. But the F-statistics in column (2) of table 4.2 are markedly lower than F-statistics for the country dummies in column (1), save for the measure of overall plant effectiveness, where they barely differ. These data thus imply that for all but overall plant effectiveness the country dummies reflect more than "normal" regional variation in labor practices and outcomes across establishments.

The remainder of table 4.2 examines another measure of the difference in estimated country or U.S. state/region effects on the variables: the unweighted variance of the estimated coefficients on the country dummies. For comparison, we also calculated the unweighted variance of the estimated coefficients for the state/region dummy variables in the United States. Columns (3) and (4) of table 4.2 show huge differences between these measures: the variance of the country dummy variables is from 3.8 to 13.9 times as great as the variance in state/regional dummy variables within the United States. The greater variation in outcomes across the countries in which the multinational operates than across the states/regions in the United States in which it operates suggests that some of the variation across countries is due to genuine country effects rather than to regional effects that occur within the same country.[8]

Finally, to make sure that our results are not dependent on the specific variables under investigation, we analyzed all of the survey questions relating to labor practices, attitudes, and performance. There are seventy-nine such variables. The results of this analysis are reported under the heading "All 79 outcomes" at the bottom of table 4.2. For the variables that give a clear ordering of outcomes, we use F-statistics to measure the country or regional contribution to overall variation. For variables without such an ordering, we use chi-square statistics. As a summary of these computations, the table gives the mean F-statistic or chi-squared statistic for the relevant variables and records the proportion of outcomes in which the variation

---

8. We also find, in results not reported here, that the variation among Continental European countries is similar to the variation among English-speaking countries, suggesting that the variation reflects real country effects and not underlying differences due to broader regional or cultural factors.

across countries exceeds the variation across states/regions in the United States. The results show that taking all of the variables, the variation due to countries exceeds that due to U.S. regions, as it does for the variables on which we focus.

In short, our data show that labor practices, attitudes, and economic performance vary across establishments by country by more than one would expect from either of two null hypotheses: that there are no country effects or that country effects are no larger than region effects within the United States.

## 4.4   Worker Responses to Practices

We turn next to this question: do these policies have the same relationship to the behavior or performance of workers in different countries? Taking practices as exogenous, we estimate the following equation that relates company practices/policies to worker reports on their performance and on the behavior of fellow employees and establishment effectiveness.

$$(2) \qquad P_{ic} = a + bX_{ic} + cY_{ic} + u_{ic},$$

where $P$ is a measure of performance, $i$ refers to the worker; $c$ to the country in which the establishment is located, $a$ is a constant, the $X_{ic}$ are covariates for the individual, and $Y_{ic}$ measures the policies/practices described earlier— labor management relations, high-performance workplaces, compensation relative to market compensation. The error term $u_{ic}$ in this specification is assumed to be independent and identically distributed. (The establishment regressions in the next section control for correlated errors within establishments.)

We estimated equation (2) separately for workers in the fourteen countries in the data with more than a single establishment, so as to reduce the danger that the calculations reflect establishment effects rather than country effects. Each regression contains all three of the independent variables: the measures of employee-management relations, the high performance work index, and total compensation relative to the market, so that the results reflect the impact of each of these policies while accounting for the impact of the other policies. On the basis of studies that link good workplace policies and workplace outcomes in single-nation studies, we expect that employee-management relations and high performance work practices will be positively related (Appelbaum et al. 2000; Huselid 1995; Ichniowski, Shaw, and Prennushi 1997; Cappelli and Neumark 2001). On the basis of analyses of gift exchange (Akerlof 1982), we expect that establishments with above-market compensation will also have better outcomes.

The regression coefficients in table 4.3 show that the vast majority of outcomes are significantly positively related to measures of labor relations and high performance workplace practices in all countries. For example, in

**Table 4.3**  Regression coefficients linking policies to performance measures

| | Likely to stay | Willing to work hard | Willing to innovate | Antishirking index | Coworkers work hard | Facility effectiveness |
|---|---|---|---|---|---|---|
| *Ee-mgt rels. coefficient* | | | | | | |
| All countries | 0.22*** | 0.19*** | 0.03*** | 0.32*** | 0.34*** | 0.32*** |
| Australia | 0.10 | 0.18 | −0.01 | 0.36 | 0.99* | 0.56*** |
| Brazil | 0.15*** | 0.16*** | 0.01 | 0.30*** | 0.08 | 0.33*** |
| Canada | 0.30*** | 0.21*** | −0.05 | 0.63*** | 0.29** | 0.35*** |
| China | 0.17*** | 0.14*** | 0.09** | 0.13 | 0.37*** | 0.27*** |
| France | −0.04 | 0.25** | −0.15 | −0.08 | 0.88*** | 0.24*** |
| Germany | 0.28*** | 0.20*** | 0.01 | 0.17 | −0.04 | 0.34*** |
| Italy | 0.14*** | 0.16*** | −0.02 | 0.22 | 0.14 | 0.17*** |
| Korea | 0.32*** | 0.12 | 0.11 | 0.09 | 0.61*** | 0.21*** |
| Sweden | 0.20*** | 0.10 | −0.10 | 0.02 | −0.06 | 0.27*** |
| United Kingdom | 0.38*** | 0.24*** | 0.10** | 0.09 | 0.38*** | 0.31*** |
| United States | 0.25*** | 0.21*** | 0.02*** | 0.34*** | 0.38*** | 0.34*** |
| Mexico | 0.10*** | 0.13*** | 0.08*** | 0.18** | 0.20*** | 0.19*** |
| *Hi-perf. index coefficient* | | | | | | |
| All countries | 0.06*** | 0.08*** | 0.07*** | 0.31*** | 0.13*** | 0.08*** |
| Australia | 0.32 | 0.24 | −0.03 | 0.00 | 0.34 | 0.22* |
| Brazil | 0.08*** | 0.10*** | 0.04* | 0.14 | 0.05 | 0.06*** |
| Canada | 0.03 | 0.17*** | 0.08* | 0.44** | 0.31*** | 0.13*** |
| China | 0.02 | 0.07** | 0.15*** | 0.52*** | 0.09 | −0.01 |
| France | 0.23*** | 0.14* | 0.25*** | 0.45 | −0.06 | 0.03 |
| Germany | 0.00 | 0.13*** | 0.04 | 0.06 | 0.19* | 0.05* |
| Italy | 0.10** | 0.09** | 0.12*** | 0.32** | 0.03 | 0.07* |
| Korea | 0.06 | 0.06 | 0.14** | 0.12 | 0.06 | 0.19*** |
| Sweden | 0.21*** | 0.16** | 0.13** | 0.13 | 0.30** | 0.06* |
| United Kingdom | 0.06 | 0.08 | 0.02 | 0.34* | 0.21** | 0.07* |
| United States | 0.05*** | 0.07*** | 0.07*** | 0.32*** | 0.16*** | 0.08*** |
| Mexico | 0.08*** | 0.08*** | 0.06*** | 0.35*** | 0.08 | 0.10*** |
| *Total comp relative to market* | | | | | | |
| All countries | 0.09*** | 0.05*** | −0.01 | 0.00 | 0.02 | 0.03*** |
| Australia | 0.05 | 0.17 | −0.01 | −0.01 | −0.04 | −0.15 |
| Brazil | 0.14*** | 0.05 | −0.05 | −0.06 | −0.10 | 0.02 |
| Canada | 0.11** | 0.01 | −0.02 | −0.33 | −0.01 | −0.06 |
| China | 0.12*** | 0.05 | 0.02 | 0.18 | −0.14 | −0.04 |
| France | 0.10 | 0.19* | −0.09 | 0.09 | −0.31 | 0.12 |
| Germany | 0.06 | 0.10 | −0.02 | 0.04 | −0.20 | −0.01 |
| Italy | 0.18*** | −0.01 | −0.14*** | −0.01 | −0.02 | −0.09** |
| Korea | 0.03 | 0.13 | −0.12 | 0.53* | 0.57** | 0.04 |
| Sweden | 0.10 | 0.12 | −0.06 | 0.40 | −0.33* | 0.07 |
| United Kingdom | 0.03 | 0.05 | −0.09* | 0.12 | 0.35** | 0.00 |
| United States | 0.09*** | 0.05*** | 0.00 | 0.00 | 0.01 | 0.03* |
| Mexico | 0.08*** | 0.06*** | 0.06*** | 0.05 | 0.21*** | 0.02 |

*Notes:* Regressions are done separately by country. Each regression contains the three dependent variables at left, plus basic job and demog. characteristics.

\*\*\*Significant at the 1 percent level.

\*\*Significant at the 5 percent level.

\*Significant at the 10 percent level.

almost every country, workers who report more positive management labor relations or whose establishments have high-performance work practices are more likely to remain with the firm, more willing to work hard, more likely to take action against fellow workers who shirk, and more willing to make innovative suggestions. In addition, these workers are also more likely to report that their coworkers work hard, and that their establishment operates effectively. Of the seventy-two estimated coefficients on labor relations in table 4.3, forty-seven are significantly positive. Of the seventy-two estimated coefficients on our measure of high performance work practices, forty-five are significantly positive. By contrast, just nineteen of the estimated coefficients on the measure of total compensation relative to the market are significantly positive. The implication is that labor practices are more important factors in the outcome variables than levels of pay. This is consistent with empirical research within countries that compensation systems do not constitute a "silver bullet" in employment relations (see Heneman, Fay, and Wang 2002).

It is important to note that many of these estimated relationships are economically significant as well as statistically significant. For example, the coefficients for the full sample indicate that one-standard-deviation improvements in employee-management relations, high performance policies, and total compensation relative to market increase the likelihood of staying by 0.27, 0.10, and 0.10 standard deviations of that variable. The effect of employee-management relations on facility performance is especially large, with a standard deviation increase in employee-management relations linked to a 0.45 standard deviation improvement in facility performance. Across the six outcomes the effects of one-standard-deviation increases for the full sample range from 0.04 to 0.45 for employee-management relations, 0.09 to 0.15 for high-performance policies, and –0.01 to 0.10 for total compensation relative to market.

The estimated relationships show similar patterns of response to management policies or practices across countries in table 4.3 but the estimated coefficients differ in magnitude across countries. For example, employment-relations have a smaller impact on the workers' expected turnover behavior in China than in Canada, and a smaller impact on their willingness to work hard in Korea than in Canada. In France the estimates show a slight negative relation between employment-management relations and expected turnover, willingness to innovate, and the antishirking index, in contrast to the positive estimated impacts in most other countries. But the estimates indicate that the French are willing to work much harder than Americans in a high performance work system, which suggests that even the highly regulated French labor market workers will respond to a coherent system of workplace practices in a positive manner. To assess the extent of the differences in the slope coefficients across countries, we computed statistics that compare the variation in slope coefficients for each policy variable on each outcome across the countries. For comparison, we estimated regressions of equation (2) for each U.S. state/region with the standard demographic and job characteristic control variables and with all three workplace policies as independent variables. Finally, following the logic we used to analyze country dummy variables, we contrasted the variation in slope coefficients among countries to the analogous variation among states/regions in the United States. If responses truly differ by country, the cross-country variation among the slope coefficients will exceed the variation among slope coefficients among U.S. states/regions.

Table 4.4 summarizes the results of these computations. Column (1) gives the F-statistics from the test of equality of slope coefficients from a pooled regression with country dummy variables to allow for separate intercepts and with identical coefficients imposed on covariates. The F-statistics reject the equality of the slope coefficients. They show significant cross-country variation in the magnitudes of coefficients estimated in table 4.3. Column (2) gives F-statistics for the equality of slope coefficients from the comparable analysis for states/regions in the United States. The F-statistics for the regions are smaller than those for the countries. Following the logic that we used earlier to test for the existence of country intercept effects above and beyond those potentially due to regional variation within a country, we interpret this pattern to mean that there are substantial cross-country differences in the relationship between workers' responses and the relevant policies or practices. However, the differences in the estimated response parameters between the country regressions and the state regressions are smaller than the differences found in table 4.2 for the country dummy variables. This is shown most clearly in columns (3) and (4), which report the variances of the estimated slope coefficients for the countries and U.S. states/regions, respectively. The variances for the estimated coefficients are 1.2 to 9.7 times larger among countries than among U.S. states/region.

Finally, there are also differences in the consistency of the estimated relationship of policy variables to outcomes among the variables. There are relatively weak differences across the countries and across U.S. states/regions on the impact of workplace policies on willingness to work hard, implying that the policies and practices have relatively similar relationships to this outcome measure. By contrast, there are relatively strong differences across countries in the likelihood of seeking a new job and in assessment of the effectiveness of their facility. In addition, the grade on employee-management relations and total compensation relative to the market have a strong significant impact on country differences in workers' report of their coworkers' willingness to work hard, while the presence of a high performance work system does not. This pattern also exists in the U.S. states/region but the differences are more pronounced across countries. The greatest variation across countries is in the relationship of high-performance policies to workers' willingness to interfere with a shirker, which suggests that the effects

**Table 4.4**    Statistical analysis of slope coefficients

| Dependent variable | Independent variable | F-stats. for equality of coefficients | | Variance of coefficients across countries/states | | Ratio (3/4) |
|---|---|---|---|---|---|---|
| | | All countries (1) | U.S. state diffs. (2) | Countries (3) | U.S. states (4) | (5) |
| Likely to stay | Grade on ee-mgt relations | 9.90*** | 2.20** | 0.014 | 0.002 | 8.543 |
| | High-perf. index | 3.08*** | 1.98*** | 0.006 | 0.001 | 6.747 |
| | Total comp relative to mkt. | 1.89** | 1.69 | 0.005 | 0.001 | 3.505 |
| Willing to work hard for co. | Grade on ee-mgt relations | 1.97** | 1.38 | 0.002 | 0.001 | 1.234 |
| | High-perf. index | 1.16 | 0.43 | 0.001 | 0.000 | 2.844 |
| | Total comp relative to mkt. | 1.22 | 0.69 | 0.007 | 0.001 | 9.660 |
| Willing to innovate | Grade on ee-mgt relations | 3.11*** | 2.50** | 0.006 | 0.002 | 3.241 |
| | High-perf. index | 3.10*** | 3.05*** | 0.004 | 0.001 | 3.456 |
| | Total comp relative to mkt. | 2.52** | 1.68 | 0.005 | 0.001 | 3.948 |
| Antishirking index | Grade on ee-mgt relations | 1.13 | 1.31 | 0.085 | 0.016 | 5.346 |
| | High-perf. index | 2.85*** | 1.82 | 0.045 | 0.012 | 3.807 |
| | Total comp relative to mkt. | 0.78 | 1.24 | 0.055 | 0.014 | 3.887 |
| Coworkers work hard | Grade on ee-mgt relations | 4.25*** | 2.31** | 0.066 | 0.013 | 5.153 |
| | High-perf. index | 1.46 | 0.78 | 0.010 | 0.002 | 4.640 |
| | Total comp relative to mkt. | 3.12*** | 1.62 | 0.063 | 0.010 | 6.163 |
| Facility effectiveness | Grade on ee-mgt relations | 13.57*** | 3.49*** | 0.013 | 0.001 | 8.624 |
| | High-perf. index | 4.77*** | 1.25 | 0.002 | 0.000 | 6.854 |
| | Total comp relative to mkt. | 2.60** | 1.80 | 0.004 | 0.001 | 4.181 |
| No. of countries/states | | 12 | 12 | 12 | 12 | 12 |

*Note:* Based on separate regressions for each country and state, controlling for job and demographic characteristics.

***Significant at the 1 percent level.

**Significant at the 5 percent level.

*Significant at the 10 percent level.

of policies on antishirking may be greatly affected by country cultures and institutions.

In sum, we conclude that although the relationship between workers' responses and the policies and practices are qualitatively the same across the countries, the greater differences in the variation of responses across countries than across states suggests that the magnitude of responses differs across countries—that is, that slope as well as intercept terms have a country dimension.

## 4.5    Establishment Level Patterns

The analyses thus far have related workers' reports of practices and policies at their workplace to their reports of actual or expected behavior or that of their coworkers. As pointed out, however, relations found among individuals need not generalize to the establishment, much less to countries. Just as there are problems in making inferences about individual behavior from correlations in regional or other aggregated data—the ecological correlation problem[9]—there are problems in making inferences from individual level data about the responses to policies for groups. If workers at the same establishment report differently on establishment practices, we cannot readily infer from regressions based on individuals how changes in establishment policies would impact the establishment.

One way to assess the importance of this problem is to examine the consistency of workers' reports on their establishment's practices and performance within a given establishment. If workers in an establishment report consistently on the quality of its labor-management relations, this is more likely to reflect establishment policy or practice than if worker reports vary greatly within the same establishment. To see whether the reports of workers within an establishment coalesce at the establishment level, we used an ANOVA analysis to determine the extent to which establishment contributed to the variation in individual responses to particular questions conditional on the covariates used in equation (1).

Table 4.5 gives the results of this analysis for the policy/practice and performance variables on which we have focused. The table shows sizable F-statistics for establishments, implying that workers' reports about practices and outcomes have a significant establishment component. The implication is that the results from the analysis of the data for individuals are likely to generalize, at least in part, to the establishment level that are arguably more appropriate for judging how establishment level policies and practices may affect outcomes than the correlations among individuals.[10]

9. See http://en.wikipedia.org/wiki/Ecological_correlation. Also, see http://en.wikipedia.org/wiki/Ecological_fallacy.
10. See Lubinski and Humphreys (1996).

Table 4.5          **Statistical tests for establishment level effects in labor practices/policies**

| | F-stat. for establishment differences |
|---|---|
| Policies | |
| Grade on ee-mgt relations | 8.52*** |
| High-perf. index | 10.15*** |
| Total comp relative to mkt. | 6.75*** |
| Own performance | |
| Likely to stay | 7.70*** |
| Willing to work hard | 5.00*** |
| Willing to innovate | 3.73*** |
| Antishirking index | 4.14*** |
| Coworker/facility performance | |
| Coworkers work hard | 5.28*** |
| Facility effectiveness | 10.77*** |

*Note:* Based on regressions that control for job and demog. characteristics, with 245 establishment dummy variables.
***Significant at the 1 percent level.
**Significant at the 5 percent level.
*Significant at the 10 percent level.

If each establishment had a single set of practices that affected all workers the same, this would be the best way to estimate the effect of those policies or practices. But it is possible that some of the variation among individuals within an establishment reflects genuine differences in practices within the establishment. Some workers may report bad employee-management relations because their supervisor is horrible while others may report good employment-relations because their supervisor is good. If all of the within-establishment variation in reported practices were due to this, the correlations at the individual level would be superior to the correlations at the establishment level. This suggests that analyses at the level of mean establishment practices and mean levels of performance are likely to provide an underestimate of the relationship of policies and practices to behavior and outcomes.

The analyses in table 4.6 of establishment averages show that the relation between policies and practices and outcomes holds up at this level of aggregation. The top panel of table 4.6 records the regression coefficients and standard errors for the impact of our three policy or practice variables and, to allow for any differences between the United States and other countries, a dummy variable for the United States. Looking at the first column, the results show the average grade on employee-management relations in establishments is significantly associated with the average score on all six outcomes measured at the establishment level. By contrast, only one of the coefficients on high performance work systems and only one of the coefficients on total compensation relative to the market are significantly linked to the establishment level outcome variables.

Table 4.6    Relation between establishment average policies and establishment average outcomes

| | Grade on ee-mgt. relations | High perf. Index | Total comp relative to mkt | U.S. dummy |
|---|---|---|---|---|
| *Establishment level regressions predicting survey measures* | | | | |
| Likely to stay | 0.433 | −0.035 | 0.244 | −0.007 |
| | (0.050)*** | (0.035) | (0.049)*** | (0.038) |
| Willing to work hard | 0.248 | 0.047 | −0.037 | 0.233 |
| | (0.051)*** | (0.035) | (0.049) | (0.039)*** |
| Willing to innovate | 0.152 | 0.058 | −0.055 | −0.032 |
| | (0.053)*** | (0.037) | (0.052) | (0.041) |
| Antishirking index | 0.824 | 0.145 | 0.034 | −0.793 |
| | (0.187)*** | (0.131) | (0.182) | (0.143)*** |
| Coworkers work hard | 0.497 | −0.043 | −0.033 | −0.291 |
| | (0.124)*** | (0.087) | (0.121) | (0.095)*** |
| Facility effectiveness | 0.378 | 0.068 | 0.060 | 0.017 |
| | (0.051)*** | (0.035)* | (0.049) | (0.039) |
| *Division level regressions predicting company-reported data* | | | | |
| On-time delivery percentage | −0.012 | 0.0426 | 0.0079 | |
| | (0.025) | (0.017)** | (0.026) | |
| Accident rate | 4.628 | −5.735 | −0.0779 | |
| | (3.808) | (2.289)** | 3.493 | |
| Monthly change in unit labor costs | 0.0005 | 0.0004 | −0.0024 | |
| | (0.0010) | (0.0007) | (0.0011)** | |
| Monthly change in ln(sales/ employee) | −0.0041 | 0.0025 | 0.0016 | |
| | (0.0074) | (0.0049) | (0.0077) | |
| Monthly change in days sales outstanding | −0.0154 | 0.3216 | −0.7151 | |
| | (0.306) | (0.203) | (0.310)** | |

*Note:* n = 258 in establishment level regressions, and 79 in division level regressions. Each row represents separate regression, with dependent variable at left.
***Significant at the 1 percent level.
**Significant at the 5 percent level.
*Significant at the 10 percent level.

Figures 4.1 through 4.3 illustrate the strong relation between the average grade on employee-management relations across facilities and worker reports on behavior and outcomes. Figure 4.1 shows the positive link between the employee relations grade on average perception of worker effort at the work site. Figure 4.2 shows the average score on antishirking activity, while figure 4.3 shows the average perception of facility effectiveness. Differentiating establishments outside the United States from those within the United States shows no noticeable difference in the slopes of these relations.

Finally, we complemented the analysis of worker reports on their behavior and that of their workplace with analysis of company-based data on the performance of its divisions. The company provided us with measures of on-time deliveries by division, accident rates, changes in unit later costs, in sales per worker, and in sales outstanding. Because divisions encompass several

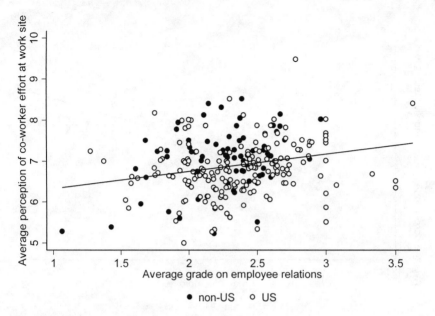

**Fig. 4.1 Employee relations and coworker effort**

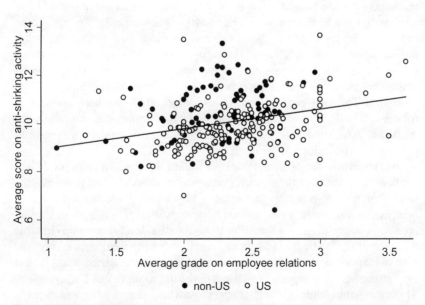

**Fig. 4.2 Employee relations and antishirking activity**

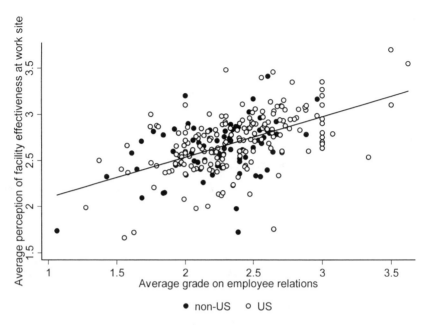

**Fig. 4.3 Employee relations and facility effectiveness**

establishments, we obtained usable data for just seventy-nine divisions. We aggregated our measures of company policies and practices to the division level and estimated equations linking policies and practices at the division level to division level outcomes. The results of these calculations are shown in the bottom panel of table 4.6. The results give a weaker and somewhat different picture of the effect of policies/practices on outcomes than in the establishment level analysis of worker-reported outcomes. The grade on employee-management relations is not significantly related to any of the outcomes. The high-performance index is associated with better outcomes for on-time delivery and accident rate while total compensation relative to market is associated with better smaller increases in unit labor costs and days sales outstanding.

Overall, while the establishment level data and the division level data confirm the positive link between management practices and policies, particularly the set of practices that create a high performance workplace, and behavior or outcomes, the effects are noticeably weaker in the establishment level regressions in table 4.6 than in the individual level regressions in table 4.3. Why is this? The most likely explanation for the weaker effects of the high performance workplace measure at the more aggregated levels is that only part of establishments, much less divisions, in fact meet that criterion. This means that some of the effect gets lost when we move from workers to more aggregate units. For example, in a 200 person establishment, the 100 workers doing final assembly of a complex mechanical device may work in a high performance work system but the other workers do not. Workers as a whole rate the facility effectiveness high (the only outcome for which high performance workplaces obtained a significant positive coefficient in table 4.6), but the workers not in the high performance work system are not especially motivated to stay with the company, work hard, innovate, or intervene with shirkers. This would produce weaker establishment level and division level correlations between high performance practices and those outcomes. From this perspective, the association between the greater use of high performance policies with better division level performance on two outcome measures is surprising.

The weak relation between total compensation relative to the market and outcome variables in table 4.6, by contrast, is consistent with the story told at the individual worker level in table 4.3, where worker reports on total compensation relative to the market were the most weakly related policy variable to measures of success. This underlines the conclusion from table 4.3 that compensation systems do not constitute a "silver bullet" in employment relations systems. Employee-management relations are linked to outcomes at the facility level as well as the individual level, while the compensation and high performance work system scores are not linked to outcomes at the facility level, showing that the effects of these high performance work system policies will be weakened when they do not cover a broad group of employees in a facility.

## 4.6    Country Level Patterns

Finally, to see whether the relations between policies/practices and outcomes also hold for country aggregates, we examine the correlations between the estimated coefficients on the country dummy variables for each of the policies/practices under study and for each of the country level outcomes. The coefficients on the dummy variables show whether a country is relatively high or low in a given practice or outcome compared to the omitted country, the United States. The correlation between the coefficients thus gives the cross-country relation between the relevant variables.

The correlations in the top panel of table 4.7 show moderately sized positive relations between each policy/practice variable and the performance or outcome measures as aggregate country variables. The strongest correlation is between the country measures of employee-management relations and the country measure of facility effectiveness. Better employee-management relations is moderately correlated with country measures of being likely to stay, and willingness to innovate and intervene with shirking coworkers. As with the establishment level analyses, the country-level measure of the high per-

Table 4.7    Correlations among policies and economic outcomes at the country level

| Outcomes[a] | Likely to stay | Willing to work hard | Willing to innovate | Antishirking index | Coworkers work hard | Facility effectiveness |
|---|---|---|---|---|---|---|
| Worker reports on labor practices at their facilities[a] | | | | | | |
| Grade on ee-mgt relations | 0.344 | 0.230 | 0.352 | 0.384 | 0.187 | 0.606*** |
| High-perf index | 0.143 | 0.118 | -0.150 | -0.027 | -0.147 | 0.020 |
| Total comp relative to mkt. | 0.103 | 0.239 | 0.613*** | 0.346 | 0.071 | 0.228 |
| Country indicators of labor conditions | | | | | | |
| Fraser Institute EFI[b] | | | | | | |
| Labor Market Regulations part | 0.061 | 0.090 | -0.004 | -0.096 | -0.442 | 0.082 |
| Global Competitiveness Report[c] | | | | | | |
| Overall Global Competitiveness Index | 0.010 | -0.571** | -0.399* | -0.213 | -0.693*** | -0.391* |
| Hiring and firing practices | -0.240 | -0.105 | -0.313 | -0.415 | -0.343 | -0.211 |
| Cooperative labor-employer relations | -0.073 | -0.458** | -0.107 | 0.001 | -0.451* | -0.396* |
| Flexibility of wage determination | -0.091 | -0.039 | -0.287 | -0.470** | -0.208 | -0.173 |
| Pay and productivity | -0.222 | -0.252 | -0.407* | -0.507*** | -0.456** | -0.420 |
| Overall mkt efficiency | -0.057 | -0.406* | -0.177 | -0.221 | -0.691*** | -0.352 |
| Restrictive labor regulations | 0.262 | -0.347 | 0.014 | 0.325 | -0.288 | -0.048 |
| Innovative factors | 0.121 | -0.434* | -0.346 | -0.194 | -0.590*** | -0.336 |
| Culture scores[d] | | | | | | |
| Power distance | 0.051 | 0.145 | -0.245 | -0.124 | 0.195 | 0.120 |
| Individualism | 0.192 | -0.064 | 0.253 | 0.370 | -0.498** | 0.075 |
| Masculinity | -0.024 | 0.613*** | 0.482* | 0.216 | 0.123 | 0.323 |
| Uncertainty avoidance | 0.213 | 0.137 | 0.058 | 0.245 | 0.155 | 0.251 |
| Long-term orientation | -0.308 | -0.108 | -0.412* | -0.552** | 0.348 | -0.448* |

*Note:* Based on nineteen countries.

[a]The outcomes and worker reports on labor practices are based on nineteen country coefficients, controlling for basic job and demographic characteristics (occupation, supervisory status, hours, tenure, union, gender, race, marital status, education, disability status).

[b]Gwartney and Lawson (2006).

[c]Lopez-Claros (2006).

[d]Hofstede and Hofstede (2005).

***Significant at the 1 percent level.

**Significant at the 5 percent level.

*Significant at the 10 percent level.

formance work system index is not correlated with country-level outcomes, presumably for the same reason—high performance work systems are concentrated among certain groups of workers and firms. Total compensation relative to the market at the country level is highly correlated with country-level measures of willingness to innovate and moderately correlated with country-level measures of antishirking. Overall, given the small number of establishments used to obtain the estimated country effects, the results are reasonably consistent with the patterns found within countries.

### 4.7    Relationship to Competitiveness Indices and Cultural Indices

The middle of table 4.7 relates the country dummy measures of performance or outcomes to aggregate measures of labor market institutions produced by the Fraser Institute as part of its Economic Freedom of the World Index and by the World Economic Forum as part of its report on global competitiveness. The Fraser Institute's index gives countries with less labor market regulation of wages, dismissal, employment, and union extension of contracts to nonparticipating parties higher scores in economic freedom.[11] The Market Efficiency component of the Global Competitiveness Index (Lopez-Claros 2006), based on public data sources and a poll of 11,000 business executives, gives higher scores to countries where executives responded that: wages are not determined by a centralized bargaining process, labor-employer relations are cooperative, hiring and firing of workers is flexibly determined by employers, and pay is related to worker productivity.[12]

The correlations in the middle of table 4.7 between global country measures of labor market institutions and this study's country-level measures of worker outcomes do not fit the view that "economic freedom" and "global competitiveness" means more economic success. The Fraser Institute's Labor Market Regulation score (for which higher values indicate less labor market regulation) is not significantly correlated with any of our estimated country measures of outcomes, and the largest correlation is a negative relation between the low levels of regulations and perceived coworker effort. The World Economic Forum's Global Competitiveness Index does even worse. It is significantly negatively correlated with the country measures of willingness to work hard, willingness to innovate, and perceived coworker effort and facility effectiveness. Similarly, the measures of individual regulations

11. "To earn high marks in the labor market regulation index (5B), a country must allow market forces to determine wages and establish the conditions of dismissal, avoid excessive unemployment benefits and refrain from the use of conscription" (Gwartney and Lawson 2006, 12). Many of the measures of the Economic Freedom of the World Index (EFWI) rely on the Global Competitiveness Index. See Gwartney and Lawson (2006, 181–82).

12. The individual country data and the text of the questions asked in the poll can be found on pp. 485–89 (Lopez-Claros 2006, chapter 1.1).

are generally negatively correlated with our outcome measures, which given the coding implies that less regulation produces worse outcomes. We do not interpret these results as indicating that less regulation indeed reduces workplace performance, but rather as demonstrating that widely cited indicators of labor practices at the aggregate level are poor measures of what goes on at the workplaces of this multinational, and potentially other firms as well. Workplace relations and practices at the establishment level are related to outcomes as opposed to more indicators of country level practices or policies.

The bottom panel in table 4.7 examines the relation between our measures of outcomes across countries and a different set of indices: the five national measures of culture that Hofstede (1984) created from his analysis of the values of IBM employees in different countries, and that have been replicated since (Hofstede and Hofstede 2005, 23, 26). These measures of cultural differences among countries are different from the Fraser Institute and the World Economic Forum measures because they are based on data on individual workers rather than judgments of how the labor economy operates. Describing the creation of these indices, Hofstede and Hofstede say, "At first sight it might look surprising that employees of a multinational—a very specific kind of people—could serve for identifying differences in national value systems. From one country to another, however, they represented almost perfectly matched samples: they were similar in all respects except nationality, which made the effect of nationality differences in their answers stand out unusually clearly." (Hofstede and Hofstede 2005, 23)

The Hofstede indicators of culture are designed to measure how national cultures address five common problems as outlined in *Cultures and Organizations: Software of the Mind* (2005).

1. *Social inequality including the relationship to authority.* This is measured by the *Power Distance Index,* which is based on research on the emotional distance that separates subordinates from their bosses with high scores indicating greater power distance.

2. *The relationship between the individual and the group.* This is measured by the *Individualism Index,* indicating that the ties between individuals are loose as opposed to societies where people are integrated into strong cohesive in-groups that protect them in exchange for unquestioning loyalty throughout their lifetimes. It is based on various work goal items with high scores indicating more individualism.

3. *Concepts of masculinity and femininity: the social and emotional implications of having been born a boy or a girl.* This is measured by the *Masculinity Index,* with higher scores indicating more masculinity. This was the sole dimension where men and women consistently scored differently, with men attaching greater importance to earnings and challenge as work goals and

women attaching greater importance to having a good working relationship with the manager and cooperation as work goals.[13]

4. *Ways of dealing with uncertainty and ambiguity.* This is the *Uncertainty Avoidance Index,* which reflects employees' level of job stress, orientation toward company rules, and intent to stay with the company over the long-term. Higher scores indicate the degree to which members of a culture feel threatened by ambiguous or unknown situations.

5. *Whether the culture is long-term or short-term oriented.* This is the *Long-Term Orientation Index,* which reflects fostering virtues oriented toward future rewards such as perseverance and thrift versus a short-term orientation of respect for tradition, saving "face," and fulfilling social obligations. This dimension expresses a "dynamic orientation towards the future" in contrast to a "static orientation towards the past and the present." Higher scores indicate an orientation toward future rewards and against tradition.[14]

The bottom of table 4.7 gives the correlations between these "Culture scores" and outcome variables. The majority of the correlations (twenty-four of thirty) are not statistically significant, indicating again the considerable gap between country-level measures and outcomes at a particular firm. Still, there are some suggestive results. The degree of individualism in the country-level culture measure is significantly negatively correlated with how hard coworkers work. Because Hofstede's measure of individualism is based on work goals that reflect a desire to *not* work for the collective, this may fit with his culture score. The degree of masculinity in a national culture is positively associated with "Willingness to work hard" and "Willingness to innovate." Because the masculinity measure is based on the importance of earnings, recognition, advancement, and challenge as work goals, this also makes sense, although the term "masculinity" seems dated as an indicator of these attributes. The Hofstede measure of uncertainty avoidance in a national culture is also not associated with any country-level economic

13. The "Masculinity" label for this index is not the label that the authors of this article would choose, because it is strongly suggestive of a strong and enduring level of differences between the sexes on these bases rather than cultural differences in how these characteristics get distributed. What we have written here is a summary of Hofstede's own description of the index. Obviously, the authors do not accept the notion that men mainly care about some aspects and women mainly care about other aspects of the workplace, or that these aspects define men or women. It is open to question whether men and women would score this differently on these items if the studies were done today.

14. This section is adapted completely from Hofstede and Hofstede (2005) as noted following. For a description of the respective dimensions and survey items along with the raw scores for the countries, see: the Power Distance Index, pp. 41–44 with country raw scores and rankings in table 2.1 on pp. 43–44; the Individualism Index, pp. 75–79 with country raw scores and rankings in table 3.1 on pp. 78–79; the Masculinity Index, pp. 118–121 with country raw scores and rankings in table 4.1 on pp. 120–21; the Uncertainty-Avoidance Index, pp. 166–69 with country raw scores and rankings in table 5.1 on pp. 168–69; the Long-term Orientation Index, pp. 210–11 with country raw scores and rankings in table 6.1 on p. 211.

outcomes, although all the outcomes are positive. Hofstede based this index on "The percentage of employees expressing their intent to stay with the company for a long-term career" (Hofstede and Hofstede 2005, 166). It is modestly positively correlated with our measure of "Likely to stay" with the firm. Finally, the cultural indictor that is most highly correlated with the outcome measures is Hofstede's "long-term orientation." This is negatively associated with the country-level economic outcomes of willing to work hard, willing to innovate, and the antishirking index, which does not seem to fit with what it is seeking to measure. Again, the lesson we draw is that workplace practices and policies trump measures of national characteristics.

Finally, we examine the relationship of the competitiveness and cultural indices to the slopes found in table 4.3, addressing the question "Do policies have a different effect on outcomes in countries with different labor market institutions or cultures?" One might think, for example, that workplace practices will have a smaller effect in countries where it is more difficult to hire and fire workers, since workers will be hard to motivate when it is difficult to fire them. The results in table 4.8 focus on slope coefficients that differed significantly among countries (table 4.4, column [1]). There are few correlations that are significantly different from zero, and the patterns do not tell a simple story, with most indices having mixed correlation signs across the six outcomes. One set of exceptions in the top third of the table are the Fraser economic freedom index, the wage flexibility index, the hiring and firing index, the pay and productivity index, and the "masculinity" score: as each of these increases, it is more likely that employee-management relations makes a difference in the outcomes. The remaining exceptions regard total compensation relative to market, which has a stronger effect on outcomes in cultures with greater "power distance" and "long-term orientation."

## 4.8  Conclusion

This study has found country differences in the labor practices, attitudes toward work, and the economic performance of workers and establishments in a data set that covers 29,353 workers in a single multinational firm. The data set has a rich variety of measures, including an innovative measure of responses to coworker shirking with results from nineteen countries. The employment relations, worker attitudes, and performance of workers varied more across countries than among states/regions in the United States and were linked in ways that suggested that workers across these countries respond to policies in broadly similar ways. Analysis of establishment averages showed that the strong relation between good labor management relations and employee behavior or outcomes holds at the establishment level as well, while the relationship of high performance workplaces and above market compensation to employee behavior generally fails to generalize to the establishment. Our comparison of country level differences showed a

**Table 4.8  Correlations with country-specific effects of policies on performance**

| | Unlikely to look for new job | Willing to work hard | Willing to Innovate | Antishirking index | Coworkers work hard | Facility effectiveness |
|---|---|---|---|---|---|---|
| | *Effect of ee-mgt. rels.* | | | | | |
| Fraser Institute[b] | | | | | | |
| Economic freedom index | 0.093 | 0.555* | 0.061 | a | 0.482 | 0.308 |
| Global Competitiveness Report[c] | | | | | | |
| Overall Global Competitiveness Index | -0.382 | -0.390 | 0.342 | a | -0.142 | -0.317 |
| Hiring and firing practices | 0.448 | 0.199 | 0.567* | a | 0.280 | 0.233 |
| Cooperative labor-employer relations | 0.509* | -0.006 | 0.192 | a | -0.397 | 0.394 |
| Flexibility of wage determination | 0.252 | 0.237 | 0.469 | a | 0.506* | 0.036 |
| Pay and productivity | 0.463 | 0.396 | 0.376 | a | 0.420 | 0.390 |
| Overall mkt efficiency | 0.424 | 0.559* | -0.181 | a | 0.149 | 0.562* |
| Restrictive labor regulations | -0.233 | 0.182 | -0.633** | a | -0.088 | 0.070 |
| Innovative factors | -0.377 | -0.447 | 0.417 | a | 0.000 | -0.257 |
| Culture scores[d] | | | | | | |
| Power distance | -0.518* | -0.264 | 0.251 | a | 0.126 | -0.507* |
| Individualism | 0.084 | 0.641 | -0.491 | a | 0.134 | 0.491 |
| Masculinity | 0.028 | 0.379 | 0.498* | a | 0.105 | 0.095 |
| Uncertainty avoidance | -0.405 | 0.007 | -0.045 | a | 0.172 | -0.389 |
| Long-term orientation | -0.108 | -0.511 | 0.479 | a | 0.046 | -0.287 |
| | *Effect of high-perf. index* | | | | | |
| Fraser Institute[b] | | | | | | |
| Economic freedom index | 0.061 | a | -0.241 | 0.359 | a | 0.306 |
| Global Competitiveness Report[c] | | | | | | |
| Overall Global Competitiveness Index | -0.207 | a | 0.020 | 0.224 | a | -0.173 |
| Hiring and firing practices | -0.337 | a | -0.320 | 0.350 | a | 0.249 |
| Cooperative labor-employer relations | -0.129 | a | -0.685** | -0.248 | a | 0.113 |
| Flexibility of wage determination | -0.214 | a | 0.028 | 0.489 | a | 0.198 |
| Pay and productivity | -0.182 | a | -0.201 | 0.130 | a | 0.200 |
| Overall mkt efficiency | 0.120 | a | -0.345 | -0.111 | a | 0.156 |
| Restrictive labor regulations | 0.352 | a | 0.169 | -0.453 | a | -0.073 |
| Innovative factors | -0.143 | a | 0.034 | 0.335 | a | -0.116 |

*(continued)*

**Table 4.8** (continued)

| | Unlikely to look for new job | Willing to work hard | Willing to Innovate | Antishirking index | Coworkers work hard | Facility effectiveness |
|---|---|---|---|---|---|---|
| Culture scores[d] | | | | | | |
| Power distance | -0.162 | a | 0.440 | 0.456 | a | -0.286 |
| Individualism | 0.362 | a | -0.300 | -0.093 | a | 0.100 |
| Masculinity | -0.379 | a | -0.389 | 0.272 | a | -0.046 |
| Uncertainty avoidance | 0.025 | a | 0.238 | -0.119 | a | 0.208 |
| Long-term orientation | -0.281 | a | 0.343 | 0.241 | a | -0.262 |
| *Effect of total comp. relative to market* | | | | | | |
| Fraser Institute[b] | | | | | | |
| Economic freedom index | -0.086 | a | 0.073 | a | 0.323 | -0.242 |
| Global Competitiveness Report[c] | | | | | | |
| Overall Global Competitiveness Index | 0.466 | a | 0.254 | a | 0.082 | -0.121 |
| Hiring and firing practices | -0.338 | a | 0.377 | a | 0.546* | -0.250 |
| Cooperative labor-employer relations | -0.391 | a | 0.466 | a | 0.058 | -0.135 |
| Flexibility of wage determination | -0.399 | a | 0.205 | a | 0.601** | 0.085 |
| Pay and productivity | -0.714*** | a | 0.304 | a | 0.385 | 0.055 |
| Overall mkt efficiency | -0.503* | a | 0.088 | a | -0.033 | 0.023 |
| Restrictive labor regulations | -0.094 | a | -0.276 | a | -0.512* | 0.250 |
| Innovative factors | 0.344 | a | 0.410 | a | 0.113 | -0.243 |
| Culture scores[d] | | | | | | |
| Power distance | 0.251 | a | 0.261 | a | 0.080 | 0.282 |
| Individualism | -0.027 | a | -0.203 | a | -0.274 | -0.251 |
| Masculinity | -0.002 | a | 0.309 | a | 0.258 | -0.521* |
| Uncertainty avoidance | 0.068 | a | -0.237 | a | 0.219 | 0.230 |
| Long-term orientation | 0.120 | a | 0.227 | a | 0.095 | 0.070 |

[a]Difference among country-specific coefficients on this predictor was not statistically significant, so prediction of variation among coefficients is not appropriate.

[b]Gwartney and Lawson (2006).

[c]Lopez-Claros (2005).

[d]Hofstede and Hofstede (2005).

***Significant at the 1 percent level.

**Significant at the 5 percent level.

*Significant at the 10 percent level.

similar correlation of measures of policies/practices and performance. The findings of worker and establishment level differences are striking since the company strives to implement its employment system globally through many frequent international meetings of managers and employees. By contrast, aggregate measures of labor market institutions common to global "economic freedom" and "competitiveness" scores across countries are either insignificantly or negatively correlated with our measures of performance, indicating that these variables fail to capture the reality of labor market operations on the ground in this firm.

The individual, establishment, and country comparisons support the idea that what matters are policies and practices at workplaces. Worker views of employee-management relations had, in particular, a strong relation not only to standard performance measures such as likely turnover and willingness to work hard, but also to our innovative measure of how workers would respond to a shirking coworker. The results on high performance practices and compensation, however, were more mixed. While we found strong evidence of country differences in behavior and outcome within the same firm, these differences were not well-related (or were inversely related) to national indicators of labor conditions and, in some cases, culture. To understand workplace outcomes, one does best to examine workplace policies and practices.

## Appendix

### Workplace Policies

*Grade on Employee-Management Relations.* 0–4 scale. "If you were to rate how well this company takes care of workers on a scale similar to school grades, what grade would you give in these areas? (C is an average grade.) Overall relations with employees." (A, B, C, D, F). (4 = A, 0 = F).

*High Performance Work System Index.* 0–6 scale. Composed of one point for each of the following components. *Employee Involvement Team:* "Some companies have organized workplace decision-making in ways to get more employee input and involvement. Are you personally involved in any team, committee or task force that addresses issues such as product quality, cost cutting, productivity, health and safety, or other workplace issues?" (0 = no, 1 = yes), 1 point. *Training:* "In the last 12 months have you received any formal training from your current employer, such as in classes or seminars sponsored by the employer?" (0 = no, 1 = yes), 1 point. *Information Sharing:* "If you were to rate how well this company takes care of workers on a scale similar to school grades, what grade would you give in these areas? (C is an average grade.) Sharing information with employees." (A, B, C, D, F),

1 point for A; .75 for B; .5 for C; .25 for D; and 0 for F. *Employee Selection:* "On a scale of 1 to 7 please evaluate how effective your work area or team functions in the following areas: Selecting the very best people to be part of our team/area." (1 = very ineffective; 4 = neutral; 7 = very effective), 1 point for a score of 7; .83 points for a score of 6; .66 points for a score of 5; .5 points for a score of 4; .33 points for a score of 3; .17 points for a score of 2; 0 points for a score of 1. *Profit or Gain Sharing:* "In your job are you eligible for any type of performance-based pay such as individual or group bonuses or any type of profit sharing?" (0 = no, 1 = yes), 1 point. *Job Rotation:* "How frequently do you participate in a job rotation or cross-training program where you work or are trained on a job with different duties than your regular job?" (1 = never; 2 = occasionally; 3 = frequently); 1 point for "frequently;" .5 points for "occasionally;" 0 points for "never."

*Total compensation relative to the market.* 1–5 scale. "Do you believe your total compensation is higher or lower than those of employees with similar experience and job descriptions in other companies in your region?" (1 = lower; 2, 3, 4, 5 = higher).

### Own Performance

*Unlikely to Look for New Job.* 1–4 scale. "How likely is it that you will decide to look hard for a job with another organization within the next twelve months?" (1 = already looking; 2 = very likely; 3 = somewhat likely; 4 = not at all likely).

*Willing to Work Hard.* 1–5 scale. "To what extent do you agree or disagree with this statement? 'I am willing to work harder than I have to in order to help the company I work for succeed.'" (1 = strongly disagree; 2 = disagree; 3 = neither agree nor disagree; 4 = agree; 5 = strongly agree).

*Willing to Innovate.* 1–4 scale. "I would be willing to be more involved in efforts to develop innovative products and services." (1 = Not at all; 2 = very little; 3 = to some extent; 4 = to a great extent).

*Antishirking Index.* 4–16 scale. "If you were to see a fellow employee not working as hard or well as he or she should, how likely would you be to: a) Talk directly to the employee, b) Speak to your supervisor or manager, c) Talk about it in a work group or team, d) Do nothing." (Answers on all four parts of this question were coded on a 1–4 scale for a summated rating with 1 = not at all likely; 2 = not very likely; 3 = somewhat likely; 4 = very likely. The last item was reverse-coded).

### Evaluation of Coworkers and Facility Performance

*Coworkers Work Hard.* 0–10 scale. "At your workplace, how hard would you say that people work?" Please rate on a scale of 0 to 10. (0 = not at all hard; 10 = very hard).

*Facility Effectiveness.* 0–4 scale. "If you were to rate the facility you work in on a scale similar to school grades, what grade would you give in these areas? Getting the job done that has to get done efficiently. (C is an average grade.)" (4 = A; 3 = B; 2 = C; 1 = D; 0 = F).

# References

Akerlof, G. A. Labor contracts as partial gift exchange. *The Quarterly Journal of Economics* 97 (4): 543–69.

Appelbaum, E., T. Bailey, P. Berg, and A. L. Kalleberg. 2000. *Manufacturing advantage: Why high performance work systems pay off.* Ithaca, NY: Cornell University Press.

Cappelli, P., and D. Neumark. 2001. Do "high-performance" work practices improve establishment-level outcomes? *Industrial and Labor Relations Review* 54 (4): 737–75.

Freeman, R. B., D. Kruse, and J. Blasi. 2006. Worker responses to shirking. Paper prepared for the Russell Sage Foundation/NBER Conference. 6–7 October, New York City.

Gwartney, J. D., and R. A. Lawson. 2006. *Economic freedom of the world: 2006 annual report.* Vancouver, British Columbia: The Fraser Institute.

Heneman, R. L., C. R. Fay, and Z.-M. Wang. 2002. Compensation systems in the global context. In *Handbook of industrial, work, and organizational psychology,* ed. N. Anderson, D. S. Ones, and H. K. Sinnangil, 5–34. Thousand Oaks, CA: SAGE.

Hofstede, G. 1984. *Culture's consequences: International differences in work-related values.* Beverly Hills, CA: SAGE.

———. 1991. *Culture and organizations: Software of the mind.* London: McGraw-Hill.

Hofstede, G., and G. J. Hofstede. 2005. *Cultures and organizations: Software of the mind.* New York: McGraw Hill.

Huselid, M. 1995. The impact of human resource management practices on turnover, productivity, and corporate financial performance. *Academy of Management Journal* 38 (3): 635–72.

Ichniowski, C., K. Shaw, and G. Prennushi. 1997. The effects of human resource management practices on productivity: A study of steel finishing lines. *American Economic Review* 87 (3): 291–313.

Kruse, D., J. Blasi, and R. Park. 2006. Shared capitalism in the U.S. Paper prepared for the Russell Sage Foundation/NBER Conference. 6–7 October, New York City.

Lopez-Claros, A. 2006. *The global competitiveness report 2006–2007.* New York: Palgrave Macmillan.

Lubinski, D., and L. G. Humphreys. 1996. Seeing the forest from the trees: When predicting the behavior or status of groups, correlate means. *Psychology, Public Policy, and Law Journal* 2:363–76.

Wallace, A. R. 1858. On the tendency of varieties to depart indefinitely from the original type, part of the Darwin-Wallace paper, On the tendency of species to form varieties, and on the perpetuation of varieties and species by natural means of selection. *Journal of the Proceedings of the Linnean Society (Zoology)* 3 (July): 53–62.

# Within-firm Labor Productivity across Countries
# A Case Study

Francine Lafontaine and Jagadeesh Sivadasan

## 5.1 Introduction

According to *Franchise Times,* the 200 largest U.S.-based franchise chains in 2004 operated 356,361 outlets and generated a total of 327,058 million U.S. dollars in sales worldwide. Of these, eighty-six were fast-food chains, operating a total of 180,772 outlets and generating sales of 162,409 million U.S. dollars. The largest franchise chain in the world in 2004 was McDonald's, with 30,220 outlets worldwide and total sales of 45,932 million U.S. dollars. The international fast-food industry is important, however, not only because of its sheer size, but because of the role it plays in the daily lives of consumers worldwide. Many fast-food brands are among the best recognized brands around the world, and fast food is a very visible part of the global economy. Another fact that make these chains particularly interesting is that they produce basically the same output using the same technology in all their outlets worldwide.[1] This homogeneity in output, coupled with variations

Francine Lafontaine is a professor of business economics and public policy at the Ross School of Business, University of Michigan. Jagadeesh Sivadasan is an assistant professor of business economics and public policy at the Ross School of Business, University of Michigan.

Stephen M. Ross School of Business, University of Michigan, e-mail: laf@umich.edu, jagadees@umich.edu. We are grateful to the Sloan Foundation and the NBER for their generous support, and to Company officials—who shall remain nameless—for allowing us to learn about their organization, and providing us with the data to carry out this research. We also thank Kathryn Shaw, Richard Freeman, Amil Petrin, Jan Svejnar, and participants at seminars at the University of Michigan, International IO Conference (Northeastern University), and Stanford University for their comments, David Leibsohn, Eun-Hee Kim, and Jon Plichta for their help with the data, and Robert Picard for his assistance. All remaining errors are our own.

1. Of course, they adapt their menus to local tastes to varying degrees. But their main menu items are served worldwide and they only introduce local menu items that are easily handled

in outlet characteristics and in regulatory environment across countries, provide a unique opportunity to investigate how business practices, outlet characteristics, and regulatory contexts affect productivity. Moreover, the fast-food industry is a fairly labor intensive, low margin industry, making it a setting where labor productivity is particularly important.

In this study, and in contrast to other contributions to this volume where authors emphasize the effect of changes in business practices over time within a firm, we use weekly data from outlets of an international retail food chain to analyze how labor productivity—defined as the number of items produced per worker-hour—varies across countries. Specifically, we consider how various outlet characteristics, such as outlet age, the experience level of workers, and the average order size, as well as the form of governance (which varies across outlets) affect productivity. In addition, given the important role of labor costs in determining profitability in this industry, we analyze how labor regulations related to hiring and firing—that is, those rules that affect the capacity of the outlet manager to schedule workers flexibly and add or subtract hours on the schedule, affect observed average labor productivity and outlet-level output. To maintain confidentiality restrictions on the data, throughout the chapter we refer to the multinational firm under study as "the Company" and the product sold in the retail outlets as "item(s)." Also for confidentiality reasons, we are unable to provide certain details on the operations of the Company. However, we rely heavily on our understanding of the industry and the firm, based on interviews with industry insiders, and on the trade press, in our modeling and interpretation of results.

To motivate our empirical analyses, we examine the optimization problem of individual outlets assuming a simple multi-input Cobb-Douglas production function. Outlet-level profit maximization leads to a linear specification for labor productivity, which should be increasing in labor wages and declining in output price.[2] If outlets have some local market power, then average labor productivity would also depend on the elasticity of demand, with those facing less elastic demand curves cutting back on production and thus exhibiting higher productivity levels on average.

In addition to considering the effect of input and output prices, we model how other factors can affect observed labor productivity through their influ-

---

within the constraints imposed by their production processes and facilities, using basically the same technologies.

2. Note that the equilibrium labor productivity is independent of the Hicks-neutral total factor productivity (TFP) term in the Cobb-Douglas production function. Specifically, ceteris paribus, outlets with higher levels of TFP would be larger than those with lower levels of TFP, but would move further down the marginal product curve so that the revenue marginal product of labor equals the prevailing wage rate. Under this condition, the Cobb-Douglas specification yields the same average labor productivity for high and low TFP outlets facing the same wages and output prices. This is because the marginal product of labor is a constant times the average labor productivity (i.e., $dQ/dL = \alpha Q/L$).

ence on what we refer to as overhead labor.[3] In other words, given what we know about what is expected of workers, we take for granted that some of the labor costs we observe for each outlet is dedicated to generating complementary services, which, per the firm's measurement process, we refer to as execution quality. Other aspects of quality, which the firm refers to under the heading of "compliance," do not require additional labor hours. Incorporating this fact into our analyses, we find that (a) execution quality has a negative effect on our measure of labor productivity, as expected, but compliance has no such effect; (b) outlet age beyond the first year of operation and increases in the number of experienced employees do not have a statistically significant effect on labor productivity; and (c) larger order sizes on average improve labor productivity. The effect of governance form is ambiguous, and the choice of governance form appears to be correlated with unobserved country fixed effects.

Next, we consider the effect of different labor regulations across countries on observed labor productivity. We expect labor market rigidities to increase the effective cost of employing workers above the prevailing wage rate. We find that indeed labor regulations that reduce flexibility in hiring and firing workers raise the equilibrium labor productivity levels, consistent with our expectation that the laws raise the effective cost of labor. Accordingly, we find that increases in the rigidity of labor regulations lowers labor demand conditional on input and output prices. Our estimates imply that increasing the index of labor regulations from the twenty-fifth to its seventy-fifth percentile level reduces conditional labor demand by about 12.4 percent.

Finally, we use the high frequency of our data to develop an empirical strategy that allows us to estimate the net impact of the labor law rigidity on output at the outlet level. Assuming optimizing behavior by outlets, three major factors influence the effect of labor regulations on output: the effect of regulations on the effective wage locally, the elasticity of output with respect to inputs (in the production function), and the own-price elasticity of demand. Using our most conservative approach to estimating demand elasticities, and a range of coefficient estimates for the other factors, we conclude that an increase in labor regulation from the p25 level ( = 0.28) to p75 level ( = 0.59) leads to a net reduction in outlet-level output (conditional on outlet level wages, output prices, capital, and demand shifters) of about 1.5 percent to 2.6 percent. These results are consistent with the negative effect of job security laws on employment found by Lazear (1990). Our conservative

3. The standard approach in productivity studies is to examine total factor productivity (TFP) using a production function specification. Here, we lack data on store level capital and hence would be unable to disentangle TFP from unobserved capital. Data constraints thus lead us to focus on labor productivity, as data on both output and labor input are available. However, as discussed previously, TFP does not affect observed average labor productivity. Hence we capture the influence of factors such as product quality and governance through their potential effect on overhead labor.

estimates also are close to the 2 percent effect on consumption calibrated by Hopenhayn and Rogerson (1993) for a job security tax equivalent to one year's wages for the United States.[4]

In the next section, we present a simple model that captures how key factors affect measured labor productivity, labor demand, and output. In section 5.3 we discuss the data and provide some details about the operations of the Company. We present results in section 5.4. Section 5.5 concludes.

## 5.2    Model and Empirical Specifications

In this section, we present a simple model of production and demand for a typical retail food outlet that allows us to analyze the effects of outlet characteristics such as experience, execution quality, compliance, and governance, as well as country-level labor regulations on outlet-level decisions. As we describe further below, we treat such characteristics as exogenous or predetermined at the time managers make input and output decisions given that our data are weekly. More generally, we use our theoretical framework to derive empirical specifications for labor productivity, labor demand, and output that highlight some industry facts and practices, per Company officials, and take into account the strengths and weaknesses of our data.

### 5.2.1    Basic Specification

We assume that food items (output) are produced in each outlet each period according to a simple three-input Cobb-Douglas production function, with materials $M$, capital $K$ and labor $L$ as the three inputs.

$$(1) \qquad Q = \theta L^{\alpha} K^{\beta} M^{\gamma},$$

where we assume that $\alpha$, $\beta$, and $\gamma$ are all greater than 0, and $\alpha + \gamma < 1$.[5] For simplicity, we omit outlet and time subscripts, keeping those implicit throughout our discussion of the model.

Initially, we take the output market as competitive; that is, we assume a horizontal demand curve. This assumption is not unreasonable in our context since there are many close substitutes for the output of any fast-food outlet, from outlets of other chains and from more local restaurant and food offerings. Still, we relax this assumption further below. For now, however, under this assumption, outlet-level profits are given by:

$$(2) \qquad \Pi = P \cdot Q - wL - rK - sM.$$

---

4. Our research is related also to Card and Krueger (1997), as some of the studies in that book were concerned with the effect of changes in minimum wage laws on employment levels in fast-food chains. While they found no effect of such changes on employment, other studies (e.g., Deere, Murphy, and Welch 1995) have found negative effects of minimum wages on employment.

5. The latter ensures that second order conditions for interior solutions hold.

We assume that for each outlet, capital is semi-fixed. That is, when the outlet manager makes weekly decisions, she is not free to choose capital—the size of the store or the amount of equipment is taken as given—but she can vary labor and materials. In fact, from our discussions with industry insiders, one of the most important jobs of a store manager (or franchisee) in the fast-food industry is to keep labor and materials costs low. In particular, they use data from the same week last year, and information about how the last few weeks this year compared to their experience the previous year, along with any information they have about the timing of special events in their market to forecast demand at their outlet one or two weeks ahead. They then plan their labor and materials purchases for the next one or two weeks based on these forecasts.[6]

Since each outlet is a small business, and thus a small employer and buyer locally, we assume material and labor are supplied at constant price through competitive input markets. At the optimum, the first-order condition for labor and material choices are binding so that the marginal cost of labor (material) is equal to the marginal revenue product of labor (material).

(3) $$P(\alpha\theta L^{\alpha-1}K^{\beta}M^{\gamma}) = w$$

(4) $$P(\gamma\theta L^{\alpha}K^{\beta}M^{\gamma-1}) = s.$$

Substituting for output and rearranging terms, equation (3) yields the following specification for average labor productivity ($Q/L$):

(5) $$\log\left(\frac{Q}{L}\right) = \log(w) - \log(P) - \log(\alpha) + e,$$

where $e$ is a residual from measurement or represents optimization errors.[7]

Equation (5) implies that in a cross-country context such as ours, if one assumes that the technology used within each outlet is the same everywhere for this type of chain (or more precisely that the parameter $\alpha$ is the same

---

6. See, for example, Deery and Mahony (1994) on the importance of labor flexibility in retail generally, and Hueter and Swart (1998) for information on how Taco Bell uses operations research models to optimize its labor usage and minimize its labor costs. The authors estimate that the company saved $40M in labor costs between 1993 and 1996 through the labor management system it developed at the time.

7. In this specification, deviations from unit values in estimated parameters for wage and output price could be due to measurement error in prices and wages, or to a mis-specification of the production function. For example, it can be shown that the general Constant Elasticity of Substitution (CES) production function yields the same specification as we use here, except that the coefficient on price and wage would be the coefficient of substitution. That is, if we assume $Q = (\alpha L^{s} + \beta K^{s} + \gamma M^{s})^{1/s}$, then the specification in equation (5) is modified to $\log(Q/L) = \psi \log(w) - \psi \log(P) - \psi \log(\alpha) + e$, where $\psi = (s-1)/s$. We maintain the Cobb-Douglas assumption in part because it fits the data reasonably well, as will be clear following, and because it allows us to evaluate the effect of labor regulations on output per the method outlined in section 5.2.4. The Cobb-Douglas functional form is not an unusual assumption in the literature examining firm performance (see, e.g., Olley and Pakes [1996], and Fabrizio, Rose, and Wolfram [2007]).

across countries), labor productivity would be higher in countries where the wage rate $w$ is high and/or the price per item $P$ is low. In other words, we should observe higher labor productivity where the cost of labor is high relative to the price of output.

As noted previously, each outlet in our data is a very small firm, and the Company itself is just one of many different companies offering different food options to customers, as was made clear in our discussions with Company managers. In some applications, an identification issue for equation (5) can arise from the endogeneity of wages. In our context, however, we view the assumption that each outlet faces a horizontal labor supply curve in its local labor market as highly plausible, given the size of these outlets relative to the total retail marketplace. Further, we focus our attention on wage differences across countries, which are even less likely to be affected by the amount of labor employed by individual outlets (or even by the total employment of the Company in any one country).[8]

### 5.2.2    Overhead Labor and Outlet Characteristics

Fast-food production, while relatively straightforward, nonetheless requires some coordination as well as the provision of various complementary services, such as clean areas to consume the food, clean restrooms, well-stocked condiment bars, and so on. The production of these complementary services also entails the use of labor. To allow for this, we modify the basic model above to add the assumption that part of observed labor represents overhead labor that does not directly contribute to producing output. This modeling approach draws on Aghion and Howitt (1994), and has been viewed as a fairly realistic representation of production processes in the context of the retail sector (see Foster, Haltiwanger, and Krizan 2002).

We assume that overhead labor is utilized in several different ways in the Company's outlets, and that this affects how some outlet characteristics should be factored into our production function framework. Let observed total labor at the outlet be $\hat{L}$ and the optimal labor level (net of overhead labor) be $L$. We assume that the number of overhead employees is a fraction $\rho$ of the optimal labor level. Then, the specification for observed labor productivity, in (5), becomes:

$$(6) \qquad \log\!\left(\frac{Q}{\hat{L}}\right) = \log(w) - \log(P) - \log(\alpha) - \log\!\left(\frac{\hat{L}}{L}\right) + e$$

$$= \log(w) - \log(P) - \log(\alpha) - \log(1 + \rho) + e.$$

---

8. One approach to instrumenting for wages could be to use the average wage for the region (similar to the approach in Hausman [1996]). But since we use the predicted wage based on average wage for cities reported by the Economist's Intelligence Unit (EIU), our wage measure is already purged of any variation from outlet-specific factors.

The impact of various outlet characteristics on measured outlet-level average labor productivity thus depends on their effect on the fraction of overhead labor $\rho$. Factors that increase the fraction of overhead labor would reduce average labor productivity, and vice versa. In what follows, we discuss the expected effects of outlet-level variables such as output quality, experience of employees, governance, and so on.

(i) Quality ($S_e$, $S_c$): Outlets in a franchise chain all operate under a common brand whose value depends crucially on consistent operations and consistent, positive consumer experiences across outlets. As a result, outlets are required to maintain quality levels to the parent company's standards, and franchisors spend both time and resources monitoring the operations of each outlet. At the Company, outlets are audited on a periodical basis, and various individual scores are summarized under two major headings: (a) Execution ($S_e$), which measures how well the outlet meets product specifications (size, presentation, portion sizes), speed of customer service requirements, cleanliness of customer areas, and so on; and (b) Compliance ($S_c$), which captures the extent to which the outlet abides by policies concerning temperature and length of storage for food products, employee safety rules, employee grooming and attire, and so on.

Given what these scores represent, we view execution quality as a second output produced by workers at the outlet. Thus, we expect that increasing execution quality level would, all else equal, require more labor resources to be diverted from actual item production. For example, customer wait times might be improved by hiring extra staff to take orders or work behind the counter. Similarly, better scores on store and customer area cleanliness require more labor resources to be allocated to related tasks. Hence, we expect the fraction of what we call overhead labor $\rho$ to increase with increases in execution quality levels, so that:

$$\frac{\mathrm{d}\rho}{\mathrm{d}S_e} > 0 \Rightarrow \frac{\mathrm{d}\log\frac{Q}{L}}{\mathrm{d}S_e} < 0.$$

We expect compliance, on the other hand, to be less labor intensive—no labor is required to comply with grooming and dress code policies, for example. In fact, for the latter, it is likely less time consuming to rely on the sources of inputs suggested or required by the Company than it would be for an outlet to find its own sources. In that sense, we believe compliance does not really involve the use of extra labor. At the same time, it should contribute to the value of the franchise (i.e., it should increase demand via the value of the brand, as franchisors all argue compliance does). In that context, compliance with company policies could reduce wastage in the long run, including potential waste in the use of labor. This, then, could be reflected in lower (total) labor. Thus, we expect compliance potentially to contribute positively to labor productivity; that is:

$$\frac{d\rho}{dS_c} \leq 0 \Rightarrow \frac{d \log\frac{Q}{L}}{dS_c} \geq 0.$$

(ii) Average order size ($\Omega$): We expect less labor (overhead and crew) to be required in outlets where the average order size is larger. For example, larger orders should be associated with larger production batches and reduced handling. As mentioned by company managers, larger orders are also particularly suited to the chain-like production process in fast-food outlets. Thus, we expect:

$$\frac{d\rho}{d\Omega} < 0 \Rightarrow \frac{d \log\frac{Q}{L}}{d\Omega} > 0.$$

(iii) Governance structure (G): The ownership structure of the Company's outlets varies from country to country, and in many cases from outlet to outlet within a country. There are five major types of governance structures (the last part of the chain indicates the owner of the outlet): (1) Parent Company → Local Franchisee (about 4 percent of outlets in the data); (2) Parent Company → Master Franchisee (about 43 percent); (3) Parent Company → Master Franchisee → Local Franchisee (about 44 percent); (4) Parent Company → Area Developer (about 7 percent); and (5) Parent Company owns and operates the outlet (about 2 percent). Note that the vast majority of outlets operate under master franchise agreements, where a firm or individual pays a fee for the right to a territory (often a whole country). Within this territory, the master franchisee may operate outlets directly or sell outlets to franchisees who then operate them. Master Franchisees most often do both, and act as a franchisor to the franchisees whom they recruit, sharing the franchise fees and royalties paid by their franchisees with the Company. Area developers are also granted the right to a territory (for a fee) but they are not allowed to sell franchises within this territory. Instead, an area developer necessarily owns and operates all the outlets in his territory.

Given the distribution of governance structures in our data, and the fact that within-country variation in governance form in particular takes the form of franchisee-owned versus nonfranchisee owned outlets, in what follows we focus on this distinction only.

The expected effect of franchisee ownership on average labor productivity is somewhat ambiguous, however. In general, franchisees are expected to put forth a greater level of effort in running their outlets (including monitoring crew labor), and hence one should find greater efficiency in the use of overhead and other labor for outlets owned and operated by franchisees.[9] This, in turn, implies that we should find higher levels of observed labor productivity for franchised outlets. Denoting franchisee-owned outlets by the dummy $D_{f'ee}$, then, holding all other factors constant, we expect:

$$E(\rho \mid D_{f'ee} = 1) < E(\rho \mid D_{f'ee} = 0)$$

$$\Rightarrow E\left(\log\frac{Q}{L} \;\middle|\; D_{f'ee} = 1\right) > E\left(\log\frac{Q}{L} \;\middle|\; D_{f'ee} = 0\right).$$

Two sets of factors may affect this prediction, however. One relates to data and measurement issues, while the other has to do with how outlet governance itself is selected by the firm. In terms of data and measurement, as discussed later, we measure labor inputs as total labor costs at the outlet divided by a country-level measure of wages. This approach to measuring labor usage, which is dictated by data constraints, may affect our results in two ways. First, outlets owned by franchisees may have downward-biased labor cost figures as these costs may exclude the compensation or full opportunity cost of franchisees' time. Since the latter typically undertake activities performed by paid managers in other outlets, but may be compensated for their effort at least partly through profits, the data on labor costs may underestimate total labor cost. Once divided by the wage rate, they would yield an underestimate of hours of labor used, and thus give rise to an upward biased measure of average labor productivity. Such a bias, of course, would reinforce our previous prediction that we should expect higher labor productivity in franchised outlets. The issue then is that if we find such higher productivity in franchised outlets, it will not be possible to determine whether this result arises from a real difference in productivity, per our hypothesis, or from a labor cost measurement problem.

Second, it could be that franchisees are better able to identify and hire workers at lower wage rates and substitute for lower labor quality through closer monitoring. In this case, the effective wage paid to workers in franchisee-owned outlets would be lower than for nonfranchised outlets. The net impact of this is ambiguous. As reflected in equation (6), we would expect these outlets to have greater output on the margin, given the lower marginal cost of production, and thus lower average levels of labor productivity. However, if franchisee-owned firms do indeed use relatively lower paid workers, our measured employment levels for franchisee-owned outlets would be biased downward given our reliance on country-level wages to infer employment from labor costs, so that measured labor productivity for these could be upward biased.

The other problem with our predictions is that as stated, our hypothesis

9. See Shelton (1967) and Krueger (1991) for some evidence that costs may be lower in franchised outlets.

takes governance form as given. Yet while the effect of franchisee ownership on overhead labor may be efficiency enhancing, one expects the presence of different governance forms within and across countries to be an endogenous response to *unmodeled* incentive constraints, as well as regulatory and market conditions. Thus, in equilibrium, labor efficiency advantages of franchisee-owned outlets may be offset by other costs to the parent company, and different governance forms would be chosen in different countries/contexts depending on the relative benefits and costs of particular governance forms. Still, on this issue, it is important to recognize that governance forms are not changed frequently—franchise contracts typically last for ten to twenty years—and thus it is reasonable to treat them as fixed by the time weekly decisions about labor and materials are made.

(iv) Experience ($E_{emp}$, $E_{store}$): It is typical in studies of labor productivity to consider how learning and employee experience levels affect productivity. In our data, we have access to information about employee and outlet-level experience. The first, $E_{emp}$, is proxied by the number of workers with more than one year of experience at time $t$. The second type of measure, $E_{store}$, captures experience/learning embodied in the outlet itself and is proxied by the age of the outlet. It is standard to assume that greater experience levels for the employees should help eliminate unnecessary overhead and improve efficiency. Similarly, learning at the outlet level should reduce overhead labor.[10] Thus we have:

$$\frac{d\rho}{dE} < 0 \Rightarrow \frac{d\log\frac{Q}{L}}{dE} > 0.$$

Incorporating the above factors into equation (6) and adopting a linear approximation, we get the following log-linear specification for measured average labor productivity:

$$(7) \quad \log\left(\frac{Q}{L}\right) = \log(w) - \log(P) - \log(\alpha) + a_{se}S_e + a_{sc}S_c + a_{\Omega}\log(\Omega)$$
$$+ a_{dfee}D_{f'ee} + a_{ee}E_{emp} + a_{es}E_{store} + e.$$

As discussed, we expect:

$$a_{se} < 0, a_{sc} > 0, a_{\Omega} > 0, a_{dfee} > 0, a_{ee} > 0, a_{es} > 0.$$

### 5.2.3  Imperfectly Competitive Output Markets

The restaurant and fast-food industry are typically viewed as ones that fit the assumptions of monopolistic competition quite well. It is, indeed, the Company's outlets operate under a brand, and as such, the product

10. Another variable capturing store/country level experience is the number of years the company has been in the country, which we examine in some of our robustness regressions.

they sell is differentiated. Given this, our model should allow for imperfect competition in the output market, or a downward-sloping demand at the outlet level. Thus, we now let outlet-level demand be given by:

$$(8) \qquad P = A \cdot Q^{1/\mu},$$

where $\mu$ is the elasticity of demand, which must be greater than one in absolute value.[11] With this demand curve, the first-order conditions in equations (3) and (4) are modified such that the labor productivity equation (5) becomes:

$$(9) \qquad \log\left(\frac{Q}{L}\right) = \log(w) - \log(P) - \log\left(1 + \frac{1}{\mu}\right) - \log(\alpha) + e.$$

Our data (see section 5.3) include measures for all the variables in equation (9) except for demand elasticity. One way to control for this unobserved parameter in our productivity regressions would be to include location-time fixed effects that implicitly control for potential demand shifters. However, the inclusion of such fixed effects would limit our ability to study the effect of labor regulation, which is fixed at the country level, and other factors of interest such as quality, which is fixed for store-quarters; governance, which is fixed at the store level; and experience, which would have little meaningful variation within a store-quarter. An alternative approach, which we adopt, is to control for demand elasticity using data on materials choices. Rearranging the modified first-order condition for materials gives:

$$(10) \qquad \left(1 + \frac{1}{\mu}\right) = \frac{sM}{\gamma PQ} = \frac{1}{\gamma}\left(\frac{\text{MaterialCost}}{\text{Revenue}}\right) = \frac{m_{sh}}{\gamma}.$$

Combining equations (5) and (10), we get a modified specification for observed labor productivity:

$$(11) \qquad \log\left(\frac{Q}{L}\right) = \log(w) - \log(P) - \log(m_{sh}) + \log(\gamma) - \log(\alpha) + e.$$

Accordingly, equation (7) becomes:

$$(12) \qquad \log\left(\frac{Q}{L}\right) = \log(w) - \log(P) - \log(m_{sh}) + \log\left(\frac{\gamma}{\alpha}\right) + a_{se}S_e$$
$$+ a_{sc}S_c + a_\Omega \log(\Omega) + a_{dfee}D_{fee} + a_{ee}E_{emp} + a_{es}E_{store} + e.$$

Estimating equation (12) with our cross-country data implicitly assumes that the production function parameters $\gamma$ and $\alpha$ are either constant across countries, or are uncorrelated with other regressors. As noted earlier, given the nature of the business, which is replicated from one location to another with a strong desire for consistency and conformity by the Company, the notion that the different outlets function under similar technology, processes, and standards is consistent with Company policy and with various statements made by Company managers.

### 5.2.4    Impact of Labor Regulations

In addition to studying the effect of outlet characteristics (as described above) on measured labor productivity, another goal of this study is to examine the effect of laws that increase labor market rigidity on measured labor productivity, labor demand, and output. We emphasize the potential effect of labor regulation for the Company because labor costs are a large part of total costs at fast-food outlets, and, given the very low margins in this industry, firms—including the Company—expand significant effort on labor cost minimization. At Taco Bell, for example, labor costs were estimated to be about 30 percent of every dollar of sales at the time Hueter and Swart (1998) examined labor scheduling at this company. They were also described as among the "largest controllable costs" at that company. Moreover, despite chain efforts, business practices in labor management can vary tremendously across outlets, leading to important differences in costs and labor turnover rates.[12] Under these circumstances, regulations further affecting labor flexibility could have a large impact on both labor practices and costs. Our goal is to assess and quantify the latter effect.

We measure labor market rigidity using an index developed in Botero et al. (2004) (see appendix), which combines measures of the difficulty or cost of using part-time employment, increasing hours worked, and hiring and firing workers. Note that, in theory, the effect of labor laws could be offset by individual outlets through contracts and agreements on side payments with their workers (Lazear 1990). In the absence of offsetting agreements—whether this is because of bargaining inefficiencies or incomplete contracts—these laws could affect labor demand at the outlet level, and, consequently, measured labor productivity.

A rich literature in labor economics has examined both theoretically and empirically the link between labor market regulations and employment (see Heckman and Pagés [2003] for a review). Both the theoretical and empirical work is divided on the net impact of labor rigidities on employment. It is easy to see how firing costs, for example, may increase as well

---

12. See Berta (2007) reporting on research conducted by Prof. Jerry Newman.

as decrease employment. On the one hand, increased firing costs would provide an immediate incentive not to fire workers when there is a negative demand (or productivity) shock. On the other hand, firms anticipate future firing costs and therefore hire less workers than required when times are good (positive demand/productivity shocks). The overall effect on employment in a cross-section of firms depends on which of these effects predominates.

For our purposes, motivated by Lazear's (1990) findings of a negative employment effect of labor rigidities, we model the rigid labor laws as increasing the effective marginal cost (or the shadow cost) of labor as perceived by an individual outlet.[13] Thus, we have:

$$w_{\text{eff}} = w_{\text{obs}} \cdot \exp(\varphi \text{Reg}),$$

where we expect $\varphi > 0$. Since higher wages leading to lower labor levels increase the equilibrium marginal product of labor, greater rigidity in labor markets would lead to higher average equilibrium labor productivity. Thus, expanding the specification for labor productivity in equation (12) to include the effect of labor rigidity, we get:

$$(13) \quad \log\left(\frac{Q}{L}\right) = \log(w_{\text{obs}}) - \log(P) - \log(m_{\text{sh}}) + \log\left(\frac{\gamma}{\alpha}\right) + a_{\text{se}}S_{\text{e}}$$
$$+ a_{\text{sc}}S_{\text{c}} + a_{\Omega}\log(\Omega) + a_{\text{dfee}}D_{\text{f'ee}} + a_{\text{ee}}E_{\text{emp}}$$
$$+ a_{\text{es}}E_{\text{store}} + \varphi \text{Reg} + e.$$

While the effect of labor regulation is expected to increase the equilibrium average labor productivity, the rigidity in the labor markets caused by the regulation has detrimental effects that are best shown in the labor demand equation (conditional on output and prices). To see this, we rearrange equation (13) above to yield:

$$(14) \quad \log L = \log Q - \log(w_{\text{obs}}) + \log(P) + \log(m_{\text{sh}}) - \log\left(\frac{\gamma}{\alpha}\right) - a_{\text{se}}S_{\text{e}}$$
$$- a_{\text{sc}}S_{\text{c}} - a_{\Omega}\log(\Omega) - a_{\text{dfee}}D_{\text{f'ee}} - a_{\text{ee}}E_{\text{emp}} - a_{\text{es}}E_{\text{store}}$$
$$- \varphi \text{Reg} - e.$$

The ultimate effect of the regulation, however, is to decrease output at the outlet level. This can be seen by solving for output:

---

13. Given the nature of these laws, a careful examination of their impact would require analysis and calibration of a dynamic labor choice model (as in, e.g., Hopenhayn and Rogerson [1993]). Unfortunately, data limitations, especially with regard to outlet-level capital stock, prevent us from pursuing such analyses here.

(15)  $\log Q = \dfrac{1}{1 - \alpha' - \gamma'}$

$\cdot [\log(\theta) + \beta \log(K) - \alpha \log(w_{\text{eff}}) - \gamma \log(s) - (\alpha + \gamma)\log(A)]$

$= \dfrac{-\alpha\varphi}{1 - \alpha' - \gamma'}(\text{Reg}) + \dfrac{1}{1 - \alpha' - \gamma'}$

$\cdot [\log(\theta) + \beta \log(K) - \alpha \log(w_{\text{obs}}) - \gamma \log(s) - (\alpha + \gamma)\log(A)],$

where $\alpha' = \alpha[1 + (1/\mu)]$, and $\gamma' = \gamma[1 + (1/\mu)]$.

The effect of labor regulation on output thus depends on four parameters: $\alpha$, $\gamma$, $\varphi$, and $\mu$. In particular, the negative effect of labor regulation on output becomes larger the larger $\alpha$ and $\gamma$ are. In other words, the greater the elasticity of output with respect to the two variable factors, the greater is the distortion in output due to regulation. Also, the negative impact of the regulations is greater the larger the (absolute value of the) own-price elasticity of demand. This is because when demand is less elastic, the outlet can pass the increased labor costs on to the consumer without having to reduce its output level as much. Thus, the effect of the regulation on output will be felt the most in those cases where the own-price elasticity of demand is very high; that is, when output markets are very competitive, on account of the availability of close substitutes, or because of the preferences of the consumers.[14]

Given our goal of estimating the impact of the regulations on output, one approach would be to directly estimate equation (15). This is unfortunately not possible with our data since we do not observe store-level capital ($K$), nor store-specific materials price(s), nor store-level demand shifters ($A$). One plausible way to condition out these unobserved variables would be to include store-period fixed effects in our regressions, but then we would be unable to identify the coefficients on many of our variables of interest, including the index of labor regulation given that this index is the same for all outlets in a country and constant over the two years of data we have.

Given that the direct estimation of equation (15) is infeasible, we estimate the four parameters determining the net impact of labor regulations on output as follows:

(i) Parameter $\varphi$ is recovered as the coefficient of the regulation index in

---

14. In general, Marshall's (1920) four laws summarizing the determinants of own-price elasticity of factor demand apply: (a) Substitutability of other factors for labor. This does not explicitly appear in our model because the Cobb-Douglas production function we use is a special case where the elasticity of substitution between factors is one; (b) Elasticity of demand for the final good. This effect shows up in our previous derivations; (c) The share of labor in total costs. This effect shows up in the denominator; that is, via $(1 - \alpha' - \gamma')$; (d) Supply elasticity of other factors. Here we assume that the other variable factor (materials) is supplied with infinite elasticity.

the labor demand specification described by equation (14) or the specification for labor productivity in equation (13).[15]

(ii) We recover the technology parameters $\alpha$ and $\gamma$ by estimating the original Cobb-Douglas production function directly, namely:

$$(16) \qquad \log(Q) = \log(\theta) + \alpha \log(L) + \beta \log(K) + \gamma \log(M) + \varepsilon.$$

Here again, the challenge is that capital $K$ is not observed. Also, we only observe the total cost of materials, or $sM$, not the quantity of such inputs directly. However, in this case we do not have any variable of interest that does not change by country or across time periods. We can therefore address these data issues by making use of the high frequency of our data and assuming that: (a) capital does not vary for any given store within a season or month, so that capital gets absorbed by store-year-season or store-year-month fixed effects; and (b) similarly, materials prices do not change for any given store within a season or month, so that variations in such costs after including store-year-season or store-year-month fixed effects reflect changes in material quantities only.

With these assumptions, we obtain $\gamma$ as the coefficient on materials costs, and $\alpha$ as the coefficient on labor costs, in the production function specification in equation (16), after including store-year-season or store-year-month fixed effects.

(iii) Finally, for the elasticity of demand parameter, we estimate a simple iso-elastic demand function:

$$(17) \qquad \log(Q) = -\mu \log(A) + \mu \log(P) + \eta.$$

The identification issue here involves potential omitted variables, in particular unobserved demand shifters that might affect $A$. We address this issue in many ways. First, we eliminate store effects via first differences. Moreover, we rely again on the high frequency of our data, and include store-year-month or store-year-season fixed effects. In a first-difference equation, these will capture store-specific trends within months or seasons.[16] Alternatively, as detailed further below, we use (first-differenced) materials costs per unit of output, and average output price in all other stores in the country in the same month, as instruments for price in equation (17).[17]

---

15. As noted earlier, we believe it is reasonable to treat wages as exogenous in our context. Moreover, we maintain the assumption that the technology parameters are either constant across countries, or uncorrelated with the other variables of interest, most importantly the labor regulation index.

16. We have verified that our results are very similar when we do not use first differences, and/or when we include fewer fixed effects. However, we chose to present results where we use all these controls for unobserved effects given that our data allow us to do so.

17. Our average output price instrument is similar to the average price instrument used by Hausman (1996) and hence is vulnerable to Bresnahan's (1996) critique. The key element of the critique is that there is a reason why the price at one outlet may be correlated with the prices at other outlets, which is the basis on which these prices could serve as an instrument for price at outlet i. So suppose that each outlet chooses price—the presumption we are making when we

## 5.3     Data Description and Definition of Variables

The main source of data for this study is an internal data set from an international retail fast-food chain. We have weekly outlet-level financial data on inputs and output levels for every outlet in every foreign country for the years 2002 and 2003. In addition, we have information on both ownership and quality of operations (execution and compliance) from audits that the Company performs for each outlet on average once every three months.[18]

In our analyses, we want to ensure that we compare outcomes obtained under similar circumstances. For that reason, starting with all outlets, we eliminated all observations that pertained to potentially unusual situations, such as outlets operating with a different type of facility (e.g., limited menu facilities), or observations related to unusual time periods (i.e., at start-up or within a short time from the closing of an outlet). Specifically, we exclude observations that are within the first year of operation for an outlet, and those observations pertaining to the last year of an outlet's operations. We also removed outlets that changed ownership the year before or after our period of analysis, as such changes are often accompanied by various disruptions, including renovations and temporary outlet closure. Additionally, a number of outlets and countries do not have information on all the variables we rely on. We exclude these as well.

Summary statistics for key variables in our study are presented in table 5.1. In what follows, we define each of the variables and explain how it is measured. To analyze labor productivity, we require a measure of output and labor input at the outlet level. The data already include a measure of the number of items produced by each outlet every week. Of course, in reality, the outlets offer a menu of different products to their customers. The company, however, translates this into a single metric, which it refers to internally as "items." We therefore follow the company's internal processes and use "number of items" as our measure of outlet-level output each week. As for labor input, our data include information on total labor cost ($w \cdot L$) for each outlet. To transform this into a measure of labor input, we need a measure of average hourly wages paid by each outlet to their workers. Since we do not have access to outlet-level data on wages, we use labor cost per hour data for 2002 and 2003 from the CityData data set, which is maintained by

---

allow downward sloping demand curves that are acted upon in the model—but the Company sets national advertising level, which is not observed. This advertising level then will affect all local demands similarly, explaining why they move together. The prices at other outlets, however, will not be a good instrument for the price at outlet i under these circumstances, as the same omitted variable—unobserved advertising—affects both. Since material costs are more likely to be driven by shifts in input supply or by differences in output composition, our material costs instrument is less vulnerable to the Bresnahan critique.

18. The average number of days between two audits is 101 days; however, there is significant variation in this figure, probably because the parent firm keeps its audit process somewhat random (standard deviation of about eighty days).

**Table 5.1          Summary statistics**

| Variable | N | Mean | SD | Median | Min | Max |
|---|---|---|---|---|---|---|
| Log(Quantity = Number of items sold per week) | 225,487 | 6.764 | 0.744 | 6.724 | 0.693 | 10.238 |
| Log(Labor hours: Uses wages imputed using EIU data) | 154,526 | 5.188 | 0.719 | 5.129 | −6.141 | 9.351 |
| Log(Material cost in USD) | 233,861 | 7.790 | 0.683 | 7.882 | −4.174 | 13.177 |
| Log(Items per hour: Uses wages imputed using EIU data) | 140,070 | 1.577 | 0.968 | 1.402 | −3.823 | 12.109 |
| Log(Price = Sales/item in USD) | 225,421 | 2.106 | 0.548 | 2.185 | −1.472 | 8.349 |
| Log(Wage: Imputed for whole country using EIU city data) | 197,522 | 1.929 | 1.183 | 2.729 | −0.598 | 3.401 |
| Log(Material cost/sales)[a] | 233,794 | −1.114 | 0.205 | −1.082 | −1.628 | −0.626 |
| Total execution points/100: Interpolated | 82,681 | 0.494 | 0.127 | 0.520 | 0.000 | 0.700 |
| Total compliance points/100: Interpolated | 82,681 | 0.226 | 0.042 | 0.232 | 0.000 | 0.300 |
| Outlet age in days/10,000 | 190,738 | 0.243 | 0.159 | 0.210 | −0.025 | 0.754 |
| Number of experienced employees (1plus)/100: Interpolated[a] | 82,681 | 0.050 | 0.049 | 0.040 | 0.000 | 0.210 |
| Experience (years) in country | 235,378 | 13.979 | 4.052 | 14.000 | 2.000 | 20.000 |
| Log(Average order size = Number of items/transaction) | 211,514 | 0.356 | 0.336 | 0.311 | −5.358 | 5.201 |
| Dummy (Franchisee-owned = 1) | 82,681 | 0.496 | 0.500 | 0.000 | 0.000 | 1.000 |
| Index of labor regulations (Botero et al 2004) | 219,223 | 0.421 | 0.159 | 0.443 | 0.161 | 0.828 |
| Log(Exchange rate) | 242,031 | 2.350 | 2.650 | 2.200 | −1.240 | 14.360 |

*Note:* SD = standard deviation.

[a]These variables are winsorized by 1 percent on the upper and lower limit of the distribution to minimize influence of outliers.

the Economist Intelligence Unit. This source contains country-level wage, and hence allows us to calculate employment for twenty-seven different countries in our sample.[19]

We obtain output price, $P$, by dividing the data on total sales value by the reported number of items sold.[20] The material cost per item(s) also is obtained by dividing total material costs by the number of items sold.[21] The material share of revenue is obtained by dividing material costs by sales revenue. To minimize the effect of outliers, we winsorize the log material share of revenue by 1 percent on the tails of the distribution.

The parent company performs audits of outlets and compiles scores on various measures of operational performance that can be interpreted as

19. As mentioned below, we checked the robustness of our results to our measure of wages using two alternative sources of labor cost data. Results were generally consistent with those reported below. See next section.

20. Since the product mix varies from outlet to outlet and from week to week, our output price measure captures differences in price levels but also some amount of variation in output mix.

21. Note that while the theory suggests using marginal wages and prices, data limitations lead us to use (proxies for) average wage and observed average output and materials prices.

quality measures. As mentioned earlier, these measures are translated into total scores on two dimensions: (a) Execution (which includes measures of item quality, speed of execution of orders, and cleanliness of outlet), and (b) Compliance (which includes compliance with product storage and handling requirements, grooming and uniforms, and employee security policies). We use the separate scores on execution and compliance as our measures of quality ($S_e$ and $S_c$). As these audits are performed only every several months (while our other data are weekly), we assign the same score to the outlet as long as a new audit is not performed, and refer to the resulting variables as interpolated. Some audit data are available for about 68.3 percent of the outlets (1,842 out of 2,695). However, all outlets were not audited with high frequency, so that even after interpolation, audit data is available for only 34 percent of the observations (i.e., 82,681 out of 242,031 outlet-week observations).

Average Order Size, $\Omega$, is defined as the number of items sold in the week divided by the total number of transactions. As for governance, as discussed earlier, we define a dummy variable ("d_franchisee") denoting outlets that are owned and operated by a local franchisee as opposed to being owned and operated directly by the Company, an area developer, or a master franchisee. As this variable is available through audit reports, it is defined only for the set of observations for which we also have quality data.

Our data include several measures of experience. Three variables capture the experience of the labor force: (a) tenure of manager at the outlet, (b) tenure of manager as an employee of the chain, and (c) the number of employees with greater than one year of tenure at the outlet. The data also include information on the opening date for every outlet. Thus, we have data on (d) the age of each outlet, as well as (e) years of experience of the Company in the country (inferred from the earliest opening data among outlets within a country). Unfortunately, we found large coding errors for the manager tenure variables. Consequently, in our analyses we focus on a single measure of employee experience, namely the number of employees with greater than one year of experience. We also rely on data on the age of the outlet as our measure outlet-level experience, as these data are richer than information on the number of years since the Company began operations in each country. To minimize the influence of outliers, we again winsorize the employee experience variable (number of experienced employees) by 1 percent on the tails of its distribution.

Finally, as discussed in section 5.2.4, we measure the intensity of labor regulation using an index constructed by Botero et al. (2004). The definitions of the different components of this index are detailed in the appendix. Unfortunately, while the Company had operations in about fifty-nine countries around the world during the period of our study (2002 to 2003), audit data is available for only forty-five countries. Of these forty-five countries, data on labor regulation is available for twenty-nine countries, of which data on wages is available for twenty-seven. Thus, data limitations restrict the sample used in most of our analysis to twenty-seven or less countries.[22]

## 5.4    Empirical Results

In this section, we first examine the effects of quality, average order size, experience, and the choice of organizational or governance form, on labor productivity. We then discuss our results concerning the effects of labor regulations on labor productivity. Finally, we estimate the effect of labor regulation on output, following the procedure outlined in section 5.2.4.

### 5.4.1    Effect of Quality, Average Order Size, Governance, and Experience

We show the effects of various outlet characteristics on observed labor productivity in table 5.2. We include various subsets of our variables of interest in the different columns in part because our sample sizes are much reduced in some cases, so we want to show that our results are robust across specifications. Moreover, in the first seven columns our regressions include country-month fixed effects to control for country-specific characteristics along with potential seasonal effects.[23] In columns (8) and (9), we control for region-season fixed effects to provide comparisons to the specifications in tables 5.3 and 5.4.[24]

In all the specifications, we find a significant positive effect for wages and negative effect of output prices, as predicted by theory. In fact, our simple model implies a coefficient of 1 and $-1$ on wage and price, respectively. The coefficients for these variables in table 5.2 are remarkably close to unity, suggesting that the Cobb-Douglas specification provides a reasonable approximation in our context.[25]

The materials cost to sales ratio introduced to capture imperfect output

22. As requested by one of the referees, for the key dependent variables in our analysis, we undertook a test for stationarity using the methodology proposed by Im, Pesaran, and Shin (2003), which rejected the null of nonstationarity for all the variables. These results are in an appendix available on request from the authors. The Im, Pesaran, and Shin (2003) test allows for heteroscedasticity, serial correlation, and nonnormality. Because the period fixed effects we use vary across specifications, we tested with and without allowing for such effects. The null was rejected in all cases at p values less than 1 percent.

23. A regression of labor productivity on country fixed effects by itself shows that across-country differences account for about 83 percent of the variation, and country-month effects about 85 percent. Thus, the R-squareds in table 5.2 should be interpreted accordingly. Note that in these regressions, the wage effect is identified off of variation in wages across the two years in our data, as our fixed effects are defined as country-month or country-season, not country-year-month or country-year-season. If we use the latter, we get similar results for other variables, but in this case the wage coefficient is not identified in the first seven columns.

24. The variables of interest here—quality, order size, governance, and experience—vary at the outlet level, so we are able to include country-month fixed effects. In the next section, we will be examining labor regulations, which are constant within country; in those regressions we can include only region-season fixed effects.

25. See footnote 7, supra, for more on this.

**Table 5.2    Labor productivity: Effect of quality, experience, and governance**

| | (1) | (2) | (3) | (4) | (5) | (6) | (7) | (8) | (9) |
|---|---|---|---|---|---|---|---|---|---|
| Log(Wage in USD) | 0.993*** | 1.073*** | 1.142*** | 0.926*** | 1.125*** | 0.960*** | 0.976*** | 0.687*** | 0.685*** |
| | (0.14) | (0.14) | (0.14) | (0.14) | (0.13) | (0.22) | (0.21) | (0.06) | (0.06) |
| Log(Price in USD) | -0.943*** | -0.932*** | -0.941*** | -0.911*** | -0.939*** | -0.737*** | -0.752*** | -0.823*** | -0.328*** |
| | (0.03) | (0.05) | (0.05) | (0.06) | (0.05) | (0.07) | (0.07) | (0.10) | (0.10) |
| Log(Materials cost/sales) | | | | | | | -0.108* | | -0.035 |
| | | | | | | | (0.06) | | (0.10) |
| Total execution points | | -0.189* | | | | -0.203** | -0.207** | -0.108 | -0.117 |
| | | (0.10) | | | | (0.10) | (0.10) | (0.13) | (0.12) |
| Total compliance points | | 0.062 | | | | -0.002 | -0.015 | 0.489 | 0.489 |
| | | (0.20) | | | | (0.19) | (0.19) | (0.31) | (0.30) |
| Outlet age (day/10,000) | | | 0.079 | | | 0.057 | 0.056 | -0.054 | -0.050 |
| | | | (0.07) | | | (0.07) | (0.07) | (0.07) | (0.07) |
| No. of experienced employees | | | 0.105 | | | 0.122 | 0.111 | 0.354 | 0.347 |
| | | | (0.09) | | | (0.09) | (0.09) | (0.25) | (0.24) |
| Log(Average order size) | | | | 0.129* | | 0.294*** | 0.289*** | 0.429*** | 0.430*** |
| | | | | (0.07) | | (0.07) | (0.06) | (0.15) | (0.15) |
| Franchisee-owned | | | | | 0.014 | 0.015 | 0.013 | 0.160*** | 0.164*** |
| | | | | | (0.07) | (0.06) | (0.06) | (0.05) | (0.05) |
| Constant | 1.499*** | 1.310*** | 1.064*** | 1.531*** | 1.121*** | 1.018* | 0.896 | 1.592*** | 1.569*** |
| | (0.27) | (0.32) | (0.33) | (0.27) | (0.33) | (0.56) | (0.55) | (0.13) | (0.14) |
| Fixed effects | Country-Month | Country-Month | Country-Month | Country-Month | Country-Month | Country-Month | Country-Month | Region-Season | Region-Season |
| Observations | 140,015 | 49,013 | 49,013 | 136,152 | 49,013 | 48,560 | 48,069 | 48,560 | 48,069 |
| $R^2$ | 0.90 | 0.92 | 0.92 | 0.90 | 0.92 | 0.92 | 0.92 | 0.89 | 0.89 |
| Number of clusters | 27 | 26 | 26 | 26 | 26 | 24 | 24 | 24 | 24 |

*Notes:* Dependent variable is log labor productivity = log (items per hour of labor). Labor hours are obtained by dividing labor cost by hourly wages. Hourly wages are imputed for the countries using data for certain cities obtained from the EIU. Robust standard errors in parentheses (clustered at country level). Column (7) includes region-season fixed effects, with two regions (North and South) and four seasons.

***Significant at the 1 percent level.

**Significant at the 5 percent level.

*Significant at the 10 percent level.

markets (see section 5.2.3) is only marginally significant, and becomes insignificant in particular in regressions where we control only for region-season effects. If we interpreted this to mean the coefficient is indeed zero, it would suggest that our more basic model, based on the notion that the market is perfectly competitive, may be appropriate for these data.

As for outlet characteristics, we find some evidence that higher execution quality scores are associated with lower labor productivity, which is consistent with our expectation that improving execution quality may require extra overhead labor (columns [2], [6], and [7]). Using the coefficients from column (7), which is our most complete specification for labor productivity, a one standard deviation (0.13) increase in execution points decreases log labor productivity by about 2.7 percent ($-0.21 \times 0.13$). Compliance, on the other hand, does not seem to have any statistically significant effect on labor productivity.

We also find no statistically significant effect of either of our measures of experience on labor productivity in any of the regressions. Note that here, we focus on steady-state effects as we have excluded from the data those outlets that had not been operating for at least one year. The lack of significance of outlet age suggests that there is not much overhead-saving learning within outlets over time, at least beyond the first year of operation for these types of retail outlets. Our results do not inform us on, nor preclude the existence of, significant efficiency improvements in the first few weeks or months after an outlet is established.

We find that order size is positively correlated with labor productivity, in line with our expectation that less overhead labor is required to produce a given quantity of items when the average order size is larger. The effect here is statistically and economically significant; a one standard deviation increase in the log order size (0.34) increases labor productivity by about 9.9 percent (using the coefficient estimate of 0.29 from column [7] again).

Finally, the coefficient on the dummy variable for franchisee-ownership of an outlet is not statistically significant in the specifications that include country fixed effects. In columns (8) and (9), where we include only region (North and South) and season (winter, spring, summer, and fall) fixed effects, we find a positive and significant effect for franchisee ownership. While the latter result is consistent with the idea that there are better incentives for controlling overhead labor in franchisee owned outlets, we are cautious about this interpretation given that the effect disappears when we control for country fixed effects. It appears that omitted country-specific factors may be determining the choice of the franchisee ownership governance form, and that these same country characteristics may also be correlated with higher average labor productivity level (even after controlling for wages, prices, and other variables).

Overall, we conclude that (a) execution quality has a negative effect on labor productivity—this is as expected as the production of what the Company refers to as execution quality involves extra labor costs; (b) outlet age beyond the first year of operation and increases in the number of experienced employees do not have a statistically significant effect on labor productivity; and (c) larger order sizes improve labor productivity. The effect of governance form is ambiguous, and the choice of governance form appears to be correlated with unobserved country fixed effects.

### 5.4.2  Effect of Labor Regulation on Labor Productivity

As discussed in section 5.2.4, we expect labor regulations to increase the effective wage rate faced by the outlets of the Company, and accordingly, we expect labor productivity to be higher for outlets located in countries with more rigid labor regulations. We present results from investigating the impact of labor law regulations on measured labor productivity (equation [13]) in table 5.3. Since labor regulations are constant at the country level, unlike in table 5.2, we are unable to control for local factors using country fixed effects in these regressions, and rely instead on region/season fixed effects.

The results in table 5.3 are consistent with our expectations.[26] In all the specifications, we find that the coefficient on the index of labor regulations is positive and significant. The magnitude of the effects drops as we add more controls, especially when we add a control for governance type. Nevertheless, the effect is statistically very significant, and is also economically important. A one standard deviation increase in the labor regulation index (0.16) increases labor productivity by 6.1 percent ($0.16 \times 0.38$), using the most conservative estimate for the effect of labor regulations (from column [6]).

In columns (6) and (8), we include two additional control variables: the log weekly exchange rate and log per capita GDP. Under the various labor productivity specifications (e.g., equation [13]), the units in which wages and prices are measured do not affect the equation; any scaling factor applied to wages is offset if the same factor is applied to output price. Thus, if our specifications are valid, our results should be unaffected by whether prices and wages are measured in local currency units or in U.S. dollars. However, if our regressions are misspecified, the units of measurement may bias our results. This is because local outlet-level decisions may be based on prices and wages perceived in local currency units. Because the price and wage variables enter the specification in logarithmic form, one way to control for possible biases introduced by fluctuations in the weekly exchange rates is to include the log of the exchange rate among the regressors, as we do in columns [6] and [8]. The log per capita GDP variable moreover controls for omitted variables that might be correlated with the income of local consum

26. A simple table of productivity means across different quartiles of the regulation index (available on request from the authors) reveals an increasing pattern over the first three quartiles and then a decrease. These unconditional means are likely to be confounded by omitted wage and output prices, hence we focus here on the conditional effects.

**Table 5.3    Labor productivity: Effect of labor regulations**

| | (1) | (2) | (3) | (4) | (5) | (6) | (7) | (8) |
|---|---|---|---|---|---|---|---|---|
| Index of labor regulation | 0.713** | 0.611** | 0.626** | 0.699** | 0.449** | 0.383*** | 0.420** | 0.387** |
| | (0.28) | (0.27) | (0.29) | (0.26) | (0.21) | (0.14) | (0.17) | (0.14) |
| Log(Wage in USD) | 0.829*** | 0.809*** | 0.803*** | 0.784*** | 0.785*** | 0.599*** | 0.702*** | 0.572*** |
| | (0.03) | (0.04) | (0.04) | (0.03) | (0.04) | (0.08) | (0.05) | (0.08) |
| Log(Price in USD) | −1.053*** | −1.046*** | −1.046*** | −0.944*** | −1.045*** | −0.886*** | −0.838*** | −0.928*** |
| | (0.04) | (0.05) | (0.05) | (0.04) | (0.05) | (0.08) | (0.09) | (0.083) |
| Log(Material cost/sales) | | | | | | | −0.123** | −0.149* |
| | | | | | | | (0.07) | (0.08) |
| Total execution points | | 0.049 | | | | −0.101 | −0.028 | −0.118 |
| | | (0.13) | | | | (0.14) | (0.12) | (0.13) |
| Total compliance points | | 0.397 | | | | 0.463 | 0.393 | 0.449 |
| | | (0.29) | | | | (0.29) | (0.31) | (0.29) |
| Outlet age (days/10,000) | | | 0.099 | | | 0.04 | 0.077 | 0.062 |
| | | | (0.11) | | | (0.08) | (0.08) | (0.08) |
| No. of experienced employees | | | 0.277 | | | −0.073 | 0.063 | −0.134 |
| | | | (0.29) | | | (0.15) | (0.19) | (0.14) |
| Log(Average order size) | | | | 0.230*** | | 0.305*** | 0.423*** | 0.284*** |
| | | | | (0.07) | | (0.10) | (0.13) | (0.10) |
| Franchisee-owned | | | | | 0.128** | 0.11** | 0.152*** | 0.131** |
| | | | | | (0.05) | (0.05) | (0.05) | (0.06) |
| Log(Exchange rate) | | | | | | −0.014 | | −0.012 |
| | | | | | | (0.01) | | (0.01) |
| Log(GDP per capita in USD) | | | | | | 0.129 | | 0.152* |
| | | | | | | (0.08) | | (0.08) |
| Constant | 1.80*** | 1.78*** | 1.86*** | 1.60*** | 1.93*** | 3.42*** | 1.26*** | 3.68*** |
| | (0.14) | (0.19) | (0.16) | (0.12) | (0.13) | (1.20) | (0.11) | (1.12) |
| Observations | 138,871 | 48,367 | 48,367 | 135,008 | 48,367 | 47,914 | 47,423 | 47,423 |
| $R^2$ | 0.87 | 0.89 | 0.89 | 0.87 | 0.89 | 0.9 | 0.9 | 0.9 |
| Number of clusters | 26 | 25 | 25 | 25 | 25 | 23 | 23 | 23 |

*Notes:* Dependent variable is log labor productivity = log (items per hour of labor). Labor hours are obtained by dividing labor cost by hourly wages. Hourly wages are imputed for the countries using data for certain cities obtained from the EIU. Robust standard errors in parentheses (clustered at country level). The sample is divided into two regions (North and South) and four seasons, and all specifications include region-season fixed effects. The index of labor regulation is taken from Botero et al. (2004).

\*\*\*Significant at the 1 percent level.
\*\*Significant at the 5 percent level.
\*Significant at the 10 percent level.

ers and that could affect labor productivity and yet also be correlated with labor regulations. For example, countries with lower GDP per capita may have bad public infrastructure that impacts labor productivity.

The results in columns (6) and (8) indicate that controlling for variations in exchange rate and for differences across countries in per capita income does not significantly affect the coefficient on the labor regulation measure (or other variables of interest).[27] This in turn suggests that our more basic specifications and results capture the main effects of interest in the data.

### 5.4.3    Impact of Labor Regulations on Labor Demand

The results in table 5.3 confirm our expectation that labor regulations raise the effective cost of labor. As discussed in section 5.2.4, this effect should also be visible in the demand for labor (i.e., in equation [14]). The results from examining the labor demand specification, shown in table 5.4, are very consistent with those in table 5.3. Conditional on output, outlets in countries with more rigid labor laws hire less labor. As expected from our simple model, the magnitude of the coefficients also is similar between the two tables. Using the most conservative estimate of $\varphi$ in table 5.4 (0.40), and given the interquartile range in the labor regulation (0.31), we find that an increase in the index of labor regulations from the twenty-fifth to the seventy-fifth percentile is associated with a reduction in conditional labor demand of about 12.4 percent.

### 5.4.4    Impact of Labor Regulations on Output

As discussed in section 5.2.4, to evaluate the effect on output, in addition to the coefficient on the labor regulation index $\varphi$ in table 5.3 (or table 5.4), we need to obtain production function parameters $\alpha$ (output elasticity with respect to labor input) and $\gamma$ (output elasticity with respect to materials), as well as an estimate of the elasticity of demand ($\mu$).

The results from estimating the production function parameters following the specification in equation (16) are shown in table 5.5. As mentioned earlier, given our data limitations, we control for the amount of capital and also for the prices of materials by including store-year-month fixed effects in all specifications. The one exception is column (6), where we include store-year-season fixed effects to check the robustness of our coefficient estimates. Since store-year-month effects would be better controls for store-level capital and material prices, in what follows we focus on the results from columns (1) to (5).

We find a range of estimates for $\alpha$, from 0.123 to 0.205, depending on the set of control variables we include. We find a much narrower range of values for the $\gamma$ parameter, from 0.505 to 0.608. In other words, the $\gamma$ parameter

---

27. The lack of significance of per capita GDP and its lack of impact on other coefficients is not surprising given that the wage variable is already a close proxy for local income levels.

**Table 5.4    Labor demand—conditional on output**

| | (1) | (2) | (3) | (4) | (5) | (6) | (7) | (8) |
|---|---|---|---|---|---|---|---|---|
| Index of labor regulation | -0.693*** | -0.585*** | -0.609*** | -0.682*** | -0.415** | -0.405** | -0.413** | -0.400** |
| | (0.21) | (0.19) | (0.21) | (0.21) | (0.16) | (0.16) | (0.17) | (0.16) |
| Log(Quantity) | 0.754*** | 0.771*** | 0.765*** | 0.763*** | 0.766*** | 0.789*** | 0.777*** | 0.785*** |
| | (0.03) | (0.04) | (0.05) | (0.03) | (0.03) | (0.03) | (0.03) | (0.03) |
| Log(Wage in USD) | -0.751*** | -0.754*** | -0.756*** | -0.742*** | -0.725*** | -0.678*** | -0.707*** | -0.685*** |
| | (0.03) | (0.03) | (0.03) | (0.03) | (0.03) | (0.06) | (0.03) | (0.06) |
| Log(Price in USD) | 0.866*** | 0.878*** | 0.878*** | 0.852*** | 0.870*** | 0.814*** | 0.797*** | 0.804*** |
| | (0.04) | (0.06) | (0.06) | (0.04) | (0.03) | (0.06) | (0.06) | (0.07) |
| Log(Material cost/sales) | | | | | | | -0.035 | -0.037 |
| | | | | | | | (0.10) | (0.10) |
| Total execution points | | 0.000 | | | | 0.048 | -0.004 | 0.045 |
| | | (0.09) | | | | (0.14) | (0.11) | (0.14) |
| Total compliance points | | 0.053 | | | | -0.041 | 0.002 | -0.032 |
| | | (0.35) | | | | (0.30) | (0.32) | (0.30) |
| Outlet age (days/10,000) | | | -0.036 | | | -0.008 | -0.005 | -0.001 |
| | | | (0.09) | | | (0.04) | (0.05) | (0.05) |
| No. of experienced employees | | | 0.352* | | | 0.391** | 0.326 | 0.373** |
| | | | (0.19) | | | (0.18) | (0.19) | (0.17) |
| | | | | | | | | (continued) |

Table 5.4    (continued)

| | (1) | (2) | (3) | (4) | (5) | (6) | (7) | (8) |
|---|---|---|---|---|---|---|---|---|
| Log(Average order size) | | | | -0.039 | | -0.132 | -0.153 | -0.134 |
| | | | | (0.07) | | (0.10) | (0.10) | (0.10) |
| Franchisee-owned | | | | | -0.142*** | -0.128* | -0.137*** | -0.124** |
| | | | | | (0.05) | (0.05) | (0.05) | (0.05) |
| Log(Exchange rate) | | | | | | 0.008 | | 0.008 |
| | | | | | | (0.01) | | (0.01) |
| Log(GDP per capita in USD) | | | | | | -0.028 | | -0.021 |
| | | | | | | (0.07) | | (0.07) |
| Constant | 0.084 | -0.093 | -0.035 | 0.045 | -0.073 | -0.560 | -0.035 | -0.465 |
| | (0.26) | (0.39) | (0.42) | (0.26) | (0.27) | (1.09) | (0.25) | (1.06) |
| Observations | 138,871 | 48,367 | 48,367 | 135,008 | 48,367 | 47,914 | 47,423 | 47,423 |
| $R^2$ | 0.81 | 0.85 | 0.85 | 0.81 | 0.86 | 0.86 | 0.86 | 0.86 |
| Number of clusters | 26 | 25 | 25 | 25 | 25 | 23 | 23 | 23 |

*Notes:* Dependent variable is log labor hours. Labor hours are obtained by dividing labor cost by hourly wages. Hourly wages are imputed for the countries using data for certain cities obtained from the EIU. Robust standard errors in parentheses (clustered at country level). The sample is divided into two regions (North and South) and four seasons, and all specifications include region-season fixed effects.

***Significant at the 1 percent level.

**Significant at the 5 percent level.

*Significant at the 10 percent level.

**Table 5.5**   Production function estimates

| | (1) | (2) | (3) | (4) | (5) | (6) |
|---|---|---|---|---|---|---|
| Log(Labor hours) | 0.123** | 0.204** | 0.205** | 0.125** | 0.198** | 0.172** |
| | (0.05) | (0.08) | (0.08) | (0.05) | (0.08) | (0.07) |
| Log(Materials cost in USD) | 0.608*** | 0.563*** | 0.563*** | 0.541*** | 0.505*** | 0.535*** |
| | (0.07) | (0.10) | (0.10) | (0.07) | (0.10) | (0.10) |
| Total execution points | | -0.017 | | | 0.043 | 0.018 |
| | | (0.04) | | | (0.03) | (0.02) |
| Total compliance points | | -0.007 | | | 0.027 | -0.046 |
| | | (0.11) | | | (0.12) | (0.05) |
| Outlet age (days/10,000) | | | -2.331** | | -3.044** | -0.224 |
| | | | (1.00) | | (1.10) | (0.49) |
| No. of experienced employees | | | -0.037 | | 0.038 | -0.009 |
| | | | (0.05) | | (0.06) | (0.06) |
| Log(Average order size) | | | | 0.708*** | 0.721*** | 0.735*** |
| | | | | (0.05) | (0.08) | (0.09) |
| Log(Exchange rate) | | | | | 0.486** | 0.464*** |
| | | | | | (0.20) | (0.10) |
| Log(GDP per capita in USD) | | | | | -0.059 | 0.311* |
| | | | | | (0.04) | (0.16) |
| Constant | 1.423*** | 1.329* | 1.985*** | 1.701*** | 0.437 | 3.945 |
| | (0.47) | (0.65) | (0.65) | (0.49) | (1.49) | (2.41) |
| Fixed effects | Store-year-month | Store-year-month | Store-year-month | Store-year-month | Store-year-month | Store-year-season |
| Observations | 138,274 | 48,523 | 48,523 | 134,469 | 48,070 | 48,070 |
| $R^2$ | 0.98 | 0.98 | 0.98 | 0.99 | 0.99 | 0.98 |
| Number of clusters | 27 | 26 | 26 | 26 | 24 | 24 |

*Notes:* Dependent variable is log output. Output is measured as number of items sold per week, per Company's internal definition and records. Labor hours are obtained by dividing labor cost by hourly wages. Hourly wages are imputed for the countries using data for certain cities obtained from the EIU. Store-month fixed effects in all specifications except column (6), which, for comparison purposes, contains region-season fixed effects. Robust standard errors in parentheses (clustered at country level).

***Significant at the 1 percent level.
**Significant at the 5 percent level.
*Significant at the 10 percent level.

estimate is not very sensitive to the inclusion or not of various controls. Also, results in columns (5) and (6) are similar, indicating that estimates are not sensitive to whether we control for store level year-month or year-season effects. The $\alpha$ and $\gamma$ parameters appear to be reasonable, compared to Cobb-Douglas parameter estimates in the production function literature.[28]

Our production function specification could potentially be affected by endogeneity of input choice, an issue lucidly reviewed in Griliches and Mairesse (1997). The availability of very high frequency data allows us to control for potential unobserved shocks using very detailed outlet-period fixed effects. So long as the remaining residual is unanticipated by the firm, the inclusion of detailed fixed effects would address the endogeneity issue (Griliches and Mairesse 1997). Because we lack data on capital and investment, implementing the Olley-Pakes approach is impractical. The need for outlet-period fixed effects to control for outlet specific capital further makes implementing the Levinsohn-Petrin, or the more recently proposed Ackerberg-Caves-Frazer approach, problematic as well. Accordingly, to check the robustness of our estimates, we adopt the Blundell and Bond (2000) Generalized Method of Moments (GMM) approach that uses suitably lagged input variables (levels for differenced equations and differences for equations in levels) as instruments. The models that passed specification tests (level specifications with 2 to 3 and 2 to 4 lags of differenced dependent variables as instruments) yielded labor coefficient estimates of 0.181 and 0.179, which are within the range obtained with our other specifications. (The GMM results are available on request from the authors.)

Next we turn to estimating the elasticity of demand in table 5.6. Here, the coefficient on the price variable is the elasticity of demand ($\mu$). A key issue in demand estimation is omitted-variable bias arising from unobserved demand shifters that are correlated with both price and quantity. We address this first by eliminating store-specific effects via differencing, and then given the high-frequency of our data, we further control for potential demand shifters that could induce store-specific trends over time within months or seasons through store-year-season or store-year-month fixed effects. In columns (3) and (4), moreover, we restrict our sample to periods such that the change in price is more than 5 percent. We do this because, as noted earlier, we do not observe output price directly, but instead measure it by dividing weekly sales revenue by items sold. Since the latter measure is noisy, in the sense that output mix changes are not reflected in the "items" variable, some of the variation we see in our price data reflects changes in output mix at the store level instead of real price changes. We assume that our restricted samples in columns (3) and (4) are more likely to correctly capture actual variation in price and quantity rather than changes in output mix, and in that sense the results should yield more valid estimates of $\mu$. Finally, as

28. See, for example, Levinsohn and Petrin (2003).

**Table 5.6    Demand elasticity estimates**

|  | OLS, FE | | | | IV, FE | |
| --- | --- | --- | --- | --- | --- | --- |
|  | (1) | (2) | (3) | (4) | (5) | (6) |
| Log price (first difference) | -1.002*** | -1.011*** | -1.022*** | -1.033*** | -1.078*** | -1.080*** |
|  | (0.04) | (0.04) | (0.04) | (0.04) | (0.04) | (0.04) |
| Constant | 0.001*** | 0.001*** | 0.000*** | 0.000*** | | |
|  | (0.00) | (0.00) | (0.00) | (0.00) | | |
| Fixed effects | Store-year-season | Store-year-month | Store-year-season | Store-year-month | Store-year-month | Store-year-month |
| Observations | 176,338 | 176,338 | 56,046 | 56,046 | 169,200 | 169,200 |
| $R^2$ | 0.42 | 0.49 | 0.65 | 0.74 | 0.40 | 0.41 |
| Number of clusters | 26 | 26 | 26 | 26 | 26 | 26 |
| Shea's first stage partial $R^2$ | | | | | 0.40 | 0.41 |
| First stage $F$ statistic (joint significance of instruments) | | | | | 110.42 | 60.3 |
| Hansen's $J$ statistic | | | | | | 0.86 |
| $p$-value for Hansen's $J$ statistic | | | | | | 0.35 |

*Notes*: Dependent variable is first difference of log output. Output is measured as number of items sold per week, per Company's internal definition and records. Columns (3) and (4) restrict the sample to periods in which the magnitude of the change in price is above 5 percent. One instrument is used in column (5), namely materials cost per item for outlet $i$ (first difference). The same instrument is also used in column (6), along with mean output price (first difference) for the same country-year-week (excluding outlet $i$). Robust standard errors in parentheses (clustered at country level). FE = Fixed Effects Estimation; IV = Instrumental Variable Estimation.

***Significant at the 1 percent level.

**Significant at the 5 percent level.

*Significant at the 10 percent level.

discussed briefly in section 5.2.4, an alternative approach to identifying the demand elasticity parameter is to use an instrumental variables approach. In column (5), we use the average cost of materials per item in outlet $i$ as an instrument for price per item at a given store. Note that this instrument has the added advantage that it varies with output mix. In column (6), we add the average price per item in all other stores in the country-month cell as a second instrument. Here we look at the Hansen's J overidentification test and cannot reject the null of the validity of the instruments. Note that for both columns (5) and (6), the joint significance of the instruments in the first stage is high, as is the first-stage Shea's partial R-square, suggesting that our instruments are not weak. Finally, the results imply that material costs per item is a more important instrument than price at other outlets. This is reassuring given that, as argued previously, our material cost instrument is not so subject to the Bresnahan (1996) critique.

Our specifications yield demand elasticity estimates for the entire sample ranging from –1.00 to –1.08.[29] Contrary to the expected effect from omitted demand shifters, however, we find that using instruments here increases the magnitude of the estimated elasticity.

Given our estimates of the four key parameters, table 5.7 summarizes the range of estimates for the coefficient of labor law regulation per equation (15), and accordingly the expected effect of a change in the labor regulation index on outlet-level output. In sum, we find that an increase in labor regulation from the p25 level ( = 0.28) to p75 level ( = 0.59) leads to a net reduction in outlet level output (conditional on outlet level wages, input prices, capital and demand shifters) of 1.53 percent to 2.65 percent if we use our demand elasticity estimates, and by up to 5 to 8 percent if we assume that demand for the items is infinitely elastic. Note that our lower range of estimates is close to the 2 percent effect on consumption calibrated by Hopenhayn and Rogerson (1993) for a job security tax equivalent to one year's wages for the United States.

### 5.4.5  Robustness

Our results were obtained using different sets of controls and fixed effects, and in some cases, different instruments. We found that our results were quite robust to these differences. In this section we explore two remaining issues explicitly.

First, as discussed previously, we relied on wage data not only as a regressor in some of our regressions, but also to generate a measure of labor hours per outlet per week from our labor cost data. To verify that our results are robust

---

29. Note that our estimates of the (short-run) demand elasticity suggest that outlets are operating in the elastic portion of their demand curve, as firms with market power are expected to do. This finding, however, is different from results obtained in Chintagunta, Dubé, and Singh (2003) for supermarkets, and from those of Levitt (2006), which he obtained in the context of a bagel shop.

**Table 5.7          Calibrated effect of labor regulation on output**

|  | Low | High |
|---|---|---|
| Parameter φ | −0.383 | −0.400 |
| Parameter α | 0.123 | 0.205 |
| Parameter γ | 0.608 | 0.505 |
| Interquartile range (p75–p25) in index of labor regulation | 0.310 | 0.310 |
| *Assuming competitive output market (infinite demand elasticity)* | | |
| Parameter $\frac{1}{\mu}$ | 0.000 | 0.000 |
| Coefficient on index of labor regulation in equation (15) | −0.175 | −0.283 |
| Effect of p25 to p75 change in index of labor regulation on output | −5.28% | −8.39% |
| *Estimating demand elasticity using equation (10)* | | |
| Parameter $\frac{1}{\mu}$ | −0.426 | −0.384 |
| Coefficient on index of labor regulation in equation (15) | −0.081 | −0.146 |
| Effect of p25 to p75 change in index of labor regulation on output | −2.48% | −4.42% |
| *Using estimated demand elasticity (table 5.6)* | | |
| Parameter $\frac{1}{\mu}$ | −0.926 | −0.926 |
| Coefficient on index of labor regulation in equation (15) | −0.050 | −0.087 |
| Effect of p25 to p75 change in index of labor regulation on output | −1.53% | −2.65% |

to different measures of wages, we reproduced our analyses in tables 5.2, 5.3, and 5.4 using two alternative measures of wages. The first was obtained from Ashenfelter and Jurajda (2001), which provided data for seventeen countries in our sample. We extended this measure to the other countries in our data using GDP per capita data from the UN World Development Indicators. More precisely, we used a simple model to predict wages based on GDP per capita for the remaining countries in our sample.[30] The second measure of wages we used are minimum wages, from the International Labour Organization (ILO). For this measure to be valid for our purposes, we must assume that wages paid at the outlets are the same as the minimum wage (or equivalently, a common multiple of the minimum wage across outlets and countries). We found that the signs and magnitudes of our results were broadly robust to using these alternative wage data sources, though the statistical significance varied across some specifications. In particular, the estimates obtained with these variables were much noisier. For this reason, and because we believe that the actual wage data we obtained from our main source were more appropriate for our purposes, we chose to focus on the previous results.

30. Regressing wages on GDP per capita yields a very good fit—an R-square of about 85 percent.

Second, we examined the effect of another measure of labor market regulation—a cross-country index measuring the extent to which minimum wage laws impact the operations of business—obtained from the Heritage Foundation's *Index of Economic Freedom* database. Since we measure wages at the country level, however, using data on average labor cost or a model based on GDP, our measure of wages paid by outlets (and hence amount of labor) could be systematically downward (upward) biased in countries with relatively higher minimum wage standards given that such standards likely apply in fast food. Thus, we expect the minimum wage regulation index to be positively correlated with measurement error in wages, and hence to be positively correlated with equilibrium labor productivity. Our results were in line with these expectations—we found that countries with more severe minimum wage standards had higher labor productivity levels. Thus, strong minimum wage standards appear to have a similar qualitative impact on retail food outlets as laws constraining the hiring and firing of workers.[31]

## 5.5   Conclusion

In this study, we used weekly data from the outlets of an international retail food chain to analyze how labor productivity—defined as the number of items produced per worker-hour—varies with outlet characteristics and organizational factors such as experience levels of the workers, average order size, governance, execution, and compliance differences, and a cross-country index of the severity of labor regulations.

We found that (a) execution quality has a negative effect on labor productivity, as expected; (b) outlet age beyond the first year of operation and increases in the number of experienced employees do not have a statistically significant effect on labor productivity; and (c) larger order sizes improve labor productivity. The effect of governance form is ambiguous, and the choice of governance form appears to be correlated with unobserved country fixed effects.

Consistent with Company managers' statements about the importance of controlling labor costs in this industry, we also found that labor laws have a significant and economically important positive effect on outlet-level labor productivity in this international fast-food chain, an effect we showed is due

31. We also redid all our analyses using a measure of the inflexibility in hiring and firing workers obtained from the Global Competitiveness Report (GCR) published by the World Economic Forum (WEF) in collaboration with the Center for International Development (CID) at Harvard University and the Institute for Strategy and Competitiveness, Harvard Business School. This measure is obtained by surveying managers of multinational firms and hence is constructed differently from the Botero et al. (2004) index that we use (which is based on tabulating labor laws and regulations across countries). The GCR measure is not highly correlated with the index of labor regulation from Botero et al. (2004), and there was no statistically significant effect of labor inflexibility on outlet level output and labor demand using this measure.

to the resulting decision of outlets to reduce the amount of labor they use in outlets located in countries with more rigid laws. We found that increasing the index of labor regulations from the twenty-fifth percentile ( = 0.28) to its seventy-fifth percentile level ( = 0.59) reduces conditional labor demand by about 12.4 percent.

Our data set has unusually high frequency (weekly) data on output and costs that would not be available in most contexts. We exploit this to address some potentially restrictive limitations in the data. The key limitations include the lack of direct data on labor (hours), quantity of materials, the amount of capital, rental rates, and profits at the outlet level. We also lack information on competition/market structure at the local (outlet) level. In particular, our empirical strategy to estimate the effect of labor law rigidity on outlet-level output utilizes outlet-year-season or outlet-year-month fixed effects to condition out unobserved heterogeneity induced by missing data. With this approach, we found that an increase in labor regulation from its twenty-fifth percentile value (= 0.28) to its seventy-fifth percentile level (= 0.59) leads to a net reduction in outlet-level output (conditional on outlet level wages, input prices, capital, and demand shifters) of about 1.5 percent to 2.6 percent (using the lowest estimates of demand elasticity, which yield the most conservative estimates of the effect on output).

Consistent with these findings of a negative impact of labor market rigidities on employment and output, in a companion paper we document that these rigidities lead to hysteresis in labor costs for the outlets of this Company, and specifically reduce the responsiveness of labor costs to changes in both output and output price in economically important ways (see Lafontaine and Sivadasan 2009). Though we cannot rule out the possibility that other factors, including other forms of regulation that might be present in markets with high labor regulation, might be affecting the firm's operations, our work nevertheless suggests that policies that increase labor market rigidities lead to substitution away from labor and cause a net reduction in output levels. These effects, moreover, are documented using data from existing outlets. If labor regulations affect the profitability of the Company's operations, they also likely affect decisions on another margin, namely entry and expansion decisions. Discussion with Company officials and preliminary analyses suggest that indeed the firm has been slower to enter and has established fewer stores in countries with more rigid labor regulations. We conclude that the easing of labor market rigidities would likely yield some increase in employment and boost output in this industry.

# Appendix

### Definition of Employment Laws Index

This index taken from Botero et al. (2004).

Alternative Employment Contracts

Measures the existence and cost of alternatives to the standard employment contract, computed as the average of: (1) a dummy variable equal to one if part-time workers enjoy the mandatory benefits of full-time workers; (2) a dummy variable equal to one if terminating part-time workers is at least as costly as terminating full-time workers; (3) a dummy variable equal to one if fixed-term contracts are only allowed for fixed-term tasks; and (4) the normalized maximum duration of fixed-term contracts.

Cost of Increasing Hours Worked

Measures the cost of increasing the number of hours worked. We start by calculating the maximum number of "normal" hours of work per year in each country (excluding overtime, vacations, holidays, etc.). Normal hours range from 1,758 in Denmark to 2,418 in Kenya. Then we assume that firms need to increase the hours worked by their employees from 1,758 to 2,418 hours during one year. A firm first increases the number of hours worked until it reaches the country's maximum normal hours of work, and then uses overtime. If existing employees are not allowed to increase the hours worked to 2,418 hours in a year, perhaps because overtime is capped, we assume the firm doubles its workforce and each worker is paid 1,758 hours, doubling the wage bill of the firm. The cost of increasing hours worked is computed as the ratio of the final wage bill to the initial one.

Cost of Firing Workers

Measures the cost of firing 20 percent of the firm's workers (10 percent are fired for redundancy and 10 percent without cause). The cost of firing a worker is calculated as the sum of the notice period, severance pay, and any mandatory penalties established by law or mandatory collective agreements for a worker with three years of tenure with the firm. If dismissal is illegal, we set the cost of firing equal to the annual wage. The new wage bill incorporates the normal wage of the remaining workers and the cost of firing workers. The cost of firing workers is computed as the ratio of the new wage bill to the old one.

Dismissal Procedures

Measures worker protection granted by law or mandatory collective agreements against dismissal. It is the average of the following seven dummy variables, which equal one: (1) if the employer must notify a third party before dismissing more than one worker; (2) if the employer needs the approval of a third party prior to dismissing more than one worker; (3) if the employer must notify a third party before dismissing one redundant worker; (4) if the employer needs the approval of a third party to dismiss one redundant worker; (5) if the employer must provide relocation or retraining alternatives for redundant employees prior to dismissal; (6) if there are priority rules applying to dismissal or lay-offs; and (7) if there are priority rules applying to reemployment.

Employment Laws Index

Measures the protection of labor and employment laws as the average of: (1) alternative employment contracts; (2) cost of increasing hours worked; (3) cost of firing workers; and (4) dismissal procedures.

# References

Aghion, P., and P. Howitt. 1994. Growth and unemployment. *Review of Economic Studies* 61 (3): 477–94.

Ashenfelter, O., and Š. Jurajda. 2001. Cross-country comparisons of wage rates: The Big Mac index. Princeton University. Working Paper, October.

Berta, D. 2007. Research professor "undercover" fast-food work yields HR lessons. *Nation's Restaurant News,* March 26.

Blundell, R., and S. Bond. 2000. GMM estimation with persistent panel data: An application to production functions. *Econometric Reviews* 19 (3): 321–40.

Botero, J. C., S. Djankov, R. La Porta, F. Lopez-de-Silanes, and A. Shleifer. 2004. The regulation of labor. *The Quarterly Journal of Economics* 119 (4): 1339–82.

Bresnahan, T. 1996. Comment, Valuation of new goods under perfect and imperfect competition. In *The Economics of New Products,* ed. T. F. Bresnahan and R. J. Gordon, 207–48. Chicago: University of Chicago Press.

Card, D., and A. B. Krueger. 1997. *Myth and measurement: The new economics of the minimum wage.* Princeton, NJ: Princeton University Press.

Chintagunta, P. K., J. P. Dubé, and V. Singh. 2003. Balancing profitability and customer welfare in a supermarket chain. *Quantitative Marketing and Economics* 1 (1): 111–47.

Deere, D., K. M. Murphy, and F. Welch. 1995. Sense and nonsense on the minimum wage. *Regulation* 18 (1): 47–56.

Deery, S. J., and A. Mahony. 1994. Temporal flexibility: Management strategies and employee preferences in the retail industry. *Journal of Industrial Relations* 36:332–52.

Fabrizio, K. R., N. L. Rose, and C. D. Wolfram. 2007. Do markets reduce costs? Assessing the impact of regulatory restructuring on US electric generation efficiency. *American Economic Review* 97 (4): 1250–77.

Foster, L., J. Haltiwanger, and C. J. Krizan. 2002. The link between aggregate and micro productivity growth: Evidence from retail trade. NBER Working Paper no. 9120. Cambridge, MA: National Bureau of Economic Research, August.

Griliches, Z., and J. Mairesse. 1997. Production functions: The search for identification. In *Essays in Honour of Ragnar Frisch,* Econometric Society Monograph Series, ed. S. Strom, 169–203. Cambridge: Cambridge University Press.

Hausman, J. A. 1996. Valuation of new goods under perfect and imperfect competition. In *The Economics of New Products,* ed. T. F. Bresnahan and R. J. Gordon, 207–48. Chicago: University of Chicago Press.

Heckman, J. J., and C. Pagés. 2003. Law and employment: Lessons from Latin America and the Caribbean—An introduction. In *Law and employment: Lessons from Latin America and the Caribbean,* 1–108. Chicago: University of Chicago Press.

Hopenhayn, H., and R. Rogerson. 1993. Job turnover and policy evaluation: A general equilibrium analysis. *The Journal of Political Economy* 101 (5): 915–38.

Hueter, J., and W. Swart. 1998. An integrated labor-management system for Taco Bell. *INTERFACES* 28 (1): 75–91.

Im, K. S., M. H. Pesaran, and Y. Shin. 2003. Testing for unit roots in heterogeneous panels. *Journal of Econometrics* 115 (1): 53–74.

Krueger, A. B. 1991. Ownership, agency and wages: An examination of the fast food industry. *Quarterly Journal of Economics* 106:75–101.

Lafontaine, F., and J. Sivadasan. 2009. Do labor market rigidities have microeconomic effects? Evidence from within the firm. *American Economic Journal—Applied,* forthcoming.

Lazear, E. 1990. Job security provisions and employment. *The Quarterly Journal of Economics* 105 (3): 699–726.

Levinsohn, J., and A. Petrin. 2003. Estimating production functions using inputs to control for unobservables. *Review of Economic Studies* 70 (2): 317–42.

Levitt, S. D. 2006. An economist sells bagels: A case study in profit maximization. NBER Working Paper no. 12152. Cambridge, MA: National Bureau of Economic Research, April.

Marshall, A. 1920. *Principles of economics, 8th. edition.* London: Macmillan.

Olley, G. S., and A. Pakes. 1996. The dynamics of productivity in the telecommunications equipment industry. *Econometrica* 64 (6): 1263–97.

Shelton, J. P. 1967. Allocative efficiency vs. "X-Efficiency". Comment. *American Economic Review* 57 (5): 1252–58.

# Productivity Differences in an International Pharmaceutical Firm

Tor Eriksson and Niels Westergaard-Nielsen

## 6.1 Introduction

The differences in productivity growth between the United States and Europe since the early 1990s have been explained by differences in the speed of adopting the new information and communication technologies and in making full use of the new technologies (see, e.g., Feldstein [2003], van Ark, O'Mahoney, and Timmer [2008]). The argument is that in order to fully exploit the possibilities to enhance productivity with the help of the new information and communication technologies, implementation of the latter have to be accompanied by changes in work organizations and practices: decentralized decision making, more teamworking, and jobs with broader skills. Thus, higher rates of adoption of Information and Communication Technology (ICT) and, hence, stronger productivity growth in the United States has been facilitated by the less regulated American labor markets, which make it easier to implement the changes in work organizations that, combined with ICT, elevate productivity. Another factor reinforcing the difference between the two continents are the stronger management incentives in U.S. firms, owing to the more widespread use of stock options, bonuses, and other incentive pay programs for managers. Naturally, there are also other factors that can have contributed to the increase in productivity, such as changed policy regime and deregulation of several markets, but

Tor Eriksson is a professor of economics at the Aarhus School of Business, University of Aarhus. Niels Westergaard-Nielsen is a professor of economics and director of the Center for Corporate Performance at the Aarhus School of Business, University of Aarhus.

Acknowledgments: We are grateful to the firm giving us time and data for this study, Frederic Warzynski for helpful discussions, and participants of the NBER-Sloan project, as well as a referee for valuable comments on an earlier version of this chapter.

for an understanding of the U.S.-Europe differential, differences in labor market regulations and institutions are the prime candidates. Following, we will provide some micro-level evidence on this issue, making use of a cross-country comparison of developments of a Danish and a U.S. plant within a single firm.

It should be noted, however, that from a general U.S.-Europe comparison perspective, Denmark has rather atypical labor market institutions and regulations. In this respect Denmark is not a typical European country and as a matter of fact does not do a good job in representing the other Scandinavian countries either. A key characteristic of Danish industrial relations is the so-called "Danish model," according to which many issues related to the labor market are regulated not by legislation, but by agreements between employers and their employees. This is true not only for wages, but for regulation of working time, employment protection, notification of lay-offs, and so forth. However, the "Danish model" does not completely exclude regulation; legislation regulates holidays and work environment and safety, but these are exceptions. Another distinguishing feature of Danish labor markets is the combination of labor market flexibility and income security, oftentimes called "flexicurity." Job security legislation is very liberal by European standards: there is no experience rating in the unemployment insurance system, the replacement ratios of the unemployment benefits are among the highest in the world, and most social insurance benefits, vacation rights, and pensions are transferable across employers. Hence, costs of labor mobility are relatively low for both employers and employees.

Our analysis is also related to another recent literature on the importance of new work practices and new work organizations for corporate performance; for a review, see Ichniowski and Shaw (2003). These studies point to flattening of hierarchies, broadening and enrichment of job designs, increased functional flexibility, teamwork, and empowerment of workers as sources of improving productivity. The idea behind many of the new work practices used is often the opposite of the traditional way of thinking in economics, according to which, ever since Adam Smith's pin factory study, productivity improvements chiefly are thought of as arising from specialization.

Now, of course, nobody is claiming that the work practices and new payment systems associated with them or empowerment of workers always work to the benefit of the firm. Thus, several studies conclude that in order for changes in work organizations to have profound effects, they have to be bundled with changes in other practices (training, compensation, etc.); see Ichniowski and Shaw (2003). An important restriction on empowering workers is that profitability is likely to decline before productivity stops improving (Freeman and Lazear 1995). Introduction of performance pay is sometimes associated with great improvements of a company's performance

(Lazear 2000); other times abandoning performance pay and adoption of input-based pay leads to better performance (Freeman and Kleiner 2005). Changes in information and communication technologies has indeed made it possible to decentralize the organization of firms, but can also enable firms to reduce their worker's decision-making authority and to monitor them more closely than before (Hubbard 2000, Acemoglu et al. 2007).

The lesson from the burgeoning literature on new workplace practices, empowerment of workers, and the impact of the new information and communication technologies seems to be that sometimes adopting them is good, but other times it is not. Thus, the conjecture that differences in the rate of adoption of new work organizations to support the introduction of information and communication technologies could explain differences in productivity does not necessarily follow.

## 6.2    The Firm and the Industry

The firm we are concerned with in the current study is a large multinational firm in the pharmaceutical industry, the mother company of which is located in Denmark. For convenience, we henceforth call the firm AB. Internationally, this firm faces strong competition from three or four other producers, but so far AB has been quite successful. Thus, AB is considered as one of the big players in the market for the specific medicine it produces. The international market for the drug AB is producing is one of the fastest growing in the whole pharmaceutical industry. In Denmark AB is not only known for its successful performance during several years in a row, but is also widely considered to be among the best employers in the country because of its labor-friendly policies. Furthermore, AB is known for its corporate social responsibility and its focus on environmental issues in particular. But also equal opportunity and concerns for work-life balance are important elements of AB's profile. When AB has opened a production plant in a new country, it has to a large extent transferred the same company values to the new location. At the same time, AB has had to account for differences in the economic environment its plants are operating.

### 6.2.1    The Production Technology

All the raw material for the medicine is produced by a single AB factory located in Denmark and is delivered as a crystalline product to all the other AB plants in different parts of the world. These plants in turn make different dilutions of the crystals for different products. This formulation, as it is called, is carried out in a separate unit at each production plant. In all plants there is still another unit where the filling process takes place. Each plant has a number of filling lines, which used to be plant-specific; that is, designed and built for that factory only. Now this has changed as there are standardized filling machines that can be bought from manufacturers and can be adapted to the local circumstances.

Because of the strict regulations characterizing the pharmaceutical industry, a considerable part of the processes have to be done in an antiseptic environment. This requires special building features as well as special training by workers. In the production of the medicine in our case firm, there are two antiseptic levels, and the workers have to meet certain qualification requirements for working at both of them. It usually takes two years to take the tests that qualify the worker for the highest level of antiseptic work. The antiseptic requirements make the filling vulnerable to faulty techniques and hence, filling is much more complex and expensive than, for instance, beer bottling. Consequently, for the profitability of the production process, maintaining high quality while simultaneously reducing operation time of machines and workers are key.

### 6.2.2   Regulation

In the two plants we are examining, the products are to be marketed in the U.S. market, and as a consequence, both the production of the raw material and the filling operations are regulated by the U.S. Food and Drug Administration (FDA). The regulation implies that there are strict requirements as to data collection, procedures, and employees' awareness and knowledge about working in antiseptic environments. The FDA approval takes a long time to obtain, but is lost in a relatively short time and is, therefore, considered as one of the biggest assets in the industry; indeed, survival is conditional on it. Thus, production quality is crucial. In order to meet the FDA standards AB has to invest large resources in hiring and training the right people. Five to eight years ago, the main focus of the company's strategy was on securing and maintaining the FDA approval. Thus, the major part of managerial resources was used on improving the quality aspects of production.

Today, the personnel are the single most important input in production of the drug since machinery and equipment for the filling lines can be bought on the market. Earlier, the filling lines were customer built; hence, a firm could compete on the quality side by design and construction of superior equipment. As this is no longer the case, improving productivity on the existing lines has become a central parameter of competition. The main vehicle in these efforts at AB has been a reengineering project using the lean production approach (henceforth referred to as the LEAN project). There are many tools in this process. Basically, it is the manner technicians and the filling staff work together, the way teams are organized, what teams do when a member is absent, employee training, and the placement of working hours.

Where FDA regulations do not apply, national or EU authorities are performing similar regulations and controls. For our study it is important to notice that the FDA is applying the same standards to the two plants studied. Next, we turn to look at the two plants in more detail.

## 6.3   The Two Case Plants

The AB company has several production sites in Denmark, one plant in the United States, and a number of additional plants in a number of other countries. In our research reported following we have predominantly focused on the U.S. plant and the main Danish plant, which is the oldest plant in the firm. At a later stage it turned out to be easier to obtain comparable data from one of the other Danish plants, which also resembles the American plant in several respects. Thus, in section 6.4.2, we will also make use of some information from this other Danish plant.

The main production processes at the two plants studied are formulation and filling of the medicine. At the two plants the medicine is filled on two types of vials: a traditional one and a modern, easier-to-use vial, henceforth called P1 and P2, respectively. One thing the two plants have in common is that they both supply to the U.S. market. Consequently, also the Danish plant has to meet all the requirements of the FDA; in fact, the plant in Denmark is the only one within AB and outside the United States that is delivering the drug to the American drug market.

In order to understand how differences in productivity and efficiency over time as well as between plants arise, it is important to know what the sources of nonproduction are. Consider the operations of a filling during a week. Of the total 168 hours available for production a considerable part is not due to:

Maintenance of the equipment
Validation of equipment
Testing new products
Changeover and setup (that is, time between batch runs)
Cleaning

The proportion of the week when the equipment is not available for production can easily be as high as 20 to 30 percent. Consequently, technological and organizational changes that reduce the time the equipment is idle are crucial. Another reason for low productivity is interruptions in production, especially filling, which give rise to losses during operation. This form of downtime makes up a considerable proportion of the total time when the equipment is available for production. Finally, for total efficiency, quality of the products play a role as some part of the production during a batch will be scrapped because it does not meet the high antiseptic and other quality standards. Thus, reduction of losses due to nonavailability of equipment, losses during operation, and quality losses constitute important ways of improving productivity.

Although the two plants have many things in common, there are also some distinct differences. One is that the Danish plant has seven lines of filling stations while the U.S. plant only has four. Another difference is that the plant in the United States is operating around the clock with work organized in two twelve-hour shifts, whereas in the plant in Denmark work is organized in two eight-hour shifts, with cleaning commencing after the second shift. The reason for this is historical: the highest antiseptic level is in the middle of the old plant building and is physically located in a big room that has to be cleaned at the same time. The American plant is younger and built in such a way that there are four distinct lines that can be run and cleaned separately.

A third difference is that the Danish plant is also doing trial fillings and is, therefore, frequently producing relatively small batches. The batch size is important not only because it affects the frequency of changeovers, but also because the filling line always has to be cleaned between two batch runs. This is because regulation stipulates that one should be able to track each batch from the formulation to the final product stage. This is not without consequences for how production can be organized and affects operation times. Moreover, as the plant in Denmark is not working around the clock, a new, larger batch will not be started up if the previous batch is finished in the middle of the day. Instead, the time will be used for maintenance. We actually saw this happen when we visited the Danish plant. The consequence is that there will be downtime that cannot always be productively used. At the U.S. plant this problem seldom arises.

Because of the differences in shift systems as well as in filling technologies, one would expect that productivity is lower at the Danish plant. Hence, it is somewhat surprising that in fact the American plant used to have the lowest productivity among all AB plants, whereas the Danish plant under study ranked in the middle. This has, however, changed after the organizational changes in the U.S. plant that took place in spring 2003. In section 6.3.1, we will explain in more detail how this was accomplished.

### 6.3.1   Industrial Relations

Industrial relations differ vastly between the two locations. In the U.S. plant there are no trade unions and the general attitude of the management is rather to provide workers with benefits of one or the other type to keep the unions out. Furthermore, the factory is located in a state where union activity is considerably lower than the national average. At the Danish plant the situation is completely different. Here workers are organized in strong unions and there is a long tradition of cooperating with the local union representative who is elected by the workers to represent them toward the management. This is a model that for many decades has worked well in many Danish firms. The model rests on the mutual trust (social capital) that has been built up over the years.

The differences in industrial relations[1] are also reflected in the organi-

---

1. The differences in span of control are likely not to be only due to differences in industrial relations, but also due to the fact that the skill level of the production workers at the U.S. plant is considerably lower than that of their Danish colleagues.

zational structure of the two plants.[2] While the average span of control of managerial employees at the Danish plant varies between twenty-four and thirty during years 2003 to 2007, the corresponding figures for the U.S. plant vary between five and six. As the production technologies are basically the same, this naturally implies that the proportion of managerial employees is higher at the U.S. plant. This in turn means that the annual promotion rates from worker to managerial employee is substantially higher in the U.S. plant (2.4 to 3.5 percent) than in the Danish plant (0.3 to 0.4 percent).

As we know from the relational contracts literature (Baker, Gibbons, and Murphy 2002), when a relationship is built on reputation and trust, major changes are oftentimes difficult and costly to implement.

### 6.3.2   The Danish Plant

The Danish plant has for many years had a reputation for paying high wages to their production workers—as much as 20 percent more than in other companies employing similar workers[3]—and for offering good working conditions in general.[4] As a consequence, it should have no problems in recruiting highly productive workers. However, a considerable portion of the workers have been hired as a result of being referred to by existing workers. In several cases the incumbents (the teams) actually chose new employees, or at least had a nontrivial influence on who was recruited. As a result, many workers knew each other before they became colleagues and were sometimes even family with each other. Of course, this meant that those who were employed were not necessarily always the best hires available and, moreover and probably more importantly, because the employees had strong ties to each other, their bargaining power toward their superiors was unusually strong.

Surprisingly, until recently nothing had been done to test workers before they were employed.[5] In fact, testing was actually forbidden according to an agreement between the firm and the local trade union representatives. Many production workers have some form of postcompulsory vocational education, or are skilled workers with apprenticeship training. As a result of the low worker turnover, the workforce at the plant typically has long tenures.

Nonproduction personnel are well paid too, but at competitive rates. Also for this category of employees the turnover rate is relatively low—on average

2. See Smeets and Warzynski (2008) for a detailed analysis that also includes other AB plants than those in focus here.

3. Firm AB uses performance pay for most of its employees at the Danish plant. Production workers are the exception. Thus, all team members receive the same pay.

4. As one of the managerial employees told us, the wages are too high insofar that the demotivated workers have no incentives to leave because of the large drop in earnings they would suffer. His estimate of the proportion of demotivated and poor employees locked in by the high wages was in the 5 to 10 percent range.

5. Buying peace at the Danish plant was very important for the top management of the firm. As one manager we interviewed expressed it: "every time there is the slightest (industrial relations) problem in this plant it will be discussed at the board level."

3 percent, annually—indicating that there are also other attractive features with the workplace than the compensation.

In general, the Danish labor market is not characterized by strong job security legislation. In fact, regulation of the termination of employment relationships is one of the most liberal in Europe and is at par with the United Kingdom and Switzerland. But at AB, employment protection is extensive and is an important part of the company's personnel policies. Thus, if an employee does not fit his or her present job, he or she is offered another job within the firm and the firm pays for the training for the new job. If this does not work out either, the person can be laid off, but will typically receive help in the reallocation.

### 6.3.3   The U.S. Plant

In hiring workers the American plant has to compete with a number of other pharmaceutical plants in the nearby area, which is one of the major pharmaceutical clusters in the United States. As a result, they tend to recruit from the same pool of workers and wages are on par with those of the competing firms. However, according to the plant's HR-manager the nonwage benefits are somewhat higher at AB's U.S. plant than in the competing plants in the same region.

Average tenure for all employees is three years and the average age of all employees is 39.6. As can be seen from table 6.1, worker turnover was rather high in 1999 to 2000 but has decreased thereafter. At the time of the interview it was to land at 17 percent for the year 2004. Thus, the employee turnover rates at the U.S. plant are vastly higher than at the Danish plant. The earlier higher turnover should be seen in the perspective that the U.S. plant has only existed for twelve years. The increase in mobility in 2004 is chiefly among hourly paid workers and is probably due to some depreciation in compensation and working conditions. The reduction of employee turnover from 1999 to 2002 was due to policies specifically aiming at retaining workers.

The predecessor of the current HR-manager had tried to implement self-managed teams that were principally designed in the same way as at the Danish plant. This organizational change turned out be a failure and was quickly abandoned. A management team member summarized these events by saying: "self-managed teams are risky in regulated industries." In order to reduce employee turnover, a new layer of supervisors, corresponding to the "team leaders" at the plant in Denmark, was recruited in 2003. There was also a change in the compensation program to include a bonus scheme, which contributed to a reduction in turnover. Another factor contributing

**Table 6.1          Employee turnover at the U.S. plant (in percent)**

| 1999 | 2000 | 2001 | 2002 | 2003 | 2004 |
|------|------|------|------|------|------|
| 30.1 | 20.2 | 12.1 | 10.2 | 13.4 | 17.0 |

to problems of retaining employees was that too many hires were ramped up at the same time, which led to lower average quality of the hires and consequently higher turnover.

Retaining employees in a highly competitive labor market like the pharmaceutical cluster the AB plant is located in is, of course, a major challenge. The hourly paid workers at the U.S. plant are paid less in terms of base salary than workers at the major local competitors, but are on the other hand paid higher bonuses and are offered more generous retirement benefits. A negative feature of working at AB's American plant is that it is only closed for two days (Christmas and Thanksgiving) per year. This makes working there "like working at a hospital," something that is not popular among the employees.

One of the elements in the compensation package that used to make the plant an attractive workplace was that annual paid time out (PTO)—forty hours per year—was also paid to hourly paid workers. However, this changed as of 2005. Now, PTO cannot be used anymore for reasons of bad weather, and in order to use PTO the employee has to notify the plant twelve hours in advance, otherwise the first two hours are deducted from the attendance record in the following year. More important for retaining workers is the relatively generous 401K Retirement Savings Program: the employer matches 8 percent (gross) of the earnings and furthermore, matches 1 percent for the employee's optional 2 percent contribution. This program is more generous than that of other firms in the local labor market and explains the success in retaining workers as it is likely to attract workers who consider staying in the industry during their entire labor market careers. A problem in attracting and retaining hourly paid workers is that there are relatively few promotion possibilities[6] for them. To improve on this, the earlier requirement that supervisors should have a college degree has been relaxed.

The U.S. plant's HR-manager complained about difficulties in recruiting enough qualified workers. Training courses have been organized in collaboration with the local community college and firms in the nearby pharmaceutical cluster in order to solve this problem.

The technicians, the supervisors, and the managers are all employed "at will," which means that they can be fired or laid off without notice, but to the best of our knowledge this has rarely happened.

## 6.4    Analysis—the Main Findings

### 6.4.1    Decision to Change

After a period of several years during which AB had been mainly focusing on the quality aspect of its production, increasing productivity and lowering

---

6. There are three grade levels and a worker can advance to the highest grade in five years' time.

production costs became the new focal point. The shift in focus was launched as a reengineering project in the lean production tradition, which was started at both plants in 2003. The main emphasis was on improving the work processes in order to enhance productivity. The motivation for starting this process in the filling process was that it was widely recognized that there was lots of idle time in the filling lines. It was conceived that one reason was that the "self-managed teams" had largely been in charge of the time planning and time use, with poor utilization of time as a consequence.

With the lackluster productivity record in the U.S. plant, there is little doubt that the management in the plant felt strongly that they had to make a turnaround. As a consequence, a number of changes were initiated. First of all a new production manager was employed. He had experience of working for many years in the utilities industry and more recently at a major consultancy firm. It was frequently pointed out to us that one of his "advantages" was that he had no previous experience of the pharmacy industry. This enabled him to take a fresh view of things and to take initiatives unseen in the industry before. He employed a number of new managers, including the current human resources manager.

Early on in the process, it was realized that one important element in a strategy to improve productivity was to change production to an around-the-clock operation, as this would foster communication and continuity in operations. Earlier, the plant was using a multiple shifts system with eight- and twelve-hour shift arrangements. As from early 2003, a standardized shifts system with twelve-hour shifts only and a work schedule following a two-week repeating cycle was introduced. As a consequence of this change, the labor force had to be doubled. Because none among the existing workers wanted to work on the night shift, two completely new teams had to be recruited. Ordinary workers were mainly recruited from the other pharmaceutical firms in the area and some were also employed directly from school (a 180 hours education preparing employees for work in the pharmaceutical industry provided by a local community college). The new employees were only hired for the night shift but they were promised to be moved to the day shift according to seniority and as vacancies opened up. There was a small wage premium of one dollar per hour for working at the night shift, but otherwise employment conditions were the same as for the day shift workers. In late 2004, the night shift premium was increased to $2.50 per hour to reduce worker turnover.

Technicians were recruited among ex-military personnel. The submariners in particular proved to be good workers in the filling lines "because they were used to dealing with problems without calling for assistance." Supervisors were also recruited among ex-military officers, mainly those with a technical college education.

After a relatively short introduction and training at the community college, the two-shift, round-the-clock production started in 2003. The productivity of the night shift fairly quickly reached levels comparable to those of the day shift. Together with the day shift, the U.S. plant was now producing at 50 percent of its capacity. It is believed that approximately 80 percent capacity utilization is the maximum, because of the FDA regulations, cleaning, and so forth.

The program for enhancing productivity also included changes in the organization of work at the filling lines. The aim was to simplify batch production procedures in order to reduce the number of errors. Training of employees became more standardized and training programs were written down and hence became more formalized. In that sense one can say that the work organization got a more Taylorist flavor than before. But some other changes went in the opposite direction. Thus, jobs typically became broader; for example, maintenance workers were now also expected to do filling work. This was not popular among the workers, but was nevertheless implemented by the management. The idea was to put more emphasis on preventive maintenance and to shorten the waiting time when a technician was needed. Another unpopular change was a shortening of breaks.

In order to support these changes and the LEAN program in general, the bonus program as from 2004 gives a bonus for LEAN participation and promotes cross-functional cooperation. Performance measurement is on the level of the individual worker, but performance bonuses accrue to teams. All the changes mentioned previously—in work organization, jobs, shifts, and remuneration—were controversial, and there was a lot of resistance that, as already noted, also took the form of an increase in workforce turnover. Thus, as predicted by theory (Lazear 2000), changes in compensation and work organization were accompanied by sorting of workers.

### 6.4.2   The Change: Different Outcomes

As can be seen from figure 6.1, total production at the U.S. plant has increased steadily since production started. Employment has almost tripled since the first years. Productivity has increased, too—see figure 6.2—but not uninterruptedly. In fact, productivity increased strongly during the first years of operation, most likely as a consequence of the management gaining more experience of running the plant and other employees of carrying out their tasks more efficiently. As from 2000, there is a considerable dip and productivity recovers slowly (and is higher only four years later). The dip in productivity coincides with the years of high labor turnover and the failure of organizing work in self-managed teams. The substantial improvement after the implementation of the turnaround in 2003, which happened without an increase in the workforce, indicates that high worker turnover and team organization can be detrimental for productivity in this type of production.

We also have access to monthly data: for the U.S. plant for 2004 and 2005, and for the Danish plant for 2004 to 2006. One should remember that the

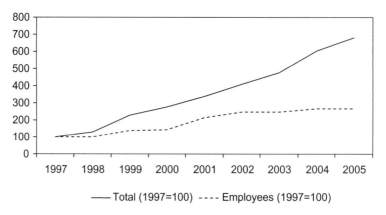

**Fig. 6.1    Development in employment and production at the U.S. plant, 1997–2005**

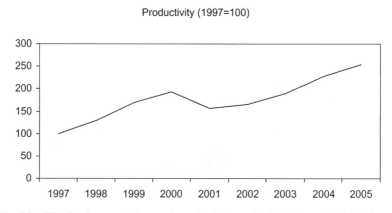

**Fig. 6.2    The development of annual productivity at the U.S. plant, 1997–2005**

new production scheme was implemented in the very first months of 2003, and so, the figures for 2003 are likely to be affected by the management and workers (many of whom at the U.S. plant were newly hired) gaining experience from the new scheme. As can be seen from figures 6.3 and 6.4, production of both products at both plants displays considerable variation across months. Although not easily discernible from the figures, there is an increase in production over time.

As was discussed in section 6.3, productivity at the plants is determined by the up-time of the equipment and the efficiency by which the equipment is operated. Somewhat surprisingly, comparable information about operating machine hours does not exist for both plants. Figure 6.5 gives the monthly availability of machines at the U.S. plant. From this it can clearly be seen

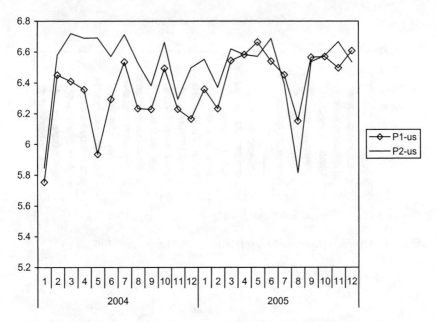

**Fig. 6.3   Total monthly production at the U.S. plant, 2004–2005**

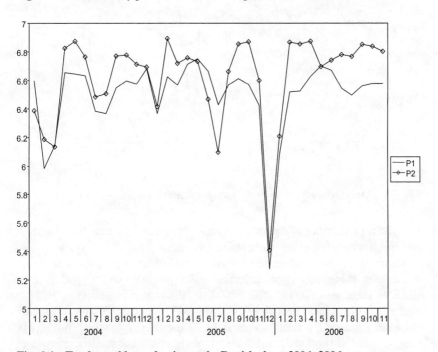

**Fig. 6.4   Total monthly production at the Danish plant, 2004–2006**

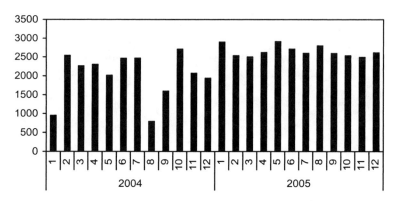

Fig. 6.5    Operating machine hours, U.S. plant, 2004 average = 100

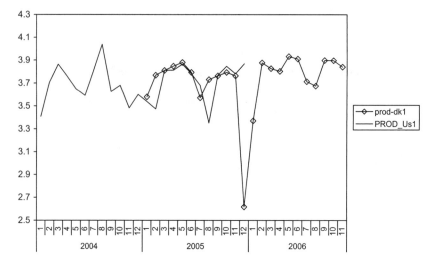

Fig. 6.6    Monthly productivity at the U.S. plant, 2004–2005

that the total number of operating hours of the machines has been increasing and has become much more stable over time.

Monthly data on labor productivity as measured by production per effective working hours are available for 2004 to 2005 (both products) for the U.S. plant and 2005 to 2006 (2004 to 2006) for production of P1 (P2) at the Danish plant. These data are displayed in figures 6.6 and 6.7, which show very similar levels of productivity. As for changes, labor productivity has been flat at the U.S. plant, whereas there is a weak positive growth at the Danish plant. Not too strong conclusions should be drawn from this as we do not have corresponding data from 2006 for the U.S. plant. With

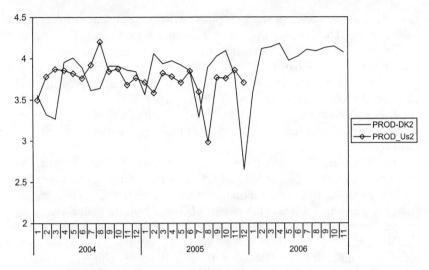

**Fig. 6.7    Monthly productivity at the Danish plant, 2004–2006**

**Table 6.2**              Reasons for downtime in the Danish and the U.S. plant in 2004
                          (in percent)

| Reason | U.S. plant | Danish plant |
|---|---|---|
| Manning problems | 8.2 | 23.5 |
| Lack of supplies | 11.8 | 29.0 |
| Technical problems | 64.6 | 14.5 |
| Other reasons | 15.4 | 31.0 |
| Total | 100 | 100 |

this caveat in mind, it seems that the major accomplishment of the U.S. plant's turnaround was an improvement in the maintenance and repair of the machinery (at least up to 2005). The group of new technicians employed and the reorganization of work have probably been key to the successful development at the U.S. plant.

Firm AB provided us with some scattered information on the handling and manning of the machines—the reasons for downtime at the U.S. and the Danish plant (see table 6.2). Unfortunately this is available for 2004 only and although we have tried our best to make the two statistics comparable, the comparison should be treated with due caution. The main reason for downtime at the Danish plant is technical problems followed by "other reasons." The HRM issues in the form of manning are considered to be substantially less important. Lack of manning is mainly due to sick absence and shortage of replacements. In the U.S. plant, "lack of supplies" is the most important cause of downtime and stops the production processes a number of times during the two month period covered by the statistics. Lack of personnel is another major factor at the U.S. plant, whereas technical problems are unimportant. This accords with our conclusions regarding the U.S. plant.

The improvements in performance of the U.S. plant in general have clearly influenced the decision of the board of the AB to expand production at the plant. Thus, during the first day of our visit at the plant our program had to be rescheduled due to the visit of the governor of the state, who made the announcement that there will be an expansion of the plant in the next few years, which will result in an increase of employment at the plant by a third by 2008.

Attempts to increase productivity were also made at the Danish plant, and as we have seen from figures 6.3 and 6.5, were met with some success. The goal here too was to increase actual production time (up-time) at each line from the previous 7.1 hours per day to 17.7 hours within a four-year time period. One central idea was to change the production into more shift work, similar to what had been done at the American plant. But it turned out to be much more difficult to get through with such dramatic changes in working hours. The management simply found itself faced with the well-paid workers regarding current working hour schedules as a right they were not going to give up willingly. As work peace was a key feature of this "model employer" firm, the strategy was to avoid conflicts as far as possible. The main thing that came out of these efforts was that workers at two filling lines are now working in a different way "as an experiment." In this experiment, new team leaders and new working schedules have been introduced.

The first change at the Danish plant was to give the team leaders more decision rights than before and conversely, to take some of the authority from the self-managed teams.[7] New employees, all with a university degree, were hired into the positions as team leaders. One of the first changes was the introduction of a new time schedule for the teams manning the two "experimental" filling lines. Instead of the usual two eight-hour shifts with Saturday and Sundays free, a nine-hour working day with two fifteen-minute breaks and one thirty-five-minute break was adopted. Furthermore, unlike at the other lines, manning of the experimental lines is secured at all times. In many ways this means that the "right to manage" has been moved back to management. The authority of the teams is reduced considerably while the power of team leaders is strengthened. There are, however, also some costs associated with this transformation. Because the teams are not responsible anymore for the covering of sick-days for the team members, absence from work becomes visible again and has to be dealt with (by team leaders).

The transformation process has been difficult because workers did not

---

7. It should be noted that also the other plants in Denmark originally had production work organized in self-managed teams, but have abandoned the multitasking philosophy in recent years. For instance, this was the case in a relatively new plant that makes use of a new filling technology, which all the managers we talked with expected to be the next generation technology that will be adopted more widely in the industry. Self-managed teams have not been adopted in the firm's plants outside Denmark (except, as mentioned previously, at the U.S. plant where it was abandoned in 2003).

want to abstain from what they considered to be well-deserved privileges. Thus, the local union representatives have not cooperated in the introduction of the new system, and occasionally actively resisted it. (Thus, there were even short strikes among production workers, which have not taken place in many years.) On the other hand, national level unions have provided some support in facilitating the changes. Help from lawyers specializing in labor relations has been instrumental in accomplishing even small changes. In addition to changes in time schedules and decision rights, another novelty is performance management meetings in order to focus on productivity improvements, development of standards for batch shifts, shortening of idle time, and increasing monitoring.

During our one-hour visit inside the plant, we observed a number of interruptions in filling, and it is obvious that the process of filling is critical for increasing up-time and improving productivity. On the technical front, a new filler line was introduced in June 2004. The filler line uses a superior technology and is twice as fast as the old ones. The new line can be considered as an implicit threat of job losses at other lines if their productivity is not improved. Still another threat facing the workers at the plant in Denmark is the company's plans to start up new production and expand current production sites abroad, including those in low-wage countries. Clearly, the likelihood of substitution of jobs from the Danish plant to other countries has created some additional pressure on the workers to accept management's plans for changes.

Next we briefly consider another Danish plant mentioned in the introduction to section 6.3. The main reason is that we were not, despite considerable efforts, able to obtain comparable data from our Danish main case plant, and therefore wanted to look at developments at this other plant as a kind of robustness check. Technologically the second Danish plant is identical to the U.S. plant; both produce products P1 and P2 and unlike the Danish main case plant, they do not do trial fillings (i.e., short batches). The month-to-month variations in production are also large at this Danish plant and production has increased in the period from 2004 to 2006.

It should be noted that some of the problems encountered in implementing the LEAN project at the main case plant were not present at this second plant. In particular, the resistance to the changes associated with the LEAN project was substantially weaker. Consequently, we would expect to observe a stronger improvement in productivity here. Unfortunately we do not have access to monthly series for the old product (P1) for 2004. But as can be seen from figure 6.8, the productivity development in 2005 and 2006 for this product shows no signs of improvement and does not lend support to our expectations of superior productivity performance here (compared to the other Danish plant). On the other hand, there is a strong increase in productivity for P2. However, this is most likely due to learning curve effects, as we are here observing production of a new product. Curiously enough, there were no signs of a similar learning effect at the U.S. plant.

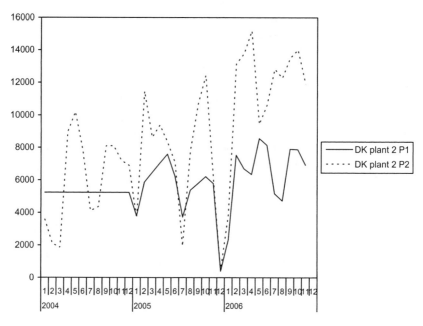

**Fig. 6.8    Monthly labor productivity at the second Danish plant**

## 6.5    Summary and Conclusions

The Danish and the American plants are more or less identical with respect to technology, product, IT, and also largely regarding overall management style. Firm AB has throughout the entire firm a labor-friendly approach to HRM with a strong emphasis on training, a relatively high level of nonwage benefits, and considerable promotion possibilities (especially for nonproduction workers) within the firm. It has strong values with respect to equal opportunities and so forth. However, there are also a number of differences between the two plants due to the different environments of operation. One difference is that workers at the Danish plant are paid higher than market wages, whereas at the American plant compensation is the competitive wage. The educational level of workers is another difference. This is considerably higher at the Danish plant. Management at the U.S. plant uses a lot of resources to keep trade unions out, while at the Danish plant resources have, at least until recently, been spent on cooperation and dealing with the local trade unions, which at times have acted quite militantly in resisting changes. The management structures are about the same down to the level of team leader. Both plants used to have self-managed teams, but these have been abandoned in the U.S. plant and in the Danish plant management is trying to disempower the teams. The main difference seems to be in how the change has been implemented at the two plants.

The management at the U.S. plant was able to take back the right to manage quite swiftly, and was also able to introduce a new shift system and to hire and train completely new teams. The changes in work organizations and in job design were met with considerable resistance. Although the U.S. plant is a nonunion workplace, it had (according to its management) many features in common with unionized workplaces because it used to be organized as "silos;" that is, in departments with very little interaction. Therefore, absence of organized labor is not necessarily the sole explanation for why the transformation of the U.S. workplace was more successful than the Danish one. The recruitment was the major difficulty in this process because of the shortage of skilled workers.

At the Danish plant the major problem seems to be to get workers—and the local trade union in particular—to accept the proposed changes in the right to manage. As a result, changes have been introduced gradually and slowly and had to be implemented as an experiment. Why does it appear to be a greater challenge to change the organizational culture at the Danish plant? The presence of quite militant local union representatives is most certainly part of the story. Another factor that presumably has had some influence is that this is a much older plant with an organizational culture, the roots of which therefore go deeper. Originally the American plant had the same company policy as the mother company, but these policies stood out as quite different from the normal U.S. practices, while the differences in Denmark were smaller.

Still another contributing factor is how the change was designed; especially the absence of positive economic incentives that would make acceptance of the changes easier is a major difference as compared the U.S. plant. On the other hand, the Danish plant was already paying considerably higher wages than their local competitors, which clearly put some restrictions on this option. Hence, the incentives were more of the threat of job loss type. To which extent these implicit threats were conceived of as credible is hard to tell; one circumstance speaking in favor of that they were not, is the fact the plant is at the headquarters of the firm and that some of the operations in the firm are only carried out at the Danish plant and, therefore, are expected to remain there.

# References

Acemoglu, D., P. Aghion, C. Lelarge, J. van Reenen, and F. Zilibotti. 2007. Technology, information and the decentralization of the firm. *Quarterly Journal of Economics* 122 (4): 1759–99.

Baker, G., R. Gibbons, and K. Murphy. 2002. Relational contracts and the theory of the firm. *Quarterly Journal of Economics* 117 (1): 39–83.

Feldstein, M. 2003. Why is productivity growing faster? *Journal of Policy Modeling* 25 (5): 445–52.

Freeman, R., and M. Kleiner. 2005. The last American shoe manufacturers: Decreasing productivity and increasing profits in the shift from piece rates to continuous flow production. *Industrial Relations* 44 (2): 307–30.

Freeman, R., and E. Lazear. 1995. An economic analysis of works councils. In *Works councils: Consultation, representation, and cooperation in industrial relations,* ed. J. Rogers and W. Streeck, 27–51. Chicago: University of Chicago Press.

Hubbard, T. 2000. The demand for monitoring technologies: The case of trucking. *Quarterly Journal of Economics* 115 (2): 533–60.

Ichniowski, C., and K. Shaw. 2003. Beyond incentive pay: Insiders' estimates of the value of complementary human resource management practices. *Journal of Economic Perspectives* 17 (1): 155–80.

Lazear, E. 2000. Performance pay and productivity. *American Economic Review* 90 (5): 1346–61.

Smeets, V., and F. Warzynski. 2008. Wages, career dynamics and organizational differences between countries in a large multinational. Unpublished Manuscript.

van Ark, B., M. O'Mahoney, and M. Timmer. 2008. The productivity gap between Europe and the United States: Trends and causes. *Journal of Economic Perspectives* 22 (1): 25–44.

# 7

# Measuring the Productivity of Software Development in a Globally Distributed Company

Alec Levenson

## 7.1 Introduction

The trend toward outsourcing outside of manufacturing, which has been emblazoned in the newspaper headlines and magazine covers in recent years, started with software development. Long before there were reports about accounting and research and development (R&D) jobs moving from the United States to developing countries such as India and China, software was the story. The predominant reason for the movement of such knowledge work jobs, including software-related, is labor costs. With large and growing numbers of highly educated and technically adept scientists and engineers in low labor cost countries, and plummeting costs for high speed telecommunications infrastructure that allows for instantaneous communication around the globe, the allure of being able to develop and produce the same product at lower costs has been too tempting for many companies to resist.

This chapter analyzes the experience of one company that has moved extensively to take advantage of lower labor costs for technical talent by spreading its software R&D work worldwide. The research issues addressed are (a) whether there are differences in performance between the company's software development sites in the United States, Western Europe, and other countries; (b) the factors leading to those differences; (c) the company's rationale for locating software development work in those locations; and (d) the future prospects for software development work at those locations.

Alec Levenson is a research scientist at the Center for Effective Organizations of the University of Southern California.

The author would like to thank Nora Osganian for excellent research assistance, and participants at the NBER Summer Institute for helpful comments. Funding for the research was provided by the Sloan Foundation.

The motivation for the research comes from the Sloan Foundation's desire to better understand productivity differences in the United States and Western Europe. After focusing on economy-wide and industry-wide differences in productivity that have left many questions unanswered, the current focus is on within-company differences: comparing two sites within the same organization that produce similar outputs on different continents, are there productivity differences and, if so, why? The company in question has sites in both the United States and France, and thus appeared to be an ideal candidate for studying such differences.

In the case of software development, the work that is done at "remote" sites (i.e., away from the headquarters of a company) often is a component of a larger product, which certainly was the case for the company that formed the basis for this case study. Thus, fully understanding site-level productivity differences requires analyzing the company's decisions to locate work remotely, not just in France but in other sites doing development work for the same set of products on which the U.S. and French teams worked. This meant expanding the scope of the study to include sites in the Czech Republic and India.

Because of interdependencies in the components produced at the remote sites, measuring productivity at the site level proved to be quite difficult. Should productivity be measured on the basis of meeting project goals for timeliness, cost, and design specifications for a particular component? Should it be measured based on the ability of the project integration teams to get the component to work seamlessly with the software? Is it possible to have site-level productivity measures when the final product is produced from components that are combined across sites? A framework for addressing these issues was derived from the organizational behavioral literature on teams and distributed work. The analysis focused on the tradeoffs between closer access to customers and markets, wage cost savings from locating the work in lower labor cost locations, and increased coordination and integration costs from distributing software development globally. Because of the challenges involved, the research used measures of self-reported effectiveness measured with respect to group-level objectives, derived from a survey administered to the group members, and from interviews conducted with both managers and employees at the sites. The combination of survey and interview data provides a detailed case study of the issues involved in distributing software R&D work across the United States, Western Europe, and less-developed countries.

## 7.1   Previous Literature

While economists are the intended audience for this chapter, the existing literature on which the research approach is based lies predominantly outside of economics. The reason for this is because economics has only fairly recently begun to model the internal working of organizations, with a primary focus on principal-agent and property rights issues that have implications for organization design, including the boundaries of the firm, the allocation of decision making, and the structuring of incentives within the firm. The decision issue in this case, however, deals primarily with aspects of job design and organization design that address what Lawrence and Lorsch (1967) call the challenges of differentiation and integration: which tasks in the R&D and production process should be differentiated as separate from each other and thus can be located in different parts of the organization both conceptually and potentially also physically, and which tasks need to be integrated (and thus are conceptually tightly linked) with potential implications for physical proximity as well.

While a detailed analysis of the economic and organizational behavioral literatures on organization design is well beyond the scope of this chapter, it is worth noting how economics does (and does not) address the issue of groups and teams within organizations. Economics typically focuses on issues of where decision making happens in organizations (e.g., centrally or decentralized). While groups are sometimes addressed, the groups that exist within economic models are collections of individuals whose actions aggregate to form a collective output with complete efficiency (Marschak and Radner 1972; Gibbons 2003). In particular, "all team theoretic models share one key feature: they ignore the interests of the team members—there is no shirking, free-riding, lying, lobbying or strategizing of any kind . . . the organization is a machine; its parts can be designed (and their interactions controlled)" (Gibbons 2003, 761). Unfortunately, anyone who has worked in groups, including academic departments, knows that these team theoretic models fall far short of describing the range of behaviors that exist and that impede efficiency in the real world.

The organizational behavioral literature, in contrast, has an entire discipline devoted to the study of groups and the difficulties in getting group members to behave in the ways the organization intends. Indeed, there are separate strands that focus, for example, on mandatory participation groups (often called teams) versus voluntary participation groups (called, among other things, social networks and learning networks). In these literatures, a group typically consists of three or more individuals, though two-person groups have been studied.[1]

For an economist, the theoretical justification for studying groups is grounded in specialization. Groups are the answer to this question: what happens when profit maximization requires individuals to rely closely on

---

1. The most common example of two-person groups from the teams literature is airline pilots. If the focus is expanded to include interactions between two individuals who are not peers, then there are entirely separate literatures on relationships that exist both as defined by the formal hierarchy of the firm (supervisor-subordinate relationships) and relationships that emerge voluntarily as a response to the organizational structure and individual's desire for outcomes such as career advancement (mentor relationships).

the output of others (interdependence) and it is not feasible to assign full accountability for the overall product in piecemeal fashion? The traditional assembly line is a good example of interdependence: the ability of any assembly line worker to complete his or her task is directly tied to the actions of the worker immediately before him or her on the assembly line. Yet the traditional assembly line is not designed to assign accountability for the overall product to each individual worker, at least not in a profit maximizing way. The problem is that defects in the overall product quality often are not detected until well after they have occurred in the production process. While an individual worker can be held accountable for performing a very narrow task, such as inserting a screw, the worker cannot be held accountable in a cost effective way if minor deviations in the quality of the work are revealed only after the complete product has been assembled.

Traditional economic models would posit the use of monitoring and monetary incentives to produce the desired outcome. Yet examples from the real world show that organizations often deal with the problem by focusing on outcomes that can be measured only at the group level, and that necessitate holding a collection of individuals jointly responsible for the group output. In the case of assembly lines, the team-based approach, which was pioneered by the Japanese auto manufacturers, has become a standard adopted in manufacturing around the world. In this approach, groups of workers are jointly responsible and held accountable for assembling parts (or all) of the car in a way that allows for internal quality control within the group that can be accurately verified by others outside the group.

Other examples include the design of new products, which requires input from individuals with various specialized skill sets (engineering, marketing, design, finance, etc.), yet that also can only be measured as successful or not when the final product is produced, and the piloting of large jet planes. In the new product case, if it fails in the marketplace, it may be due to the standalone contributions of individual team members falling short, or to the fact that the individuals did not properly work together (cross-functionally) in the design of the product. The former is a failure of contribution, which can be measured at the individual level; the latter is a failure of cooperation, which can be measured only at the group level and that might not be accurately assessed by someone external to the group. In the jet plane case, the firm does not need, neither is it optimal, to know how the pilot and copilot divide the flying tasks, so long as the plane reaches its destination safely. The problem from the firm's perspective is how to create the right set of incentives for the individuals in the group to work together to achieve the outcome. The answer, as the organizational behavioral literature has shown, often is to create a team (Hackman and Oldham 1980; Hackman 1987).

According to the organizational behavioral literature, a team is "a collection of individuals who are interdependent in their tasks, who share responsibility for outcomes, who see themselves and are seen by others as an intact social entity embedded in one or more larger social systems (for example, business unit or the corporation), and who manage their relationships across organizational boundaries" (Cohen and Bailey 1997, 241). For economists, the latter two parts of the definition require further explanation. An "intact social entity" is another way of saying that the members of the group have to interact with each other in often fluid ways in order to accomplish the shared objectives. Having to "manage their relationships across organizational boundaries" means that traditional hierarchical approaches to organizing, evaluating, and rewarding individuals may not help, and might even hinder, achieving the group's objectives; successful performance may require ignoring or redefining those approaches.

Because economists typically prefer causal models, the prospects of focusing on fluid social interactions and how relationships get managed raises the uncomfortable specter of endogeneity. As such, to the extent that economists have focused on team issues, it has been limited to looking for ways that nontraditional approaches to designing work can improve productivity, of which teams form a core element as in the auto assembly case described previously. These nontraditional approaches have been called both high performance work systems and innovative HR approaches, and typically are characterized by bundles of work practices that deviate from the norm found in the job design approach used in traditional assembly lines (e.g., Appelbaum and Batt 1994; Cappelli and Neumark 2001; Kochan et al. 1996; Ichniowski, Shaw and Prennushi 1997). While there is some debate regarding the size of effects and the impacts on profitability (Cappelli and Neumark 2001), the economic and organizational behavioral literatures typically find a positive correlation between the use of these bundles of work practices, including teams, and productivity. Beyond this, however, economics largely is silent with respect to the role that teams play in organizations.

One reason why economists have been persuaded regarding the importance of innovative human resource practices and teams is the empirical evidence that comes almost exclusively from manufacturing showing their impact on productivity. Yet the use of teams is pervasive throughout all segments of the economy, not just manufacturing (Cohen and Bailey 1997). In knowledge-based work, which is a growing portion of all jobs, teams are useful in many contexts, including R&D and customer service and sales; and, in the extreme, teams can form the basic organizing principle for an entire organization (Mohrman, Cohen, Mohrman 1995). In these settings, however, with the exception of sales, the types of productivity measures that economists prefer are difficult to impossible to come by.

The organizational behavioral literature on teams, in contrast, has spent much time wrestling with the issue of measuring productivity in settings where physical output measures are lacking. The most common approach is to survey the team members and others in the firm (supervisors, coworkers, customers, etc.) who are knowledgeable about the team's objectives and performance, asking them to rate the team on an "effectiveness" scale—meaning ability to accomplish the team's objectives. While such measures are more subjective than physical output measures, they have the advantage of enabling the rater to take into consideration organizational and external (market-based) factors that might otherwise confound effective comparison of outcomes for teams operating under different circumstances. Thus, a team that is hindered by unforeseen circumstances beyond its control could be rated more leniently than one that had smooth sailing. Similarly, any rating of effectiveness at achieving targets that can be measured using time or other counts (e.g., number of innovations) is done in relative terms, given that the rater should have a sense about how other people and teams should perform under comparable conditions. This means that effectiveness ratings can be very useful for comparing the drivers of performance across teams that have dissimilar and/or multiple objectives.

In addition to the outcome measures, the organizational behavioral literature focuses heavily on identifying the team characteristics and intermediate factors that impact productivity (Gladstein 1984; Keller 1986; Campion, Medsker, and Higgs 1993; Straus and McGrath 1994; Campion, Papper, and Medsker 1996; Guzzo and Dickson 1996; Cohen and Bailey 1997; Janz, Colquitt, and Noe 1997), factors that are not familiar to economists but that should appeal to economists' desires to better understand the black box of group dynamics. These include, but are hardly limited to, the measures used in this chapter, which are described in detail following.

In addition to the general factors that impact team effectiveness, the organizational behavioral literature recently has addressed the extent to which teams that operate in traditional settings (i.e., colocated) are different from teams that are geographically dispersed (i.e., one or more member is in a different location). A main focus of this literature is understanding how such geographically dispersed teams divide the work across locations, how they use technology to facilitate communication, and how time and distance impact team effectiveness (Hiltz, Johnson and Turoff 1986; Valacich et al. 1994; Saphiere 1996; Graetz et al. 1998; Cappel and Windsor 2000; McDonough, Kahn, and Barczak 2001; Schmidt, Montoya-Weiss, and Massey 2001; Bell and Kozlowski 2002; Driskell, Radtke, and Salas 2003; Gibson and Cohen 2003; Martins, Gilson, and Maynard 2004).

## 7.3   Research Questions and Methods

The research issues addressed in this study are as follows: are there differences in performance between the company's software development sites located in the United States, Western Europe, and other countries? If so, what drives those differences? Why would a company choose to locate software development work in such locations? And what are the prospects for future software development work in these locations?

To answer these questions a multimethod research approach was used, including interviews, site visits, and a survey at a large multinational technology company. The company, which must remain anonymous, was chosen because two of its business units have software development engineers in the United States, France, and Norway. Interviews with senior leaders of the firm revealed, however, that in order to understand software development location decisions, additional sites in the Czech Republic and India had to be included because development engineers in those locations worked in close cooperation with the engineers in the United States and France. The distribution of work across sites within the two business units is as follows:

- California (three sites)—Business Units A and B
- Texas—Unit B
- France—Unit B
- Czech Republic—Unit A
- Norway—Unit A
- India—Unit B

The research approach taken for this study is atypical of standard empirical economics studies that use existing data to test well-defined research questions. Rather, given the complexity of the work design, interdependencies across sites, and lack of existing data, the approach used elements of both "grounded theory" (Glaser and Strauss 1967; Strauss 1987; Marshall and Rossman 1995) and case study methodology (Yin 2003), which qualitative researchers in general and organizational behavior researchers in particular employ in situations such as this (Lee 1999). Lee (1999) and Yin (2003) provide excellent reviews of and frameworks for applying the methodologies involved in such research; the interested reader is encouraged to start with those sources for in-depth details. For purposes of brevity, the discussion here will focus on the steps taken for this particular study, and how they relate to the guidelines provided by those literatures.

The first step in the research process consisted of a review of the organizational behavioral literature on teams to identify the domain of factors that have been associated with team performance (see previous citations; Mohrman, Cohen, and Mohrman 1995; and Gibson and Cohen 2003). The second step consisted of interviews with the senior leadership of the company to identify business units and sites that had operations in both the United States and Western Europe and that produced similar products. The interviews also focused on the nature of the work and interdependencies across sites, and the history behind the company's rationale for locating software development work in each site. The latter was used for conclusions about strategy, motivation for starting and maintaining work at the different sites, and prospects for continued work at the sites. The former was used to narrow the domain of questions to address in the site visits, along with the types of workers (jobs/roles) to be interviewed during the site visits. The interview protocols addressed the following areas, using a semi-structured, open-ended format:

- The individual's background, role on the team, and job responsibilities
- The team's objectives and structure
- Communication, information sharing, and conflict resolution between team members at different sites and among members within a site
- The benefits and costs of distributed work
- Team leadership and processes such as goal setting, coordination, and decision making
- Trust among the team members
- Performance management, rewards, and other HR practices that impact team effectiveness
- Lessons learned on how to improve the effectiveness of distributed teams

Site visits were conducted in California, Texas, France, and the Czech Republic, and included interviews with both managers and development engineers. For the Norway and India sites, telephone interviews were conducted with the site managers. The interview results were used to define the issues to be addressed in the survey, which was subsequently sent anonymously to all development engineers and on-site managers at each site. A copy of the survey and summary statistics for each question is in appendix B.

Figure 7.1 shows the model that was used to specify the regressions. It draws heavily from the work of Mohrman, Cohen, and Mohrman (1995), Gibson and Cohen (2003), and other contributions from the organizational behavioral literature on teams. There are three main parts of the model: (a) the group-related variables that are hypothesized to impact effectiveness ("effectiveness drivers"), (b) measures of the degree of distributed work, and (c) individual attitudes and intention to leave. The latter are included to investigate the impact that having team members located apart from each other may have on employees' satisfaction and desire to remain with the organization, potentially key issues in a knowledge work environment where turnover could negatively impact productivity. The model can be summarized using the following equations, which were used to guide the statistical analysis:

(1)     Team effectiveness = $f$(effectiveness drivers, individual attitudes,

degree of distributed work)

(2)     Intention to leave = $g$(individual attitudes, degree of distributed

work)

These equations and the diagram in figure 7.1 have the implicit assumption that both team effectiveness and intention to leave the organization are caused by the other variables. There are long intellectual histories in both economics and organizational behavior that support that perspective. For example, trust is viewed by the organizational behavior literature as a

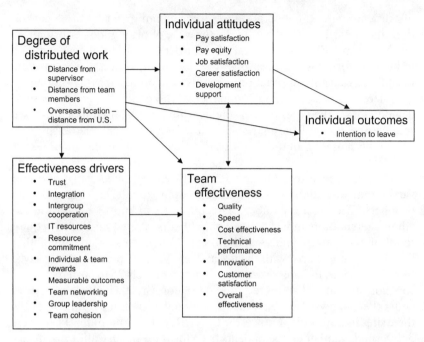

**Fig. 7.1    Distributed team effectiveness model**

key indicator that often precedes good group performance; in this view, trust among group members is a foundation upon which good performance is based (e.g., Mayer, Davis, and Schoorman 1995; Rousseau et al. 1998; Saparito, Chen, and Sapienza 2004; Mayer and Gavin 2005; Krishnan, Martin, and Noorderhaven 2006; Langfred 2007; Schoorman, Mayer, and Davis 2007). Within the economics literature, trust per se has been less of a focus than shirking in principal-agent, efficiency wage, and other models (e.g., Shapiro and Stiglitz 1984; Bulow and Summers 1986; Radner 1992; Prendergast 1999). In a group context, the absence of shirking could easily be conceptualized (and measured) as trust; viewed this way, many economic models support trust preceding performance.

In reality, however, it is reasonable to expect that there may be feedback loops from performance to employees' attitudes (the individual attitudes) and team processes, attitudes, and behaviors (the effectiveness drivers). For example, if team members are rewarded for their contributions only after the group's objectives have been achieved, their responses to the "individual and team rewards" construct questions could reflect the impact of prior performance on their most recently received compensation.[2] Similarly, the levels

---

2. At a practical level, the very high alpha (.90) for that construct in this sample indicates that the individual survey items that comprise the construct are all highly correlated. Thus, in the context of teams in this firm, rewards for individual performance appear to be very closely tied into rewards for group performance, and vice versa.

of trust, intergroup cooperation, resource commitment by the organization, and so forth, may all improve in the wake of prior good performance;[3] indeed, this is the "virtuous spiral" that Lawler (2003) describes as common in high-performing organizations. The methodological issues involved in identifying causality in situations like this have been extensively addressed elsewhere (e.g., Cappelli and Neumark 2001). For the present purpose of demonstrating the types of measurement that can be used in team-based settings, the intent of the analysis is to test for a statistical relationship, not determine causality. In that context, the previous simplified equations are sufficient.

The data needed to estimate the model were collected using an online survey that was administered in 2004 to approximately 750 to 800 team members. The precise number of recipients is unknown because it was administered anonymously—the company distributed an e-mail request to all of the team members and on-site managers using an e-mail alias list that was not shared with the researchers. Valid responses were received from 204 people, for a response rate of approximately 25 to 30 percent. The company indicated that this response rate is consistent with their experience with other surveys. The respondents predominantly came from two of the three sites in California, France, the Czech Republic, and India. There were only a small number of respondents from the third site in California, Texas, and Norway, limiting the ability to draw direct inferences about these sites. At least one response was received from fifteen unique teams, with thirteen teams providing at least five responses per team.

The survey collected three measures of geographic dispersion: (a) location of the person, (b) distance of the respondents from their immediate supervisors (measured in number of time zones), and (c) whether the respondents regularly communicated with team members elsewhere (also measured in number of time zones). The latter were used to create dummy variables indicating the furthest distance from team members with whom the person interacted regularly. This person-specific measure of geographic dispersion was preferred to a team-level aggregate for two reasons. First, the interviews revealed that some of the teams included in the survey were predominantly colocated, with only a handful (sometimes only one or two) of members located elsewhere. Second, even within the highly geographically dispersed teams with, for example, no more than half their members at one location and the rest on different continents, many team members, according to the interviews, did not regularly communicate with other team members in far flung locations; this communication was typically reserved for the project lead or other team member playing a "tutorial integrating role." Using a person-specific measure of geographic dispersion ensured that these

---

3. Or, as in the case of downsizing, poor business unit performance can reduce trust among the remaining employees (Mishra and Spreitzer 1998).

differences in personal experience with distributed work were accurately reflected in the data and analysis.

The attitudinal measures that the survey sought to measure were drawn predominantly from previous research on teams and distributed teams in the organizational behavioral literature. The standard approach when collecting attitudinal measures is to ask multiple questions designed to address the same concept, and then use factor and reliability analysis to verify that the individuals' responses to the separate questions are sufficiently correlated that they can be combined together in indexes (using simple averages of the individual questions). The results of the factor and reliability analysis produced the following measures ("constructs") for the regression analyses. The individual survey items that form each construct are detailed in appendix A. The results of the Oblimin-rotated exploratory factor analysis using Principal Axis Factoring[4] indicated that the items included in each construct factored with relatively high loadings within each construct and low cross-loadings across constructs (typically less than .3). The alphas from the reliability analyses[5] are reported in appendix A.

1. *Trust:* Trust is supposed to be a key factor that measures whether team members can work together effectively in both colocated and distributed contexts.

2. *Integration:* Measures the extent to which team members who come from different disciplinary backgrounds can resolve their different perspectives.

3. *Intergroup cooperation:* The integration construct measures within-team cooperation; this construct measures cooperation between functions and sites within the organization, which often go beyond the team members.

4. *IT support:* Measures the extent to which the team members perceive the organization provides sufficient technology support.

4. Broadly speaking, there are two types of "rotations" available to use when conducting exploratory factor analysis, both of which are designed to identify distinct groups of survey items that can be combined together based on common variance. Though there is a history of heated debate regarding the implicit assumptions underlying each approach, in practice both types of rotation yield similar results when dealing with relatively "clean" sets of survey items; that is, groups of survey items that have a high degree of within-group correlation (high within-group factor loadings) and a low degree of between-group correlation (low between-group factor loadings).

5. Calculating reliabilities (or "alphas") is a counterpart to exploratory factor analysis: any group of survey items that has high within-group correlation (factor loadings) usually has high reliability (alpha). The rule of thumb that has emerged over time with organizational behavioral research is to view constructs with alphas of .70 or higher as acceptable. It should be noted, however, that there is a direct analogy between this guideline and the guideline regarding "acceptable" *p*-values for hypothesis testing: though .05 has emerged over time as the dominant *p*-value cutoff used by most researchers, important information is conveyed by *p*-values in the .10 to .05 range, and in the .05 to .01 range. It is approximate, but reasonable, to say that the analogy to a *p*-value of .10 is an alpha of .60, while the analogy to a *p*-value of .01 is an alpha of .80 (or even .90).

5. *Resource commitment:* Similar to the previous construct, but focused broadly on any type of resource the team might need to be effective.

6. *Individual and team rewards:* Finding the right balance of individual versus group-based rewards is a key challenge when designing teams. This construct measures the extent to which the person perceives adequate alignment of rewards at both the individual and group level with both the individual's and the team's efforts and contributions.

7. *Measurable outcomes:* Having measurable outcomes should make it easier for team members to focus their efforts on actions that enhance effectiveness.

8. *Team networking:* Measures the extent to which the team works with other people in the company that can help it achieve its objectives.

9. *Group leadership:* Measures team member attitudes regarding leaders' roles in facilitating the team's work.

10. *Team cohesion:* Measures the extent of conflict among members of the team.

11. *Intention to leave:* A precursor to turnover, intention to leave has been shown to be a fairly reliable predictor in a number of settings.

12. *Pay satisfaction:* An attitudinal measure of whether the person is receiving wages at or above the reservation wage.

13. *Job satisfaction:* Though economists typically focus solely on the wage or total monetary compensation, models of job matching can be easily enhanced to include search for nonmonetary aspects in addition to monetary ones. This construct measures the overall quality of the match across all job aspects.

14. *Career satisfaction:* In addition to point-in-time issues related to a job match, the job may provide opportunities for career advancement through skill building that is needed for subsequent jobs.

15. *Development support:* On-the-job learning is a conscious activity that typically is acknowledged by economists only in the guise of formal training. However, the organizational behavioral literature has long recognized that there are active processes in which the employee can engage, including working with mentors and getting feedback on ways to improve skills on the job. This construct addresses those issues.

16. *Work-life imbalance:* Economic models of the labor market rarely address hours constraints, except in the constant of dual job holding (Paxson and Sicherman 1996). Such models focus on binding upper limits on hours worked that are created by overtime laws. Virtually ignored is the issue of binding lower limits on hours worked, something that has been noted in the nonacademic literature as a concern for professional workers (Schor 1991), and which has been addressed in the organizational behavioral literature as work-life imbalance.

For the effectiveness measures, the respondents were asked to rate their team along seven dimensions: (i) overall, (ii) quality, (iii) speed, (iv) cost,

(v) technical performance, (vi) innovation, and (vii) customer satisfaction, using a 0 to 100 scale. These measures were initially identified as candidates based on a review of the teams literature, and were subsequently verified during the interviews with the senior executives of the company. To check the accuracy of the team members' perspectives, senior level managers (who did not take the survey) familiar with the team's objectives and processes were asked to rate the teams using the same effectiveness measures. These individual ratings were combined with those of the on-site managers to produce team-level aggregate (mean) manager ratings, which were compared to team-level aggregate employee ratings. The correlation between the manager and employee means across the seven outcome measures and fifteen teams was .41, which indicates a reasonable amount of agreement. While we would have preferred even greater consistency between manager and employee ratings of team effectiveness, given the small sample size we opted for combining the employee and on-site manager data when conducting the regression analyses. Because the on-site managers were active team members, including writing software computer code side-by-side with the nonmanagers, including their observations in the analysis seems warranted.

## 7.4  Results

*Why did the company conduct software development work in these locations?*

*Interview results:* The interviews with the firm's senior leaders indicated that seeking lower labor costs for software development work was one reason for moving such work overseas, though proximity to customers and acquisitions strategies played comparable if not larger roles. The company's headquarters is in the United States and much of its U.S.-based software development work is located in traditional centers of technology industry concentration, including the Bay Area in Northern California, Massachusetts, and Texas. When the company first set up operations in Western Europe, the initial offices had software sales and customer support responsibility only. In subsequent years, some of the end-stage development work was moved to Western Europe, including offices in France and Ireland. This included localization, which means adapting the software program to meet local language and other preferences. In keeping with the principles of distributed work, these end-stage processes are self-contained in the sense that they typically can be performed by stand-alone teams in the target countries with equal or better performance than if such work were performed closer to headquarters in the United States.

The success with moving end-stage software development work to Western Europe suggested to the firm's senior leadership that it might be feasible to move some of the earlier-stage development work as well. Aside from proximity to customers, the leadership perceived labor quality that was comparable to that available in the United States, with labor costs that were below those in the United States.[6] The perceptions of labor quality came both from organic growth (hiring of additional software development engineers to work on existing products) and from acquisitions. In the case of Norway and the Czech Republic, part of the reason for the company's presence was due to acquiring companies based in those countries that had software products the U.S. company wanted to integrate into its own product offerings. In these cases, opening and maintaining "official" company operations offered the greatest chance of retaining the acquired firms' founders and employees, who were critical to the success of the integrated products. Thus, expansion in Western and Eastern Europe occurred both incrementally and in discrete jumps.

Incremental expansion only continued, however, as the company became adept at managing the work being done remotely. In each case, as a new site was established abroad, there was an initial learning curve regarding the best way to set up the technology and communications infrastructure, learn the local laws and labor regulations, and iron out the kinks of managing work that was being conducted many time zones away. Consistent with the literature on distributed teams (Gibson and Cohen 2003), the company learned the hard way the benefits of bringing team members together for face-to-face (FTF) meetings to establish trust, shared understanding, and integration among members working across large time, space, and culture differences. It also learned the need for ongoing FTF work by both team members and managers at regular intervals, which is accomplished by bringing people together at both the U.S. and abroad sites, depending on the stage of work and other considerations such as enabling the abroad team members to develop relationships with senior leaders in the United States, which both facilitates the team achieving its objectives and the individuals' ability to advance their careers within the firm.

With the perceived successful operation of software development sites in Western Europe, the company gained confidence that it could use its expertise in distributed software development to pursue even lower labor costs in India and China. In both of those cases, labor costs appear to have been more of a primary motivation than they were for the expansion into Western Europe. Interestingly, though, anecdotal evidence suggests that with the rapid expansion of outsourcing and software development work, particularly in India, labor costs have been rising much faster there in recent years than in the United States or Western Europe, eroding some, though hardly all, of the labor cost advantages. This apparently was the case with the site in Ireland, which started out with lower labor costs than the United

---

6. Historical data on labor cost differences was not available. However, the senior leaders' recollection is that the labor cost differences in the early years produced savings that were significant, though nowhere near as much as the current labor cost differences with Eastern Europe (approximately 50 percent of U.S. labor costs), India, and China (both approximately 33 percent of U.S. labor costs).

States, but by the time of the study had labor costs within 90 percent of the United States.

*Are there differences in performance between the company's software development sites located in the United States, Western Europe, and other countries?*

*Interview results:* Labor cost differences are only one factor, albeit an important one, that impacts site performance. The other main benefit that emerged from the interviews was access to talent (skills) that are comparable or even better than the average talent available in the United States. Countering these advantages are the higher nonlabor costs from doing work over large distances. Because all software components produced abroad by this company eventually have to be integrated back into the components produced in the United States, the costs of coordinating and integrating the work produced at remote sites is greater than at sites in the United States.

A key factor in the higher integration costs is lack of overlap of the standard workday. For the Western European and California sites, there is only about one hour of overlap at the end of the day in Europe and the beginning of the day in California, during which all synchronous problem solving has to take place. This creates a significant burden on the team members who play the integrating roles, which can impact their job and career satisfaction, not to mention their productivity. The story that emerged from the interviews is that these employees do whatever it takes to get the work done (including sacrificing time with family and friends to work either late at night or early in the morning), but that they are subject to potentially greater burnout and turnover than the other employees.

Despite these difficulties, employees on both sides of the Atlantic who discussed their frustrations with the small overlap in the working day also said that they managed to work through the problems, finding a manageable equilibrium for the most part. Those on teams with members in California and India, in contrast, had no such equilibrium: the time difference is twelve hours, meaning that there is absolutely no overlap in the standard workday. The interviews suggested that these employees would be susceptible to the biggest imbalances between work and nonwork demands, with the highest potential for dissatisfaction and turnover.

*Survey results:* Descriptive statistics from the survey for each country are reported in table 7.1. The results of ANOVA tests for equality of each variable mean across the four countries are reported in the final column. The first seven rows report the outcome measures; the ANOVA results indicate that there is no statistically significant difference in the team effectiveness measures across the different sites. The point estimates in some cases differ by more than a small amount (e.g., the France site mean for speed is 70.6 percent effectiveness, compared to 80.5 for the Czech Republic site), but the standard deviations are equally large. This indicates a significant amount of within-site (and within-country, in the case of the United States, which

**Table 7.1**         **Descriptive statistics**

| Mean (Standard deviation) | United States | France | Czech Republic | India | ANOVA: test difference in country means ($p$-value) |
|---|---|---|---|---|---|
| Overall effectiveness | 73.9 | 79.5 | 75.2 | 78.3 | .66 |
| | (20.3) | (10.9) | (17.6) | (8.4) | |
| Quality | 77.1 | 84.4 | 79.8 | 76.8 | .56 |
| | (18.4) | (8.5) | (12.7) | (9.1) | |
| Speed | 73.9 | 70.6 | 80.5 | 77.6 | .45 |
| | (22.5) | (12.4) | (16.4) | (11.8) | |
| Cost effectiveness | 77.9 | 81.5 | 75.9 | 87.6 | .29 |
| | (20.3) | (14.9) | (29.9) | (9.5) | |
| Technical performance | 79.5 | 84.5 | 80.8 | 80.0 | .84 |
| | (18.4) | (14.6) | (16.0) | (8.6) | |
| Innovation | 72.6 | 64.4 | 71.8 | 64.4 | .48 |
| | (24.2) | (27.4) | (18.5) | (24.6) | |
| Customer satisfaction | 73.1 | 80.7 | 62.6 | 74.3 | .14 |
| | (21.5) | (13.0) | (23.3) | (8.1) | |
| Trust | 4.1 | 4.3 | 4.1 | 4.0 | .86 |
| | (0.84) | (0.57) | (0.56) | (0.62) | |
| Integration | 4.5 | 4.4 | 4.3 | 4.1 | .00*** |
| | (0.48) | (0.46) | (0.41) | (0.53) | |
| Intergroup cooperation | 3.7 | 3.8 | 3.5 | 3.9 | .47 |
| | (0.93) | (0.67) | (0.59) | (0.61) | |
| IT support | 3.5 | 4.0 | 3.2 | 3.2 | .20 |
| | (1.09) | (0.60) | (0.92) | (0.90) | |
| Resource commitment | 2.4 | 2.9 | 2.9 | 2.9 | .05* |
| | (1.08) | (0.86) | (0.91) | (0.78) | |
| Individual and team rewards | 2.8 | 2.7 | 2.7 | 3.2 | .40 |
| | (1.00) | (1.09) | (0.95) | (0.94) | |
| Measurable outcomes | 3.7 | 4.2 | 3.7 | 3.9 | .35 |
| | (1.04) | (0.94) | (0.70) | (0.73) | |
| Team networking | 3.9 | 4.0 | 3.6 | 3.7 | .24 |
| | (0.75) | (0.69) | (0.66) | (0.56) | |
| Group leadership | 3.8 | 4.5 | 4.0 | 3.8 | .24 |
| | (1.06) | (0.96) | (0.69) | (0.96) | |
| Team cohesion | 3.3 | 3.7 | 3.7 | 3.5 | .02** |
| | (0.70) | (0.62) | (0.50) | (0.38) | |
| Intention to leave | 2.8 | 2.7 | 2.5 | 3.0 | .66 |
| | (1.20) | (1.23) | (1.07) | (0.90) | |
| Pay satisfaction | 3.1 | 2.7 | 2.9 | 2.0 | .00*** |
| | (1.25) | (1.08) | (1.30) | (0.84) | |
| Job satisfaction | 3.7 | 4.1 | 3.9 | 3.4 | .30 |
| | (1.03) | (0.66) | (0.77) | (0.80) | |
| Career satisfaction | 3.1 | 3.1 | 3.2 | 3.2 | .97 |
| | (1.22) | (1.07) | (0.87) | (0.75) | |
| Development support | 2.5 | 2.5 | 2.6 | 2.9 | .44 |
| | (1.07) | (1.26) | (1.01) | (1.04) | |
| Work-life imbalance | 3.3 | 3.2 | 3.3 | 3.4 | .98 |
| | (1.17) | (0.88) | (0.81) | (0.96) | |
| Supervisor located in same time zone, but different location | 0.15 | 0 | 0 | 0 | .02** |
| | (0.36) | (0) | (0) | (0) | |

**Table 7.1**          (continued)

| Mean (Standard deviation) | United States | France | Czech Republic | India | ANOVA: test difference in country means ($p$-value) |
|---|---|---|---|---|---|
| Supervisor located 1–3 or 4–7 time zones away | 0.09 (0.29) | 0.10 (0.32) | 0 (0) | 0 (0) | .19 |
| Supervisor located 8–9 or 10–12 time zones away | 0.01 (0.12) | 0 (0) | 0.31 (0.47) | 0.41 (0.50) | .00*** |
| Distance of communication with team members: 4–7 time zones away | 0.04 (0.20) | 0 (0) | 0 (0) | 0 (0) | .48 |
| Distance of communication with team members: 8 or more time zones away | 0.70 (0.46) | 0.80 (0.42) | 0.77 (0.43) | 0.82 (0.39) | .60 |
| Small change in product life cycle | 0.13 (0.34) | 0.11 (0.33) | 0 (0) | 0.32 (0.48) | .01** |

*Notes:* Number observations: United States (144), France (10), Czech Republic (26), India (22). Observations from Norway (2) not included in calculations for this table.

***Significant at the 1 percent level.

**Significant at the 5 percent level.

*Significant at the 10 percent level.

has multiple sites) differences in effectiveness ratings. Separate anovas, not reported in the table, testing differences across the three main sites in the United States found a similar pattern of no statistically significant differences in any of the effectiveness ratings ($p$-value $>$ .10 in each case).

The results from analyzing the drivers of team effectiveness are presented in table 7.2. In each case the ten effectiveness drivers are regressed on the effectiveness measure in the first stage, and then the indicators for degree of collaboration across time zones, distance from supervisor, and location are entered in the second stage.

The results in table 7.2 indicate that the relationships between the effectiveness drivers and (perceived) outcome measures are consistent with the existing literature on teams. In particular, trust, intergroup cooperation, IT support, resource commitment, team networking, and team cohesion all are statistically significantly positively related to at least one of the effectiveness measures. All of the coefficients are either statistically significantly positive or not significantly different from zero; none are negative and statistically significant.

The indicators for geographic dispersion and location do not provide much support for the notion that having the software development work located in far-flung locations negatively impacts team effectiveness. Having to regularly communicate with team members either four to seven or eight or more time zones away does not appear to impact effectiveness, relative to those who do not regularly communicate with team members

**Table 7.2**  Team effectiveness regressions

| | Overall effectiveness | | Quality | | Speed | | Cost effectiveness | | Technical performance | | Innovation | | Customer satisfaction | |
|---|---|---|---|---|---|---|---|---|---|---|---|---|---|---|
| Trust | 4.34* | 5.12** | 3.69* | 4.18* | 2.73 | 4.24 | 2.87 | 4.02 | 4.80** | 5.14** | -.35 | 1.57 | 2.79 | 4.22 |
| | (2.28) | (2.39) | (2.12) | (2.21) | (2.73) | (2.66) | (3.29) | (3.44) | (2.32) | (2.43) | (3.09) | (3.19) | (2.95) | (3.07) |
| Integration | -2.88 | -3.15 | .53 | .13 | -3.86 | -5.36 | -4.53 | -4.12 | -.00 | -.94 | 5.66 | 3.82 | 1.81 | -.11 |
| | (3.04) | (3.25) | (2.93) | (3.09) | (3.70) | (3.69) | (3.95) | (4.20) | (3.14) | (3.33) | (4.15) | (4.34) | (4.02) | (4.31) |
| Intergroup cooperation | 2.10 | 3.09* | 1.08 | 2.21 | -1.68 | -1.37 | -1.02 | -.14 | .82 | 1.48 | 6.23*** | 6.35** | 5.47** | 5.89** |
| | (1.69) | (1.82) | (1.62) | (1.71) | (2.05) | (2.04) | (2.15) | (2.25) | (1.75) | (1.87) | (2.34) | (2.46) | (2.15) | (2.27) |
| IT support | .67 | .28 | .91 | .45 | 1.40 | .31 | 3.74** | 3.60* | 2.44* | 1.84 | .22 | -1.34 | 1.42 | .24 |
| | (1.42) | (1.51) | (1.33) | (1.42) | (1.69) | (1.69) | (1.79) | (1.93) | (1.40) | (1.50) | (1.86) | (1.96) | (1.78) | (1.88) |
| Resource commitment | 4.44*** | 3.55** | 2.84** | 2.08 | 5.14*** | 4.08** | .65 | -.48 | 1.95 | .88 | 2.18 | 1.41 | 3.45* | 4.63** |
| | (1.48) | (1.65) | (1.41) | (1.60) | (1.76) | (1.84) | (2.00) | (2.16) | (1.49) | (1.65) | (2.02) | (2.21) | (1.85) | (2.09) |
| Individual and team rewards | 1.81 | 1.53 | 2.33 | 2.43 | .38 | 1.00 | 3.42 | 2.81 | 1.48 | 2.05 | 1.95 | 2.60 | .88 | 1.16 |
| | (1.66) | (1.73) | (1.58) | (1.64) | (1.98) | (1.94) | (2.07) | (2.17) | (1.69) | (1.78) | (2.32) | (2.36) | (2.08) | (2.17) |
| Measurable outcomes | 1.25 | 1.64 | 1.20 | 1.07 | -.34 | -.47 | 3.35 | 3.98 | 1.62 | 1.30 | .84 | 1.45 | -.99 | -.99 |
| | (1.83) | (1.94) | (1.72) | (1.81) | (2.21) | (2.17) | (2.34) | (2.51) | (1.86) | (1.98) | (2.53) | (2.62) | (2.36) | (2.45) |
| Team networking | 3.96* | 3.43 | 2.80 | 2.57 | 6.89** | 6.51** | 1.82 | 1.47 | 1.22 | 1.05 | 2.07 | .50 | 5.13* | 3.81 |
| | (2.29) | (2.39) | (2.14) | (2.22) | (2.69) | (2.61) | (2.88) | (3.04) | (2.31) | (2.43) | (3.12) | (3.15) | (3.03) | (3.12) |
| Group leadership | .26 | .12 | -2.40 | -2.56 | 2.19 | 2.29 | .19 | .21 | -.03 | .12 | .21 | .86 | .95 | 1.62 |
| | (1.67) | (1.74) | (1.54) | (1.58) | (2.08) | (2.00) | (2.20) | (2.29) | (1.76) | (1.82) | (2.30) | (2.32) | (2.21) | (2.29) |
| Team cohesion | 3.06 | 1.95 | 2.96 | 1.10 | 4.24 | 4.21 | 2.71 | 1.40 | 2.05 | 1.28 | 9.04** | 9.24** | -.90 | -2.18 |
| | (2.77) | (2.94) | (2.60) | (2.79) | (3.27) | (3.29) | (3.91) | (4.11) | (2.98) | (3.15) | (3.78) | (3.94) | (3.45) | (3.63) |
| Supervisor located in same time zone, but different location | | -8.47* | | -8.04* | | -15.0*** | | -7.61 | | -7.97 | | -18.4*** | | -10.18* |
| | | (4.80) | | (4.77) | | (5.61) | | (6.06) | | (4.96) | | (6.78) | | (6.02) |
| Supervisor located 1–3 or 4–7 time zones away | | .11 | | -5.97 | | -19.6*** | | 4.36 | | .10 | | -1.86 | | -4.15 |
| | | (6.61) | | (6.35) | | (7.48) | | (7.96) | | (6.59) | | (8.27) | | (7.89) |

| | | | | | | | | | | | | | |
|---|---|---|---|---|---|---|---|---|---|---|---|---|---|
| Supervisor located 8–9 or 10–12 time zones away | .54 (6.27) | | -2.67 (5.68) | | -5.23 (6.73) | | -.90 (7.99) | | -8.81 (6.35) | | -4.27 (7.72) | | 9.19 (7.79) |
| Distance of communication with team members: 4–7 time zones away | -.75 (10.03) | | .50 (9.68) | | 6.09 (11.42) | | 1.68 (11.83) | | -5.16 (9.98) | | -10.32 (12.67) | | -11.13 (11.95) |
| Distance of communication with team members: 8 or more time zones away | -3.68 (3.76) | | -2.53 (3.65) | | -5.37 (4.44) | | -3.98 (4.81) | | -4.05 (3.81) | | -1.69 (5.18) | | -1.75 (5.04) |
| West Europe (France or Norway) | -1.01 (6.30) | | 5.66 (6.46) | | -14.64* (7.60) | | -1.94 (7.59) | | -1.74 (6.28) | | -16.26* (8.43) | | -6.27 (9.44) |
| East Europe (Czech Republic) | 4.97 (5.40) | | 6.88 (4.98) | | 2.66 (5.85) | | 11.19* (6.60) | | 6.37 (5.38) | | .50 (6.86) | | -11.42* (6.79) |
| India | 3.00 (6.09) | | -.51 (5.75) | | 1.34 (6.85) | | 8.58 (7.33) | | 2.79 (6.15) | | -4.62 (7.78) | | -10.57 (8.43) |
| Small change in product life cycle | 2.54 (4.56) | | 3.45 (4.24) | | -11.27** (4.98) | | 3.31 (5.48) | | 1.02 (4.55) | | -3.33 (6.28) | | 8.91 (5.56) |
| Constant | 12.53 (15.53) | 18.97 (17.88) | 32.50* (16.64) | 23.25 (14.61) | 35.23* (20.51) | 20.50 (18.90) | 37.97** (18.95) | 38.00* (21.55) | 33.79* (18.06) | 22.24 (15.96) | -28.76 (21.03) | -15.54 (24.10) | 12.53 (23.78) |
| Adjusted $R^2$ | .253 | .234 | .172 | .162 | .241 | .147 | .165 | .163 | .173 | .157 | .225 | .250 | .170 |
| N | 140 | 140 | 147 | 147 | 142 | 142 | 109 | 109 | 135 | 135 | 126 | 126 | 120 |

*Note:* Standard errors are in parentheses.

***Significant at the 1 percent level.

**Significant at the 5 percent level.

*Significant at the 10 percent level.

so far away. Similarly, having a supervisor eight or more time zones away also does not differentiate effectiveness, relative to those who are colocated with their supervisors. Interestingly, those whose immediate supervisor is at a different location but in the same time zone (typically those at the California sites) report lower overall effectiveness, quality, speed, innovation, and customer satisfaction. As the results in table 7.3 show, this most likely is because these same people report worse IT support and resource commitment (in the regression context that controls for the other included variables), whereas team members in both the Czech Republic and in India report higher resource commitment than the software engineers located at the company's headquarters.[7] With the company focusing so heavily on trying to make things work for team members located on different continents, the results in tables 7.1 and 7.2 suggest that they may be missing an opportunity to improve performance by mending the fences that are much closer to home (i.e., those who are in the same time zone but not located at headquarters).

Very few of the location indicators are significant in table 7.2. Team members in France[8] report lower speed and innovation, which is consistent with the interviews. Some of the U.S.-based leadership expressed high degrees of satisfaction with the French sites' quality, but low satisfaction with their responsiveness. The Czech Republic site, in contrast, was viewed as having software engineers who were less complacent, more "hungry" to succeed regardless of the personal sacrifices that might be needed. Perhaps in part because of this, the respondents at the Czech Republic site reported higher cost effectiveness. They also, however, reported lower customer satisfaction; their drive to succeed within the cost parameters thus may produce unintended costs downstream with lower sales. This story is consistent with one senior leadership interviewee who expressed frustration at what appeared to be an ongoing need to have senior technical experts in the United States intervene in the Czech Republic team's work to fix problems that occurred with higher frequency than other sites such as France.

At this point it is worth noting the impact of both IT and HR practices in impacting effectiveness for these teams. For IT support, at first glance it may seem surprising that variation in this is related to effectiveness only on the cost and technical performance fronts. Yet this company, like most, strives for consistency in practices across sites within the same business unit; if a certain level of technology support is provided in the United States because

7. Note, however, that this effect only exists for those who are located in India and the Czech Republic who do not have to communicate on a regular basis with team members in the United States—the coefficients on communicating with team members both four to seven and eight or more time zones away are negative and significant.

8. The indicator in the tables is for team members in either France or Norway; however, the vast majority of these are in France so those respondents undoubtedly dominate the estimated relationships.

**Table 7.3    Effectiveness drivers regressions**

| | Trust | Integration | Intergroup cooperation | IT support | Resource commitment | Individual and team rewards | Measurable outcomes | Team networking | Group leadership | Team cohesion |
|---|---|---|---|---|---|---|---|---|---|---|
| Supervisor located in same time zone, but different location | .37** (.18) | –.04 (.11) | .24 (.23) | –.93*** (.24) | –.68*** (.23) | –.04 (.24) | –.05 (.23) | .02 (.17) | –.03 (.24) | –.02 (.16) |
| Supervisor located 1–3 or 4–7 time zones away | .07 (.24) | .13 (.15) | .11 (.30) | –.34 (.31) | .47 (.30) | –.12 (.32) | –.33 (.30) | .23 (.23) | .11 (.31) | –.04 (.20) |
| Supervisor located 8–9 or 10–12 time zones away | –.29 (.24) | .03 (.14) | –.16 (.28) | –.16 (.31) | –.60** (.30) | .38 (.30) | –.42 (.29) | .26 (.22) | –.09 (.30) | –.05 (.20) |
| Distance of communication with team members: 4–7 time zones away | .35 (.36) | –.00 (.23) | .59 (.45) | –.19 (.47) | –.88* (.45) | .56 (.52) | –.30 (.46) | –.24 (.34) | .82* (.47) | .15 (.31) |
| Distance of communication with team members: 8 or more time zones away | .20 (.14) | –.07 (.09) | .14 (.17) | –.32* (.18) | –.52*** (.17) | .09 (.19) | –.07 (.17) | –.02 (.13) | .15 (.18) | .05 (.12) |
| West Europe (France or Norway) | .30 (.24) | –.09 (.15) | .20 (.29) | .09 (.31) | .40 (.29) | –.06 (.30) | .39 (.29) | –.10 (.22) | .70** (.30) | .44** (.21) |
| East Europe (Czech Republic) | .14 (.19) | –.23* (.12) | –.17 (.23) | –.38 (.25) | .59** (.24) | –.21 (.25) | .10 (.24) | –.37** (.18) | .22 (.24) | .40** (.16) |
| India | .14 (.22) | –.40*** (.13) | .28 (.25) | –.36 (.29) | .72** (.29) | .20 (.29) | .40 (.27) | –.28 (.20) | .10 (.26) | .17 (.18) |
| Constant | 3.86*** (.13) | 4.59*** (.08) | 3.51*** (.17) | 3.92*** (.18) | 2.91*** (.17) | 2.70*** (.18) | 3.77*** (.17) | 3.92*** (.12) | 3.67*** (.18) | 3.27*** (.11) |
| Adjusted $R^2$ | .044 | .047 | –.008 | .062 | .133 | –.010 | –.001 | –.007 | .009 | .017 |
| N | 189 | 193 | 194 | 189 | 189 | 186 | 191 | 193 | 194 | 191 |

*Note*: Standard errors are in parentheses.

***Significant at the 1 percent level.

**Significant at the 5 percent level.

*Significant at the 10 percent level.

that is what it takes to get the job done, the expectation of the company's leaders is that the same level of support will be provided at all sites. Thus, within-company analyses such as these often suffer from a range restriction problem: most employees should experience much lower variation in practices within a company than if we were to compare employees across companies.

For HR practices the range restriction issue may be less stark, but still important. Range restriction is an issue because the desire to promote common ways of communicating and rewarding performance lead to consistency of HR practices across sites. The need to do some adaptation to local preferences, however, has the potential to introduce more variation in HR practices than might be expected for IT support. For the French site, in particular, the national restrictions on firing have significantly impacted how the company uses the site. Initially there was no expectation that a downturn in business would lead to headcount adjustment problems in France. Yet this is precisely what happened a few years prior to the study, when the company tried to remove costs at many of its sites around the globe in response to a business downturn. The difficulties in laying off software engineers in France led the company to manage the site differently, focusing on keeping headcount the same or even falling through natural attrition. Yet despite this emphasis, the French site continues to be given highly technical components of the work in no small part because of the stability of the employees and their high level of expertise. Thus, both IT and HR practices appear to matter, but in ways that do not necessarily impact measured productivity at a single point in time, as these data do.

Moving to the attitudinal data, table 7.4 reports the correlation of overall team effectiveness with the intention to leave, satisfaction, perceived development support, and work-life imbalance variables. As expected, and consistent with previous research, there is a reasonably large positive correlation with satisfaction and development support, and negative correlation with intention to leave. As Lawler (2003) has argued, these results are consistent with mutually reinforcing HR practices and employee actions: a supportive environment creates the conditions for effective performance, which makes it easier for the firm to spend money and take the time to do things to keep its employees happy, which improves retention, which helps performance, and so forth. This perspective is further supported by the results in table 7.5, which show a strong negative correlation between intentions to leave the firm and satisfaction, development support, and work-life balance (column [1]), regardless of how geographically dispersed the team members are (column [2]).

Finally, the results in table 7.6 indicate that geographic dispersion of team members is not related to satisfaction, development support, or work-life imbalance. The one difference that stands out is for team members located

**Table 7.4**        **Correlations of overall team effectiveness and individual attitudes**

| Pearson (N) | Overall team effectiveness | Intention to leave | Pay satisfaction | Job satisfaction | Career satisfaction | Development support |
|---|---|---|---|---|---|---|
| Intention to leave | −.22*** (160) | | | | | |
| Pay satisfaction | .09 (160) | −.33*** (190) | | | | |
| Job satisfaction | .37*** (161) | −.67*** (192) | .33*** (190) | | | |
| Career satisfaction | .22*** (161) | −.48*** (190) | .37*** (191) | .49*** (191) | | |
| Development support | .31*** (160) | −.45*** (191) | .32*** (189) | .44*** (192) | .49*** (190) | |
| Work-life imbalance | .09 (160) | .19*** (191) | −.11 (189) | −.03 (192) | −.05 (190) | −.05 (191) |

***Significant at the 1 percent level.
**Significant at the 5 percent level.
*Significant at the 10 percent level.

in India, who reported lower pay satisfaction and job satisfaction. This is consistent with anecdotes that wages are rising relatively fast in India. The results indicate that the firm's HR policies regarding pay may not be responding quickly enough to changes in the external environment.

*What are the prospects for future software development work in these locations?* The survey results indicated that, on average, there are not many differences in reported effectiveness for work that is done at the different sites. This, in large part, likely is due to the interdependent nature of work that takes place not just at those sites, but in the United States as well. Given the company's strong preference for making overall product decisions and doing the final integration work in the United States, it is hard to foresee a scenario in which such integration costs could be lowered without a major shift in the way overall product development decisions are made. Thus, to the extent that the company continues to do this kind of software development work in general, the data and interviews suggest that there is no reason to expect a pullback from working in these regions.

That said, the desire to seek lower labor costs suggests that future growth in software engineering headcount is liable to take place in the Czech Republic, India, and China. On the one hand, at the time of the study the Czech Republic's labor costs were about one half those in the United States, whereas the labor costs in India and China were lower, at about one third those in the United States. Countering the lower labor costs of India and China, however, the Czech Republic is closer to the United States, which makes synchronous communication much easier to do, even if it is concentrated at

Table 7.5    Intention to leave regressions

| | | |
|---|---|---|
| Pay satisfaction | −.05 | −.03 |
| | (.05) | (.06) |
| Job satisfaction | −.61*** | −.62*** |
| | (.07) | (.08) |
| Career satisfaction | −.16** | −.13* |
| | (.07) | (.07) |
| Development support | −.17** | −.19*** |
| | (.07) | (.07) |
| Work-life imbalance | .16*** | .13** |
| | (.05) | (.06) |
| Supervisor located in same time zone, but different location | | −.32 |
| | | (.20) |
| Supervisor located 1–3 or 4–7 time zones away | | .12 |
| | | (.26) |
| Supervisor located 8–9 or 10–12 time zones away | | −.13 |
| | | (.25) |
| Distance of communication with team members: 4–7 time zones away | | −1.06*** |
| | | (.37) |
| Distance of communication with team members: 8 or more time zones away | | .09 |
| | | (.16) |
| West Europe (France or Norway) | | −.09 |
| | | (.26) |
| East Europe (Czech Republic) | | −.06 |
| | | (.21) |
| India | | −.02 |
| | | (.27) |
| Organization tenure | | −.09 |
| | | (.08) |
| Years of experience working on distributed teams | | .02 |
| | | (.02) |
| Constant | 5.54*** | 5.76*** |
| | (.32) | (.42) |
| Adjusted $R^2$ | .526 | .540 |
| $N$ | 179 | 179 |

*Note:* Standard errors are in parentheses.
***Significant at the 1 percent level.
**Significant at the 5 percent level.
*Significant at the 10 percent level.

the end of the day in Europe and beginning of the day in the United States. This suggests that the type of work that is done in the Czech Republic may have greater complexity than the work that is done in India or China—unless the company moves toward allowing complete pieces of software to be developed in those sites that are the furthest removed from headquarters. In France, the prospects appear to be continued work, but no expansion in the number of software engineers, and thus a low or diminished profile with respect to the company's overall software development efforts.

**Table 7.6**                    **Individual attitudes regressions**

| | Pay satisfaction | Job satisfaction | Career satisfaction | Development support | Work-life imbalance |
|---|---|---|---|---|---|
| Supervisor located in same time zone, but different location | .56** | −.27 | .36 | .05 | −.07 |
| | (.28) | (.22) | (.27) | (.25) | (.26) |
| Supervisor located 1–3 or 4–7 time zones away | .46 | .60** | .02 | −.53 | −.19 |
| | (.37) | (.29) | (.35) | (.33) | (.34) |
| Supervisor located 8–9 or 10–12 time zones away | .28 | .33 | .29 | .37 | .52 |
| | (.34) | (.27) | (.33) | (.31) | (.32) |
| Distance of communication with team members: 4–7 time zones away | −.25 | .27 | .47 | −.11 | −.34 |
| | (.57) | (.44) | (.53) | (.50) | (.52) |
| Distance of communication with team members: 8 or more time zones away | −.30 | .19 | −.11 | −.30 | .01 |
| | (.21) | (.17) | (.20) | (.19) | (.19) |
| West Europe (France or Norway) | −.40 | .30 | .11 | .12 | .06 |
| | (.37) | (.29) | (.34) | (.32) | (.33) |
| East Europe (Czech Republic) | −.19 | .04 | .09 | −.01 | −.19 |
| | (.29) | (.23) | (.27) | (.25) | (.26) |
| India | −1.06*** | −.43* | .07 | .28 | −.15 |
| | (.31) | (.26) | (.30) | (.30) | (.30) |
| Constant | 3.20*** | 3.58*** | 3.10*** | 2.71*** | 3.31*** |
| | (.21) | (.16) | (.19) | (.18) | (.18) |
| Adjusted $R^2$ | .082 | .036 | −.020 | .005 | −.019 |
| N | 193 | 193 | 193 | 192 | 192 |

*Note:* Standard errors are in parentheses.
***Significant at the 1 percent level.
**Significant at the 5 percent level.
*Significant at the 10 percent level.

## 7.5   Conclusions

This study has found evidence in favor of the following conclusions:

1. International differences in productivity do not appear to be a big factor in explaining cross-sectional patterns of software development work location.

2. To the extent that geographic dispersion matters, spreading work out to the point where there is no overlap in the standard workday may put limits on the productivity of individual team members. However, the teams as a whole appear capable of dealing with such pressures without significantly impacting the teams' overall effectiveness.

3. Even though the data did not reveal average productivity differences across sites, this says nothing about marginal productivity differences. Given a set of strengths and weaknesses associated with conducting software development work in various sites, one would expect the firm to distribute the work in such a way that average productivity (and contributions to profit-

ability) are equalized. Without a natural experiment that varies the type of work in a controlled way, it may be very difficult to detect marginal productivity differences.

# Appendix A
## *Glossary, Scales, and Reliabilities*

Trust, Integration, and Cooperation

Trust (alpha = .90)
E2.   We can count on the people in our team to perform their jobs proficiently.
E10.  Team members trust each other to contribute worthwhile ideas.
E12.  We can trust that the members of our team have the knowledge and skills to complete their work.
E3.   Team members always do what they say they will do.
E5.   The people on our team are reliable in their work.
E7.   Team members believe that others on our team will follow through on their commitments.

Integration (alpha = .58)
I2.   I try to investigate an issue with others to find a solution acceptable to all.
I3.   I try to integrate my ideas with those of others to come up with a decision jointly.

Intergroup Cooperation (alpha = .70)
D12.  There is good cooperation between functions.
D15.  There is good cooperation between sites.

IT Support and Resources

IT Support (alpha = 71)
G3.   We receive prompt technical assistance when our computer systems are not working.
G9.   Company provides adequate information technology support.

Resource Commitment (alpha = .75)
G1.   Company has committed the resources required to do this work.
G5r.  *We can't count on continuity of the resources we need. *(reversed)*
G8r.  *We have to fight to hold on to the resources we need. *(reversed)*

Rewards and Goal Setting

Individual and Team Rewards (alpha = .90)
F2.   How much pay I receive depends almost entirely on how well I perform my job.
F4.   My contributions to this team are rewarded by the company.
F7.   My pay level is determined by my individual job performance.
F13.  My pay depends on the success of the teams I work with.
F17.  Members of this team are rewarded commensurate with their contributions
F18.  Teams are rewarded in line with their performance here.

Measurable Outcomes (alpha = .74)
F8.   Our team's work has measurable team outcomes.
F16.  Our team has quantifiable targets.

Networking, Conflict, and Leadership

Team Networking (alpha = .59)
F3.    My team forms alliances with people in different units at the company to work toward mutual objectives.
F6.    My team maintains contacts with people in other parts of the company who can be a useful source of information, resources, and support.

Group Leadership (alpha = .77)
D6.    My immediate supervisor attempts to resolve disagreements in a constructive manner.
D7r.   *Our leader is hesitant about taking initiative in the group. *(reversed)*
D11r.  *Our leader fails to take necessary action. *(reversed)*

Team Cohesion (alpha = .82)
D1r.   *How often do people in your team disagree about opinions regarding the work being done? *(reversed)*
D2r.   *How much are personality conflicts evident in your team? *(reversed)*
D3r.   *How frequently are there conflicts about ideas in your team? *(reversed)*
D4r.   *How much tension is there among members in your team? *(reversed)*
D9.    My team attempts to resolve disagreements in a constructive manner.

Satisfaction, Equity, and Support

Intention to Leave (alpha = .82)
J7.    I plan to look outside the company for a new job within the next year.
J16.   It is likely that I will quit my job in the next twelve months.

Pay Satisfaction (alpha = .94)
J2.    I am satisfied with my total compensation.
J12.   I am satisfied with my current salary.

Pay Equity (alpha = .74)
J1.    I believe I am fairly paid compared to my peers at company who are at equivalent job levels and who are equivalently skilled.
J9.    I believe I am fairly paid compared to my peers in other companies who are at equivalent job levels and who are equivalently skilled.

Job Satisfaction (alpha = .84)
J4.    All in all, I am satisfied with my job.
J19.   In general, I like working here.

Career Satisfaction (alpha = .84)
J6.    I am satisfied with the progress I have made toward meeting my overall career goals.
J13.   I am satisfied with the progress I have made toward meeting my goals for advancement.

Development Support (alpha = .81)
J15.   The company has a good process for mentoring employees.
J20.   The company has a good process for identifying employees' development needs.

Work-Life Imbalance (alpha = .85)
J3.    My work takes up time that I would like to spend with family/friends.
J18.   My family/friends dislike how often I am preoccupied with my work while at home.
J21.   On the job I have so much work to do that it takes away from my personal interests.

# Appendix B
## *Survey Items and Summary Statistics*

A.   Details of the Work

1.  Please select your team: (NOTE: If you are on multiple teams, please answer this survey regarding the team on which you spend most of your time.) *(required)*
2.  At what location do you primarily work? *(required)*

| | | | |
|---|---|---|---|
| 3.9% | Texas | 17.2% | California site #2 |
| 10.8% | India | 1.0% | Norway |
| 4.9% | France | 2.5% | California site #3 |
| 37.7% | California site #1 | 9.3% | Other (please specify): |
| 12.7% | Czech Republic | | |

3.  What is your *main* function on this team? *(required)*

| | | | |
|---|---|---|---|
| 42.6% | Development Engineer | 1.5% | Technology Specialist |
| 3.4% | Release Engineer | 4.4% | Architect |
| 2.5% | Human Interface Engineer | 10.3% | Engineering Manager |
| 6.4% | Sustaining Engineer | 2.5% | QA Manager |
| 12.3% | Quality Engineer | 0% | Documentation Manager |
| 0% | Localization Engineer / Testing | 1.5% | Product Manager |
| 1.0% | Marketing | 7.8% | Other (please specify): |
| 3.9% | Documentation | | |

4.  How long has this team been in existence? *(round off to nearest number of months)*   3.73 years
5.  How long have you been on this team? *(round off to nearest number of months)*   2.65 years
6.  At what stage in the product life cycle is your team's work? (choose one response only)
    - 24.1%   First release / entirely new product
    - 7.0%   Updating an existing product with minor changes
    - 62.8%   Updating an existing product with major changes
    - 6.0%   Sustaining an existing product with little to no changes
    - 0%   End of product life cycle / Ending an existing product
7.  Where is your immediate supervisor located? (choose one response only)
    - 72.8%   Colocated with me (same site)
    - 10.9%   Different location, same time zone
    - 5.4%   Different location, one to three time zones away
    - 1.5%   Different location, four to seven time zones away
    - 5.0%   Different location, eight to nine time zones away
    - 4.5%   Different location, ten to twelve time zones away
8.  Approximately what percentage of the members of your team are colocated?   61.2%
9.  Do you communicate regularly with members of your team at other sites?   83.8%   Yes   16.2%   No
    If yes, where are the other members located? (choose all that apply)
    - 34.3%   Different location, same time zone
    - 30.4%   Different location, one to three time zones away
    - 15.2%   Different location, four to seven time zones away

34.8%  Different location, eight to nine time zones away

42.6%  Different location, ten to twelve time zones away

10. Are you actively involved in ensuring that communication occurs between your team and other members of the company?   67.3%  Yes    32.7%  No

If yes, where are the other members located? (choose all that apply)

37.3%  Colocated with me (same site)

25.0%  Different location, same time zone

25.5%  Different location, one to three time zones away

13.2%  Different location, four to seven time zones away

30.4%  Different location, eight to nine time zones away

31.9%  Different location, ten to twelve time zones away

B.  Outcomes

Compared to what is possible (100 percent), estimate how effective your team has been at each of the following using a percentage. For example, if Team X meets 80 percent of its quality goals compared to what is possible, enter 80 percent in the first item. If they do not apply, leave blank.

|  | Percent Effectiveness |
|---|---|
| 1. Quality | 77.9% |
| 2. Speed (cycle time, time to market, etc.) | 75.0% |
| 3. Cost effectiveness | 79.1% |
| 4. Technical performance | 80.1% |
| 5. Innovation | 71.3% |
| 6. Customer satisfaction | 72.3% |
| 7. Overall effectiveness | 75.0% |

C.  Degree of Distributed Work

For items 1–6, rate using two columns: How important are each of the following technologies to getting your work done in this team? In the second column, indicate the percentage of your time spent on each technology (the total across all six technologies should equal 100 percent).

|  | Not Important | Somewhat Important | Important | Very Important | Extremely Important | Mean | % of Time Spent on Each Technology |
|---|---|---|---|---|---|---|---|
| 1. E-mail | 0 | 0 | 3.5 | 19.7 | 76.8 | 4.73 | 48.5% |
| 2. Telephone | 5.2 | 11.9 | 34.5 | 34.5 | 13.9 | 3.40 | 12.9% |
| 3. Knowledge repositories (e.g., intranet, shared databases) | 4.3 | 14.4 | 24.1 | 41.7 | 15.5 | 3.50 | 14.4% |
| 4. Collaborative software (e.g., remote presentation software) | 22.8 | 37.0 | 18.5 | 15.8 | 6.0 | 2.45 | 6.8% |
| 5. Video conferencing | 58.3 | 19.8 | 14.4 | 6.4 | 1.1 | 1.72 | 2.6% |
| 6. Face to face | 3.1 | 17.8 | 31.4 | 24.1 | 23.6 | 3.47 | 20.6% |
|  |  |  |  |  |  |  | Total 100% |

7. To what extent are you reliant on electronic communication to accomplish your collaboration in your team?

| 0 | 0.5 | 9.8 | 25.4 | 64.2 | 4.53 |
|---|---|---|---|---|---|
| Not At All | Some Extent | Moderate Extent | Considerate Extent | Very Great Extent | Mean |

D. Processes

Please respond to the following regarding the processes inside your team:

| | Never | Rarely | Sometimes | Often | Constantly | Mean |
|---|---|---|---|---|---|---|
| 1. How often do people in your team disagree about opinions regarding the work being done? | 1.0 | 17.9 | 48.0 | 29.1 | 4.1 | 3.17 |
| 2. How much are personality conflicts evident in your team? | 5.6 | 49.2 | 33.0 | 8.6 | 3.6 | 2.55 |
| 3. How frequently are there conflicts about ideas in your team? | 3.6 | 23.0 | 51.0 | 19.4 | 3.1 | 2.95 |
| 4. How much tension is there among members in your team? | 10.3 | 49.2 | 30.8 | 7.2 | 2.6 | 2.43 |
| 5. My team's dealings with other teams go smoothly | 4.1 | 10.2 | 11.7 | 47.4 | 26.5 | 3.82 |
| 6. My immediate supervisor attempts to resolve disagreements in a constructive manner | 4.1 | 8.6 | 9.6 | 32.0 | 45.7 | 4.07 |
| 7. Our leader is hesitant about taking initiative in the group | 38.1 | 28.4 | 11.3 | 15.5 | 6.7 | 2.24 |

Please indicate the extent to which you agree or disagree with the following statements:

| | Strongly Disagree | Slightly Disagree | Neither | Slightly Agree | Strongly Agree | Mean |
|---|---|---|---|---|---|---|
| 8. Members are free to be assertive about what they think and feel | 1.5 | 5.1 | 7.7 | 36.4 | 49.2 | 4.27 |
| 9. My team attempts to resolve disagreements in a constructive manner | 2.1 | 6.2 | 8.7 | 46.7 | 36.4 | 4.09 |
| 10. When there's a problem, members talk about it | 1.0 | 8.8 | 10.3 | 39.7 | 40.2 | 4.09 |
| 11. Our leader fails to take necessary action | 36.7 | 31.6 | 15.3 | 10.2 | 6.1 | 2.17 |
| 12. There is good cooperation between functions | 4.6 | 10.8 | 13.3 | 46.2 | 25.1 | 3.76 |
| 13. Members are able to say what they think | 1.5 | 6.2 | 6.7 | 36.9 | 48.7 | 4.25 |
| 14. My immediate supervisor proposes a reasonable approach to resolve disagreements | 4.6 | 8.2 | 17.4 | 35.9 | 33.8 | 3.86 |
| 15. There is good cooperation between sites | 4.1 | 12.3 | 13.1 | 40.0 | 30.0 | 3.78 |
| 16. Our leader lets others take away the leadership of the group | 23.4 | 24.0 | 21.9 | 23.4 | 7.3 | 2.67 |
| 17. My team proposes a reasonable approach to resolve disagreements | 2.6 | 4.2 | 19.9 | 47.6 | 25.7 | 3.90 |

| | Strongly Disagree | Slightly Disagree | Neither | Slightly Agree | Strongly Agree | Mean |
|---|---|---|---|---|---|---|
| 18. There is good communication between the people that need to work together | 2.6 | 6.7 | 8.8 | 54.1 | 27.8 | 3.98 |

## E.  Enabling Conditions

Please indicate the extent to which you agree or disagree with the following statements:

| | Strongly Disagree | Slightly Disagree | Neither | Slightly Agree | Strongly Agree | Mean |
|---|---|---|---|---|---|---|
| 1. There is agreement about our priorities in our team | 5.1 | 15.4 | 12.3 | 40.0 | 27.2 | 3.69 |
| 2. We can count on the people in our team to perform their jobs proficiently | 2.1 | 7.2 | 8.2 | 37.6 | 44.8 | 4.16 |
| 3. Team members always do what they say they will do | 2.1 | 10.9 | 12.4 | 47.7 | 26.9 | 3.87 |
| 4. We have a shared understanding of what we are trying to accomplish | 3.1 | 8.8 | 10.9 | 42.5 | 34.7 | 3.97 |
| 5. The people on our team are reliable in their work | 2.1 | 3.6 | 9.3 | 41.5 | 43.5 | 4.21 |
| 6. There is an agreed way of getting the work done in our team | 1.6 | 8.9 | 14.1 | 43.5 | 31.9 | 3.95 |
| 7. Team members believe that others on our team will follow through on their commitments | 2.1 | 4.2 | 9.9 | 50.3 | 33.5 | 4.09 |
| 8. Everyone on our team has similar goals | 6.3 | 14.7 | 23.0 | 36.1 | 19.9 | 3.49 |
| 9. We have good acceptance of process and methods in our team | 6.8 | 17.7 | 18.2 | 34.9 | 22.4 | 3.48 |
| 10. Team members trust each other to contribute worthwhile ideas | 2.1 | 6.8 | 11.5 | 45.3 | 34.4 | 4.03 |
| 11. In our team, members agree on work standards and procedures | 3.7 | 13.7 | 16.8 | 43.2 | 22.6 | 3.67 |
| 12. We can trust that the members of our team have the knowledge and skills to complete their work | 2.1 | 4.2 | 6.8 | 42.4 | 44.5 | 4.23 |

## F.  Collaboration Structure

Please indicate the extent to which you agree or disagree with the following statements:

| | Strongly Disagree | Slightly Disagree | Neither | Slightly Agree | Strongly Agree | Mean |
|---|---|---|---|---|---|---|
| 1. Members have to obtain information and advice from each other in order to complete their work | 1.0 | 5.8 | 7.9 | 44.0 | 41.4 | 4.19 |
| 2. How much pay I receive depends almost entirely on how well I perform my job | 22.8 | 23.3 | 23.8 | 21.2 | 8.8 | 2.70 |
| 3. My team forms alliances with people in different units at the company to work toward mutual objectives | 1.6 | 11.4 | 23.8 | 45.6 | 17.6 | 3.66 |

| | Strongly Disagree | Slightly Disagree | Neither | Slightly Agree | Strongly Agree | Mean |
|---|---|---|---|---|---|---|
| 4. My contributions to this team are rewarded by the company | 15.5 | 20.7 | 28.0 | 28.5 | 7.3 | 2.91 |
| 5. Each member of this team is held personally accountable for team results | 5.2 | 17.1 | 24.4 | 38.9 | 14.5 | 3.40 |
| 6. My team maintains contacts with people in other parts of the company who can be a useful source of information, resources, and support | 0.5 | 3.6 | 12.4 | 55.7 | 27.8 | 4.07 |
| 7. My pay level is determined by my individual job performance | 18.8 | 21.5 | 23.0 | 30.4 | 6.3 | 2.84 |
| 8. Our team's work has measurable team outcomes | 4.2 | 14.1 | 15.6 | 42.7 | 23.4 | 3.67 |
| 9. The members of our team change frequently | 29.2 | 31.8 | 14.6 | 16.7 | 7.8 | 2.42 |
| 10. My immediate supervisor forms alliances with people in different units at the company to work toward mutual objectives | 2.6 | 8.4 | 19.9 | 42.9 | 26.2 | 3.82 |
| 11. On this team, we share the responsibility for our deliverables | 2.1 | 7.3 | 11.9 | 43.0 | 35.8 | 4.03 |
| 12. The contributions of each member to this team are valued by their subunit | 3.2 | 7.9 | 22.1 | 41.6 | 25.3 | 3.78 |
| 13. My pay depends on the success of the team I work with | 18.9 | 18.9 | 24.2 | 28.4 | 9.5 | 2.91 |
| 14. In order to complete our work, we have to obtain information and advice from each other | 0 | 5.3 | 7.4 | 43.7 | 43.7 | 4.26 |
| 15. My immediate supervisor maintains contact with people in other parts of company who can be a useful source of information | 2.1 | 5.8 | 16.8 | 42.9 | 32.5 | 3.98 |
| 16. Our team has quantifiable targets | 3.1 | 10.5 | 19.4 | 39.3 | 27.7 | 3.78 |
| 17. Members of this team are rewarded commensurate with their contributions | 16.4 | 22.8 | 37.0 | 19.6 | 4.2 | 2.72 |
| 18. Teams are rewarded in line with their performance here | 19.6 | 24.9 | 31.2 | 19.6 | 4.8 | 2.65 |

G.   Resources and Work Environment

| | Strongly Disagree | Slightly Disagree | Neither | Slightly Agree | Strongly Agree | Mean |
|---|---|---|---|---|---|---|
| 1. The company has committed the resources required to do this work | 22.4 | 24.0 | 13.5 | 27.1 | 13.0 | 2.84 |
| 2. It seems that everything is changing around here | 2.1 | 8.4 | 22.5 | 31.4 | 35.6 | 3.90 |
| 3. We receive prompt technical assistance when our computer systems are not working | 8.9 | 15.6 | 16.1 | 38.5 | 20.8 | 3.47 |
| 4. Many aspects of the company are changing at the same time | 2.1 | 4.1 | 17.1 | 34.2 | 42.5 | 4.11 |

| | Very Dissatisfied | Dissatisfied | Neither | Satisfied | Very Satisfied | Mean |
|---|---|---|---|---|---|---|

5. We cannot count on continuity of the resources we need — 7.9, 13.2, 21.1, 34.7, 23.2, 3.52

6. We waste considerable time in doing our work because of information technology problems that are not fixed — 20.3, 34.9, 21.4, 16.7, 6.8, 2.55

7. Priorities keep being changed — 5.7, 11.9, 22.3, 36.3, 23.8, 3.61

8. We have to fight to hold on to the resources we need — 6.8, 10.4, 22.4, 31.8, 28.6, 3.65

9. Company provides adequate information technology support — 6.3, 14.8, 21.7, 41.3, 15.9, 3.46

10. The people who use my work keep changing their requirements — 10.9, 25.5, 32.8, 20.3, 10.4, 2.94

## H.  Satisfaction With Distributed Work

Please indicate how satisfied you are with the following characteristics of distributed work:

| | Very Dissatisfied | Dissatisfied | Neither | Satisfied | Very Satisfied | Mean |
|---|---|---|---|---|---|---|
| 1. Amount of travel | 6.7 | 10.9 | 30.6 | 33.7 | 18.1 | 3.46 |
| 2. Flexibility | 1.5 | 6.2 | 13.3 | 41.0 | 37.9 | 4.08 |
| 3. Gaining technology skills | 2.6 | 14.4 | 20.0 | 42.6 | 20.5 | 3.64 |
| 4. Developing new relationships | 3.6 | 10.8 | 21.6 | 47.4 | 16.5 | 3.62 |
| 5. Face to face social opportunities | 6.2 | 21.5 | 25.1 | 34.9 | 12.3 | 3.26 |
| 6. Interruptions to personal life | 6.2 | 17.1 | 37.8 | 29.5 | 9.3 | 3.19 |
| 7. Visibility of my work | 7.2 | 17.9 | 25.1 | 40.5 | 9.2 | 3.27 |
| 8. Technological dependence | 2.1 | 6.8 | 39.8 | 42.4 | 8.9 | 3.49 |

## I.  Personal Characteristics

Please indicate the extent to which the following describe you personally:

| | Strongly Disagree | Slightly Disagree | Neither | Slightly Agree | Strongly Agree | Mean |
|---|---|---|---|---|---|---|
| 1. It is inappropriate to express negative emotions in the workplace | 9.8 | 26.3 | 17.0 | 31.4 | 15.5 | 3.16 |
| 2. I try to investigate an issue with others to find a solution acceptable to all | 0 | 1.0 | 2.6 | 42.3 | 54.1 | 4.49 |
| 3. I try to integrate my ideas with those of others to come up with a decision jointly | 0 | 0.5 | 2.6 | 49.2 | 47.7 | 4.44 |
| 4. I am eager to tell outsiders that this is a good place to work | 6.7 | 10.3 | 32.0 | 31.4 | 19.6 | 3.47 |
| 5. I am satisfied with the chances I have to do something that makes me feel good about myself as a person | 6.7 | 16.6 | 18.1 | 36.8 | 21.8 | 3.50 |
| 6. I am satisfied with the chances I have to accomplish something worthwhile | 7.3 | 15.0 | 18.1 | 40.9 | 18.7 | 3.49 |

## J.   Attitudes

Please indicate the extent to which you agree or disagree with the following statements:

|  | Strongly Disagree | Slightly Disagree | Neither | Slightly Agree | Strongly Agree | Mean |
|---|---|---|---|---|---|---|
| 1. I believe I am fairly paid compared to my peers at the company who are at equivalent job levels and who are equivalently skilled | 13.9 | 23.2 | 24.7 | 25.8 | 12.4 | 2.99 |
| 2. I am satisfied with my total compensation | 12.3 | 28.7 | 17.9 | 28.2 | 12.8 | 3.01 |
| 3. My work takes up time that I would like to spend with family/friends | 8.2 | 14.4 | 21.6 | 41.2 | 14.4 | 3.39 |
| 4. All in all, I am satisfied with my job | 6.1 | 12.7 | 15.7 | 47.7 | 17.8 | 3.58 |
| 5. Developing employee skills is a high priority for managers at the company | 16.8 | 20.4 | 21.4 | 27.0 | 14.3 | 3.02 |
| 6. I am satisfied with the progress I have made toward meeting my overall career goals | 10.7 | 24.4 | 17.8 | 36.5 | 10.7 | 3.12 |
| 7. I plan to look outside the company for a new job within the next year | 17.4 | 18.5 | 31.8 | 19.5 | 12.8 | 2.92 |
| 8. I am satisfied with the chances I have to accomplish something worthwhile | 6.7 | 15.9 | 23.1 | 41.0 | 13.3 | 3.38 |
| 9. I believe I am fairly paid compared to my peers in other companies who are at equivalent job levels and who are equivalently skilled | 13.3 | 15.9 | 32.8 | 27.2 | 10.8 | 3.06 |
| 10. I have very little control over the hours I am expected to work | 20.1 | 36.6 | 20.1 | 17.5 | 5.7 | 2.52 |
| 11. My job enables me to use all my capabilities | 13.3 | 26.7 | 15.9 | 33.3 | 10.8 | 3.02 |
| 12. I am satisfied with my current salary | 18.1 | 26.9 | 18.1 | 24.4 | 12.4 | 2.86 |
| 13. I am satisfied with the progress I have made toward meeting my goals for advancement | 9.8 | 24.4 | 21.2 | 31.6 | 13.0 | 3.13 |
| 14. I am satisfied with the chances I have to do something that makes me feel good about myself as a person | 7.3 | 15.6 | 20.3 | 45.3 | 11.5 | 3.38 |
| 15. The company has a good process for mentoring employees | 24.0 | 28.1 | 29.7 | 13.5 | 4.7 | 2.47 |
| 16. It is likely that I will quit my job in the next twelve months | 26.6 | 22.4 | 29.2 | 13.0 | 8.9 | 2.55 |
| 17. My work enables me to use my full range of expertise | 13.5 | 26.0 | 20.3 | 29.2 | 10.9 | 2.98 |
| 18. My family/friends dislike how often I am preoccupied with my work while at home | 14.5 | 18.7 | 23.3 | 28.0 | 15.5 | 3.11 |
| 19. In general, I like working here | 3.1 | 6.7 | 13.5 | 49.7 | 26.9 | 3.91 |
| 20. The company has a good process for identifying employees' development needs | 21.6 | 26.8 | 27.8 | 20.6 | 3.1 | 2.57 |
| 21. On the job I have so much work to do that it takes away from my personal interests | 9.8 | 16.6 | 22.3 | 30.1 | 21.2 | 3.36 |

| | Strongly Disagree | Slightly Disagree | Neither | Slightly Agree | Strongly Agree | Mean |
|---|---|---|---|---|---|---|
| 22. I am satisfied with the chances I have to learn new things at work | 4.2 | 17.8 | 20.9 | 42.4 | 14.7 | 3.46 |

## K.  Demographics

1. How long have you been with the company?
   - 7.4%  1 year or less
   - 16.3%  2–3 years
   - 40.1%  4–5 years
   - 36.1%  6 or more years
2. How many teams/projects are you involved with?   3.03  (number of teams)
3. How many of these operate primarily distributed?   2.20  (number of distributed teams)
4. How many years of experience do you have working on distributed teams?   5.77  years
5. What is the level of your education? (Please indicate highest completed.)
   - 2.0%  High school or equivalent
   - 3.5%  Some college or technical training, but no degree, beyond high school (1–3 years)
   - 2.0%  Associate's Degree or equivalent (2–year degree)
   - 44.1%  Graduated from 4-year college (BA, BS, or other Bachelor's degree)
   - 41.6%  Master's degree or equivalent
   - 6.9%  Doctorate degree or equivalent
6. How old were you on your last birthday?
   - 0%  19 years or younger
   - 2.0%  20 to 24
   - 13.3%  25 to 29
   - 24.1%  30 to 34
   - 23.2%  35 to 39
   - 16.3%  40 to 44
   - 10.8%  45 to 49
   - 7.4%  50 to 54
   - 2.5%  55 to 59
   - 0.5%  60 years or older
7. Country you live in now:
   Canada (0.5%); Czech Republic (11.8%); France (4.9%); India (10.3%); Norway (1.0%); United States (67.2%)
8. Country/region you were born in:
   - 1.0%  Africa and Middle East
   - 29.7%  Asia
   - 27.2%  Europe and Russia (including United Kingdom)
   - 1.0%  Latin America (including Central and South America, and Mexico)
   - 40.1%  United States and Canada
   - 1.0%  Other: _____
9. Is English your first or native language?   46%  Yes
   If no, do you speak English fluently?   96%  Yes

# References

Appelbaum, E., and R. Batt. 1994. *The new American workplace: Transforming work systems in the U.S.* Ithaca, New York: Cornell ILR Press.

Bell, B. S., and S. W. J. Kozlowski. 2002. A typology of virtual teams: Implications for effective leadership. *Group and Organization Management* 27 (1): 14–49.

Bulow, J., and L. H. Summers. 1986. A theory of dual labor markets with application to industrial policy, discrimination, and Keynesian unemployment. *Journal of Labor Economics* 4 (3) Part 1:376–414.

Campion, M. A., G. J. Medsker, and A. C. Higgs. 1993. Relations between work group characteristics and effectiveness: Implications for designing effective work groups. *Personnel Psychology* 46 (4): 823–50.

Campion, M. A., E. M. Papper, and G. J. Medsker. 1996. Relations between work team characteristics and effectiveness: A replication and extension. *Personnel Psychology* 49 (2): 429–52.

Cappel, J. J., and J. C. Windsor. 2000. Ethical decision making: A comparison of computer-supported and face-to-face group. *Journal of Business Ethics* 28 (2): 95–107.

Cappelli, P., and D. Neumark. 2001. Do high performance work practices improve establishment-level outcomes? *Industrial and Labor Relations Review* 54 (4): 737–75.

Cohen, S. G., and D. Bailey. 1997. What makes teams work: Group effectiveness research from the shop floor to the executive suite. *Journal of Management* 23 (3): 239–90.

Driskell, J. E., P. H. Radtke, and E. Salas. 2003. Virtual teams: Effects of technological mediation on team performance. *Group Dynamics: Theory, Research, and Practice* 7 (4): 297–323.

Gibbons, R. 2003. Team theory, garbage cans and real organizations: Some history and prospects of economic research on decision-making in organizations. *Industrial and Corporate Change* 12 (4): 753–87.

Gibson, C. B., and S. G. Cohen. 2003. *Virtual teams that work: Creating conditions for virtual team effectiveness.* San Francisco, CA: Jossey-Bass.

Gladstein, D. 1984. A model of task group effectiveness. *Administrative Science Quarterly* 29 (4): 499–517.

Glaser, B. G., and A. L. Strauss. 1967. *The discovery of grounded theory: Strategies for qualitative research.* Chicago: Aldine.

Graetz, K. A., E. Boyle, C. Kimble, P. Thompson, and J. Garloch. 1998. Information sharing in face-to-face, teleconferencing, and electronic chat groups. *Small Group Research* 29 (6): 714–43.

Guzzo, R. A., and M. W. Dickson. 1996. Teams in organizations: Recent research on performance and effectiveness. *Annual Review of Psychology* 47:307–38.

Hackman, J. R. 1987. The design of work teams. In *Handbook of organizational behavior* ed. J. W. Lorsch, 315–42. Englewood Cliffs, NJ: Prentice-Hall.

Hackman, J. R., and G. R. Oldham. 1980. *Work redesign.* Reading, MA: Addison-Wesley.

Hiltz, S. R., K. Johnson, and M. Turoff. 1986. Experiments in group decision making: Communication process and outcome in face-to-face versus computerized conferences. *Human Communication Research* 13 (2): 225–52.

Ichniowski, C., K. Shaw, and G. Prennushi. 1997. The effects of human resource management practices on productivity. *American Economic Review* 87 (3): 291–313.

Janz, B. D., J. A. Colquitt, and R. A. Noe. 1997. Knowledge worker team effectiveness: The role of autonomy, interdependence, team development, and contextual support variables. *Personnel Psychology* 50 (4): 877–904.

Keller, R. T. 1986. Predictors of the performance of project groups in R&D organizations. *Academy of Management Journal* 29 (4): 715–26.

Kochan, T. A., C. Ichniowski, D. Levine, C. Olson, and G. Strauss. 1996. What works at work: A critical review. *Industrial Relations* 35 (3): 299–333.

Krishnan, R., X. Martin, and N. G. Noorderhaven. 2006. When does trust matter to alliance performance? *Academy of Management Journal* 49 (5): 894–917.

Langfred, C. W. 2007. The downside of self-management: A longitudinal study of the effects of conflict on trust, autonomy, and task interdependence in self-managing teams. *Academy of Management Journal* 50 (4): 885–900.

Lawler, Edward E. III. 2003. *Treat people right.* San Francisco, CA: Jossey-Bass.

Lawrence, P. R., and J. W. Lorsch. 1967. *Organization and environment.* Boston, MA: Harvard Business School Press.

Lee, T. W. 1999. *Using qualitative methods in organizational research.* Thousand Oaks, CA: SAGE.

Marschak, J., and R. Radner. 1972. *Economic theory of teams.* New Haven, CT: Yale University Press.

Marshall, C., and G. B. Rossman. 1995. *Designing qualitative research,* Second edition. Thousand Oaks, CA: SAGE.

Martins, L. L., L. L. Gilson, and M. T. Maynard. 2004. Virtual teams: What do we know and where do we go from here? *Journal of Management* 30 (6): 805–35.

Mayer, R. C., J. H. Davis, and F. D. Schoorman. 1995. An integrative model of organizational trust. *Academy of Management Review* 20 (3): 709–34.

Mayer, R. C., and M. B. Gavin. 2005. Trust in management and performance: Who minds the shop while the employees watch the boss? *Academy of Management Journal* 48 (5): 874–88.

McDonough, E. F., III, K. B. Kahn, and G. Barczak. 2001. An investigation of the use of global, virtual, and collocated new product development teams. *The Journal of Product Innovation Management* 18 (2): 110–20.

Mishra, A. K., and G. M. Spreitzer. 1998. Explaining how survivors respond to downsizing: The roles of trust, empowerment, justice, and work redesign. *Academy of Management Journal* 23 (3): 567–88.

Mohrman, S. A., S. G. Cohen, and A. M. Mohrman, Jr. 1995. *Designing team-based organizations: New forms for knowledge work.* San Francisco, CA: Jossey-Bass.

Paxson, C. H., and N. Sicherman. 1996. The dynamics of dual-job holding and job mobility. *Journal of Labor Economics* 14 (3): 357–93.

Prendergast, C. 1999. The provision of incentives in firms. *Journal of Economic Literature* 37 (1): 7–63.

Radner, R. 1992. Hierarchy: The economics of managing. *Journal of Economic Literature* 30 (3): 1382–1415.

Rousseau, D. M., S. B. Sitkin, R. S. Burt, and C. Camerer. 1998. Not so different after all: A cross-discipline view of trust. *Academy of Management Review* 23 (3): 393–404.

Saparito, P. A., C. C. Chen, and H. J. Sapienza. 2004. The role of relational trust in bank-small firm relationships. *Academy of Management Journal* 47 (3): 400–10.

Saphiere, D. M. H. 1996. Productive behaviors of global business teams. *International Journal of Intercultural Relations* 20 (2): 227–59.

Schmidt, J. B., M. M. Montoya-Weiss, and A. P. Massey. 2001. New product development decision-making effectiveness: Comparing individuals, face-to-face teams, and virtual teams. *Decision Sciences* 32 (4): 575–600.

Schoorman, F. D., R. C. Mayer, and J. H. Davis. 2007. An integrative model of organizational trust: Past, present, and future. *Academy of Management Review* 32 (2): 344–54.

Schor, J. B. 1991. *The overworked American: The unexpected decline of leisure.* New York: Basic Books.

Shapiro, C., and J. E. Stiglitz. 1984. Equilibrium unemployment as a worker discipline device. *American Economic Review* 74 (3): 433–44.

Strauss, A. L. 1987. *Qualitative analysis for social scientists.* New York: Cambridge University Press.

Strauss, S. G., and J. E. McGrath. 1994. Does the medium matter? The interaction of task type and technology on group performance and member reactions. *Journal of Applied Psychology* 79 (1): 87–97.

Valacich, J. S., J. F. George, J. F. Nunamaker, Jr., and D. R. Vogel. 1994. Physical proximity effects on computer-mediated group idea generation. *Small Group Research* 25 (1): 83–104.

Yin, R. K. 2003. *Case study research: Design and methods,* third edition (Applied social sciences research methods series, v.5). Thousand Oaks, CA: SAGE.

# 8

# International Differences in Lean Production, Productivity, and Employee Attitudes

Susan Helper and Morris M. Kleiner

## 8.1 Introduction

In this chapter, we report on a study of U.S.-European productivity differences, conducted at five plants belonging to a single multinational firm. We investigate whether human resource policy changes within a firm in concert with other manufacturing transformations have affected the organization's ability to prosper financially and provide job satisfaction for its employees.

All five plants we study make similar products (sensors and actuators for automobiles), using similar processes. We look at the impact of a value-added gain-sharing plan (VAG) that was introduced at different times among the plants in a way that had many features of a natural experiment. Our analysis draws on multiple plant visits over eight years, surveys of almost all of the workforce, and confidential financial data. Our study thus offers an unusual opportunity to examine the internal operations of a low-wage, nonunion firm, using data from both management and workers.

A major issue for our firm has been finding the appropriate method of

Susan Helper is AT&T Professor of Economics at Case Western Reserve University, and a research associate of the National Bureau of Economic Research. Morris M. Kleiner is the AFL-CIO Chair Professor of Labor Policy at the Humphrey Institute of Public Affairs, University of Minnesota, and a research associate of the National Bureau of Economic Research.

We are very grateful to the managers and workers of the firm we call SP for their extraordinary cooperation and to Professor Sue Fernie of the London School of Economics (LSE) for undertaking the worker attitude survey in the United Kingdom. We also thank the NBER/Sloan Project on International Differences in the Business Practices and Productivity of Multinational Firms for financial support. We thank a referee, Fredrik Andersson, for very helpful comments. In addition, we are grateful to Wei Chi, Alexander Lefter, and Yingying Wang for excellent research assistance. We do not wish to implicate any of the above in our conclusions or our errors.

compensation to complement its other strategic initiatives. In 1987, the firm began a major change in its product market strategy; it now designs its own products (which are complex assemblies of plastic and electronic parts) and modifies them frequently, rather than producing individual electronic components to customer blueprints. It has also vastly increased its quality levels and reduced its inventory. These changes are common in this industry, and result from pressure from the firm's customers, such as Ford and General Motors (though our firm was above average in its response).

As a result of these product-market changes, the firm introduced changes in its human resource policies, changing its methods of compensation, increasing automation, introducing work in groups, and (late in our study) increasing training. In some of the plants, compensation received by production workers has fallen dramatically; in others it has increased slightly. (Wages even at the best-paid U.S. plant are less than 40 percent of the U.S. manufacturing average.)

We present information on the dates of the introduction of the VAG in figure 8.1. The firm has employed a variety of methods of pay (both piece rates and time rates) in plants making similar products in similar ways. It changed these plants to a plant-wide gain-sharing system at different times. We use these changes as a quasi-experiment, to examine the impact of changes in human resource policies on productivity and worker well-being. We will examine the impact on the plants that changed over early, treating the later adopters as a control group, using a time-series cross-section statistical methodology (Bertrand, Duflo, and Mullainathan 2002; Athey and Imbens 2006).

We find that the U.S. plants were more productive and profitable than ones in the United Kingdom, and that the introduction of VAG enhanced plant level performance across all the plants. Moreover, the transition to VAG

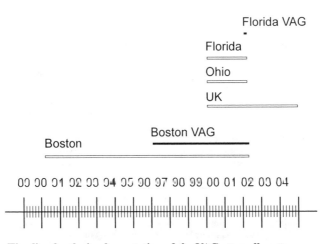

**Fig. 8.1    Timeline for the implementation of the VAG at small parts**

influenced employee attitudes toward pay and work by similar amounts in both the U.S. and UK plants.

In the next section, we review relevant literature. In section 8.3, we discuss basic characteristics of the industry and our plants, and the nature and timing of their adoption of the value-added gain-sharing plan and complementary policies such as automation, worker recognition programs, and training. In section 8.4, we discuss our methods, both qualitative (multiple visits to each plant, discussions with both management and workers) and quantitative. In section 8.5 we present results, and in section 8.6, our conclusions.

## 8.2    Review of the Literature

### 8.2.1    Firm Performance

The impact of human resource practices on organizational performance has received considerable attention from academics for more than twenty years. Starting with a research volume published by the Industrial Relations Research Association entitled *Human Resources and the Performance of the Firm* (Kleiner et al. 1987), many researchers have examined the effects of human-resource policies on the economic performance of the firm.

Two types of policies have been examined extensively: compensation and employee involvement. With respect to compensation, several studies have found that pay based on individual output ("piece-rates") is the best way to maximize firm performance (Ehrenberg 1990; Conyon and Freeman 2001; Seiler 1984; and Lazear 2000). On the other hand, some studies have suggested that time rate methods of pay allow the enterprise to increase the number of products produced and thereby increase the value-added production of the enterprise (Freeman and Kleiner 2005; Helper and Kleiner 2003). An alternative to piece rates or time rates is value-added gain-sharing or some form of profit-sharing with employees (Kaufman 1992; Kruse 1993; Kleiner, Helper, and Ren 2001; and Helper and Kleiner 2003).

Although economists see the method and level of compensation as a central factor in developing the correct incentive structures, research about the impact of compensation on firm performance has found mixed results. This is largely a result of most researchers' inability to control for the way in which the compensation system interacts with the other human resource and production systems in the firm. As we discuss below, the profit-maximizing form of compensation is contingent on the nature of the product and on which complementary HR policies are adopted.

Another type of policy is participation in running the enterprise. A number of studies have found a positive impact of such employee involvement on productivity and firm performance (see, e.g., Appelbaum and Batt 1994; Appelbaum et al. 2000; Ichniowski et al. 2000; Black and Lynch 2004a).

Most of these studies, each based in a single industry, find that employee involvement increased the productivity of the firm. However, other studies using a national sample with a diverse set of firms have shown very little impact of employee involvement on firm level productivity, but a larger influence of financial participation on productivity (Freeman, Kleiner, and Ostroff 2000; Cappelli and Neumark 2001).

An alternative approach to looking just at compensation or just at employee involvement is examining bundles of human resource practice. Some papers have found that there is a set of high performance workplace practices (HPWP) that, if all implemented together, result in higher returns than do a set of traditional practices (MacDuffie 1995; Arthur 1994; Cutcher-Gershenfeld 1991; and Ichniowski, Shaw, and Prennushi 1997). Other papers (Kleiner, Leonard, and Pilarski 2002; Jones and Kato 1995) show mixed results.

Similarly, analyses of nationally representative data have found mixed results regarding the effect of these practices. In a time-series cross-industry sample, Black and Lynch (2004b) found that a combination of policies (such as profit-sharing for nonmanagerial employees and group meetings) led to increased productivity, especially in unionized firms. However, Cappelli and Neumark (2001) found less positive results. There also is evidence of a long run equilibrium level of employee involvement that firms move toward with establishments adding and dropping specific types of involvement policies based on their own circumstances (Chi, Freeman, and Kleiner 2007).

Two factors help to differentiate the studies, which have found positive results of employee involvement on productivity and profits: (a) number of industries studied, and (b) the extent to which authors are able to distinguish actual implementation of policies from the intent to implement such policies.

One explanation for the difference between the single-industry and multi-industry studies is that the type of employee involvement that matters for productivity varies by industry. (For example, in some industries [e.g., apparel], job rotation and on-line problem-solving may increase productivity, while in others [e.g., steel], off-line problem-solving is most important [Appelbaum et al. 2000].)

In addition, many studies simply ask managers what policies they have in place, without looking at the extent of implementation. In contrast, it is reasonable to expect that fully adopting a bundle of complementary policies places a premium on management skill, and that not all managers will be equally successful in doing so.

Our study allows us to look especially at this second reason for mixed results. We are able to control for detailed industry, product, and process, yet can observe different managerial behavior across our plants. Thus, we extend the traditional analysis of one plant over time to an analysis of similar plants over time, of which some changed and others did not. In addition, we have information from both workers and management about the nature and the extent of these changes; thus we capture not only management's intent to change, but also other views of how effective these changes were.

### 8.2.2    Impacts on the Establishment's Employees

Employee welfare should be considered as part of any overall calculus of the impact of changes in human resource policies (Appelbaum, Bernhardt, and Murnane 2003). Moreover, employees' perceived well-being is closely correlated with behaviors such as turnover and absenteeism, which affect establishment outcomes (Brief 1998).

A recent survey of American workers in large firms found that U.S. workers want to be employed in establishments where they have a say in running the organization. Over 60 percent of the surveyed workers said they wanted committees in which workers have varying levels of independence from management in deciding work tasks (Freeman and Rogers 1999). However, these results were for a diverse sample of employees, and there was little attempt to examine the effect of changes in human resource policies, or to examine these changes for a homogeneous group of workers who were all subject to the same policy transformations.

### 8.3    Context: The Auto Parts Industry and the Plants We Study

During the 1980s and 1990s, U.S. automakers sharply reduced their degree of vertical integration in three ways: (a) having more components manufactured by outside firms, (b) having the joining of those components ("subassembly") done by outside firms, and (c) having more design work done by outside firms (MacDuffie and Helper 2006; Helper and Levine 1992).

These changes created an opportunity for the firm we analyze, which we call SP (for "Small Parts"). Firm SP is a $600 million manufacturer of electrical and electronic products, such as ignition switches and a product that indicates when a car door is ajar, which are sold largely to vehicle manufacturers (automakers and truck manufacturers). The oldest part of the firm was founded in 1909, and has undergone a number of changes in its markets and products over the years.

Firm SP announced a major change in strategy in 1987 (SP annual report, 1995). The new strategy involved enhancing profitability through product differentiation. Firm SP would increasingly design its own products (instead of building to the automakers' blueprints), do more subassembly, produce a wider variety of products, and introduce new products more frequently. These changes would increase overhead, so the firm also began looking to acquire firms that made similar products, as a way of achieving economies of scale and scope. At this time, the firm also began to adopt some Japanese innovations in manufacturing, such as just-in-time inventory and total quality management (see Helper and Kleiner [2003] for more detail).

In 1997, SP went public in order to increase its access to capital. At the end of 1998, SP bought another firm that designed and manufactured sensors, thereby acquiring a plant in rural Ohio and one in suburban Florida. During the 1990s the firm also acquired some foreign operations (Europe, Mexico, and Brazil). In 1999, the firm ended the contract manufacturing operation that had originally formed the core of its business, and focused entirely on parts that the firm designed itself. Thus, the firm exemplifies many of the trends that are common in this industry: it has become an expert in the design and manufacture of its products, become global, and has grown dramatically, mostly through acquisitions, and seen labor costs fall as a percent of total costs. (Direct labor costs at SP average about 8 percent of total costs.)

This new strategy was not consistent with SP's existing pay practices, which involved piece rates for some operators and most assemblers, and time rates for other operators and all office and engineering staff. As we discuss below, piece rates can lead to excess inventory, difficulty in changing to new products, and problems in encouraging teamwork. However, managers worried that time rates alone would not provide enough incentive to avoid wasteful inventory, prevent defects, or promote incremental improvement. As a result, the firm implemented a value-added gain-sharing plan (VAG).

Management did not implement VAG in all of its plants at once. We suggest that the implementation process can be thought of as a quasi-natural experiment that can allow us to estimate the impacts of gain-sharing on both productivity and worker satisfaction. Below, we describe the implementation process and timing.

### 8.3.1    Method of Pay and Timing of VAG Introduction

The principle behind the value-added gain-sharing program was to give workers as a group a stake in their plant's performance. The details of the plan changed over the years; initially the size of the bonus pool was a function only of factors that management felt workers could influence: productivity increases, defect rates, and customer satisfaction. Later, material and capital costs were added, and the formula became so complex that "only three people in the company understand how it is calculated," as the controller of the Massachusetts plant (Ms. P) told us. Everyone in the plant (except for a few top managers, who were on a different bonus plan with greater economic incentives) received the same percentage of their pay as a bonus. In practice, the gainsharing bonus varied between zero and 15 percent of pay. (In contrast, the piece rate systems at the Massachusetts and UK plants were widely understood, and offered a 50 to 100 percent increase over base pay.)

We examine the impact of VAG introduction at each of SP's five plants, which all produce similar electronic parts for the automotive industry. The U.S. plants are located in urban Massachusetts, suburban Massachusetts, rural Ohio, and urban Florida; the UK plant is in a far suburb of London. As we mentioned earlier in figure 8.1, we give the timing of the changes in the method of compensation for each of the plants.[1]

### 8.3.2    Interaction of VAG and Other Policies

As previously mentioned, management did not implement VAG by itself, but rather as part of a series of changes in overall strategy consistent with the system of "Modern Manufacturing" described by Milgrom and Roberts (1990). Our multiple plant visits over eight years (described in section 8.4) allowed us to follow this process in real time.

Management's new strategy increased the returns to a group bonus system compared especially to piece rates, but also to time rates. This strategy was most carefully worked out in the Massachusetts plants where it was first implemented. The rationale for VAG and the coordination with supporting policies were much less well understood by management or workers in the plants that SP acquired.

Our fieldwork suggested that there were several factors that affected VAG's impact on productivity and satisfaction: (a) the nature of the changes involved in adopting "modern manufacturing;" (b) the problems caused by the new system for the existing methods of pay, such as reduced contractibility and return to individual effort; (c) the supporting employee involvement policies introduced by management; (d) impact of the change to VAG on the pay/effort bargain; and (e) the degree to which workers in the plant felt they had access to alternative employment. We discuss each of these in turn, starting with the Massachusetts experience and commenting on differences at other plants.

*Changes in Product and Process in "Modern Manufacturing"*

At the time of our first visit in 1995, the Massachusetts urban plant was toward the end of a transition begun in the mid-1980s. It had been a low-volume plant where quality requirements were not high, and where designs were generally dictated by the customer and did not change often. The new

---

1. In the urban Massachusetts plant, workers on individually-paced jobs were paid piece rates from the 1960s until early 1996. The VAG was phased in gradually (by department) between 1993 and 1995. The suburban Massachusetts facility was established in 1989, and was populated in part by workers from the urban plant. Both managers and workers were moved back and forth between the two plants; our data do not allow us to separate these plants.

The Florida and Ohio facilities were acquired by SP in late 1998. At the Florida facility the production employees were paid a time rate. On January 1, 2001, the plant shifted to a value-added gain-sharing method of pay. Workers also were paid an hourly rate at the Ohio facility. This facility did not switch to VAG until January 1, 2002.

The UK plant was acquired by SP in March 1999. The workers had been paid a piece rate for many years. At the time of our first visit in January 2003, most of the workers had been transferred from individual piece rates to a time rate plus a bonus based on their work group's performance, and some had been told that they would be paid a time rate plus VAG (a bonus based on plant-wide performance) starting in March 2003.

strategy was to become a "high-volume, precision operation," according to Mr. M, the plant manager in 1995. This transition involved changes in many areas.

*Product Strategy.* Firm SP hired engineers to design products in-house, and dramatically increased the rate at which new products were introduced (fifty in a typical year under the new strategy) and retired. These products became increasingly sophisticated, and many were patented. For example, a sensor based on the Hall Effect (using an electrical current for highly accurate, contact-less sensing) was written up in a technical journal.

*Process Flow.* The older jobs were individually paced, and consisted of a single worker sitting at a machine. He or she would add one or more pieces to a small assembly and then press a button or foot pedal to fasten the piece via welding or crimping. He or she would then place the partially-completed product in a box; when the box was full, material handlers would move it to workers who would do the next stage. During our 1995 visit we watched several of these piece-rate workers, and were impressed by the workers' speed and intensity of focus.

Management gradually brought in more automated assembly, eliminating individually-paced jobs. Instead, six to eight workers sat around a circular work cell. Some stations were completely automated; at most stations a worker assisted the machine in assembling the part. When the part was finished, it would be moved (automatically or manually) to the next station. At the last station, the operator would pack the fully-completed part into a box to be shipped directly to the customer. The cell was paced by the slowest worker. At many of the cells, a lighted overhead sign kept track of the pieces made, and compared it to the pieces that should be made to meet the day's quota. Since there was no buffer between operators, inventory in the cells was dramatically lower (and lead times faster) than under piece rates.

By 2000, these assembly jobs employed the bulk of the workforce. There was also a small plastic molding operation, in which workers monitored machines and loaded and unloaded parts. In the suburban plant there were several cells that were completely automated, and monitored by technicians who had received three months of training and were paid more than the assemblers. Other blue-collar jobs included material handling and shipping and receiving.

*Design for Manufacturing.* The key to the success of the firm, according to the CEO (Mr. P), was the tight integration of product and process. At the time of the survey, the Massachusetts plants employed over 100 design engineers. They tried to design products that were not only sophisticated (many were patented), but easy to make, and whose quality could be checked automatically, rather than relying on manual inspection (which is less accurate, particularly when thousands of parts must be checked each day). Examples of design for manufacturing included molding in small bumps on the piece whose only function was to help locate the part correctly in a machine (they had no function once the part was made), and simple fixtures that tested for the presence of certain parts (and would not let the operator go to the next step unless all parts were there).

In our 1995 visit, we saw several engineers working with operators to design such "mistake-proofing" mechanisms. In several cases, the work seemed hampered by language barriers; we saw a lot of sign language being used, as the operator and engineer struggled to communicate about quality problems. We saw fewer engineers on the shop floor in our later visits. One reason was that design-for-manufacturing principles had become codified (both by SP and others), so that more of the work could proceed without input from operators. (These principles include ideas such as making sure that parts either are perfectly symmetric, so that orientation does not matter, or are obviously asymmetric, so a fixture can be built that would not allow work to proceed on an incorrectly oriented part.) This move toward codification was given additional impetus by the fact that the design engineers in Massachusetts were increasingly called on to design parts for SP's other locations far away (including Europe and Mexico).

The other plants were in the process of making similar moves toward more frequent introduction of more sophisticated products, particularly after they were acquired by SP. Both the Ohio and Florida plants were acquired in 2000 by SP for $370 million. According to Mr. P, the purchased firm had excellent market positioning, but Jack (the paternalistic former owner) had not invested in the business in recent years, and operational effectiveness was slipping. There was growing tension between the Ohio managers and SP top management. In contrast to Mr. P's perception, the Ohioans felt that their company was making a good profit, but being dragged down by accounting charges made to reflect what SP felt were its managers' contribution to the business, and financial problems caused by SP's other plants.

The UK plant (actually three small plants about a mile apart) was located in a far distant suburb of London, in a gentrifying area. The plant had been unionized, but almost all the workers had left the union by the late 1990s, feeling that they were not getting much for their dues. Firm SP bought the plant in 2002, and replaced a paternalistic managing director (who used to bring the workers fish and chips on Fridays, and did not enforce a fast pace of work). At the time of our visit, management was just beginning to introduce work cells and just-in-time production techniques.

### Obstacles to Modern Manufacturing Caused by Method of Pay

Although economists often regard piece rates as the optimal method of pay because such rates tie together individual effort and reward, operating such a system in practice requires very special circumstances, as we discuss in the following paragraphs.

In Massachusetts, management recognized that piece rates were not well suited to their new strategy. First, the new system reduced the return to individual, uncoordinated effort. Under piece rates, individual operators had a strong incentive to figure out how to do their jobs as quickly as possible. This led to a sustained 2 to 3 percent annual productivity improvement over the decades, according to Mr. K, an older manager. But piece rates did not promote the teamwork necessary to meet customers' new demands for just-in-time delivery of high-quality products that changed frequently. Increasingly, jobs were automated. The automated work cells increased precision, but frustrated the efforts of those workers who wanted to work faster than others. Also, workers on piece rates wanted a large amount of inventory between stations, so that they were not constrained by someone working more slowly than they were. This practice led to long lead times and low quality, both because of the incentive to work as fast as possible and because the large batches meant that many bad products could be made before they were caught by inspectors.

Second, the problem of establishing contracts for jobs was magnified by the increased rate of new product introduction. Under piece rates, new product introduction created big risks for both labor (that the rate of pay per piece would be set too low) and management (that the rate would turn out to be too high, or "loose"). As Ms. P put it in 2000[2], "New product development became a hurdle with the piecework system. Employees did not want to work on new product [because they would have to learn a new job, with the risk of lower pay while they figured out shortcuts]. We had a lot of turnover in the plant at this time (late 1980s). There were no good standards for new product and there was no way to introduce new products unless we wanted to throw loose rates on them. This restricted us from doing new products."

Both workers and management in the United Kingdom reported similar reluctance to work on new products during our visits there in 2003, at the start of that plant's transition away from piece rates.

These problems of uncoordinated individual effort and contractibility were much less acute in the time rate plants (suburban Massachusetts, Ohio, and Florida). However, management felt that the new higher quality requirements would be better met by having some pay be contingent on group performance.

*Introduction of Employee Involvement Policies in Support of VAG*

When we visited the Massachusetts plants again in 1998, it was clear that VAG was the centerpiece of management's strategy to make workers more aware of their impact on plant performance. Management put a lot of effort into figuring out what they considered to be a "fair" formula (one that would yield a 10 to 15 percent payout if things went well). If the payout

---

2. This is a quote from a very useful document, "Progression of Pay for Performance," that Ms. P wrote for us in February 2000.

was too small, workers would be demoralized, and if it was too big, workers would be getting too much money. Managers also felt the formula needed to change if conditions changed, and so spent a lot of time explaining the changes and justifying them.[3]

Management also set up and continually promoted several mechanisms that provided workers the opportunity to increase the bonus pool for everyone, and recognition for doing so. Among them were "The Last Chance Club" for workers who had caught a defect just before it went out the door. One example of a response (in 1995) was a flood of volunteers willing to sort through 80,000 parts to find the 5 percent that were defective in the 90 minutes before the customer's truck came, on their own time. (This action avoided a one dollar per part air freight cost.) Members of the Last Chance Club got their names on a plaque in the lunchroom; those so inscribed (including management) seemed genuinely pleased at the honor. The gain-sharing also played an important role in changing engineers' incentives: "It used to be like pulling teeth to get engineers to leave their new products and solve problems on the floor. We need to leverage our 30 percent overhead as well as our 5 percent direct labor," said Mr. P in 1995. However, Mr. P observed in 1999 that the VAG seemed successful in getting on-time delivery, but not quality.

There were several mechanisms for management to communicate to employees. These built on some management communication initiatives started in the 1980s. Union avoidance was the initial motivation for these initiatives, according to Mr. K, a semi-retired manager now in his eighties, who had worked at the plant since the 1950s. (There had been several organizing drives in the past, but none since about 1987, a development he attributed to Mr. P's efforts to address problems quickly.) There are quarterly meetings with supervisors, monthly meetings with hourly workers (these are attended by one or two representatives from each department, chosen by management) and quarterly meetings to discuss the gain-sharing results.

Although the VAG formula was complex, almost all shop workers had a basic understanding that low productivity, defects, and delivery mistakes would cost them money. (However, especially in the early months of the program, some of the efforts made by workers seemed to go far beyond the individual monetary benefit they received (a defective part would cost each worker only about one dollar).

In 1995 in Boston, there were continuous improvement teams in which 10 to 15 percent of the workforce participated. These were not in evidence in later visits. Instead, in 1998, the plants focused on obtaining International Organization for Standardization (ISO) 9000 quality certification; there

3. The magnitude of management's effort to design and maintain the gain-sharing effort perhaps both explains its success, and why relatively few firms are able to achieve such success. See Helper and Kleiner (2003) for more details.

was some involvement by workers in writing their own job descriptions. In 2000, the plants undertook a Six Sigma initiative, which was still going on in 2002. This program involves training supervisors and management as "Six Sigma black belts" (or green belts in the case of supervisors); they learn techniques for reducing inventory and lead time, and for analyzing quality data. Operators join with supervisors and engineers to improve line layout, but according to one supervisor we talked with, they contribute very few useful ideas. Overall, the improvement efforts have helped the urban plant to reduce costs by 3 percent every year since 1986. (Interestingly, this figure is similar to the 2 to 3 percent productivity improvement that Mr. K said that operators on piece rates achieved.) At the time of survey, the plants seemed to be placing less emphasis on suggestions to change the process, and more on training to take over supervisory functions and avoid mistakes. This last is in response to quality problems that have meant the VAG payout in the suburban plant was zero in the year preceding the survey. (The urban plant continued to average 7 to 10 percent.)

Efforts to set up complementary programs that would allow workers to have an influence on plant performance were much less consistent in the other plants. In Florida, there was an effort to train workers to avoid defects. We attended a company meeting where the emphasis was on the costs to the company of defective parts. The key message was that small numbers of defects can lead to large costs that harm the VAG bonus to production employees. The emphasis during the meeting was for employees to attempt to catch mistakes, rather than think of innovations to prevent mistakes in the first place.

In Ohio, the main improvement activity at the time of our visits was the "War on Waste" program (WOW). This program was led by an engineer (Mr. S), who was truly an evangelist for lean production. In 1994 (before SP acquired it), he had gotten the plant enrolled in a program sponsored by the Toyota Supplier Support Program, even though the plant has never had Toyota business. Several Toyota engineers had helped the plant with projects to improve the flow of product through the plant. According to Mr. S's calculations, WOW has saved the plant 2 to 3 percent of sales in the two years since its inception. Almost all of the ideas seem to be generated by technicians and engineers. "We don't involve operators enough. We do it hardly at all—this is a failing," notes Mr. S. Mr. S did what he could to encourage participation, believing that "people want recognition, not more pay. You could increase pay and still have dissatisfied employees." Participation in small ways is rewarded; about 10 percent (by rough estimate) of operators were wearing a WOW T-shirt or using a WOW pencil on the day we conducted the survey. However, this program was really the brainchild of Mr. S, who called himself "the Wizard of WOW;" he received little reinforcement for his efforts from top management. When SP reorganized the management bonus pool after acquiring the company, Mr. S was no longer included, leading to a significant cut in pay and status for him.

In the United Kingdom, there was no such effort. (The VAG was not clearly explained, even to the managers who were to implement it. On one of our visits, one month before VAG was implemented; the finance director confided that "I don't understand it at all.")

At the time of our survey in spring 2003, the workers at the UK plant were very unhappy with SP management, which had eased out their "beloved managing director" and imposed a faster pace of work and more emphasis on cost-cutting. Even though many of the workers found our survey quite challenging, almost a third took the time to write comments, which were quite scathing. Two examples follow:

"The management could do with more training on how to talk to people and try to understand their personal problems and see that we are human beings and not machines to be switched off and on at will."

"They expect you to send out work [deliver output] when we go days a week without getting any parts. When they get here they are often short mouldings or water damaged. Also nobody takes any notice of anything we say or suggest. They ask for votes but have already made up their minds . . . Here they treat you as a number not a person. We get little pay for working like a Trojan. Our holidays have been altered now we have to take ours when the children are still at school . . . All we want to do is come to work, earn our money then go home but all we get is meetings and videos that nobody much is interested in."

*Impact of VAG Introduction on Levels of Pay, and the Pay/Effort Bargain*

The change to VAG had a large impact on both levels of pay, and on the pay/effort bargain as perceived by workers. These impacts differed by plant, and the magnitude of the impacts seemed largely unexpected by management.

At the Massachusetts urban plant, getting rid of the piece rate system was not easy. "From 1985 to the early 1990s, we started to educate the employees in a series of round table meetings and business meetings, that the security they felt they had in the incentive system was hurting the company and hurting them and hurting the quality of the business and that we would have to make changes to the way they made their money." (Ms. P, 2000). But some mistakes were made. "For our original steering committee, we selected [hourly] people who had trust in the plan—we didn't have the natural leaders. We had approached it as a control thing with employees," said Mr. P in 1995.

"The opportunity of expanding to a second plant in 1989 was the first chance of changing the pay system," according to Ms. P. Workers in this plant, located in a suburb, worked in cells, and were paid an hourly wage.

This wage was lower than in the urban plant, since the prevailing wage in the suburb was lower. Thus, it was difficult to get people to help with the start-up, so some were given promotions as an incentive. Piece rates also were gradually phased out at the urban plant, between 1992 and 1996.

Some operators we interviewed in focus groups in 2000 remained upset about the change. Almost all operators worked faster than the standard at which the piece rate was set. Management recognized this by setting the base time wage at 132 percent of the piece-rate base wage. They also introduced a gain-sharing program that they thought would pay an additional 10 to 15 percent. Managers said later that they did not intend to cut pay ("except that there were some people making 200 percent of the base rate, which is just unrealistic," according to Ms. P in 2002). However, management was very worried about setting the rates too high and locking themselves into a wage that was "too high."[4] (In one case, "we underestimated the impact of automating the manual O-ring assembly—it almost killed the plan," said Mr. P in 1995.) The result was 45 percent of those who filled out our survey and had worked under piece rates felt that they had suffered a pay cut. Workers who had been on piece rates were kept at the same hourly pay for two years. However, the fastest workers saw their hourly pay decline four to five dollars per hour (40 to 50 percent) over several years. According to management, only about 10 percent of operators quit due to the transition, however.[5] And newer workers, who had not yet figured out shortcuts on their job (or been assigned to a job with a "loose" rate), benefited; 27 percent of survey respondents who had worked under piece rates indicated that they made more money now than before.

Wages in 1999 for assemblers were $10.48 per hour in the suburban plant and $10.60 per hour in the urban plant (there was no seniority increment). In the urban plant, this was supplemented by a VAG payout of about one dollar per hour. The VAG was much less (often zero) in the suburban plant, due mostly to quality problems and secondarily to difficulties in accounting for the time of engineers who worked on products for SP's other plants (Ms. P, 2002). This pay rate was far below the U.S. manufacturing average of $14.40 per hour in 1999 ($15.03 for workers in industrial machinery) (Jacobs 2000). Benefits (which included paid vacation, medical, and dental) were more generous than in the average U.S. factory, but did not come close to offsetting the low pay. In addition, the Massachusetts plants are located in an area with a very high cost of living.

However, the impact on satisfaction of the pay cut for the Massachusetts

4. It seemed that "too high" meant wages more than 15 percent above the average for unskilled manufacturing workers in the area. (For example, Mr. P said in 1995 that if gain-sharing exceeded 15 percent, then it was time to cut prices to customers (rather than continue to increase compensation to workers). It is not clear how the 15 percent figure was arrived at.

5. Note that the figure of 45 percent of workers receiving a pay cut does not include any of the 10 percent who left the plant.

piece-rate workers was offset in part by a perceived decline in work effort required. There was now no incentive to work fast; instead, the goal was to work at the same pace as the team.

At the time rate plants, however, workers perceived that the new management policies (including both VAG and lean production techniques) required a significant increase in effort. Because the VAG payout was generally low in these plants, pay did not increase much to compensate for this effort. The payout was low due to quality problems; it was unclear if these problems were exogenous, or due to workers' desire to economize on effort given their low pay.

*Perceived Access to Alternative Employment*

The demographics of the workforce in each of SP's plants were quite distinct from each other. But, as we discuss below, the demographics sought out by SP (immigrants, older people, residents of rural areas) were those who had few alternative job possibilities.

In the 1990s, the line workers at the Massachusetts plants were largely immigrants. About one-third of the work force was Vietnamese and one-third Cape Verdean. The rest was a mixture of immigrants from other countries, such as Poland, and U.S.-born workers. About 60 percent was female. The workforce was recruited by word of mouth rather than advertising; many workers were related to each other. There were few blacks, though the plant was in a majority-black area. At the urban location, most workers walked or took public transportation to work. Turnover was low; at the time of our survey two-thirds of the workforce had been at SP for at least four years (see table 8.1).

The Ohio plant was located in a rural part of the state, about thirty minutes from a medium-sized city where most of the managers lived. The company was started in the mid-1960s by a man universally known as Jack, who had innovative ideas for electronics products and a paternalistic management style. Layoffs were done on a voluntary basis, and Jack was often seen on the shop floor until he semi-retired and moved south (where he opened the Florida plant).

At the Ohio plant, everyone seemed to be native born, and all but a handful were white. The average age was forty-four, higher than in Massachusetts; about 20 percent appeared to be over sixty. (Management explained that many of them worked to supplement retirement benefits obtained from working on a previous job.) Although there was a core of experienced workers (see table 8.1), turnover was very high; 30 percent of those hired in 2000 had left by the end of the year (quit or were fired). In 2001, the starting wage for an assembler was $6.85 per hour; after one year this increased to $7.80; after three years to $8.27. After twelve years, one assembler reported that she made about nine dollars per hour. This was supplemented with an annual check that was called "profit-sharing." The owner allocated a pool of money

**Table 8.1**          **Descriptive financial and nonproduction employee statistics**

| Variable | Boston Mean (S.D.) | Florida Mean (S.D.) | Ohio Mean (S.D.) | UK Mean (S.D.) | All Plants Mean (S.D.) |
|---|---|---|---|---|---|
| Assets per employee | 106.90 | 148.12 | 133.16 | 41.78 | 102.01 |
|  | (8.55) | (112.11) | (110.80) | (3.26) | (71.86) |
| Sales per employee | 14.04 | 8.07 | 9.42 | 6.48 | 10.51 |
|  | (3.73) | (1.02) | (1.39) | (1.36) | (4.18) |
| Gross profits per employee | 4.37 | 1.68 | 3.47 | 1.08 | 3.01 |
|  | (1.15) | (0.47) | (0.67) | (0.37) | (1.65) |
| Operating profits per employee | 2.77 | 1.07 | 2.71 | 0.36 | 2.00 |
|  | (1.03) | (0.51) | (0.66) | (0.26) | (1.29) |
| Value-added per employee | 8.31 | 5.68 | 5.98 | 4.14 | 6.45 |
|  | (1.34) | (0.71) | (0.90) | (0.79) | (2.01) |
| Percentage nonproduction employees | 28.94 | 19.42 | 17.64 | 21.71 | 24.26 |
|  | (1.52) | (0.64) | (1.28) | (1.44) | (4.89) |
| Sample size (months of data) | 98–111 | 37–39 | 37–39 | 44–58 | 224–245 |

*Notes:* All financial figures are in tens of thousands of dollars. Value-added = Net sales – Material cost. Boston monthly data from December 1989 to April 2000; Florida monthly data from January 1999 to March 2002; Ohio monthly data from January 1999 to March 2002; UK monthly data from March 1999 to December 2003. S.D. = standard deviation.

(based loosely on the past year's performance) which was divided among the workforce based on seniority and wages; the payment was typically equal to about two weeks' wages. In contrast to the VAG, management did not emphasize the role of workers in affecting the payment, and the size of the bonus pool was subjectively determined.

The Florida plant had many similarities to the suburban Boston plant. It was relatively new, about fifteen years old, and was capital intensive. Unlike Boston, the workforce has a large number of retirees who moved to Florida, and found that their retirement income and savings were insufficient. Consequently, the age of production employees was higher in Florida than at the other plants.

The plant manager in Florida, Mr. Z, said that the plant was built to serve as a semi-retirement location for the founder of the company. Consequently, the plant and the major offices for top management were in separate buildings. The manufacturing plant and its offices were plain, with Spartan amenities. The main office complex had carpeted workspaces with spacious windows for management, and was generally larger and had modern audio visual equipment. The corporate meeting rooms and cafeteria were in the office complex rather than in the plant.

Although most of the jobs involved watching and adjusting controls on machines and checking for defects, there were many difficult and tedious jobs. These included packing parts and loading trucks: a particularly daunting job involved putting small round sensors into a hole the size of the eye of a needle for eight hours per day.

In the United Kingdom, the base wage had not been raised for several years, and the assembler rate of 4.60 pounds in 2002 (about seven dollars at then-current exchange rates), was not much above the national minimum of 4.20. The former management saw the low wage as the plant's main source of competitive advantage, according to the new management. The base wage was raised to 4.83 per hour on January 1, 2003, with the possibility of a group bonus ranging from 0 to 40 percent, with the average at 14 percent. In contrast to the VAG, which is plant-wide, this bonus was based on the efforts of one work cell (a dozen or so people). Management's idea was to transition the workforce slowly toward a bonus based on a larger number of workers, from an individual bonus (piece rate) to a group bonus, to the VAG, which was to be implemented in spring 2003. The demographics of the workforce was overwhelmingly female ("mostly second earners," according to the HR director), and was about 20 percent Indian and 5 percent Chinese, with the remainder white British.

## 8.4    Methods

### 8.4.1    Plant Visits and Surveys

We visited each of the Massachusetts plants three times: in 1995, 1998, and 2000, and the urban plant again in 2002. We visited the Ohio and Florida plants each three times in 2002 and the UK plant three times in 2003. At each visit, we spoke with managers and toured the plant. As part of the survey process, we conducted focus groups with workers (without management present), and talked with workers as they filled out the surveys (though we did not look at how they answered the questions; the surveys were anonymous). We also made a presentation of our findings to the management of each plant, and learned from their responses.

Our methodology thus combines standard econometric multivariate approaches with the enhanced knowledge from plant visits that provides insights not gained through statistical estimation. For example, we were able to learn about the product improvements and the "war on waste" policies implemented within the Ohio plant through discussions with the plant manager and employees. General knowledge of the products produced or financial records would not be able to capture these changes in the establishments. Ironically, this close understanding of the policies and practices makes it harder to argue that the policy was implemented identically in each plant—if we had known less, we could have more convincingly argued that we have a true natural experiment.[6]

6. Thanks to Fredrik Andersson for this point.

### 8.4.2   Estimation Strategy

Our efforts to isolate the impact of the VAG on productivity and satisfaction involve two types of tests. We examine the direct impact of the various plants in the United States, relative to the UK plant, on measures of firm performance to include measures of productivity and profitability. Next we measure the impact of the changes to VAG on employee satisfaction in the U.S. versus the UK plants.

In order to suggest that this was a quasi-natural experiment, we need to show that the plants are similar except for the adoption of VAG. The production processes at all five plants are quite similar, involving assembly of small, complex electronic and plastic-molded parts. These areas of the five plants are remarkably similar. All plants also have in-house engineering. The level of productivity at the Massachusetts plants is higher than at the others, but this is due largely to the greater productivity of engineers there; these engineers increasingly design products to be produced at SP's other plants as well. Engineers made up a relatively constant 13 percent of the workforce in Massachusetts, and nonproduction workers ranged from 25 to 30 percent. In our estimates, we also control for the level of nonproduction employees in each plant. In addition, the Ohio, Florida, and United Kingdom establishments each had plastic molding departments, though Massachusetts did not. Assembly worker jobs and pace of work are remarkably similar across plants, according to the management groups. Our basic efficiency-based models were of the following form:

(1)                         $Q = f(\text{VAG}, \text{X}', \varepsilon),$

where $Q$ is productivity as measured by output or value added per worker, VAG is 0 for each month until the VAG program is introduced in that plant, and 1 afterward, $\text{X}'$ is a set of controls for plant and individual characteristics, and $\varepsilon$ is the standard error term with the usual ordinary least squares (OLS) assumptions on its structure.

## 8.5   Results

### 8.5.1   Worker and Establishment Characteristics

In table 8.1 we give the basic financial characteristics of the four plants in our study. For the UK plant, we adjust the values by the exchange rate of the pound for the dollar in each year for which we have data, and give the values in dollars. In all of our measures of productivity or profits, the UK plant is lower. We also show the percentage of nonproduction employees in each of the plants. By this measure, the UK plant ranks second to the Boston area facilities. In the final column, we show the aggregate measures of each factor for the four facilities for SP. Since there was missing data for some of our measures, we also give the range of the number of monthly observations in our sample.

### 8.5.2    Impact of Value-Added Gain-Sharing

In table 8.2, we estimate the impact of the plants and the VAG on measures of financial performance at SP. We provide estimates of several specifications of the basic model described in equation (1). We begin with a basic plant effect with controls for only assets per employee. We then add a time trend measured by the lag of the dependent variable; this captures the impact of other features of the plant's environment. For example, automakers succeeded in preventing suppliers from raising prices (the Producer Price Index for auto parts did not rise from 1990 to 2001), while input prices rose. For the period that VAG is in place, we also control for improvements made due to the VAG in the previous month, imposing a relatively stringent test of the program's efficacy.[7] In the third column of table 8.2 we include the percentage of nonproduction employees as a control. In all our specifications, the performance levels of the U.S. plants are significantly higher than those of the UK plant, which is consistent with our descriptive statistics.

Panel A shows the impact of the VAG on gross productivity as measured by sales per employee. In this case, with our fully specified model the VAG increased productivity by 18 percent. Panel B shows a similarly specified set of multivariate models for the log of gross profits per employee, where gross profits equals total revenue minus total variable costs during the month. The U.S. plants were more profitable than their UK counterpart across all specifications. Adoption of VAG increased gross profits by a statistically significant 17 percent in the most fully specified model across all the plants.

In panel C of table 8.2 we show estimates of the log of value added per employee, where value-added equals sales minus material costs. The results again show that the U.S. plants are more productive than the UK plants. The last column gives the fully specified model that shows that the VAG is associated with a 10 percent increase in value added per employee that is precisely estimated. These estimates are similar to those of Kaufman for his estimates of the effect of gain-sharing (1992). The results in table 8.3 show that the U.S. plants are more productive and that the introduction of the VAG enhanced the ability of the plants to improve on its productivity and profitability in a highly competitive marketplace.

Thus we find consistently that (a) the level of productivity and profits is higher in the U.S. plants than in the UK plants, and that (b) adoption of the VAG is associated with subsequent 10 to 18 percent improvements in those measures. (Note that the gross profit figures include the cost of administering the program, so VAG more than paid for itself.) In results not shown,

---

7. On the other hand, to the extent that errors in measuring output are serially correlated, this method overstates the impact of VAG on performance.

**Table 8.2**    **Estimates of the impact of VAG on measures of firm performance in U.S. plants relative to the UK plant**

| | | | | | | |
|---|---|---|---|---|---|---|
| A. Dependent variable: Log sales per employee | | | | | | |
| Percent nonproduction employees | | | −0.08*** | −0.03*** | −0.03** | −0.02 |
| | | | (0.01) | (0.01) | (0.01) | (0.01) |
| Lagged log sales per employee | | 0.59*** | | 0.51*** | | 0.38*** |
| | | (0.05) | | (0.06) | | (0.06) |
| Log assets per employee | 0.00 | 0.01 | −0.07** | −0.03 | −0.10*** | −0.05** |
| | (0.03) | (0.02) | (0.03) | (0.02) | (0.03) | (0.02) |
| Boston | 0.75*** | 0.31*** | 1.36*** | 0.64*** | 0.88*** | 0.55*** |
| | (0.05) | (0.06) | (0.09) | (0.11) | (0.10) | (0.10) |
| Florida | 0.23*** | 0.09** | 0.13** | 0.06 | 0.15*** | 0.09** |
| | (0.05) | (0.04) | (0.05) | (0.04) | (0.05) | (0.04) |
| Ohio | 0.39*** | 0.15*** | 0.13** | 0.07 | 0.36*** | 0.21*** |
| | (0.05) | (0.04) | (0.06) | (0.05) | (0.06) | (0.06) |
| VAG | | | | | 0.32*** | 0.18*** |
| | | | | | (0.04) | (0.04) |
| Adjusted $R^2$ | 0.66 | 0.81 | 0.72 | 0.82 | 0.78 | 0.83 |
| $N$ | 239 | 229 | 239 | 229 | 239 | 229 |
| B. Dependent variable: Log gross profits per employee | | | | | | |
| Percent nonproduction employees | | | −0.07*** | −0.04** | −0.03 | −0.02 |
| | | | (0.02) | (0.02) | (0.02) | (0.02) |
| Lagged log gross profits per employee | | 0.24*** | | 0.21*** | | 0.19*** |
| | | (0.07) | | (0.07) | | (0.07) |
| Log assets per employee | −0.08* | −0.05 | −0.15*** | −0.10** | −0.17*** | −0.12** |
| | (0.05) | (0.04) | (0.05) | (0.05) | (0.05) | (0.05) |
| Boston | 1.52*** | 1.18*** | 2.03*** | 1.54*** | 1.64*** | 1.34*** |
| | (0.07) | (0.12) | (0.15) | (0.20) | (0.18) | (0.21) |
| Florida | 0.56*** | 0.42*** | 0.47*** | 0.38*** | 0.49*** | 0.41*** |
| | (0.08) | (0.09) | (0.09) | (0.09) | (0.08) | (0.09) |
| Ohio | 1.30*** | 0.98*** | 1.08*** | 0.88*** | 1.26*** | 1.03*** |
| | (0.08) | (0.11) | (0.10) | (0.12) | (0.11) | (0.13) |
| VAG | | | | | 0.26*** | 0.17** |
| | | | | | (0.07) | (0.07) |
| Adjusted $R^2$ | 0.76 | 0.80 | 0.77 | 0.80 | 0.78 | 0.81 |
| $N$ | 236 | 225 | 236 | 225 | 236 | 225 |

we also find significant differences within the U.S. plants: the Boston plants perform significantly better throughout the period and have significantly greater improvements due to the adoption of VAG.

Table 8.3 suggests some reasons for the differential effect of VAG across plants—the differences in the levels of adoption of complementary policies, as perceived by workers. In our satisfaction survey, workers were asked to mark each of the statements in table 8.3 on a scale of 1 ("strongly disagree") to 5 ("strongly agree"). The VAG is more effective to the extent that workers understand (a) "their roles and responsibilities"; (b) what actions on their part lead to good performance (they are informed by their supervisors about their

Table 8.2          (continued)

C. Dependent variable: Log value added per employee

|  | (1) | (2) | (3) | (4) | (5) | (6) |
|---|---|---|---|---|---|---|
| Percent nonproduction employees |  |  | −0.04*** | −0.03*** | −0.02** | −0.02** |
|  |  |  | (0.01) | (0.01) | (0.01) | (0.01) |
| Lagged log value-added per |  | 0.33*** |  | 0.26*** |  | 0.21*** |
| employee |  | (0.06) |  | (0.06) |  | (0.07) |
| Log assets per employee | 0.02 | 0.02 | −0.02 | −0.01 | −0.03 | −0.03 |
|  | (0.02) | (0.02) | (0.02) | (0.02) | (0.02) | (0.02) |
| Boston | 0.68*** | 0.45*** | 1.00*** | 0.75*** | 0.80*** | 0.65*** |
|  | (0.03) | (0.05) | (0.07) | (0.10) | (0.08) | (0.10) |
| Florida | 0.30*** | 0.20*** | 0.25*** | 0.18*** | 0.26*** | 0.20*** |
|  | (0.04) | (0.04) | (0.04) | (0.04) | (0.04) | (0.04) |
| Ohio | 0.37*** | 0.24*** | 0.23*** | 0.16*** | 0.32*** | 0.24*** |
|  | (0.04) | (0.04) | (0.05) | (0.05) | (0.05) | (0.05) |
| VAG |  |  |  |  | 0.13*** | 0.10*** |
|  |  |  |  |  | (0.03) | (0.03) |
| Adjusted $R^2$ | 0.74 | 0.77 | 0.77 | 0.78 | 0.78 | 0.79 |
| N | 232 | 229 | 232 | 229 | 232 | 229 |

*Notes:* Standard errors in parenthesis. Value-added = Net sales – Material cost. Boston monthly data from December 1989 to April 2000; Florida monthly data from January 1999 to March 2002; Ohio monthly data from January 1999 to March 2002; UK monthly data from March 1999 to December 2003; Boston introduced VAG in January 1996; Florida introduced VAG in January 2001. Blank cells indicate that variable was not included in the regression.

***Significant at the 1 percent level.
**Significant at the 5 percent level.
*Significant at the 10 percent level.


**Table 8.3          Measures of complementary policies to improve productivity**

|  | Boston Mean (S.D.) | Florida Mean (S.D.) | Ohio Mean (S.D.) | UK Mean (S.D.) |
|---|---|---|---|---|
| In my work unit, people have a clear understanding of their roles and responsibilities | 3.66 (1.12) | 3.37*** (1.18) | 3.42*** (1.15) | 3.14*** (1.17) |
| I regularly get communication from my supervisor (or group leader) about my performance | 3.26 (1.34) | 2.91*** (1.24) | 2.89*** (1.28) | 2.58*** (1.26) |
| When an external customer (like Ford or Chrysler) finds a problem, I learn about it | 3.62 (1.15) | 3.28*** (1.24) | 3.13*** (1.23) | 3.08*** (1.17) |
| When a problem is found in my work unit, we change our procedures to make sure the problem does not happen again | 3.97 (1.06) | 3.55*** (1.12) | 3.43*** (1.09) | 3.31*** (1.20) |

*Note:* Standard errors are in parentheses.
***Significant at the 1 percent level.
**Significant at the 5 percent level.
*Significant at the 10 percent level.

performance); (c) when certain actions are necessary (e.g., they find out when an external customer finds a defect); and (d) how to ensure that the problem does not happen again (so that VAG leads not just to a one-time performance gain, but to a new improvement path). Table 8.3 shows that the U.S. average on each of these measures is significantly greater than the UK average, and that Massachusetts is significantly higher than Florida or Ohio.

As our interviews suggest, the higher U.S. performance is due mostly to managerial policies (the introduction and constant reinforcement of supporting policies). We found little evidence to suggest that the differences were a consequence of country-specific regulations or culture. However, our sample of just a few establishments in only one firm by itself is not sufficient to draw general conclusions about the influence of national policies on either productivity or employee satisfaction.

### 8.5.3    What Affects Employee Satisfaction?

We find that worker satisfaction varies a great deal by plant. However, the UK plant averages are significantly lower than those for the United States. Employees who perceived that they made more money under VAG were more satisfied. Workers who reported working harder under VAG also were more satisfied, although the causality here may be reversed.

The basic survey instrument we used to examine employee satisfaction was the Minnesota Satisfaction Survey (MSS). We then added questions to examine the impact of the pay systems in each plant. The baseline questions were of a Likert-type 5-point scale. The MSS has been used by industrial psychologists for more than fifty years to gauge employee satisfaction in American industry. We also asked questions of the employees about their tenure with the company, type of job, and pay policies.

In our attempt to examine the determinants of satisfaction, we examine a number of factors in addition to the effects of company policies. From the literature in psychology we know that there are individual differences that affect job satisfaction (Arvey, Carter, and Buerkley 1991). Moreover, the specific question asked of the respondents is also of importance; the central questions about job satisfaction measure different qualities such as attachment to the job, quality of supervision, and other attributes. Consequently, these factors should be accounted for in any attempt to examine what is under the control of the firm versus other exogenous factors. Even though the overarching policies adopted by the firm were at the plant level, group or team effects are also likely to influence satisfaction with work (Judge et al. 2001).

In table 8.4 we show employment characteristics of the more than 1,800 employees (90 percent of the workforce) who responded to the satisfaction survey at the U.S. and UK plants. The UK plant had the highest percentage of assemblers, but the lowest percentage of temporary workers. Except for

Table 8.4                Employee characteristics at SP

|  | Boston (all) | Boston (urban) | Boston (suburban) | Florida | Ohio | UK |
|---|---|---|---|---|---|---|
| Sample size | 518 | 233 | 285 | 482 | 634 | 199 |
| Assemblers | 67.71% | 63.29% | 71.35% | 44.33% | 53.55% | 73.51% |
| Part-time workers |  |  |  | 1.07% | 0.59% |  |
| Temporary workers | 14.49% | 16.53% | 12.96% |  |  | 5.37% |
| Worked on piece rate | 66.02% | 67.38% | 64.91% |  |  | 76.88% |
| Worked on hourly rate | 74.13% | 70.82% | 76.84% |  |  | 68.84% |
| Tenure: less than 1 year | 12.17% | 12.02% | 12.30% | 16.51% | 3.74% | 12.95% |
| Tenure: 1 to 4 years | 30.00% | 26.92% | 32.54% | 37.39% | 34.47% | 25.91% |
| Tenure: 4 to 6 years | 20.65% | 13.94% | 26.19% | 17.66% | 16.91% | 15.03% |
| Tenure: 6 to 10 years | 12.39% | 11.54% | 13.10% | 21.79% | 19.84% | 12.44% |
| Tenure: more than 10 years | 24.78% | 35.58% | 15.87% | 6.65% | 25.04% | 33.68% |

*Note:* Blank cells indicate that variable was not included in the regression.

Table 8.5                ANOVA analysis of the impact of working in the establishment on employee satisfaction

|  | DF | Sum of squares | Mean square | *F* Value | Pr > *F* |
|---|---|---|---|---|---|
| Model | 1,356 | 18,131.48 | 13.37 | 14.93 | < .0001 |
| Person | 1,337 | 13,476.77 | 10.08 | 11.26 | < .0001 |
| Question | 15 | 3,963.00 | 264.20 | 295.04 | < .0001 |
| Place | 4 | 691.70 | 172.92 | 193.11 | < .0001 |
| Error | 20,051 | 17,954.86 | 0.90 |  |  |
| Corrected total | 21,407 | 36,086.34 |  |  |  |
| $R^2$ | 0.50 |  |  |  |  |

*Note:* The ANOVA sample include employee satisfaction data from two plants in Massachusetts and one each in Florida, United Kingdom, and Ohio. DF = degrees of freedom; Pr = probability.

the Florida plant (the newest one), tenure with the plant was similar across the plants in our sample.

Table 8.5 presents an ANOVA multivariate analysis of the role of both individual and plant characteristics in contributing to explaining overall employee satisfaction. We show the role of the plant, individual, or question in explaining overall job satisfaction. The ANOVA shows that the workplace as measured by the plant where you work is important in contributing to overall satisfaction. Although the exact type of satisfaction asked about (and individual worker characteristics) are significant, the role of the plant-level environment significantly contributes to the overall level of employee satisfaction, suggesting that where you work matters beyond your personal characteristics.

**Table 8.6**    **Impact of working on piece rates on job satisfaction of production employees in the Massachusetts establishments**

|  | Job satisfaction (1) | Job satisfaction (2) |
|---|---|---|
| Piece rate | 0.24 | 0.24 |
|  | (0.24) | (0.24) |
| Vietnamese | 0.38 | 0.26 |
|  | (0.16)* | (0.16) |
| Cape Verde | 0.11 | 0.02 |
|  | (0.17) | (0.17) |
| Tenure less than 1 year | 0.05 | 0.13 |
|  | (0.21) | (0.22) |
| Tenure between 1 and 6 years | 0.26 | 0.23 |
|  | (0.14) | (0.14) |
| Lack of other jobs |  | 0.22 |
|  |  | (0.05)** |
| Adj. $R^2$ | 0.02 | 0.07 |
| $N$ | 361 | 361 |

*Note:* Standard errors are in parentheses.
***Significant at the 1 percent level.
**Significant at the 5 percent level.
*Significant at the 10 percent level.

### 8.5.4 Internationalization of the American Workplace: The Job Satisfaction of Immigrants

At the inner city Boston and suburban plant we were able to gather more detailed information on the job satisfaction of employees. A high percentage of the employees were immigrants from Vietnam and Cape Verde, and were not proficient in English. Consequently, we translated our questionnaire into Vietnamese and Portuguese,[8] and respondents chose the language in which they wanted to take the survey. Thus, we are able to differentiate individuals in the plant by their degree of assimilation to English. In addition, we compare the degree of satisfaction with work with English-reading and writing individuals within the plant to persons whose main language is Vietnamese and Portuguese. Further, we compare their level of satisfaction to persons in the other plants whose main language is English.

The regression results of language on job satisfaction for the Boston facility are presented in table 8.6. The estimates show that having worked under piece rates does not have a significant impact on satisfaction. Moreover, we find that the English speakers were the least satisfied, but that language served as a proxy for fewer job opportunities. When we added a variable for

8. The Cape Verdeans spoke several dialects of Portugese.

the lack of other jobs in the second column, the impact of language was not statistically significant.[9]

### 8.5.5    Did the Change in HR practices Influence Overall Satisfaction?

As part of the effort to examine the overall effects of the HR practices on employee satisfaction we analyze the change in the method of pay on employee satisfaction. The basic model is of the following form:

$$(2) \qquad\qquad \Delta\text{Sat} = f(\text{VAG}, X', \varepsilon),$$

where the change in satisfaction, $\Delta$Sat, is a function of the change in compensation, and plant controls and characteristics, and the $\varepsilon$ is the error term.

Using the previous model, we examine the relative impacts of working harder and making more money on overall satisfaction. The estimates in table 8.7 show the impact of the change in satisfaction at the Boston, Florida, and UK facilities after the VAG. We show the coefficient estimates from equation (2), where the dependent variable is $\Delta$Sat and the independent variables are the response to working harder under the new system and the increase in pay. In all cases, the values for the independent variables for working harder and making more money are statistically significant. Working harder seems to increase job satisfaction, perhaps tied to the strong view about having pride in the company, but having more pay is of greater importance.

There seems to have been important impacts of the changes to a VAG system of pay on productivity and employee satisfaction. Profitability also increased, especially when compared to the industry. Firm SP's profitability increased because the move away from piece rates allowed the plants to offer more diverse new products that had higher profit margins (Freeman and Kleiner 1998). In addition, worker's compensation costs at the urban plant were cut in half after the move away from piece rates, for a savings of $200,000 per year (an amount equal to 10 percent of the direct labor payroll).[10]

### 8.6    Conclusions

Our results show that the UK plant was less productive and profitable relative to the U.S. operations. We also find that changing to VAG increased productivity and gross profits even in the most restrictive specification. The

---

9. In the appendix we estimate the same model but give the satisfaction measure as a Rasch index rather than a summated index for overall satisfaction, and find similar results.

10. According to data provided by the company, workers' compensation expenses incurred averaged $203,000 per year from 1996 to 1999 (after the transition to gain-sharing was completed), and $413,000 from 1989 to 1995. (These figures are uncorrected for either inflation or the growth in hours worked over this period; these are similar-sized adjustments that move in opposite directions.)

**Table 8.7**          **Impact of changes in satisfaction after moving to VAG**

| From piece rate to VAG Massachusetts | Change in job satisfaction after VAG | Change in job satisfaction after VAG |
| --- | --- | --- |
| Working harder under VAG | 0.20** | |
| | (0.08) | |
| Making more money under VAG | | 0.55*** |
| | | (0.08) |
| Making suggestions | −0.02 | 0.01 |
| | (0.07) | (0.06) |
| Vietnamese | 0.76*** | 0.29 |
| | (0.28) | (0.26) |
| Cape Verde | 0.23 | −0.23 |
| | (0.29) | (0.27) |
| Adj. $R^2$ | 0.07 | 0.29 |
| $N$ | 131 | 127 |

| From time rate to VAG Florida | Change in job satisfaction after VAG | Change in job satisfaction after VAG |
| --- | --- | --- |
| Working harder under VAG | 0.47*** | |
| | (0.07) | |
| Making more money | | 0.49*** |
| | | (0.07) |
| Making suggestions | 0.03 | 0.09* |
| | (0.05) | (0.05) |
| Adj. $R^2$ | 0.22 | 0.25 |
| $N$ | 158 | 161 |

| From piece rate to VAG UK | Change in job satisfaction after VAG | Change in job satisfaction after VAG |
| --- | --- | --- |
| Working harder under VAG | 0.53*** | |
| | (0.08) | |
| Making more money | | 0.58*** |
| | | (0.07) |
| Making suggestions | −0.05 | −0.05 |
| | (0.06) | (0.06) |
| Adj. $R^2$ | 0.30 | 0.36 |
| $N$ | 110 | 110 |

*Note:* Standard errors are in parentheses.
***Significant at the 1 percent level.
**Significant at the 5 percent level.
*Significant at the 10 percent level.

move away from piece rates allowed introduction of new products more quickly, and allowed inventory reduction. The VAG was particularly effective when management undertook a lot of activities complementary to the VAG (explained how the VAG worked, created the Last Chance Club)—especially in Massachusetts. The impact of the pay cut from getting rid of piece rates was offset by the reduction in work effort required.

## 8.6.1   National Differences

We find it hard to attribute the differences we found (lower worker satisfaction and lower productivity in the UK plants) to national institutions. We did not hear complaints from managers (many of whom were familiar with conditions in the United States) about restrictive work rules, and did not observe any differences in work rules—management in all plants seemed to have complete freedom to assign workers anywhere in the plant. The U.S. plants had made a commitment to workers to avoid layoffs. This was especially true in the two acquired plants; the previous owner made it known that he had a year's worth of salaries in the bank, which he used to cushion downturns. The UK plants had no such commitments.

Instead, we think that the diversity of outcomes is a reflection in large part of sample selection bias. Firm SP chose a low-productivity UK plant to buy, because they believed that their management skills would allow the U.S. firm to turn around the UK firm so that it returned economic value greater than its cost of purchase. (A similar logic was evident in the purchase of the Ohio and Florida plants, which also had lower productivity than Massachusetts.) A variety of sources attested to the low quality of the British management team: SP top executives, workers we interviewed, and our own observation of disorganization, poor communication, and capricious behavior. Pay levels had not kept pace with inflation, and were significantly below the national and regional averages for manufacturing.

We did find one factor that is linked to institutions: access to immigrant labor and other workers with limited alternatives. Across all of our plants, access to alternative employment was negatively correlated with satisfaction. We found this result both directly (satisfaction was negatively correlated with answers to our question about how easy it would be to find an equivalent or better job) and indirectly. In the Massachusetts plants, we translated the survey into Portuguese and Vietnamese; those who took the survey in these languages were more satisfied than those whose English skills were good enough to take the survey in English. However, the UK plants also had access to immigrants. In England we were unable to distinguish survey responses from immigrants—but we did find that immigrants expressed more satisfaction in our interviews.

The case of SP suggests the following generalizations:

1. Managers often introduce new plans without (a) understanding the importance of complementary efforts, or (b) thinking through the incentive effects on workers (they are more concerned with making sure they do not pay "too much," and fall victim to the multitask problem (they pay too much attention to minimizing costs that can easily be measured, while ignoring costs that are harder to measure, or that would constrain management autonomy if measured, like overhead). These pitfalls affect even highly successful managers, such as those at SP. By most measures, SP has

been a financially successful company. Although the second half of 2000 and 2001 were tough years and profits were relatively low, this was true for almost all firms in the auto industry. In other years, the firm's return on equity was between 12 and 20 percent. Firm SP achieved this performance without being a particularly high-productivity operation; value added per shop worker at the Ohio plant is only $70,000, not far above the median for component producers, according to benchmarking data from the Industrial Technology Institute (Helper and Stanley 2004).

Although management bought the Ohio, Florida, and UK plants because it thought they could use their superior administrative tools to turn these plants around, it appears that they did not fully understand the roots of their success in Boston. In Boston, plant management was highly visible, and introduced many complementary policies, including constantly referring to the importance of the VAG, and the nature of worker actions required to increase it. As a result of their success in Boston, the top two managers there were promoted into corporate offices of an expanding company, where they visited the acquired plants only once a month, pushing VAG on them as a sort of magic bullet.

2. It is possible to introduce a kind of "lean from above," that mimics some of the Toyota results on inventory and quality by having management do much of the continuous improvement efforts that are done by workers at Toyota. Firm SP has focused on inventory reduction and having engineers design for manufacturing. These efforts have allowed SP to use a relatively unskilled, low-paid workforce to produce at low cost. Firm SP has not, on the other hand, placed much emphasis (particularly recently) on broad-based participation, where ideas for continuous improvement come from both line workers and engineers.

What are the benefits of SP for workers? The factors affecting satisfaction appear quite similar in the United States and United Kingdom. One way to characterize them is that "workers at SP do fairly well compared to their alternatives." An optimist would emphasize the "do well" part, pointing out that SP's wages are high by world standards, that SP's worker satisfaction levels are similar to national averages, and that many SP workers stay there for a long time. From the perspective of SP employees, it seems there are several reasons why many stay. First, the firm pays good benefits, including health care, pension, and paid vacation. (Pay and benefits were low in the UK plant, but so were effort requirements until new management came in.) The extra pay provided by the VAG is important. In the Massachusetts suburban plant, applications for openings fell dramatically after the VAG payout fell from almost 7 percent to zero. Second, the firm has found work-forces that perceive themselves as having few labor market options. The firm hired many immigrants in Massachusetts and the UK, retirees and other rural workers in Ohio, and older workers and retirees in Florida. Third, in the Massachusetts plants the sense of community provided by working with others of the same ethnic group—and sometimes the same family—in a plant that is perceived as well managed provides many first-generation Americans a sense of economic and cultural security.

A pessimist would also agree that "workers at SP do fairly well compared to their alternatives"—but would focus on how bad the alternatives are. In this view, the worker satisfaction measures capture mostly that workers do not feel they can do much better. From this point of view, the impact of the changes in product and HR strategies is to give managers and stockholders more new products without paying a higher wage (and in the case of the urban plant, paying a lower wage). Workers report that they work harder, and now that they work for a public company rather than a paternalistic owner, they are subject to layoffs. However, at least the firm survives, offering a fairly high probability of continued employment with health and pension benefits.

## Appendix

**Table 8A.1**   Impact of working on piece rates on job satisfaction of production employees in the Massachusetts establishments—Rasch index measures of job satisfaction

|  | Rasch measure of job satisfaction (1) | Rasch measure of job satisfaction (2) |
|---|---|---|
| Piece rate | 0.09 | 0.11 |
|  | (0.20) | (0.20) |
| Vietnamese | 0.33** | 0.19 |
|  | (0.14) | (0.14) |
| Cape Verde | −0.04 | −0.04 |
|  | (0.14) | (0.14) |
| Tenure less than 1 year | 0.27 | 0.36** |
|  | (0.18) | (0.18) |
| Tenure between 1 and 6 years | 0.28** | 0.28** |
|  | (0.12) | (0.12) |
| Lack of other jobs |  | 0.23*** |
|  |  | (0.04) |
| Adj. $R^2$ | 0.03 | 0.11 |
| $N$ | 376 | 358 |

*Note:* Standard errors are in parentheses.
***Significant at the 1 percent level.
**Significant at the 5 percent level.
*Significant at the 10 percent level.

# References

Appelbaum, E., and R. Batt. 1994. *The new American workplace.* Ithaca, NY: Cornell University Press.

Appelbaum, E., T. Bailey, P. Berg, and A. Kalleberg. 2000. *Manufacturing advantage: Why high performance work systems pay off.* Ithaca, NY: Cornell University Press.

Appelbaum, E., A. Bernhardt, and R. J. Murnane, eds. 2003. *Low-wage America: How: employers are reshaping opportunity in the workplace.* New York: Russell Sage Foundation.

Arthur, J. B. 1994. Effects of human resource systems on manufacturing performance and turnover. *Academy of Management Journal* 37 (3): 670–87.

Arvey, R., G. W. Carter, and D. Buerkley. 1991. Job satisfaction: Dispositional and situational influences. In *International review of industrial organizational psychology,* ed. C. L. Cooper and I. T. Robertson, 359–83. New York: Wiley.

Athey, S., and G. W. Imbens. 2006. Identification and inference in nonlinear difference-in-differences models. *Econometrica* 74 (2): 431–97.

Bertrand, M., E. Duflo, and S. Mullainathan. 2002. How much should we trust difference-in-difference estimates? NBER Working Paper no. 8841. Cambridge, MA: National Bureau of Economic Research, March.

Black, S. E., and L. M. Lynch. 2004a. How workers fare when employers innovate. *Industrial Relations* 43 (1): 44–66.

Black, S. E., and L. M. Lynch. 2004b. What's driving the new economy? The benefits of workplace innovation. *The Economic Journal* 114: F97–116.

Brief, A. P. 1998. *Attitudes in and around organizations.* Thousand Oaks, CA: SAGE.

Cappelli, P., and D. Neumark. 2001. External job churning and internal job flexibility. NBER Working Paper no. 8111. Cambridge, MA: National Bureau of Economic Research, February.

Chi, W., R. B. Freeman, and M. M. Kleiner. 2007. Adoption and termination of employee involvement programs. NBER Working Paper no. 12878. Cambridge, MA: National Bureau of Economic Research, January.

Conyon, M. J., and R. B. Freeman. 2001. Shared modes of compensation and firm performance: UK evidence. Working Paper no. 8448. Cambridge, MA: National Bureau of Economic Research, August.

Cutcher-Gershenfeld, J. 1991. The impact on economic performance of a transformation in workplace relations. *Industrial and Labor Relations Review* 44 (2): 241–60.

Ehrenberg, R. G., ed. 1990. Do compensation policies matter? *Industrial and Labor Relations Review* 43 (3): 3–12.

Freeman, R. B., and M. M. Kleiner. 1998. From piece rates to time rates: An exploratory study. *Industrial Relations Research Association Proceedings* 50–59.

———. 2005. The last American shoe manufacturers: Decreasing productivity and increasing profits in the shift from piece rates to continuous flow production. *Industrial Relations* 44 (2): 307–30.

Freeman, R. B., M. M. Kleiner, and C. Ostroff. 2000. The anatomy of employee involvement and its effects on firms and workers. NBER Working Paper no. 8050. Cambridge, MA: National Bureau of Economic Research, December.

Freeman, R. B., and J. Rogers. 1999. *What workers want.* Ithaca, NY: ILR Press, Russell Sage Foundation.

Helper, S., and M. M. Kleiner. 2003. When management strategies change: Employee well-being at an auto supplier. In *Low wage America: How employers are reshaping opportunity in the workplace,* ed. E. Appelbaum, A. Bernhardt, and R. J. Murnane 446–78. New York: Russell Sage Foundation.

Helper, S., and D. I. Levine. 1992. Long-term supplier relations and product market structure. *Journal of Law, Economics, and Organization* 8 (3): 561–81.

Helper, S., and M. Stanley. 2004. Creating innovation networks among manufacturing firms: How effective extension programs work. In *Economic development through entrepreneurship,* ed. S. Shane, 50–62. Northampton: Edward Elgar.

Ichniowski, C., T. A. Kochan, D. I. Levine, C. Olson, and G. Strauss. 2000. *The American workplace: Skills, compensation, and employee involvement.* Cambridge: Cambridge University Press.

Ichniowski, C., K. Shaw, and G. Prennushi. 1997. The effects of human resource management practices on productivity: A study of steel finishing lines. *American Economic Review* 87 (3): 291–322.

Jacobs, E. 2000. *The handbook of U.S. labor statistics.* Lanum, MD: Bernam Press.

Jones, D.C., and T. Kato. 1995. The productivity effects of employee stock-ownership plans and bonuses: Evidence from Japanese panel data. *American Economic Review* 85 (3): 391–414.

Judge, T., C. Thorson, J. Bono, and G. K. Patton. 2001. The job satisfaction-job performance relationship: A qualitative and quantitative review. *Psychological Bulletin* 127 (3): 376–407.

Kaufman, R. 1992. The effects of IMPROSHARE on productivity. *Industrial and Labor Relations Review* 45 (2): 311–22.

Kleiner, M. M., R. Block, M. Roomkin, and S. Salsburg. 1987. Industrial relations and firm performance. In *Human resources and the performance of the firm,* ed. S. G. Allen and M. M. Kleiner, 319–43. Madison, WI: Industrial Relations Research Association.

Kleiner, M. M., S. R. Helper, and Y. Ren. 2001. From piece rates to group incentives: Can the company and its employees gain? *Industrial Relations Research Association Proceedings:* 183–91.

Kleiner, M. M., J. Leonard, and A. Pilarski. 2002. How industrial relations affect plant performance: The case of commercial aircraft manufacturing. *Industrial and Labor Relations Review* 55 (2): 195–218.

Kruse, D. L. 1993. *Profit sharing: Does it make a difference? The productivity and stability effects of employee profit-sharing plans.* Kalamazoo, MI: W. E. Upjohn Institute for Employment Research.

Lazear, E. P. 2000. Performance pay and productivity. *American Economic Review* 90 (5): 1346–61.

MacDuffie, J. P. 1995. Human resource bundles and manufacturing performance: Organizational logic and flexible production systems in the world auto industry. *Industrial and Labor Relations Review* 48 (2): 197–221.

MacDuffie, J. P., and S. Helper. 2006. Collaboration in supply chains: With and without trust. In *The firm as a collaborative community: Reconstructing trust in the knowledge economy,* ed. C. Heckscher and P. Adler, 417–65. New York: Oxford University Press.

Milgrom, P., and J. Roberts. 1990. The economics of modern manufacturing: Technology, strategy, and organization. *The American Economic Review* 80 (3): 511–28.

Seiler, E. 1984. Piece rate vs. time rate: The effect of incentives on earnings. *The Review of Economics and Statistics* 66 (3): 363–76.

# Contributors

Ann Bartel
Graduate School of Business
Columbia University
3022 Broadway, 816 Uris Hall
New York, NY 10027

Joseph Blasi
School of Management and Labor
  Relations
Rutgers University
Levin Building
New Brunswick, NJ 08540

Nick Bloom
Department of Economics
Stanford University
579 Serra Mall
Stanford, CA 94305-6072

James B. Bushnell
University of California Energy
  Institute
2547 Channing Way
Berkeley, CA 94720

Ricardo Correa
International Banking and Finance
  Section
Division of International Finance
Board of Governors of the Federal
  Reserve System
20th Street and Constitution Avenue,
  NW
Washington, D.C. 20551

Tor Eriksson
Department of Economics
Aarhus School of Business
University of Aarhus
Prismet Silkeborgvej 2
8000 Århus C Denmark

Richard B. Freeman
NBER
1050 Massachusetts Avenue
Cambridge, MA 02138

Susan Helper
Weatherhead School of Management
Case Western Reserve University
11119 Bellflower Road
Cleveland, OH 44106-7235

Casey Ichniowski
Graduate School of Business
3022 Broadway Street, 713 Uris Hall
Columbia University
New York, NY 10027

Morris M. Kleiner
University of Minnesota
Humphrey Institute
260 Humphrey Center
301 19th Street South
Minneapolis, MN 55455

Tobias Kretschmer
Department of Management
University of Munich
Schackstrasse 4/III
D-80539 Munich Germany

Douglas Kruse
School of Management and Labor
    Relations
Rutgers University
94 Rockafeller Road
Piscataway, NJ 08854

Francine Lafontaine
University of Michigan Ross School of
    Business
701 Tappan Street
Ann Arbor, MI 48109-1234

Alec Levenson
Center for Effective Organizations
Marshall School of Business
University of Southern California
3415 South Figueroa Street, DCC-200
Los Angeles, CA 90089-0871

Kathryn L. Shaw
Graduate School of Business
Littlefield 339
Stanford University
Stanford, CA 94305-5015

Jagadeesh Sivadasan
University of Michigan Ross School of
    Business
701 Tappan Street
Ann Arbor, MI 48109-1234

John Van Reenen
London School of Economics
Centre for Economic Performance
Houghton Street
London WC2A 2AE England

Niels Westergaard-Nielsen
Department of Economics
Aarhus School of Business
University of Aarhus
Prismet Silkeborgvej 2
8000 Århus C Denmark

Catherine Wolfram
Haas School of Business
University of California, Berkeley
Berkeley, CA 94720-1900

# Author Index

# Subject Index